Accounting: AS Level and A Level

AS Level and A Level
Accounting

Harold Randall

CAMBRIDGE
UNIVERSITY PRESS

CAMBRIDGE UNIVERSITY PRESS
Cambridge, New York, Melbourne, Madrid, Cape Town, Singapore,
São Paulo, Delhi, Dubai, Tokyo

Cambridge University Press
The Edinburgh Building, Cambridge CB2 8RU, UK

www.cambridge.org
Information on this title: www.cambridge.org/9780521539937

First published 2005
7th printing 2010

Printed in Dubai by Oriental Press

A catalogue record for this publication is available from the British Library

ISBN 978-0-521-53993-7 Paperback

ACKNOWLEDGMENTS

Cover image © Philip James Corwin/CORBIS

Past examination questions are reproduced by permission of the University of Cambridge Local
Examinations Syndicate.

Contents

Preface

This book is written for students of accounting who face problems by asking 'How do I do this?'. Here are the approaches to the problems that such students are likely to meet in the CIE AS and A level accounting examinations. Students need to practise the approaches until they have mastered them. No textbook can do the students' work for them!

Accounting AS Level and A Level covers the entire CIE syllabus. Ideally, students should already have taken O level or IGCSE accounting before starting on AS level or A level studies. Many do not have such a background and this text has such students in mind in the early chapters. The essentials of double-entry bookkeeping are covered in sufficient detail to equip students to progress to more advanced work. It must be emphasised, however, that thorough mastery of the basics is absolutely necessary if real progress is to be made with the subsequent chapters.

The text follows the order of the CIE syllabus but allows for some flexibility in the sequence in which the topics are studied. Whichever the order in which the chapters are taken, it is of paramount importance that the whole of the syllabus is covered before the examination. Every topic is likely to find its place in at least one of the papers each session. It is invariably the case that too many candidates enter the examinations inadequately prepared – with inevitably disappointing results. A grid is provided to show how the chapters cover the AS level and A level syllabuses.

Answers to exercises within chapters, and answers to multiple-choice questions, are provided at the end of the textbook. The answers to the additional exercises at the ends of chapters are provided in a teacher's supplement available on the Cambridge University Press website at **http://www.cambridge.org/accounting_as_alevel**

Many years as an examiner (and lecturer) have made me keenly aware of the difficulties experienced by examination candidates, and the text seeks to address these difficulties as they arise in the topics covered. Particular difficulties are identified as they occur in the chapters; in addition, every chapter has 'Examination hints'. My approach has been from the dual standpoints of teacher and student. If it is any consolation and encouragement to students, I have experienced the frustrations and difficulties that many encounter in their studies, but I hope I have proved that determination to succeed brings its reward. Students should ask the question 'Why?' even more times than they ask 'How?' because an understanding of the reasons underlying accounting practices makes the rules more memorable. 'How do I do this' will give way to 'I know how to do this!'

I wish to express my great appreciation to George Brownlee, Ken Frame, Ian Harrison and Don Payne for reading my manuscript and making many helpful suggestions.

To my readers, I send my best wishes for success.

Harold Randall

Topics grid

The grid below show how the chapters of this text cover the topics in the syllabuses for AS level and A level accounting. The syllabuses do not present the topics or their contents in the order in which they should be taught, and the order in which the chapters are shown in the grid is intended only to show how the syllabuses are covered. Teachers will decide their own order to suit their particular teaching plans, which will usually follow, more or less, the chapters in sequence.

Some topics are either wholly or partly outside the AS level syllabus but none of the topics is outside the A level syllabus.

Syllabus	Chapter	AS level	A level
THE ACCOUNTING SYSTEM			
A. Recording Financial Information	1	All	All
	2	All	All
	3	All	All
	4	All	All
	5	All	All
	10	All	All
	11	All	All
	12	All	All
B. Accounting Principles	9	All	All
C. Control Systems	6	All	All
	13	All	All
	14	All	All
	15	All	All
FINANCIAL ACCOUNTING			
D. Preparation of Financial Statements	7	All	All
	8	All	All
	16	All	All
	17	All	All
	18	All	All
	19	All	All
	20	All	All
	21	All	All
	22	All	All
	23	All	All
	24	N/A	All
E. Capital	25	§§25.1-25.5, 25.11	All
F. Business Purchase	26	N/A	All
G. Published Company Accounts	27	N/A	All
FINANCIAL REPORTING AND INTERPRETATION			
H. Interpretation and Analysis	28	§§28.1-28.6, 28.8, 28.9, 28.10, 28.11	All
I. Company Financing	29	N/A	All
ELEMENTS OF MANAGERIAL ACCOUNTING			
J. Costing Principles and Systems	30	All	All
	31	All	All
	32	N/A	All
	33	§§33.1-33.5, 33.10	All
K. Budgeting	34	N/A	All
L. Standard Costing	35	N/A	All
M. Investment Appraisal	36	N/A	All

Part I
The accounting system

1 Double-entry bookkeeping: cash transactions

> **In this chapter you will learn:**
> • that every transaction has two aspects
> • that double-entry bookkeeping records both aspects of a transaction
> • what ledger accounts are
> • the meanings of the terms 'debit' and 'credit'
> • how to record cash transactions in ledger accounts.

1.1 What is double-entry bookkeeping?

Double-entry bookkeeping is a system of recording transactions that recognises that there are two sides (or aspects) to every transaction. For example, you give your friend $10 in exchange for his watch. This involves you giving him $10 (one aspect) and your friend receiving $10 (the other aspect). The transfer of the watch involves him giving you the watch (one aspect) and you receiving his watch (the other aspect). Every transaction involves giving and receiving. It is important that you *recognise* and *record* both aspects of every transaction in your bookkeeping.

1.2 Ledger accounts

Transactions are recorded in **ledger accounts**. An account is a history of all transactions of a similar nature. A ledger is a book that contains accounts. An account separates what is received from what is given. For example, a Cash account records cash received and cash paid, as shown:

Cash					
Debit			**Credit**		
		$			$
Mar 1	Cash received from customers	240	Mar 2	Cash paid to suppliers	80
Mar 4	Cash received from customers	118	Mar 3	Wages paid	116

The left-hand side of the account is called the debit side and is used to record cash received (that is, coming into the account). The right-hand side of the account is the credit side and shows cash paid (that is, going out of the account). All accounts have a debit side on the left to record what is received, and a credit side on the right to record what is given. In practice, the words 'debit' and 'credit' are not shown because bookkeepers do not need to be reminded of them.

1.3 How to record cash transactions

Bookkeeping treats businesses as 'persons' with separate identities from their owners. For example, if Abdul is a trader, all his business transactions are recorded as those of the business and not as Abdul's own transactions.

In the example that follows, some transactions are recorded in ledger accounts. Make sure you understand the bookkeeping entries, and observe the wording carefully. This is important as you must be able to record transactions in ledger accounts correctly.

Example

(Here all transactions are recorded from the point of view of Abdul's business, not from the point of view of the people with whom the business deals.)

Transaction 1 April 1. Abdul starts business as a trader by paying $10 000 into a Bank account which he opens for the business. Abdul gives, and the business receives, $10 000. An account for Abdul will be opened (his Capital account) and credited with his 'capital'. The business Bank account will be debited.

Abdul – Capital					
		$			$
			Apr 1	Bank	10 000

Bank					
		$			$
Apr 1	Abdul – Capital	10 000			

Note. Each entry is dated and shows the name of the other account in which the double entry is completed. Make sure you show these details for every entry you make in a ledger account.

Entries in ledger accounts are known as **postings**, and bookkeepers are said to 'post' transactions to the accounts.

Transaction 2 April 2. Abdul buys a motor vehicle for the business and pays $2000 from the business Bank account. A Motor Vehicles account must be opened.

Bank

		$			$
Apr 1	Abdul – Capital	10 000	Apr 2	Motor Vehicles	2000

Motor Vehicles

		$			$
Apr 2	Bank	2 000			

Transaction 3 April 3. Abdul buys stock (goods which he will re-sell in the normal course of trade) for $3000 and pays by cheque.

Bank

		$			$
Apr 1	Abdul – Capital	10 000	Apr 2	Motor Vehicles	2000
			Apr 3	Purchases	3000

Purchases

		$			$
Apr 3	Bank	3 000			

Note. Purchases of stock are always debited to a Purchases account. An account called Stock account is used for a special purpose, which will be explained in chapter 7.

Transaction 4 April 4. Abdul sells a quantity of stock for $800 and banks the cash.

Bank

		$			$
Apr 1	Abdul – Capital	10 000	Apr 2	Motor Vehicles	2000
Apr 4	Sales	800	Apr 3	Purchases	3000

Sales

		$			$
			Apr 4	Bank	800

Sales of stock are always credited to Sales account, never to Stock account.

Transaction 5 April 7. A customer returns some goods and receives a refund of $40.

Bank

		$			$
Apr 1	Abdul – Capital	10 000	Apr 2	Motor Vehicles	2000
Apr 4	Sales	800	Apr 3	Purchases	3000
			Apr 7	Sales Returns	40

Sales Returns

		$			$
Apr 7	Bank	40			

Note. Goods returned are not debited to Sales account but to Sales Returns account. This account is also known as Goods Inwards account.

Transaction 6 April 8. Abdul returns some goods costing $100 to a supplier and receives a refund.

Bank

		$			$
Apr 1	Abdul – Capital	10 000	Apr 2	Motor Vehicles	2000
Apr 4	Sales	800	Apr 3	Purchases	3000
Apr 8	Purchases Returns	100	Apr 7	Sales Returns	40

Purchases Returns

		$			$
			Apr 8	Bank	100

Note. Goods returned to a supplier are credited to Purchases Returns account. This account is also known as Goods Outwards account.

Transaction 7 April 10. Abdul buys another motor vehicle for the business and pays $4000 by cheque.

Bank

		$			$
Apr 1	Abdul – Capital	10 000	Apr 2	Motor Vehicles	2000
Apr 4	Sales	800	Apr 3	Purchases	3000
Apr 8	Purchases Returns	100	Apr 7	Sales Returns	40
			Apr 10	Motor Vehicles	4000

Motor Vehicles

		$			$
Apr 2	Bank	2 000			
Apr 10	Bank	4 000			

Note. As explained in §1.2, an account is a history of all transactions of a similar nature. Therefore it is not necessary to open another account for the second motor vehicle. Similarly, all purchases of office equipment are posted to Office Equipment account, and all purchases of office furniture are posted to Office Furniture account. You will encounter other examples such as plant and machinery, and fixtures and fittings.

Transaction 8 April 11. Tania lends the business $5000.

Bank

		$			$
Apr 1	Abdul – Capital	10 000	Apr 2	Motor Vehicles	2000
Apr 4	Sales	800	Apr 3	Purchases	3000
Apr 8	Purchases Returns	100	Apr 7	Sales Returns	40
Apr 11	Tania – Loan	5 000	Apr 10	Motor Vehicles	4000

Tania – Loan

		$			$
			Apr 11	Bank	5000

Transaction 9 April 12. Abdul pays rent on a warehouse by cheque, $1000.

Bank

		$			$
Apr 1	Abdul – Capital	10 000	Apr 2	Motor Vehicles	2000
Apr 4	Sales	800	Apr 3	Purchases	000
Apr 8	Purchases Returns	100	Apr 7	Sales Returns	40
Apr 11	Tania – Loan	5 000	Apr 10	Motor Vehicles	4000
			Apr 12	Rent Payable	1000

Rent Payable

		$			$
Apr 12	Bank	1 000			

Transaction 10 April 14. Abdul sublets part of the warehouse and receives $300 rent.

Bank

		$			$
Apr 1	Abdul – Capital	10 000	Apr 2	Motor Vehicles	2000
Apr 4	Sales	800	Apr 3	Purchases	3000
Apr 8	Purchases Returns	100	Apr 7	Sales Returns	40
Apr 11	Tania – Loan	5 000	Apr 10	Motor Vehicles	4000
Apr 14	Rent Receivable	300	Apr 12	Rent Payable	1000

Rent Receivable

		$			$
			Apr 14	Bank	300

Note. Rent receivable is not posted to the Rent Payable account. It is important to keep income and expenditure in separate accounts.

Transaction 11 April 15. Abdul pays wages by cheque, $1200.

Bank

		$			$
Apr 1	Abdul – Capital	10 000	Apr 2	Motor Vehicles	2000
Apr 4	Sales	800	Apr 3	Purchases	3000
Apr 8	Purchases Returns	100	Apr 7	Sales Returns	40
Apr 11	Tania – Loan	5 000	Apr 10	Motor Vehicles	4000
Apr 4	Rent Receivable	300	Apr 12	Rent Payable	1000
			Apr 15	Wages	1200

Wages

		$			$
Apr 15	Bank	1 200			

Transaction 12 April 16. Abdul withdraws $600 from the business Bank account for personal use.

Bank

		$			$
Apr 1	Abdul – Capital	10 000	Apr 2	Motor Vehicles	2000
Apr 4	Sales	800	Apr 3	Purchases	3000
Apr 8	Purchases Returns	100	Apr 7	Sales Returns	40
Apr 11	Tania – Loan	5 000	Apr 10	Motor Vehicles	4000
Apr 14	Rent Receivable	300	Apr 12	Rent Payable	1000
			Apr 15	Wages	1200
			Apr 16	Drawings	600

Drawings

		$			$
Apr 16	Bank	600			

Note. Money drawn out of a business by the owner for personal use is debited to a Drawings account, not to the owner's Capital account.

Exercise 1

Open the necessary ledger accounts and post the following transactions to them.

May 1	Martine started business as a florist by paying $3000 into a business Bank account.
2	Charline lent the business $1000.
	Martine then had the following transactions.
3	Paid rent, $100.
4	Purchased shop fittings, $400.
	Purchased stock of flowers $300.
5	Received refund of $20 for flowers returned to supplier.
6	Sold some flowers and received $40.
7	Paid wages, $60.
8	Withdrew $100 for personal use.

Exercise 2

Complete the entries for the following table. The first item has been done for you.

	Debit account	Credit account
1. Noel pays a cheque into his business Bank account as capital	Bank	Noel – Capital
2. Purchases some stock and pays by cheque		
3. Sells some stock and banks the takings		
4. Pays rent by cheque		
5. Purchases shop fittings and pays by cheque		
6. Cashes cheque for personal expenses		
7. Pays wages by cheque		
8. Returns stock to supplier and banks refund		
9. Receives rent from tenant and banks cheque		
10. Refunds money to customer by cheque for goods returned		
11. Motor vehicle purchased and paid for by cheque		
12. Pays for petrol for motor vehicle and pays by cheque		

1.4 Examination hints

- All transactions are recorded from the point of view of the business, not from those of its customers and suppliers.

- When recording transactions think very carefully about which account 'gives' and which account 'receives'. Credit the account that 'gives' and debit the account that 'receives'.
- Make sure you complete the double entry for every transaction before starting to record the next one.
- Date every entry and enter the name of the other account in which the double entry is completed in the details column.
- If you make a mistake in an exercise, study the answer given at the end of the book and make sure you understand what you should have done *and why*.

1.5 Multiple-choice questions

1 Joel occupies part of Natasha's business premises. Which entries in Natasha's books record the rent Joel pays her?

	Debit account	Credit account
A	Bank	Rent Payable
B	Bank	Rent Receivable
C	Rent Payable	Bank
D	Rent Receivable	Bank

2 Yasmina purchased some office equipment for use in her business. The equipment was faulty and she returned it to the supplier who refunded the cost to Yasmina.

Which entries in Yasmina's books record the return of the equipment?

	Debit account	Credit account
A	Bank	Purchase Returns
B	Bank	Office Equipment
C	Purchases Returns	Bank
D	Office Equipment	Bank

3 A trader withdraws money from his business Bank account for personal expenses.

Which entries record this in his books?

	Debit account	Credit account
A	Bank	Capital
B	Bank	Drawings
C	Capital	Bank
D	Drawings	Bank

4 A trader returns goods to the supplier and receives a refund.

Which entries record the refund in the trader's books?

	Debit account	Credit account
A	Bank	Purchases
B	Bank	Purchases Returns
C	Purchases	Bank
D	Purchases Returns	Bank

1.6 Additional exercises

1 Open the necessary ledger accounts and post the following transactions to them.

June 1 Farook commenced business by paying $15 000 into his business Bank account.

Amna lent the business $5000.

Farook then had the following business transactions:

2 Purchased premises and paid $8000.

3 Bought office furniture for $2000 and paid by cheque.

4 Paid $5000 by cheque for goods for re-sale.

5 Sold some goods for $1500 and banked the proceeds.

6 Paid insurance premium by cheque, $600.

7 Bought motor van and paid $3000 by cheque.

8 Drew cheque for $50 to pay for petrol for motor van.

9 Bought some goods costing $2000 for re-sale and paid by cheque.

10 Sold goods for $2400 and banked the proceeds.

Drew cheque for wages, $400.

11 Repaid $1200 by cheque to customers for goods returned.

12 Received a refund of $900 from suppliers for goods returned.

13 Received a refund of insurance of $100.

Withdrew $200 from business bank account for personal expenses.

14 Returned some office furniture that was damaged and received a refund of $800.

15 Repaid $1000 of the loan from Amna.

2 Complete the entries for the following table with information taken from the accounts of a trader.

	Debit account	Credit account
1. Local taxes paid by cheque		
2. Bank pays interest to trader		
3. Sundry expenses paid by cheque		
4. Postage and stationery paid by cheque		
5. Telephone bill paid by cheque		
6. Carriage inwards* paid by cheque		
7. Carriage outwards** paid by cheque		
8. Interest paid by cheque to brother in respect of a loan received from him		
9. Interest paid to bank		

* Carriage inwards is the delivery cost added to the price of goods by the supplier.

** Carriage outwards is the cost of delivering goods to a customer.

2 Double-entry bookkeeping: credit transactions

> *In this chapter you will learn:*
> - how to record transactions which do not involve immediate cash payments in ledger accounts
> - the difference between trade and cash discounts and how to treat them.

2.1 What are credit transactions?

Many transactions take place without any money being paid or received at the time. For example, Lai sells goods to Chin for $500 on 31 May and gives Chin until 30 June to pay. The transaction is 'on credit'. The sale has taken place on 31 May and must be recorded in the books of both Lai and Chin at that date. No entries to record payment are made in their books until Chin pays Lai.

2.2 How to record credit transactions

In a seller's books A sale on credit is credited to Sales account and debited to an account opened for the customer. When the customer pays, his or her account is credited, and the Bank account debited.

In a customer's books A purchase on credit is debited to Purchases account and credited to an account opened for the supplier. When the supplier is paid, his or her account is debited, and the Bank account credited.

Example

Lai sells goods to Chin for $500 on 31 May and gives Chin until 30 June to pay.

In Lai's books Credit the sale to Sales account and debit it to an account for Chin.

Sales			
	$		$
		May 31 Chin	500

Chin			
	$		$
May 31 Sales	500		

The debit entry in Chin's account shows that he is a **debtor** in Lai's books; that is, Chin owes Lai $500 until he pays for the goods.

In Chin's books Debit the purchase to Purchases account and credit it to an account for Lai.

Purchases			
	$		$
May 31 Lai	500		

Lai			
	$		$
		May 31 Purchases	500

The credit entry in Lai's account shows that he is a **creditor** in Chin's books.

Goods returned

On 4 June Chin returns some of the goods costing $100 to Lai because they are damaged.

In Lai's books Credit Chin's account and debit Sales Returns account.

Chin			
	$		$
May 31 Sales	500	Jun 4 Sales Returns	100

Sales Returns			
	$		$
Jun 4 Chin	100		

In Chin's books Debit Lai's account and credit Purchases Returns account.

Lai

		$			$
Jun 4	Purchases Returns	100	May 31	Purchases	500

Purchases Returns

		$			$
			Jun 4	Lai	100

2.3 How to record payments for goods bought or sold on credit

Trade discount

Trade discount is an allowance made by one trader to another. In the above example, the goods which Lai sold to Chin may have been sold normally for $625. Lai knows that Chin, also a trader, must make a profit on the goods when he sells them. He has allowed Chin a **trade discount** of $125 (20% of $625) so that if Chin sells the goods for $625 he will make a profit of $125.

Note. Although the normal price of the goods was $625, the transaction was for $500 only, and only $500 is entered into the books of both Lai and Chin. Trade discount is *never* recorded in ledger accounts.

Cash (or settlement) discount

Lai has given Chin one month to pay for the goods. To encourage Chin to pay by 30 June, Lai may allow Chin to pay less than the amount due. This allowance is a cash (or settlement) discount. (Notice the difference between cash discount and trade discount: trade discount is not dependent on payment being made promptly, or even at all.)

Note. Cash discounts are *always* recorded in ledger accounts.

Suppose Lai has allowed Chin a cash discount of 5% provided Chin pays by 30 June, and Chin pays Lai on 28 June. Chin owes Lai $400 ($500 – $100). 5% of $400 = $20. He will therefore pay only $380.

In Lai's books Debit the discount to Discounts Allowed account.

Chin

		$			$
May 31	Sales	500	Jun 4	Sales Returns	100
			Jun 28	Bank	380
			Jun 28	Discounts Allowed	20

Bank

		$		$
Jun 28	Chin	380		

Discounts Allowed

		$		$
Jun 28	Chin	20		

In Chin's books Credit the discount to Discounts Received account.

Lai

		$			$
Jun 4	Purchases Returns	100	May 31	Purchases	500
Jun 28	Bank	380			
Jun 28	Discounts Received	20			

Bank

	$			$
		Jun 28	Lai	380

Discounts Received

	$			$
		Jun 28	Lai	20

Example

Andrew had the following transactions in May.

May 1 Purchased goods from David. The goods cost $1000 less 10% trade discount.

2 Purchased goods from Rodney for $1600 less 15% trade discount.

3 Purchased a computer for the office on credit from Bernard for $2000.

4 Sold goods to Mario for $800.

5 Returned goods which had cost $100 after trade discount to David.

6 Purchased goods from Ludovic for $700 less trade discount of 20%.

7 Sold goods to Ravin for $500.

8 Mario returned goods which had been sold to him for $40.

9 Received cheque from Ravin for amount owing, less cash discount of 5%.

10 Paid amount owing to David, less cash discount of 5%.

11 Paid amount owing to Rodney, less cash discount of 5%.
Paid Bernard for computer.

12 Received cheque from Mario for amount owing, less 5% cash discount.
Paid amount owing to Ludovic, less 5% cash discount.

These transactions are recorded as follows.

David

		$			$
May 5	Purchases Returns	100	May 1	Purchases	900
May 10	Bank	760			
May 10	Discounts Received	40			

Rodney

		$			$
May 11	Bank	1292	May 2	Purchases	1360
May 11	Discounts Received	68			

Bernard

		$			$
May 11	Bank	2000	May 3	Office Computer	2000

Ludovic

		$			$
May 12	Bank	532	May 6	Purchases	560
May 12	Discounts Received	28			

Mario

		$			$
May 4	Sales	800	May 8	Sales Returns	40
			May 12	Bank	722
			May 12	Discounts Allowed	38

Ravin

		$			$
May 7	Sales	500	May 9	Bank	475
			May 9	Discounts Allowed	25

Purchases

		$		$
May 1	David	900		
May 2	Rodney	1360		
May 6	Ludovic	560		

Purchases Returns

	$			$
	$	May 5	David	100

Sales

	$			$
		May 4	Mario	800
		May 7	Ravin	500

Sales Returns

		$		$
May 8	Mario	40		

Discounts Allowed

		$		$
May 9	Ravin	25		
May 12	Mario	38		

Discounts Received

	$			$
		May 10	David	40
		May 11	Rodney	68
		May 12	Ludovic	28

Office Computer

		$		$
May 3	Bernard	2000		

Bank

		$			$
May 9	Ravin	475	May 10	David	760
May 12	Mario	722	May 11	Rodney	1292
			May 11	Bernard	2000
			May 12	Ludovic	532

Calculations

Purchases:	Amount before trade discount	Trade discount	Cost to Andrew
	$	$	$
From: David	1000	(10%) 100	900
Rodney	1600	(15%) 240	1360
Ludovic	700	(20%) 140	560
Cash settlements:	Amount before cash discount	Cash discount (5%)	Amount paid
	$	$	$
By Ravin	500	25	475
Mario	760	38	722

Exercise 1

Post the following transactions in the books of Geraud.

June 1 Purchased goods from Khor which cost $3000 less trade discount of 10%.

5 Sold goods to Lai for $600.

10 Returned goods which had cost Geraud $200 to Khor.

15 Purchased goods from Lim which cost $2800 before trade discount of 10%.

20 Sold goods to Chin for $1300.

25 Lai returned goods which had cost him $200.

30 Geraud paid Khor and Lim the amounts due to them after deducting 5% cash discount.

Lai and Chin paid Geraud the amounts they owed him after deducting 5% cash discount.

2.4 Examination hints

- Remember to record all transactions from the point of view of the business, not from those of its customers and suppliers.
- Where trade discounts are given, record all amounts net of trade discount.
- Note carefully whether cash discount is to be deducted from settlements.
- Remember to complete the entries for cash discounts to the correct Discount accounts.
- Be accurate in all your calculations.

2.5 Multiple-choice questions

1 Davina bought goods on credit from Sharon for $600 less trade discount of $120.

Which entries record this transaction in Davina's books?

	Account to be debited	Account to be credited
A	Purchases $480	Sharon $480
B	Purchases $480 Discounts Allowed $120	Sharon $600
C	Purchases $600	Sharon $600
D	Purchases $600	Sharon $480 Discounts Received $120

2 Kristal bought goods on credit from Prisca. The goods had a list price of $1000 but Prisca allowed Kristal trade discount of 10% and cash discount of 4%.

How much did Kristal have to pay Prisca?

A $860   **B** $864   **C** $900   **D** $960

3 Shirley bought goods from Corrine. The goods had a list price of $800. Corrine allowed Shirley trade discount of 20% and cash discount of 5%.

In Corrine's books, which entries record the cheque she received from Shirley?

	Account to be debited	Account to be credited
A	Bank $608 Discounts Allowed $32	Shirley $640
B	Bank $608 Discounts Received $32	Shirley $640
C	Bank $608 Discounts Allowed $152	Shirley $760
D	Bank $608 Discounts Received $152	Shirley $760

2.6 Additional exercises

1 Fleming had the following transactions.

July 1 Purchased goods from Adams for $5000 less trade discount of 15%. Adams allowed Fleming 4% cash discount.

4 Purchased goods from Bond for $2500 less trade discount of 10%. Bond allowed Fleming 4% cash discount.

5 Returned goods which had cost $600 to Adams.

7 Purchased goods from Astle for $7000 less trade discount of 20%. Astle allowed Fleming 5% cash discount.

9 Returned goods which had cost $800 to Astle.

10 Purchased goods from Cairns for $4200 less 10% trade discount. Cairns allowed Fleming 5% cash discount.

14 Fleming settled all accounts owing to his suppliers by cheque, taking advantage of the cash discount in each case.

Required
Post the transactions listed above in Fleming's books in good form.

2 Streak had the following transactions in March.

Mar 1 Sold goods to Blignaut for $2500 less trade discount of 10%, and allowed him cash discount of 4%.

4 Sold goods to Ebrahim for $4000 less trade discount of 15%, and allowed him cash discount of 5%.

6 Ebrahim returned goods which had cost him $200.

8 Sold goods to Friend for $3200 less trade discount of 20%, and allowed him cash discount of 5%.

12 Sold goods to Flower for $2000 less trade discount of 10%, and allowed him cash discount of 4%.

14 Flower returned goods which had cost him $350.

15 Blignaut, Ebrahim, Friend and Flower settled their accounts by cheque, each taking advantage of cash discount.

Required
Post the transactions listed above in Streak's books in good form.

3 Books of prime (or original) entry

In this chapter you will learn:
- **the purpose of books of prime entry**
- **how to enter transactions in books of prime entry**
- **how to post transactions from the books of prime entry to ledger accounts.**

3.1 What is a book of prime entry?

A **book of prime entry** is used to list all transactions of a similar kind *before* they are posted to ledger accounts. They are sometimes known as books of first (or original) entry but for convenience they will be referred to as books of prime entry in this text. Because they list transactions before they are posted to ledger accounts they are *outside* the double-entry model. *It is important to remember that they are not part of double-entry bookkeeping.* There is, however, one exception to this rule, and that is the cash book, as explained later in §3.4.

The names of the books of prime entry and their uses are:

Book of prime entry	Use
Sales journal (or sales day book)	To record all sales made on credit. The entries are made from copies of invoices sent to customers.
Sales returns book (or sales returns journal, or returns inwards journal)	To record all goods returned from customers. When customers return goods that were bought on credit they are sent credit notes showing the amount credited to their account for the returns. The sales returns book is prepared from the copies of credit notes sent to customers.
Purchases journal (or purchases day book)	To record all purchases of stock in trade (goods for resale) made on credit. These are entered in the purchases journal from suppliers' invoices.
Purchases returns journal (or purchases returns book, or returns outwards journal)	To record all goods returned to suppliers. The purchases returns journal is prepared from credit notes received from suppliers.
Cash book	To record all cash transactions. (But see §3.4.)
Journal (or general journal)	To record all transactions for which there is no other book of prime entry. (Also see §3.11.)

3.2 How to write up books of prime entry

Example

Jayasuriya has sent and received the following invoices and credit notes.

Invoices sent to customers	Amount of invoice $
May 1 Atapattu	2350
May 4 de Silva	1746
May 6 Arnold	520

Credit notes sent to customers	Amount of credit note $
May 3 Atapattu	350
May 5 de Silva	146
May 7 Arnold	60

Invoices received from suppliers	Amount of invoice $
May 2 Vaas	5000
May 5 Fernando	3600
May 7 Mubarak	2200

Credit notes received from suppliers	Amount of credit note $
May 6 Vaas	1000
May 7 Fernando	600

The transactions will be entered in the books of prime entry as follows:

Sales journal	$	Sales returns journal	$
May 1 Atapattu	2350	May 3 Atapattu	350
May 4 de Silva	1746	May 5 de Silva	146
May 6 Arnold	520	May 7 Arnold	60
	4616		556

Purchases journal	$	Purchases returns journal	$
May 2 Vaas	5 000	May 6 Vaas	1000
May 5 Fernando	3 600	May 7 Fernando	600
May 7 Mubarak	2 200		1600
	10 800		

3.3 How to post from books of prime entry to ledger accounts

Example

Use the information in the books of prime entry in §3.2.

Step 1 Post each item in the books of prime entry to the supplier's or customer's account in the ledger following the procedure already learned in chapter 2, but do *not* post them to the Purchases, Purchases Returns, Sales or Sales Returns accounts.

Atapattu			
	$		$
May 1 Sales	2350	May 3 Sales Returns	350

de Silva			
	$		$
May 4 Sales	1746	May 5 Sales Returns	146

Arnold			
	$		$
May 6 Sales	520	May 7 Sales Returns	60

Vaas			
	$		$
May 6 Purchases Returns	1000	May 2 Purchases	5000

Fernando			
	$		$
May 7 Purchases Returns	600	May 5 Purchases	3600

Mubarak			
	$		$
		May 7 Purchases	2200

Step 2 Post the total of each book of prime entry to the Sales, Sales Returns, Purchases or Purchases Returns accounts, as appropriate.

Sales			
	$		$
		May 7 Sales journal total	4616

Sales Returns			
	$		$
May 7 Sales returns journal total	556		

Purchases		
	$	$
May 7 Purchases journal total	10 800	

Purchases Returns		
	$	$
		May 7 Purchases returns journal total 1600

Bank					
	Discounts (allowed)	Bank		Discounts (received)	Bank
	$	$		$	$
May 7 Attapattu	100	1900	May 7 Vaas	200	3800
May 7 de Silva	80	1520	May 7 Fernando	150	2850
May 7 Arnold	23	437	May 7 Mubarak	110	2090
	203			460	

3.4 The cash book

A **cash book** is the book of prime entry for all cash transactions; but we have already seen in chapter 1 that it is also an account. It is the only book of prime entry that is also part of the double-entry model.

The cash book is also used as the book of prime entry for cash discounts. A column is provided on the debit side of the Bank account to record discounts allowed, and a column on the credit side to record discounts received.

Bank					
	Discounts (allowed)	Bank		Discounts (received)	Bank
	$	$		$	$

The words 'allowed' and 'received' are usually omitted because bookkeepers know which is which.

3.5 How to enter discounts in the cash book

When a payment is received from a customer who has deducted cash discount, enter the amount of the discount in the discounts allowed column next to the amount received in the bank column.

Enter discounts received from suppliers in the discounts received column next to the amount paid in the bank column.

Example

All payments due from customers and all payments to suppliers in §3.2 were settled on 7 May. In each case, cash discount of 5% was allowed or received.

Atapattu			
	$		$
May 1 Sales	2350	May 3 Sales Returns	350
		May 7 Bank	1900
		May 7 Discounts Allowed	100

de Silva			
	$		$
May 4 Sales	1746	May 5 Sales Returns	146
		May 7 Bank	1520
		May 7 Discounts Allowed	80

Arnold			
	$		$
May 6 Sales	520	May 7 Sales Returns	60
		May 7 Bank	437
		May 7 Discounts Allowed	23

Vaas			
	$		$
May 6 Purchases Returns	1000	May 2 Purchases	5000
May 7 Bank	3800		
May 7 Discounts Received	200		

Fernando			
	$		$
May 7 Purchases Returns	600	May 5 Purchases	3600
May 7 Bank	2850		
May 7 Discounts Received	150		

Mubarak			
	$		$
May 7 Bank	2090	May 7 Purchases	2200
May 7 Discounts Received	110		

3.6 How to post discounts from the cash book to the Discounts Allowed and Discounts Received accounts

The periodic totals of the discount allowed column in the cash book are posted to the **debit** of the Discounts Allowed account; the periodic totals of the discounts received column are posted to the **credit** of the Discounts Received account. The discount columns in the cash book are not part of the double-entry model.

Discounts Allowed			
	$		$
May 7 Cash book total	203		

Discounts Received			
	$		$
		May 7 Cash book total	460

Exercise 1

Murgatroyd had the following transactions, all on credit, in March.

March 1 Purchased goods from Tikolo for $10 000 less trade discount of 20%. Tikolo allowed him 5% cash discount.

4 Sold goods to Snyman for $1200 less trade discount of 10%. He allowed Snyman 4% cash discount.

6 Purchased goods from Walters for $8000 less trade discount of 10%. Walters allowed Murgatroyd 5% cash discount.

10 Sold goods to Karg for $2500 less trade discount of 10%. He allowed Karg 4% cash discount.

11 Snyman returned goods which had cost him $200.

12 Returned goods which had cost $400 to Tikolo.

13 Purchased goods from Burger for $7000 less trade discount of 25%. Burger allowed him cash discount of 4%.

17 Sold goods to Kotze for $3000 less trade discount of 10%. He allowed Kotze 5% cash discount.

18 Purchased goods from Tikolo for $6000 less trade discount of 20%. Tikolo allowed him 5% cash discount.

20 Karg returned goods which had cost him $300.

22 Returned to Burger goods which had cost $1000.

25 Sold goods to Snyman for $1800 less trade discount of 10%. Murgatroyd allowed Snyman 5% cash discount.

31 Received cheques from Snyman, Karg and Kotze respectively in full settlement of their accounts, and sent cheques in full settlement of their accounts to Tikolo, Walters and Burger.

Required

Enter the transactions for March in Murgatroyd's books of prime entry and post them in good form to the proper accounts.

3.7 Three-column cash book

Most businesses receive cash that they do not bank and pay some of their expenses out of the unbanked cash. An account for this cash is kept in the cash book. It is usually found convenient to have columns for cash next to those for the Bank account for cash receipts and payments. The account is then a combined Bank and Cash account.

Bank and Cash							
	Disc	Cash	Bank		Disc	Cash	Bank
	$	$	$		$	$	$

3.8 How to write up a three-column cash book

The cash columns are entered in exactly the same way as the bank columns, cash received being debited, and cash payments credited, in the cash columns. When cash is banked the cash column must be credited and the bank column debited with the amount. When cash is drawn from the bank, the bank column must be credited and the cash column must be debited.

Example

On 1 May Cassius received $700 in cash from a customer. On 3 May he paid sundry expenses of $40 out of cash. On 4 May his takings were $2000. On 5 May he banked $1500 cash.

On 7 May he paid cash, $70, on sundry items. On May 8 he withdrew $500 from the bank to pay wages.

Bank and Cash

	Disc $	Cash $	Bank $		Disc $	Cash $	Bank $
May 1 Sales		700		May 3 Sundry exps.		40	
May 4 Sales		2000		May 5 Bank ¢		1500	
May 5 Cash ¢			1500	May 7 Sundry exps.		70	
May 8 Bank ¢		500		May 8 Cash ¢			500
				May 8 Wages		500	

Note. ¢ is an abbreviation for 'contra', indicating that the double entry is completed on the opposite sides of the Bank and Cash accounts.

Exercise 2

Enter the following transactions in Joshua's three-column cash book.

March		
	1	Received takings from cash sales, $1100.
	2	Paid electricity in cash, $130.
	3	Received takings from cash sales, $900.
	4	Banked cash, $1700.
	5	Paid sundry expenses in cash, $25.
	6	Drew $800 from bank for the office cash float.
	7	Paid for stock by cash, $750.

3.9 The journal

All transactions should be recorded in one of the books of prime entry before being posted to ledger accounts. The journal is the book of prime entry for transactions for which there is no other book of prime entry. Items which will require entries in the journal are

- corrections of posting errors
- adjustments to accounts (which are dealt with later)
- transfers between accounts
- purchase and sale of items other than stock-in-trade (e.g. machinery, delivery vans, etc. used in the business)
- opening entries in a new set of ledgers (e.g. when there is no more room in the existing ledgers and the balances on the accounts are transferred to new ledgers).

Each journal entry shows the account to be debited, and the account to be credited. It follows that the debits should always equal the credits. The journal is ruled as follows:

Date	Accounts	Dr* $	Cr* $

* Dr is short for debit and Cr is short for credit.

3.10 How to make journal entries

Always state the account to be debited before the one to be credited. Every entry should have a brief but informative explanation of the reason for the entry; this is called the **narrative**.

Example

1 Jonah discovered that he had credited $100 that he had received from A. Burger on 1 April to an account for L. Burger in error. The journal entry to correct the error will be:

Date	Accounts	Dr $	Cr $
April 1	L. Burger	100	
	A. Burger		100

Correction of an error. A remittance from A. Burger on this date was posted incorrectly to L. Burger's account.

2 On 4 May Jonah bought office furniture from A. Whale on credit for $400.

Date	Accounts	Dr $	Cr $
May 4	Office Furniture	400	
	A. Whale		400

Purchase of office furniture from A Whale. See A.Whale's invoice no. 123 dated 4 May.

Note. The narrative gives Jonah the information he needs to enable him to check on the details later if needs be.

3 On 13 May Jonah bought a delivery van for $3000 and paid by cheque.

(The book of prime entry for this cash transaction is the cash book but, by also entering the purchase in the journal, Jonah will be able to see more detail about this important item than if he had entered it in the cash book only.)

Date	Accounts	Dr $	Cr $
May 13	Delivery Van account	3000	
	Bank		3000

Purchase of delivery van, registration no. G1234PYD. See Wheeler's invoice no. 6789 dated 13 May.

Exercise 3

Prepare journal entries in proper form to correct the following.

1 Credit note no. 964, for $120, received from A & Co., a supplier, has been posted to A. Cotter's account in error.

2 Invoice no. 104, for $400, received from Hussain, a supplier, has not been entered in the purchases journal.

3 Invoice no. 6789, for $150, sent to Maya, a customer, has been entered in the sales journal as $105.

4 The purchase of a machine for use in the business, and costing $2300, has been debited to Purchases account in error.

5 Credit note no. 23, for $68, sent to Hanife, a customer, has been omitted from the sales returns journal.

3.11 Examination hints

- Remember that books of prime entry, except the cash book, are not part of the double-entry model.
- Recognise the correct book of prime entry for every transaction you record in ledger accounts.
- Enter invoices *net of trade discount* in the books of prime entry.
- Post the periodic totals of the sales journal, sales returns journal, purchases journal and purchases returns journal to the Sales, Sales Returns, Purchases and Purchases Returns accounts respectively.
- Remember that the discount columns in the cash book are memorandum columns only and not part of the double-entry model.
- Prepare cash books in columnar form if possible. (See §3.8.)
- Show the debit entry before the credit entry in the journal.
- Add a suitable narrative with proper detail to every entry in the journal.
- Prepare journal entries only to ledger accounts, *never to other books of prime entry*.

3.12 Multiple-choice questions

1 Tania purchased goods for $1000 less 25% trade discount. She was allowed cash discount of 10%. Which amount should she enter in her purchases journal?

A $650   **B** $675   **C** $750   **D** $1000

2 Lara purchased goods costing $1800 less trade discount of 30%. He was allowed cash discount of 5%.

How much should Lara have to pay for the goods?

A $1080   **B** $1197   **C** $1260   **D** $1800

3 Cora sent an invoice to Maria for $2000 less 20% trade discount. Cora has omitted to enter the invoice in her sales journal.

What effect will this have on her accounts?

	Maria's account		Sales account	
	Debit	Credit	Debit	Credit
A		understated $1600	understated $1600	
B	understated $1600			understated $1600
C		understated $2000	understated $2000	
D	understated $2000			understated $2000

4 Cheung has received a cheque for $1540 from Raju in full settlement of a debt of $1700.

How should this be recorded in Cheung's books of account?

	Debit	$	Credit	$
A	Bank	1540	Raju	1540
B	Bank	1700	Raju	1700
C	Bank	1540	Raju	1700
	Discounts Allowed	160		
D	Bank	2000	Raju	1540
			Discounts Received	160

3.13 Additional exercises

1 Adeel's transactions for the month of April were as follows.

April 1 Bought goods from Bilal for $3000 less 20% trade discount. Bilal allowed Adeel 5% cash discount.

2 Sold goods to Imran for $800 less 10% trade discount. He allowed Imran 5% cash discount.

3 Bought goods from Asad for $1300 less 20% trade discount. Asad allowed Adeel 5% cash discount.

5 Purchased a delivery van on credit from Syed for $6000. The invoice for the van was no. 324.

8 Returned goods which had cost $100 to Bilal.

10 Sold goods to Raza for $1100 less 20% trade discount. He allowed Raza 5% cash discount.

13 Imran returned goods which had cost him $60.

15 Purchased goods from Asma for $4000 less 25% trade discount. Asma allowed Adeel 5% cash discount.

16 Sold goods to Amna for $1500 less 20% trade discount. He allowed Amna 5% cash discount.

17 Sold goods to Raza for $1600 less 20% trade discount. He allowed Raza 5% cash discount.

21 Returned goods which had cost him $600 to Asma.

24 Amna returned goods which had cost her $300.

26 Purchased goods from Bilal for $4000 less 20% trade discount. Bilal allowed Adeel 5% cash discount.

30 Adeel settled all accounts he owed by cheque, and received cheques for all amounts owing by his customers. All discounts were taken.

Required
(a) Enter all the transactions for April into the books of prime entry.
(b) Post the books of prime entry to the ledger accounts.

2 Prepare journal entries with suitable narratives to record the following:
   1. Received from Mumtaz invoice no. 506 dated 3 March for $10 000. This was in respect of the purchase of a machine on credit.
   2. Invoice no. 495 dated 6 March for $675 for goods sold to Wayne. The invoice has been entered twice in the sales journal.
   3. Invoice no. 998 dated 7 March for $4250 in respect of a delivery van purchased from Younas and paid for by cheque.
   4. Credit note no. 103 dated 10 March for $190 sent to Browne but omitted from the sales returns journal.
   5. Invoice no. 854 dated 15 March for $1300 for goods purchased from Sandra. The invoice has been posted to Geeta's account in error.

4 Balancing accounts

Balancing accounts

> *In this chapter you will learn:*
> • how to find and record a balance on a ledger account
> • what debit balances and credit balances mean.

4.1 Why accounts need to be balanced

The cash book must be balanced periodically to find how much money is left in the bank account. Similarly, the ledger accounts are balanced to find how much the business owes other people, how much it is owed, and how much has been received from, or spent on, the various activities.

4.2 How to balance an account

Add each side of the account to find which has the lesser total. Insert on that side the amount needed to make both sides equal, or, in other words, balance. Insert the total on each side of the account and carry the balance down to the other side of the account on the next day.

Example 1

Bank

		$			$
Apr 1	Abdul – Capital	10 000	Ap 2	Motor Vehicles	2 000
Apr 4	Sales	800	Apr 13	Purchases	3 000
Apr 8	Purchases Returns	100	Apr 7	Sales Returns	40
Apr 11	Tania – Loan	5 000	Apr 10	Motor Vehicles	4 000
Apr 14	Rent Receivable	300	Apr 12	Rent Payable	1 000
			Apr 15	Wages	1 200
			Apr 16	Drawings	600
			Apr 10	Balance carried down	4 360
		16 200			16 200
Apr 11	Balance brought down	4 360			

Notes
- The account has been balanced at 10 April.
- The balance was entered on the credit side to make it balance with the debit side, and carried down to the debit side on the next day.
- The account has a *debit balance* showing how much money is left in the Bank account on 10 April.
- The totals are placed level with each other although there are more items on the credit side than on the debit side.

Example 2

Charley is a customer whose account has been balanced and is as follows.

Charley

		$			$
Jun 4	Sales	1040	Jun 6	Sales Returns	400
Jun 10	Sales	3105	Jun 14	Bank	600
Jun 19	Sales	900	Jun 14	Discount	40
			Jun 30	Balance c/d	4005
		5045			5045
Jul 1	Balance b/d	4005			

Notes
- Charley's account has a debit balance which shows that he owes the business $4005; he is a 'debtor' of the business.
- c/d is short for 'carried down' and b/d is short for 'brought down'. These abbreviations are quite acceptable in accounting.
- The credit entry on 14 June is described simply as 'discount' because it is understood that it is discount allowed.

Example 3

Sara (who supplies goods to the business)

		$				$
May 8	Purchase Returns	1000	May 1	Balance	b/d	1940
May 29	Bank	2005	May 12	Purchases		7330
May 29	Discount	125				
May 31	Balance	c/d 6140				
		9270				9270
			June 1	Balance	b/d	6140

Notes

- The credit balance shows that Sara is owed $6140; she is a creditor of the business.
- When Sara's account was balanced on the previous 30 April, a balance of $1940 was carried down and appears as an opening credit balance on her account at 1 May.

If an account has only one entry on each side and they are of equal amount, the account is simply ruled off.

Gerald

		$			$
Mar 4	Sales	1000	Mar 23	Bank	1000

An account with an entry on one side only is balanced without the insertion of totals.

Paula

		$			$
Mar 31	Balance	c/d 1500	Mar 22	Purchases	1500
			Apr 1	Balance	b/d 1500

A three-column cash book is balanced as follows.

Bank and Cash

		Discs $	Cash $	Bank $			Discs $	Cash $	Bank $
May 1	Sales		700		May 3	Sundry exps.		40	
May 4	Sales		2000		May 5	Bank ¢		1500	
May 5	A & Co.	100		2080	May 6	Z & Sons	50		600
May 5	Cash ¢			1500	May 7	Sundry exps.		70	
May 7	P Ltd	80		450	May 8	Q Bros.	40		160
May 8	Bank ¢		500		May 8	Cash ¢			500
					May 8	Wages		500	
					May 8	Balances c/d		1090	2770
		180	3200	4030			90	3200	4030
May 9	Balances b/d		1090	2770					

4.3 When are accounts balanced?

The cash book will usually be balanced at frequent intervals because it is always important to know how much money is in the Bank account. It will be balanced at weekly intervals in small businesses, daily in large ones.

Accounts for customers and suppliers are balanced monthly because of the practice of sending and receiving statements of account. The statements are copies of the accounts of customers in the sellers' books and are sent to customers so that they can reconcile their ledger accounts with those of their suppliers. Any differences can be enquired into and agreement reached between supplier and customer. The statements also remind customers that payment of outstanding balances is due.

The other accounts are usually balanced as and when required; this will always be when a trial balance is being prepared. Trial balances are explained in chapter 6.

4.4 Examination hint

- Remember that balances carried down on accounts should always be shown as brought down on the accounts on the next day. Marks may be lost in an examination if this is not done.

Note. The discount columns are not balanced. The totals are carried to the Discounts Allowed and Discounts Received accounts respectively.

5 The classification of accounts and division of the ledger

5.1 The classification of accounts

All accounts fall into one of two classes: **personal** or **impersonal**. Each of these classes can be further divided into subgroups.

Personal accounts are those for persons (including sole traders, partnerships and companies). The subgroups are as follows.

* **Accounts for debtors**, persons who owe the business money. They are usually the customers of the business, and their accounts have debit balances. These accounts collectively are known as current assets. (Other current assets include cash in hand, cash at bank and stock, as explained below under Impersonal accounts.)
* **Accounts for creditors**, persons to whom the business owes money. They are usually those who supply goods or services to the business, and their accounts have credit balances. This group includes Loan accounts. Creditors who have to be paid within one year are **current liabilities**. Creditors who do not have to be paid within one year (e.g. for a long-term loan) are **long-term liabilities**.
* The owner's **Capital and Drawings accounts**.

Impersonal accounts are all accounts other than personal accounts. The subgroups are as follows.

* **Accounts with debit balances**. These are further divided into asset accounts (real accounts) and expenses accounts (nominal accounts).

* **Asset accounts** (real accounts) are things that the business owns. This group may be further subdivided into
  – **fixed assets**, which are things acquired for use in the business and not for re-sale, such as premises, plant and machinery, vehicles, office furniture and equipment. These assets are intended to be used in the business for a number of years. Expenditure on fixed assets is **capital expenditure**.
  – **current assets**, in addition to the debtors referred to above, are those that arise in the course of trading, such as stock-in-trade, stocks of stationery, stocks of fuel, cash at bank and in hand.
* **Expenses accounts** (nominal accounts) include rent payable, wages, salaries, heating and lighting, postage and stationery, etc. This type of expenditure is **revenue expenditure**.
* **Accounts with credit balances**. These accounts record **revenue** (sales) and **other income** (rent receivable, discounts received and interest receivable). These are also nominal accounts.

The distinction between the types of accounts is very important. Care must always be taken to ensure that capital expenditure is not confused with revenue expenditure. The cost of purchasing a motor vehicle is capital expenditure and must be debited to the Motor Vehicles account. The cost of running the vehicle is revenue expenditure and must be debited to Motor Vehicles Running Expenses account.

Exercise 1

Copy and complete this table, ticking the boxes which correctly describe the given accounts in the books of a bakery.

Account	Personal	Fixed asset	Current asset	Revenue or other income	Expense
Capital					
Sales Returns					
Delivery Vans					
Purchases					
Rent Payable					
Debtors					
Stock-in-trade					
Discounts Allowed					
Drawings					
Bank					
Rent Receivable					
Creditors					
Computer					
Wages					
Discounts Received					

5.2 Division of the ledger

Except in very small businesses there are too many accounts to be kept in a single ledger. It is usual to divide the accounts among several ledgers as follows:

- sales ledger for the accounts of customers
- purchase ledger for the accounts of suppliers
- general (or nominal) ledger for the impersonal accounts for assets, revenue, other income, and expenses
- private ledger for accounts of a confidential nature – the owner's Capital and Drawings accounts and Loan accounts; also the Trading and Profit and Loss Accounts and Balance Sheets (see chapters 7 and 8)
- cash book containing the Bank and Cash accounts.

The division of the ledger as above is essential in a business which employs several bookkeepers; the work may be divided between them so that they do not all need to be working on the same ledger at the same time.

6 The trial balance

6.1 What is a trial balance?

A **trial balance** is a list of all the balances extracted from the ledgers at a particular date, and its purpose is to check that the total of the debit balances equals the total of the credit balances. The principle of double entry ensures that the two totals should agree. If the totals do not agree there must be an error somewhere in the bookkeeping.

6.2 How to prepare a trial balance

First balance all the ledger accounts including the cash book. Then list the balances with the debit balances and credit balances in separate columns. The total of the debit balances should equal the total of the credit balances. If the totals are equal, the trial balance agrees.

Example

The following trial balance has been extracted from the books of Zabine at 31 March 2003.

Account	Debit balances $	Credit balances $
Premises	70 000	
Machinery	10 000	
Office Furniture	5 000	
Sales		100 000
Sales Returns	700	
Purchases	6 900	
Purchases Returns		1 000
Trade debtors*	1 100	
Trade creditors**		1 575
Rent Payable	1 600	
Wages and Salaries	4 080	
Heating and Lighting	960	
Sundry Expenses	1 430	
Cash	500	
Bank	12 600	
Loan from Ludmilla		2 000
Capital – Zabine		13 000
Drawings	2 705	
	117 575	117 575

* The balances on the accounts in the sales ledger are listed and totalled separately; the total is entered in the trial balance as trade debtors.

** The balances on the accounts in the purchase ledger are listed and totalled separately; the total is entered in the trial balance as trade creditors.

Exercise 1

Prepare a trial balance from the following balances that have been extracted from the books of Achilles, a grocer, at 31 December.

Account	$
Premises	50 000
Motor Vans	8 000
Office Furniture	2 000
Computer	3 000
Sales	60 000
Sales Returns	700
Purchases	4 000
Purchases Returns	500
Motor Vehicle Running Expenses	4 200
Wages	1 800
Rent	2 000
Bank	1 650
Capital	20 000
Drawings	3 150

6.3 Limitations of a trial balance

As stated above, if a trial balance does not agree, there must be a mistake somewhere in the bookkeeping. Unfortunately, even if a trial balance agrees, it does not mean that there are no errors because there are six types of error that do not affect the agreement of the trial balance. They are as follows.

1. **Errors of omission.** A transaction omitted completely from the books results in there being neither debit nor credit entry for the transaction. This could happen if a transaction is not entered in a book of prime entry.

2. **Errors of commission.** A transaction is posted to the wrong account, but the account is of the same class as the account to which the posting should have been made. Example: the payment of a telephone bill is posted in error to Heating and Lighting account. Telephone account and Heating and Lighting account are both expense accounts.

3. **Errors of principle.** A transaction is posted to a wrong account which is not of the same type as the correct account. Example: revenue expenditure treated as capital expenditure. For instance, payment for petrol for a vehicle has been debited to Motor Vehicles account (a fixed asset account) instead of to Motor Vehicles Running Expenses account (an expense account).

4. **Errors of original entry.** A wrong amount is entered in a book of prime entry for a transaction. Example: a sales invoice for $200 is entered in the sales journal as $20.

5. **Complete reversal of entries.** An account which should have been debited has been credited, and the account which should have been credited has been debited. Example: a payment received from Hussain is debited to Hussain's account and credited to Bank account.

6. **Compensating errors.** Two or more errors cancel each other out. Example: an invoice for $1100 in the sales journal is posted to the customer's account as $1000. At the same time, the sales journal total is understated by $100. The debit balance on the customer's account and the credit balance on Sales account will both be understated by $100.

Exercise 2

State which type of error each of the following represents.
(a) Payment of rent has been debited to the Bank account and credited to the Rent Payable account.
(b) The purchase of a computer has been debited to the Office Expenses account.
(c) A supplier's invoice has been omitted from the purchases journal.

(d) The total of the Wages account has been overstated by $1000 and rent received of $1000 has been posted twice to the Rent Received account.
(e) Discount allowed to Amna has been credited to Asma's account.
(f) A purchase of goods for $960 has been entered in the purchases journal as $690.

6.4 Examination hints

- Learn the six types of error which do not affect the trial balance.
- Look for the cause of a difference on a trial balance by carrying out the following simple checks before spending a lot of time checking all your postings:
  - check the additions of the trial balance
  - if the difference is divisible by 2, look for a balance equal to half the difference which may have been entered on the wrong side
  - if the difference is divisible by 9, two figures may have been transposed in a balance; for example, $269 may have been copied as $296.

6.5 Multiple-choice questions

1 Which of the following accounts normally has a credit balance?
  A Discounts Allowed
  B Discounts Received
  C Purchases
  D Sales Returns

2 After which error will a trial balance still balance?
  A An invoice for $400 in the sales journal not posted to the customer's account in the sales ledger.
  B A purchase of goods from Ratna for $1000 credited to Ravin's account in the purchases ledger.
  C Payment of $60 to Josan entered correctly in the Bank account and credited to Josan's account.
  D Rent paid $660 entered correctly in the cash book but posted to Rent Payable account as $600.

3 A business has paid rent of $800. The payment has been entered in the books as follows.

Account debited	Account credited
Bank $800	Rent $800

Which type of error is this?
  A Commission
  B Compensating
  C Complete reversal
  D Principle

4 Discounts allowed of $160 for one month have been posted to the credit of the Discounts Received account. What effect has this had on the trial balance?

A $160 too much credit

B $160 too little debit

C $160 too little debit and $160 too much credit

D $320 too much credit

6.6 Additional exercises

1 The following balances at 31 December 2003 have been extracted from Hassan's books.

	$
Sales	160 000
Sales Returns	2 600
Purchases	84 000
Purchases Returns	3 400
Wages	26 000
Heating and Lighting	3 160
Rent Payable	5 000
Rent Receivable	1 000
Advertising	2 900
Postage and Telephone	2 740
Discounts Allowed	6 100
Discounts Received	5 900
Plant and Machinery	50 000
Delivery Van	9 000
Bank	2 300
Trade Debtors	7 400
Trade Creditors	3 700
Drawings	8 800
Capital	?

Required

Prepare a trial balance at 31 December 2003 from the balances extracted from Hassan's books and calculate the balance on his Capital account.

2 An inexperienced bookkeeper has extracted a trial balance at 31 December 2003 from Andrea's books. It contains some errors and does not balance.

	$	$
Premises	70 000	
Plant and Machinery	30 000	
Office Equipment	5 000	
Wages	7 600	
Rent Payable		4 000
Heating and Lighting	1 500	
Sundry Expenses	1 720	
Sales		133 000
Purchases	57 000	
Discounts Allowed		2 450
Discounts Received	1 070	
Bank	2 910	
Trade Debtors	14 000	
Trade Creditors		10 140
Purchases Returns	2 400	
Sales Returns		3 150
Rent Receivable	1 200	
Capital		80 000
Drawings		28 480
	194 400	261 220

Required

Re-write the trial balance and correct the errors so that it balances.

Part II
Financial accounting

7 Trading and Profit and Loss Accounts for sole traders

In this chapter you will learn:
- how to prepare Trading and Profit and Loss Accounts
- what the purpose of the Stock account is.

7.1 What is a Trading and Profit and Loss Account?

Most people carry on business in order to make a living. They depend upon the profit of the business for their income to enable them to buy food, clothes and other necessities. They compare the revenue earned by the business with its expenses. If the revenue exceeds expenses the business has made a profit. On the other hand, if the expenses exceed the revenue the business has made a loss and the trader has no income. Profit or loss is found by the preparation of a Trading and Profit and Loss Account covering a period of time, usually one complete year. Until now, double-entry bookkeeping may have seemed a tiresome and largely pointless exercise, but it is the only system that enables Trading and Profit and Loss Accounts to be prepared.

7.2 How to prepare a Trading and Profit and Loss Account for a sole trader

Step 1

All ledger accounts must be balanced and a trial balance prepared at the date to which the Trading and Profit and Loss Account is to be prepared.

Example

Andrew commenced business on 1 January 2003. The following trial balance has been extracted at 31 December 2003 from his books.

Account	$	$
Sales		126 000
Sales Returns	2 000	
Purchases	55 200	
Purchases Returns		2 200
Discounts Received		2 340
Discounts Allowed	3 260	
Wages	28 000	
Rent	16 000	
Heating and Lighting	3 400	
Postage and Stationery	1 070	
Motor Van Expenses	9 830	
Interest on Loan	800	
Sundry Expenses	920	
Premises	40 000	
Motor Vans	18 000	
Office Furniture	5 000	
Trade Debtors	7 400	
Trade Creditors		3 420
Bank	2 160	
Loan from Marie (repayable in 2005)		10 000
Andrew – Capital		60 000
Drawings	10 920	
	203 960	203 960

Trading and Profit and Loss Accounts are part of the double-entry model. Balances on the nominal (revenue, income and expense) accounts are transferred to them by journal entries.

Step 2 Trading Account

The Trading Account calculates the profit on the activity of buying and selling goods. The balances on the Sales, Sales Returns, Purchases and Purchases Returns accounts are *transferred* to the Trading Account by journal entry:

	$	$
Sales	126 000	
Trading Account		126 000
Trading Account	2 000	
Sales Returns		2 000
Trading Account	55 200	
Purchases		55 200
Purchases Returns	2 200	
Trading Account		2 200

(Narratives have been omitted.)

These journal entries produce a Trading Account as follows.

Andrew
Trading Account for the year ended 31 December 2003

	$		$
Sales returns	2 000	Sales	126 000
Purchases	55 200	Purchases returns	2 200

The Trading Account is improved if sales returns are deducted from sales to show the revenue actually earned (called the **turnover**). Similarly, it is better to deduct purchases returns from purchases.

Andrew
Trading Account for the year ended 31 December 2003

	$		$
Purchases	55 200	Sales	126 000
Less Purchases returns	2 200	Less Sales returns	2 000
	53 000*		124 000

* $53 000 is the cost of the goods which were available for selling.

Closing stock It is unlikely that Andrew has sold all his stock by 31 December, therefore some remains to be sold next year. This 'closing stock' must be deducted from the cost of the goods that were available for selling in the Trading Account to arrive at the cost of the goods sold. The double entry for this requires a journal entry to open a Stock account.

		$	$
31 December 2003	Stock	5000	
	Trading Account		5000

Transfer of closing stock at 31 December 2003 to Trading Account

Note. The debit to the Stock account creates a new asset that is not in the trial balance.

The closing stock is credited to the Trading Account. This is done by *deducting* it on the debit side from net purchases. The Trading Account now shows the cost of the goods which have been sold. The debit side of the account is therefore headed with the words 'Cost of goods sold' or 'Cost of sales':

Andrew
Trading Account for the year ended 31 December 2003

		$			$
Cost of sales			Sales		126 000
Purchases		55 200	Less Sales returns		2 000
Less Purchases returns		2 200			124 000
		53 000			
Less Closing stock		5 000			
		48 000			
Gross profit		76 000			
		124 000			124 000

Note. The balance on the Trading Account is gross profit, or the profit made on buying and selling goods before any other expenses are taken into account.

Step 3

The Profit and Loss Account follows the Trading Account without a break; the heading for the Profit and Loss Account is included in the Trading Account heading. The Profit and Loss Account begins with the gross profit to which is added other income, if any. Next, the overhead expenses included in the trial balance are deducted. (The balances on the ledger accounts are transferred to the Profit and Loss Account by journal entries.) The Trading and Profit and Loss Account is now as follows.

Andrew
Trading and Profit and Loss Account for the year ended 31 December 2003

	$		$
Cost of sales		Sales	126 000
Purchases	55 200	Less Sales returns	2 000
Less Purchases returns	2 200		124 000
	53 000		
Less Closing stock	5 000		
	48 000		
Gross profit	76 000		
	124 000		124 000
Less Overheads		Gross profit brought down	76 000
Wages	28 000	Discounts received	2 340
Rent	16 000		78 340
Heating and lighting	3 400		
Postage and stationery	1 070		
Motor van expenses	9 830		
Discounts allowed	3 260		
Sundry expenses	920		
Interest on loan	800		
Net profit	15 060		
	78 340		78 340

Andrew
Trading and Profit and Loss Account for the year ended 31 December 2003

	$	$
Sales		126 000
Less Sales returns		2 000
		124 000
Less Cost of sales		
Purchases	55 200	
Less Purchases returns	2 200	
	53 000	
Less Stock at 31 December	5 000	48 000
Gross profit		76 000
Add Discounts received		2 340
		78 340
Less Overheads:		
Wages	28 000	
Rent	16 000	
Heating and lighting	3 400	
Postage and stationery	1 070	
Motor van expenses	9 830	
Discounts allowed	3 260	
Sundry expenses	920	
Loan interest	800	63 280
Net profit		15 060

Trading and Profit and Loss Accounts like this have debit and credit sides like ledger accounts and are described as being in *horizontal* form. Many people reading these accounts are not accountants; they know nothing about debits and credits and find the accounts difficult to understand. It is now normal to prepare these accounts in *vertical* form, which is easier for non-accountants to understand.

Andrew's Trading and Profit and Loss Account in vertical form is shown on the right.

Notes
- Give the Trading and Profit and Loss Account a proper heading including the name of the business.
- The account is known as a period statement because it covers a period of time; it must be described as 'for the year (or other period) ended (date)(month)(year)'.
- It is part of the double-entry model and the balances on the accounts are transferred to it by journal entry.
- 'Sales less sales returns' is the **turnover** of the business.
- The words 'Cost of sales' or 'Cost of goods sold' are important and should always be shown.
- A trader may take some stock from the business for personal use. The goods taken should be deducted from purchases at cost price and added to the trader's drawings.

- The words 'Gross profit' are important and must be shown. The gross profit is the profit earned on selling goods before any other expenses are taken into account.
- Trading Accounts should only be prepared for traders, that is, people who trade in (buy and sell) goods. People who sell their services, such as accountants, lawyers, dentists and gardeners, only require Profit and Loss Accounts.
- There is no particular order in which overheads should be shown in the Profit and Loss account of a sole trader, but it is often best to place the larger amounts before the smaller.
- It is also a good plan to group similar kinds of expenses, for example, property expenses (rent, heating and lighting, and insurance) together.
- Net profit is the trader's income after all expenses have been taken into account.
- A net loss arises if the overheads exceed the gross profit.
- Always describe the final balance as 'net profit' (or 'net loss').

- *Examiners expect Trading and Profit and Loss Accounts to be prepared in vertical form; marks may be lost if they are prepared in horizontal form. You should study the vertical form carefully until you are quite familiar with it.*

Exercise 1

Corrine began trading on 1 January 2003. The following trial balance as at 31 December 2003 has been extracted from her books.

Account	$	$
Sales		200 000
Sales Returns	6 300	
Purchases	86 500	
Purchases Returns		5 790
Rent Received		3 000
Discounts Received		3 210
Discounts Allowed	5 110	
Wages	61 050	
Rent Paid	12 000	
Electricity	5 416	
Insurance	2 290	
Motor Van Expenses	11 400	
Sundry Expenses	3 760	
Loan Interest	1 000	
Land and Buildings	84 000	
Plant and Machinery	22 000	
Motor Van	19 000	
Trade debtors	12 425	
Trade creditors		4 220
Bank	5 065	
Loan (repayable in 2004)		20 000
Drawings	25 904	
Capital at 1 January 2003		127 000
	363 220	363 220

Corrine had unsold stock of $10 000 at 31 December 2003.

Required

Prepare Corrine's Trading and Profit and Loss Account for the year ended 31 December 2003 in good form.

Save your answer; it will be required again in chapter 8.

7.3 Opening stock

One year's closing stock is the next year's opening stock and it must be included in the cost of sales for that year. The debit balance on the Stock account is transferred by journal entry to the Trading Account.

Example

When Andrew (see §7.2) prepares his Trading Account for the year ended 31 December 2004 the opening stock will be transferred from the Stock account to the Trading Account:

Journal			
		$	$
31 Dec 2004	Trading Account	5000	
	Stock		5000

Stock			
	$		$
31 Dec 2003 Trading Account	5000	31 Dec 2004 Trading Account	5000

In the year ended 31 December 2004 Andrew's sales totalled $150 000 and his purchases were $62 000. Stock at 31 December 2004 was $8000. Andrew's Trading Account will be as follows.

Andrew
Trading and Profit and Loss Account for the year ended 31 December 2004

	$	$
Sales		150 000
Less Cost of sales		
Opening stock	5 000	
Purchases	62 000	
	67 000	
Less Closing stock	8 000	59 000
Gross profit		91 000

Note. In almost every case, stock shown in a trial balance is opening stock. The exception occurs when the trial balance has been extracted from the books *after* a Trading Account has been prepared, in which case the trial balance will not include Sales, Sales Returns, Purchases or Purchases Returns accounts.

Exercise 2

The following balances have been extracted from Khor's books at 31 December 2003.

	$	$
Sales		48 000
Sales Returns	1 600	
Purchases	21 000	
Purchases Returns		900
Stock at 1 January 2003		4 000

Stock at 31 December 2003 was $7500.

Required

Prepare Khor's Trading Account for the year ended 31 December 2003.

Exercise 3

The following trial balance has been extracted from the books of Perkins, a sole trader, at 31 March 2004.

Account	$	$
Premises	60 000	
Plant and Machinery	12 000	
Sales		104 000
Sales Returns	3 700	
Purchases	59 000	
Purchases Returns		2 550
Stock at 1 April 2003	6 000	
Wages	13 000	
Rent Payable	2 000	
Rent Receivable		1 800
Heating and Lighting	2 700	
Repairs to Machinery	4 100	
Interest on Loan	750	
Discounts Allowed	1 030	
Discounts Received		770
Trade debtors	1 624	
Trade creditors		1 880
Bank	5 000	
Drawings	10 096	
Long-term Loan		15 000
Capital		55 000
	181 000	181 000

Stock at 31 March 2004 was $10 000.

Required

Prepare Perkin's Trading and Profit and Loss Account for the year ended 31 March 2004.

Save your answer; it will be required again in chapter 8.

7.4 Carriage inwards and carriage outwards

When goods are purchased, the supplier may make an additional charge to cover the cost of delivery. This charge is carriage inwards and adds to the cost of the goods. Carriage inwards is added to the cost of purchases in the Trading Account.

The cost of delivering goods to a customer is carriage outwards and is debited in the Profit and Loss Account as an overhead. Carriage inwards and carriage outwards are both expense items but it is important to treat them correctly in Trading and Profit and Loss Accounts.

Example

A. Trader
Trading and Profit and Loss Account for the year ended 31 December 2003

	$	$	$
Sales		93 000	
Less Sales returns		2 700	90 300
Less Cost of sales			
Stock at 1 January 2003		3 000	
Purchases	45 200		
Less Purchases returns	3 400		
	41 800		
Carriage inwards	4 000	45 800	
		48 800	
Less Stock at 31 December 2003		7 000	41 800
Gross profit			48 500
Less Overheads			
Wages		12 000	
Rent		5 600	
Carriage outwards		2 220	
Sundry		1 760	21 580
Net profit			26 920

Exercise 4

Sara's trial balance at 31 March 2004 was as follows.

Account	$	$
Sales		40 000
Stock	5 000	
Purchases	20 500	
Wages	6 000	
Rent	10 000	
Electricity	2 600	
Carriage Inwards	1 320	
Carriage Outwards	1 080	
Sundry Expenses	1 250	
Plant and Machinery	8 000	
Office Equipment	1 000	
Trade Debtors	1 900	
Trade Creditors		800
Bank	820	
Drawings	6 330	
Capital		25 000
	65 800	65 800

Stock at 31 March 2004 was $3000.

Required

Prepare Sara's Trading and Profit and Loss Account for the year ended 31 March 2004.

7.5 Wages treated as cost of sales

Goods purchased may not be in a suitable condition for selling to customers. Further work may be required on them before they are sold. The wages paid to employees for performing this work should be debited as part of cost of sales in the Trading Account.

Example

The following balances are extracted from a trial balance at 30 April 2004.

	$	$
Sales		80 000
Stock at 1 May 2003	5 000	
Purchases	35 000	
Wages	16 000	

Stock at 30 April 2004 was $6000, and 25% of the wages were paid to staff who prepared the stock for sale to customers.

Trading Account for the year ended 30 April 2004

	$	$
Sales		80 000
Cost of sales		
Stock at 1 May 2003	5 000	
Purchases	35 000	
	40 000	
Less Stock at 30 April 2004	6 000	
	34 000	
Wages (25% of $16 000)	4 000	38 000
Gross profit		42 000

7.6 Examination hints

- Marks may be awarded in an examination for good presentation of Trading and Profit and Loss Accounts.
- Give all Trading and Profit and Loss Accounts proper headings.
- Include in the heading the name of the trader or business.
- State the period covered by the account.
- Include the words 'Cost of sales', 'Gross profit' and 'Net profit' (or 'Net loss').
- Copy the vertical layouts of the accounts given in the examples in this chapter as far as possible.
- Make sure you copy accurately all the nominal accounts included in the trial balance into your Trading and Profit and Loss Account.
- Deduct stock taken by the trader for personal use from purchases and add to drawings at cost price.
- Include *carriage inwards* as an addition to purchases in the Trading Account, but *carriage outwards* as an overhead in the Profit and Loss account.
- Do not prepare journal entries for the Trading, Profit and Loss Accounts unless you are specifically asked to do so. They have been shown in this chapter simply to help you understand how balances are transferred from ledger accounts to the Trading, Profit and Loss Accounts.

7.7 Multiple-choice questions

1 Which of the following does not appear in a Profit and Loss Account?

  A Carriage inwards

  B Carriage outwards

  C Discounts allowed

  D Discounts received

2 The following information has been extracted from the trial balance of a business:

	$
Sales	100 000
Purchases	60 000
Wages	21 000

Closing stock was $3000 more than opening stock.

One third of the wages was charged to cost of sales in the Trading Account.
What was the gross profit?

A $30 000

B $33 000

C $36 000

D $37 000

3 The Carriage inwards of a business amounted to $6000, and the Carriage outwards was $7000.

The Carriage outwards was charged in the Trading Account in error, and the Carriage inwards was debited in the Profit and Loss Account.
What has been the effect of these errors?

	Gross profit	Net profit
A	understated by $1000	understated by $1000
B	overstated by $1000	overstated by $1000
C	understated by $1000	not affected
D	overstated by $1000	not affected

4 Discounts received amount to $10 500 and discounts allowed to £13 000. The discounts received have been debited, and the discounts allowed have been credited in the Profit and Loss Account.

What has been the effect of these errors on net profit?

A understated by $2500

B overstated by $2500

C understated by $5000

D overstated by $5000

5 Carriage inwards in a trial balance is $2300. It has been entered in the Trading Account as $3200. In addition, motor expenses of $600 been posted to the Motor Vans account.

What effect has this had on the Trading and Profit and Loss Account?

	Gross profit	Net profit
A	understated by $900	overstated by $300
B	overstated by $900	understated by $300
C	understated by $900	overstated by $1500
D	overstated by $900	understated by $1500

7.8 Additional exercises

1 The following trial balance has been extracted from Hadlee's books at 31 December 2003.

	$	$
Plant and Machinery	25 000	
Office Furniture	6 000	
Stock at 1 January 2003	11 000	
Trade debtors	4 740	
Trade creditors		1 976
Bank	3 327	
Loan, repayable in 2005		5 000
Sales		72 800
Purchases	28 540	
Sales Returns	1 600	
Purchases Returns		2 144
Wages	3 100	
Rent	4 000	
Heating and Lighting	5 120	
Advertising	2 400	
Sundry Expenses	2 010	
Loan Interest	250	
Drawings	4 833	
Capital		20 000
	101 920	101 920

Stock at 31 December 2003 cost $9000.

Required

Prepare Hadlee's Trading and Profit and Loss Account for the year ended 31 December 2003.

Keep your answer; it will be needed again in chapter 8.

2 The trial balance extracted from Tikolo's books at 31 March 2004 is as follows.

Account	$	$
Sales		204 000
Sales Returns	3 600	
Purchases	120 000	
Purchases Returns		4 440
Stock at 1 April 2003	18 000	
Carriage Inwards	5 000	
Carriage Outwards	3 724	
Discounts Received		3 160
Discounts Allowed	5 020	
Wages	36 800	
Rent	8 000	
Heating and Lighting	6 450	
Sundry Expenses	1 143	
Fixtures and Fittings	9 000	
Office Furniture	2 000	
Trade debtors	1 970	
Trade creditors		2 130
Bank	2 496	
Drawings	20 527	
Capital		30 000
	243 730	243 730

During the year, Tikolo had taken goods costing $2000 for his own use. This had not been recorded in the books.

Stock at 31 March 2004 cost $20 000.

Required

Prepare Tikolo's Trading and Profit and Loss Account for the year ended 31 March 2004.

Keep your answer; it will be needed again in chapter 8.

8 Balance Sheets for sole traders

> *In this chapter you will learn:*
> • what a Balance Sheet is and why Balance Sheets are prepared
> • how to prepare a Balance Sheet for a sole trader.

8.1 What is a Balance Sheet?

A **Balance Sheet** is a list of the assets and liabilities of a business at a particular date. A trader needs to know if his business will continue to provide an income for the foreseeable future. A Balance Sheet can provide a good indication of the answer to this question.

Unlike a Trading and Profit and Loss Account, a Balance Sheet is not part of the double-entry model. After the nominal account balances have been transferred to the Trading and Profit and Loss Account, the only balances left in the ledger are those for assets and liabilities. The Balance Sheet is a list of these balances.

Although a Balance Sheet is not an account, the Trading and Profit and Loss Account and Balance Sheet are known collectively as the **final accounts** of a business.

8.2 How to prepare a Balance Sheet

List and group the assets and liabilities of the business under the headings:

- Fixed assets
- Current assets
- Current liabilities
- Long-term liabilities
- Capital

Example

The following is the Balance Sheet for Andrew's business at 31 December 2003. It is prepared from the trial balance given in §7.2 and lists all the balances remaining in the ledger after the Trading and Profit and Loss Account has been prepared.

Andrew Balance Sheet at 31 December 2003		
	$	$
Fixed assets		
Premises		40 000
Motor vans		18 000
Office furniture		5 000
		63 000
Current assets		
Stock	5 000*	
Trade debtors	7 400	
Bank	2 160	
	14 560	
Less Current liabilities		
Trade creditors	3 420	11 140
		74 140
Less Long-term liability		
Loan from Marie		10 000
		64 140
Represented by:		
Capital at 1 January 2003		60 000
Add net profit for the year		15 060
		75 060
Deduct drawings		10 920
		64 140

* Stock: see page 29.

Notes

- A Balance Sheet is a 'position' statement showing the position of a business at a particular moment in time. It is not a period statement like a Trading and Profit and Loss Account. The date at which the Balance Sheet is prepared must be included in the heading 'Balance Sheet at ....'.

- The Balance Sheet has been prepared in vertical form. Study it carefully until you are quite familiar with it and prepare all your Balance Sheets in similar style.
- The fixed assets are grouped together and totalled. The assets which are likely to have the longest useful life are placed first.
- Current assets are grouped next in an inner column and totalled. They are listed in the reverse order of **liquidity**. A **liquid asset** is one which is in the form of cash (cash in hand) or nearly so (cash at bank). Stock is not a liquid asset because it has not been sold and no money has been, or will be, received for it until it is sold. Debtors should soon become a liquid asset. The order in the Balance Sheet is: stock, debtors, bank and cash (if any).
- The current assets are not added to the fixed assets at this stage.
- Current liabilities are those that are due to be settled within one year of the date of the Balance Sheet. They are deducted from the total of current assets to give the **working capital**. In the example above, the working capital is $11 140.
- Working capital is a very important item in the Balance Sheet. The liquid current assets should exceed the current liabilities and show that the business resources adequately cover the payments it must make to its creditors. If the current assets are insufficient to meet the current liabilities, the trader may be forced to sell fixed assets to pay his creditors and that could be the beginning of the end of the business.
- Long-term liabilities are those which are not due to be settled within one year of the date of the Balance Sheet. They are deducted from the total of fixed assets and working capital.
- The assets less the liabilities are represented by the owner's capital. The capital shown in the trial balance is the balance on the Capital account brought forward from the previous year. The net profit shown by the Profit and Loss Account is added to the opening capital, but a net loss must be deducted. Profit increases capital and losses reduce capital. When the drawings are deducted, the balance on the Capital account will be carried forward as the opening capital next year.
- At the end of the year, the balances on the Profit and Loss Account and Drawings account are transferred to the Capital account (by journal entry) as shown.
- The total of the fixed and current assets $(63 000 + 14 560) less the total of the current and long-term liabilities $(3420 + 10 000) equals the closing balance on the Capital account, $64 140. This is always true, and the formula 'assets – liabilities = capital' is known as the **accounting equation**.
- At the end of the year, the balances on the Profit and Loss Account and Drawings account are transferred to the Capital account (by journal entry) as shown.

Andrew – Capital

		$			$
2003			2003		
Dec 31	Drawings	10 920	Jan 1	Balance brought down	60 000
	Balance carried down	64 140	Dec 31	Profit and Loss	15 060
		75 060			75 060
			2004		
			Jan 1	Balance brought down	64 140

Exercise 1

Prepare a Balance Sheet at 31 December 2003 for Corrine from the trial balance given in exercise 1 of chapter 7 (page 31).

Exercise 2

Prepare a Balance Sheet at 31 March 2004 for Perkins from the trial balance given in exercise 3 of chapter 7 (page 32).

8.3 Examination hints

- Marks may be awarded in an examination for good presentation of Balance Sheets.
- Give every Balance Sheet a proper heading which should include the name of the business and the date. (If the Balance Sheet follows a Trading Profit and Loss Account which is headed with the name of the business, the name need not be repeated for the Balance Sheet.)
- Prepare Balance Sheets as shown in this chapter, with headings for fixed assets, current assets, current liabilities and long-term liabilities. Show the total of each group.
- Show the working capital clearly.

8.4 Multiple-choice questions

1 The purchase of an office computer has been debited to Office Expenses instead of to Office Equipment.

What effect will this have on the Balance Sheet?

	Fixed assets	Profit	Capital
A	no effect	understated	no effect
B	no effect	understated	understated
C	understated	no effect	understated
D	understated	understated	no effect

2 The owner of a business has taken goods for his own use but no entry has been made in the books to record this. What is the effect of this on the Balance Sheet?

	Stock	Capital
A	no effect	no effect
B	no effect	overstated
C	overstated	no effect
D	overstated	overstated

3 The following information has been extracted from a Balance Sheet at 31 December 2003.

	$
Fixed assets	300 000
Working capital	30 000
Long-term loan	20 000
Profit for the year	35 000
Drawings	25 000

What was the balance on Capital account at 31 December 2003?

A $300 000   B $320 000   C $340 000

D $350 000

4 Which of the following statements is incorrect?

A assets = liabilities + capital

B capital = assets – liabilities

C capital – liabilities = assets

D liabilities = assets – capital

8.5 Additional exercises

1 Prepare the Balance Sheet at 31 December 2003 for Hadlee from the trial balance given in §7.8 (additional exercise 1, page 34).

2 Prepare the Balance Sheet at 31 March 2004 for Tikolo from the trial balance given in §7.8 (additional exercise 2 page 35).

9 Accounting principles or concepts

9.1 What are principles or concepts?

Accounting principles are basic rules that are applied in recording transactions and preparing financial statements. They are also known as concepts. These rules are necessary to ensure that accounting records provide reliable information. All businesses should apply the rules in their financial statements. The most important of these rules are now described, and should be learned, understood and applied when preparing financial statements.

9.2 Business entity

Every business is regarded as having an existence separate from that of its owner. This has already been recognised when an owner's capital has been debited in the business Bank account and credited to the owner's Capital account. The credit in the Capital account shows that the owner is a creditor of the business, which owes him the money. This can only be the case if the business is regarded as being separate from the owner as no one can owe himself money. When the owner withdraws money from the business, the amount is debited to his Drawings account. The business accounts do not show if he spends the money on food, clothes, or holidays because these are not business transactions.

(It is important to remember that this is only an accounting concept. Anyone who has a grievance against a business may legally sue a sole trader or a partner in a firm. The business is not a separate entity for that purpose.)

9.3 Money measurement

Only transactions that can be expressed in monetary terms are recorded in ledger accounts. Goods, fixed assets, debtors and creditors etc. may be recorded in ledger accounts because they have resulted from transactions that can be expressed in monetary terms.

Although there are obvious advantages in being able to record things in monetary terms, it has disadvantages. Things which cannot be expressed in monetary terms, such as the skills of workers or their satisfaction with their working conditions, are not recorded in the accounts. Some people think it would be good if these and some other 'non-monetary' items could be included in financial statements.

9.4 Historic cost

Transactions are recorded at their cost to the business. Cost cannot be disputed as invoices or other documentary evidence may be produced to support it. This treatment is said to be objective because it is based on fact and not on opinion.

The opposite of objectivity is subjectivity, which is based upon personal opinion. For example, somebody may give his friend a watch that cost $50. The friend may already have a good watch or perhaps several watches. He would not have paid $50 for another. He would probably value the gift at less than $50. On the other hand, if the friend had not already got a watch and his life depended on him having one, he might value the watch at much more than $50. Values based on personal opinions are said to be subjective and are not reliable bases on which to record transactions.

While the principle of recording transactions at their historic cost has obvious advantages, it has two disadvantages.

- It ignores the changing value of money. A good that was purchased five years ago for $100 might have been sold then for $200 making a profit of $100. If inflation since then has been 25%, today's selling price would be $250 giving an apparent profit of $150. A more realistic calculation of the profit would be to express the original cost at today's prices, $125, giving a profit of $125, which would be enough to buy no more than $100 would have bought five years ago! Historic cost may produce misleading results unless its limitations are understood.
- Like the concept of money measurement, historic cost does not allow things that cannot be expressed in monetary terms to be recorded in accounting.

9.5 Realisation

When accountants speak of realisation, they mean that something becomes an actual fact, or that something has been converted into money. For example, if a man goes into a shop and says that he will return tomorrow and buy a pair of shoes, there is no sale yet; but if the man returns the next day and buys the shoes, the sale has become a fact. By selling the shoes, the shopkeeper has converted goods into money. The sale has been **realised**. Transactions are realised when cash or a debtor replace goods or services. This principle is important as it prevents revenue from being credited in the accounts before it has been earned.

Goods on sale or return When a trader sends goods on sale or return to a customer, no sale takes place until the customer informs the seller that he has decided to buy them. The customer has the right to return the goods to the trader. The goods remain the property of the seller until the sale actually takes place. Goods on sale or return when final accounts are being prepared must be treated as stock. If they have been wrongly treated as sold the accounting treatment must be reversed. Sales and debtors must be reduced by the selling price, and closing stock must be increased by the cost price of the goods.

Example

George has sent goods on sale or return to Helen for $500 and treated the transaction as a sale. Helen has not yet accepted the goods. The goods cost George $350. The following balances have been extracted from George's trial balance: Sales $30 000; trade debtors $1000. Stock on hand has been valued at $900. The following adjustments must be made for the final accounts.

9.6 Duality

The concept of **duality** recognises that there are two aspects for each transaction – represented by debit and credit entries in accounts. The concept is the basis of the accounting equation:

assets = capital + liabilities.

The equation is also expressed in its other form: assets – liabilities = capital. Balance Sheets are prepared in this form.

The accounting equation is a very useful tool for solving some accounting problems.

9.7 Consistency

Transactions of a similar nature should be recorded in the same way (that is, consistently) in the same accounting period and in all future accounting periods. For example, the cost of redecorating premises should always be debited to an expense account for the redecoration of premises and charged to the Profit and Loss Account. It would not be correct, the next time the offices were redecorated, to debit the cost to the Premises (fixed asset) account.

Consistency in the treatment of transactions is important to ensure that the profits or losses of different periods, and Balance Sheets, may be compared meaningfully.

9.8 Materiality

Sometimes a business may depart from the generally accepted principles for recording some transactions. They may do this when the amounts involved are not considered **material** (or significant) in relation to the amounts of the other items in their Profit and Loss Accounts and Balance Sheets.

A company may prepare its Balance Sheet showing all amounts rounded to the nearest $000 or even $m. It would treat the purchase of any asset not exceeding, say, $1000 as revenue expenditure instead of adding it to its fixed assets, as it would not make any noticeable difference to the figure of fixed assets in the Balance Sheet. It would not be considered a material item.

On the other hand, the same amount of expenditure in a small business may be very significant and would need to be treated as capital expenditure in order not to distort profit and the assets in the Balance Sheet.

Sales	$	Debtors	$	Stock	$
Per trial balance	30 000	Per trial balance	1 000	As given	900
Less	500	Less	500	Add	350
Trading Account	29 500	Balance Sheet	500	Trading A/c and Balance Sheet	1 250

An amount may be considered material in the accounts if its inclusion in, or omission from, the Profit and Loss Account or Balance Sheet would affect the way people would read and interpret those financial statements.

9.9 Accruals (matching)

If the final accounts of a business are to give reliable information, the revenue and other income must be no more and no less than the business has earned in the period covered by the Profit and Loss Account. The expenses in the Profit and Loss Account should fairly represent the expenses incurred in earning that revenue. The difference between a Profit and Loss Account prepared on a cash basis and one prepared on an accruals basis will be apparent from the following example:

A business occupies premises at an annual rental of $2000. In one year it has paid $2500 because it has paid one quarter's rent in advance. It has also used $2100 worth of electricity but it has paid only $1200 because it has not paid the latest bill for $900. Its gross profit for the year is $10 000.

Profit and Loss Accounts prepared on (a) a 'cash basis', that is, on the actual payments made, and (b) on an accruals basis, would look as follows:

	(a) Cash basis		(b) Accruals basis	
	$	$	$	$
Gross profit		10 000		10 000
Less Rent	2500		2 000	
Electricity	1200	3 700	2 100	4 100
Net profit		6 300		5 900

The accruals basis is the correct one as it records the actual costs incurred in the period for rent and electricity.

Trading and Profit and Loss Accounts should be prepared on the **accruals**, or matching, basis so that expenses are matched to the revenue earned; that is, expenses should be shown in the Profit and Loss Account as they have been *incurred* rather than as they have been paid.

9.10 Prudence

The prudence concept is intended to prevent profit from being overstated. If profit is overstated, a trader may believe that his income is more than it really is, and he may withdraw too much money from the business. That would lead to the capital invested in the business being depleted. If it happens too often the business will collapse because there will not be enough money to pay creditors

or to renew assets when they are worn out. The principle is sometimes known as the **concept of conservatism**. It is safer for profit to be understated rather than overstated.

The rule is:

- profits should not be overstated
- losses should be provided for as soon as they are recognised.

Students often make the mistake of saying that the prudence concept means that profits must be understated. That is not so; the concept is meant to ensure that profits are realistic without being overstated.

9.11 Going concern

A business is a going concern if there is no intention to discontinue it in the foreseeable future. If it is short of working capital and the owner is unable to put more money into it, or to find somebody who will be prepared to lend it money, it may be unable to pay its creditors and be forced to close.

Unless stated to the contrary, it is assumed that the accounts of a business are prepared on a going concern basis. If the business is not a going concern, the assets should be valued in the Balance Sheet at the amounts they could be expected to fetch in an enforced sale, which could be much less than their real worth. Balance Sheets should always show a realistic situation, bearing in mind the weakness of the business.

9.12 Substance over form

These words are used to describe the accounting treatment of something that does not reflect the legal position.

For example, a machine bought on hire purchase remains the property of the seller until the final instalment has been paid. If the purchaser fails to pay the instalments as they become due, the seller may reclaim the machine. That is the legal position, or the 'form'.

However, the machine is being used in the purchaser's business in the same way as the other machines that have not been bought on hire purchase. From an accounting point of view and for all practical purposes, the machine is no different from the other machines; that is the 'substance' of the matter.

The practical view (the substance) is preferred to the legal view (the form) in the accounting treatment. This is known as 'substance over form'.

Example

Antonio bought a machine on hire purchase on 1 January 2003. The cash price of the machine was $50 000. Antonio paid $10 000 on 1 January 2003. The balance was to be settled by four payments of $10 100 (including interest of $100) on 1 April 2003, 1 July 2003, 1 October 2003 and 1 January 2004. The following entries should appear in Antonio's final accounts at 31 December 2003.

> Profit and Loss Account: Interest on hire purchase $400
>
> Balance Sheet: Fixed assets $50 000 (the cash price although only $40 000 has been paid)
>
> Current liabilities $10 100 (including the final instalment of $10 000 and accrued interest of $100 not paid until 1 January 2004)

9.13 Examination hints

- Learn all the concepts and make sure you understand them.
- Watch for the application of the concepts when you answer examination questions.
- Make sure you identify the correct concept when asked which one has been applied to a particular situation. (Prudence is not always the right answer!)
- Read questions carefully. Questions may require you to give a definition, or to explain, or to discuss. Each of those requirements must be met with an appropriate response.
- When asked for a definition, do not give an example instead. If asked to define 'substance over form', an answer such as 'substance over form is when an asset is bought on hire purchase' is unlikely to gain any marks because the definition is missing. The following is better: 'Subject over form is the treatment accorded to a transaction so that the real effect on the business is recorded in the accounts, rather than the strictly legal position. For example, an asset bought on hire purchase is treated as though it already belongs to the purchaser although it legally remains the property of the seller until the final instalment has been paid.' This answer gives a definition as required. (The example develops the answer further and may gain an additional mark.)

'Explain...' requires an explanation of the way a concept is applied and an explanation as to why it is necessary or important.

'Discuss...' invites an answer which includes a discussion of the advantages **and** disadvantages of a concept.

Examiners choose their words carefully and expect candidates to take note of the wording of questions.

9.14 Multiple-choice questions

1 A trader who sells food does not include food that is past its 'sell by' date in his stock in the Balance Sheet.

Which concept has he applied in valuing his stock?

A matching
B prudence
C realisation
D going concern

2 A business is about to be closed down as it has insufficient funds to pay its creditors. The owner places a very low value on his stock in the Balance Sheet. Which concept is being applied?

A going concern
B materiality
C money measurement
D subjectivity

3 The owner of a business paid his private telephone bill from the business bank account. The amount was debited to his Drawings account. Which concept was applied?

A business entity
B matching
C prudence
D realisation

4 A trader has included rent which is due but not paid in his Profit and Loss Account. Which accounting concept has been applied?

A historic cost
B matching
C money measurement
D prudence

5 The balances in a sales ledger total $16 000. A debtor who owes $800 is known to be in financial difficulty. The figure of debtors shown in the Balance Sheet is $15 200. Which concept has been applied?

A matching
B prudence
C realisation
D substance over form

6 A trader sends goods on sale or return to a customer. When the trader prepares his Balance Sheet at 31 March 2004, the customer has still not indicated that he has accepted the goods. Which concept should the trader apply when he prepares his accounts at 31 March 2004?

A consistency
B matching
C prudence
D realisation

10 Accruals and prepayments (the matching concept)

10.1 What are accruals and prepayments?

Accruals are expenses that have been incurred but not paid for. For example, an unpaid electricity bill is an accrued expense; the electricity has been consumed (the cost has been incurred), but not paid for.

Prepayments are payments made in advance of the benefits to be derived from them. Rent is an example because it usually has to be paid in advance.

10.2 How to treat an accrued expense in an account

An accrued expense is an amount that is owed to somebody; that somebody is a creditor. The creditor must be represented in the expense account by a credit balance carried down on the account.

Example

The accounting year of a business ended on 31 December 2003. In the 11 months ended 30 November 2003 payments for electricity amounted to $900. At 31 December 2003 there was an unpaid electricity bill for $130. That amount is carried down on the account as a credit balance.

Notes
- Only £900 has been paid but the Profit and Loss Account has been debited with the full cost of electricity for the year, £1030.
- A creditor for the amount owing for electricity has been created on the account by a credit balance carried down.
- The creditor will be shown in the Balance Sheet under current liabilities as an 'accrued expense' or as an 'expense creditor' to distinguish it from trade creditors.

Electricity				
2003	$	2003		$
Jan – Nov Sundry payments	900	Dec 31 Profit and Loss A/c		1030
Dec 31 Electricity owing c/d	130			——
	1030			1030
		2004		
		Jan 1 Balance b/d		130

10.3 How to treat a prepaid expense in an account

The person to whom a payment has been made in advance is a debtor of the business. The debtor is represented on the expense account by a debit balance carried down.

Example

Yousif occupies premises at a rental of $2000 per annum, the rent being payable in advance on 1 January, 1 April, 1 July and 1 October. In 2003, Yousif paid the rent on each of those dates, but on 31 December he paid the rent due on 1 January 2004. At 31 December, the landlord is a debtor for the amount of the prepayment.

Rent Payable				
2003		$	2003	$
Jan 1 Bank		500	Dec 31 Profit and Loss A/c	2000
Apr 1 Bank		500	Dec 31 Rent paid in advance c/d	500
Jul 1 Bank		500		
Oct 1 Bank		500		
Dec 31 Bank		500		
		2500		2500
2004				
Jan 1 Balance b/d		500		

Notes

- Payments during the year amount to $2500, but the Profit and Loss Account has been debited with the rent for one year only.
- The debtor (the landlord) is represented by the debit balance on the account.
- The debit balance will be included in the Balance Sheet under current assets as a prepayment to distinguish it from trade debtors.

10.4 How to record stocks of stores on expense accounts

Some expense accounts represent stocks of consumable stores. Examples are stationery, heating fuel and fuel for motor vehicles. Stocks of consumable stores may be unused at the year-end. According to the matching principle, these stocks should not be charged against the profit for the year; they are an asset and not an expense at the year-end. Carry them down as a debit balance on the account. This may result in an expense account having debit and credit balances at the year-end.

Example

In the year ended 31 December 2003, Prospero had paid $1200 for stationery. At 31 December 2003, he owed $270 for stationery and had an unused stock which had cost $400.

Stationery				
2003		$	2003	$
Jan 1- Dec 31 Bank		1200	Dec 31 Profit and Loss A/c	1070
Dec 31 Amount owing c/d		270	Dec 31 Stock c/d	400
		1470		1470
2004			2004	
Jan 1 Stock b/d		400	Jan 1 Balance b/d	270

Note. Closing balances are the opening balances of the next financial period.

10.5 How to adjust income for accruals and prepayments

Some income accounts such as rents or interest receivable may need to be adjusted for income received in advance or in arrears. Income received in advance of its due date indicates the existence of a creditor and requires a credit balance equal to the prepayment to be carried down on the account. Income accrued at the date it is due indicates the existence of a debtor and a debit balance equal to the amount should be carried down on the account.

Example

In the year ended 31 January 2004, Elizabeth had received $500 for rent from a tenant and $160 for interest on a loan. At that date, the rent prepaid amounted to $100, and $40 interest was due from the borrower. The entries in the Rent Receivable and Interest Receivable accounts at 31 January 2004 are as follows:

Rent Receivable				
2004		$	2004	$
Jan 31 Profit and Loss		400	Jan 31 Bank	500
Jan 31 Rent prepaid c/d		100		
		500		500
			Feb 1 Balance b/d	100

Interest Receivable				
2004		$	2004	$
Jan 31 Profit and Loss		200	Jan 31 Bank	160
			Jan 31 Interest accrued c/d	40
		200		200
Feb 1 Balance b/d		40		

Exercise 1

In the year ended 31 December 2003, Alex made the following payments: rent $1000; electricity $630; stationery $420. In addition he had received $300 rent from a tenant.

At 31 December 2003, Alex had prepaid rent of $200. Accrued expenses were electricity $180 and stationery $130. The stock of stationery was $140. The tenant owed rent of $100.

Required

Show how the accounts concerned will appear in Alex's books after the adjustments for accruals and prepayments have been made. Show clearly the amounts to be transferred to the Profit and Loss Account.

10.6 How to adjust a trial balance for accruals and prepayments

Examination questions often include trial balances that require to be adjusted for accruals and prepayments. A reliable examination technique (or method) to deal with this situation is important for success. Adjustments may be made on the question paper but the workings should be shown on your examination script. Two good methods are suggested here. You should try both methods, decide which one you prefer, and stick to it in your preparations for the exam.

Example

The following is an extract from a trial balance at 31 December 2003.

	$	$
Rent Payable	2400	
Heating and Lighting	1860	
Stationery	1100	
Interest Receivable		600
Rent Receivable		1200

The following amounts were owing at 31 December 2003: heating and lighting $290; stationery $100. Rent receivable of $200 had been received in advance.

At 31 December 2003, rent payable of $400 had been paid in advance; interest receivable of $120 was due but had not been received.

There was an unused stock of stationery, $230, at 31 December 2003.

Method 1 Adjust the items in the trial balance in the question. Make lists of the debtors and creditors you create. Insert stock of stationery in the trial balance. (The adjustments are shown in *italics*.)

Show your workings with your answer.

	$	$	Debtors $	Creditors $
Rent Payable	2400 – *400*		*400*	
Heating and Lighting	1860 + *290*			*290*
Stationery	1100 + *100* – *230*			100
Stock of stationery	*230*			
Interest Receivable		600 + *120*	*120*	
Rent Receivable		1200 – *200*		*200*
			520	590

Method 2 Delete the items on the trial balance after cross-referencing them to calculations shown as workings with your answer (TB trial balance; P&L Profit and Loss).

W1 Rent Payable	$	W2 Heat & Light	$	W3 Stationery	$
Per TB	2400	Per TB	1860	Per TB	1100
Less prepaid	(400)*	Add owing	290 †	Add owing	100 †
P & L	2000	P & L	2150	Less stock	(230)
				P & L	970

W4 Interest Receivable	$	W5 Rent Receivable	$
Per TB	600	Per TB	1200
Add due	120*	Less prepaid	(200) †
P & L	720	P & L	1000

Items marked * will be listed as debit balances as in method 1. Items marked † will be listed as credit balances as in method 1.

Exercise 2

Devram extracted a trial balance at 31 December 2003 from his books after he had prepared his Trading Account for the year ended on that date. It was as follows.

	$	$
Fixed assets	40 000	
Stock at 31 December 2003	7 000	
Trade debtors	1 600	
Trade creditors		1 400
Bank	2 524	
Long-term Loan		10 000
Gross profit		30 000
Rent	2 600	
Electricity	926	
Stationery	405	
Motor Expenses	725	
Interest on Loan	500	
Drawings	5 120	
Capital		20 000
	61 400	61 400

Further information

1. At 31 December 2003, rent had been prepaid in the sum of $300.

2. The following amounts were owing at 31 December 2003: electricity $242; stationery $84; motor expenses $160.

3. The long-term loan was made to the business on 1 January 2003. Interest at the rate of 10% per annum is payable on the loan.

4. The stock of unused stationery on hand at 31 December 2003 was valued at cost: $100.

Required

(a) Prepare Devram's Profit and Loss Account for the year ended 31 December 2003.

(b) Prepare the Balance Sheet at 31 December 2003.

(**Note.** Stock shown in the trial balance is the closing stock.)

10.7 Examination hints

- Read questions carefully before starting to answer them. Note any adjustments required for accruals and prepayments.
- Calculate adjustments carefully and show your workings. Even if your answer is wrong, you may gain some marks for partially correct answers if the examiner can follow your workings.

- Take care to complete the double entry for each adjustment you make to the trial balance.
- As you make each adjustment, tick the item on the question paper. Before starting to copy out the answer, check that all adjustments have been ticked on the question paper. Many candidates lose marks because they have missed some of the adjustments.

10.8 Multiple-choice questions

1 A trader prepares his accounts annually to 30 April. He pays annual rent of $12 000 and makes the payments quarterly in advance on 1 January, 1 April, 1 July and 1 October.

Which amount should be included in his accounts for the year ended 30 April 2004?

A $1000 accrual

B $1000 prepayment

C $2000 accrual

D $2000 prepayment

2 A trader commenced business on 1 February 2003. He paid rent on his premises as follows.

Date	Period	Amount
1 Feb 2003	1 Feb – 31 Mar	$1200
1 Apr 2003	1 Apr – 30 Jun	$1800
1 Jul 2003	1 Jul – 30 Sept	$1800
1 Oct 2003	1 Oct – 31 Dec	$2100
1 Jan 2004	1 Jan – 31 Mar	$2100

Which amount for rent should be shown in the Profit and Loss Account for the year ended 31 January 2004?

A $6900   **B** $7600   **C** $7800   **D** $9000

3 A business has an accounting year that ends on 30 September. Its insurance premiums are paid in advance on 1 July each year. Premiums have been paid in the past three years as follows.

Year 1 $1800

Year 2 $2000

Year 3 $2400

How much will be debited in the Profit and Loss Account for insurance in Year 3?

A $2000   **B** $2100   **C** $2300   **D** $2400

4 The accounts of a business have been prepared, but no adjustments have been made for accrued expenses at the end of the year.

What effect will these omissions have on the accounts?

	Net profit	Current assets	Current liabilities
A	overstated	no effect	understated
B	understated	no effect	overstated
C	overstated	understated	no effect
D	understated	overstated	no effect

10.9 Additional questions

1 Antonia's trial balance at 31 December 2003 was as follows.

	$	$
Sales		120 000
Purchases	62 400	
Sales Returns	7 300	
Purchases Returns		4 190
Wages	17 310	
Rent	3 200	
Heating and Lighting	2 772	
Motor Expenses	1 284	
Interest on Loan	500	
Stock	5 660	
Trade Debtors	12 440	
Trade Creditors		6 167
Bank	5 055	
Loan		10 000
Premises	24 000	
Motor Vehicles	7 400	
Drawings	7 036	
Capital		16 000
	156 357	156 357

Further information

1. Stock at 31 December 2003 was valued at $8000.
2. The loan was received on 1 April 2003 and is repayable in 2006. Interest is charged at 10% per annum.
3. Expenses owing at 31 December 2003 were as follows.

	$
Wages	558
Heating and Lighting	328

4. Rent in the sum of $800 was prepaid at 31 December 2003.

Required

(a) Prepare the Trading and Profit and Loss Account for the year ended 31 December 2003.
(b) Prepare the Balance Sheet at 31 December 2003.

2 Desmond's trial balance at 31 March 2004 was as follows.

	$	$
Plant and Machinery	36 000	
Motor Vehicles	17 000	
Stock	9 000	
Trade Debtors	7 060	
Bank	5 400	
Trade Creditors		3 950
Capital		70 000
Drawings	22 088	
Sales		219 740
Purchases	100 100	
Sales Returns	17 420	
Purchases Returns		8 777
Wages	67 000	
Rent Payable	8 000	
Rent Receivable		2 600
Interest Receivable		840
Discounts Allowed	2 826	
Discounts Received		1 040
Carriage Inwards	5 170	
Carriage Outwards	7 920	
Sundry Expenses	1 963	
	306 947	306 947

Further information

1. Stock at 31 March 2004 was valued at $11 000.
2. Expenses owing at 31 March 2004 were: rent payable $2000; carriage inwards $330; carriage outwards $280.
3. Sundry expenses of $200 had been paid in advance; interest receivable of $160 had accrued.
4. At 31 March 2004, rent receivable of $200 had been received in advance.

Required

(a) Prepare Desmond's Trading and Profit and Loss Account for the year ended 31 March 2004.
(b) Prepare the Balance Sheet at 31 March 2004.

11 Provisions for the depreciation of fixed assets

In this chapter you will learn:
- what depreciation is and why it must be provided for in accounts
- how to calculate it by the straight-line and reducing-balance methods
- how to account for the disposal of fixed assets.

11.1 What is depreciation?

Depreciation is the part of the cost of a fixed asset that is consumed during the period it is used by a business. For example, a motor car purchased for $10 000 may be worth only $8000 one year later because it is not as good as new after a year's use. The asset has suffered depreciation of $(10 000 − 8000) = $2000.

Assets may depreciate for a number of reasons.

- **Wear and tear:** assets become worn out through use.
- **Obsolescence:** assets have to be replaced because new, more efficient technology has been developed; or machines which were acquired for the production of particular goods are of no further use because the goods are no longer produced.
- **Passage of time:** an asset acquired for a limited period of time, such as a lease of premises for a given number of years, loses value as time passes. Accountants refer to this as **effluxion of time** and speak of **amortising** rather than 'depreciating' these assets.
- **Using up, or exhaustion:** mines, quarries and oil wells depreciate as the minerals etc. are extracted from them.

11.2 How does depreciation of fixed assets affect accounts?

The accounting treatment of capital expenditure, which is expenditure on fixed assets, is different from the treatment of revenue expenditure. Revenue expenditure is debited to the Profit and Loss Account as it is incurred. Capital expenditure, on the other hand, is on assets that are intended for use in a business for more than one year, usually for many years. It would be wrong to debit the whole of the cost of a fixed asset to the Profit and Loss Account in the year it was acquired; it would be against the matching principle. Nevertheless, the cost of *using* fixed assets to earn revenue must be charged in the Profit and Loss Account; that cost is the depreciation suffered in the accounting period.

11.3 How to account for depreciation

There are several methods used to calculate depreciation. The two most common are:

- straight line
- reducing balance.

Straight-line depreciation

With this method the total amount of depreciation that an asset will suffer is estimated as the difference between what it cost and the estimated amount that will be received when it is sold or scrapped at the end of its useful life. The total depreciation is then spread evenly over the number of years of its expected life.

> Calculation: (cost − estimated proceeds on disposal) ÷ estimated useful life in years.

Example 1

A machine cost $20 000. It is expected to have a useful life of five years at the end of which time it is expected to be sold for $5000 (its **residual value**). The total depreciation over five years is $(20 000 − $5000) = $15 000. The annual depreciation is $15 000 ÷ 5 = $3000.

Ledger entries for depreciation Debit the Profit and Loss Account and credit a Provision for Depreciation account with the annual depreciation each year.

In the above example, the bookkeeping entries in each of the five years will be as follows.

Profit and Loss Account	$
Overheads	
Year 1	
Provision for depreciation of machine	3000
Year 2	
Provision for depreciation of machine	3000
Year 3	
Provision for depreciation of machine	3000
Year 4	
Provision for depreciation of machine	3000
Year 5	
Provision for depreciation of machine	3000

Machinery at Cost

		$			$
Year 1	Bank	20 000			

Provision for Depreciation of Machinery

			$				$
Year 1	Balance	c/d	3 000	Year 1	Profit and Loss		3 000
Year 2	Balance	c/d	6 000	Year 2	Balance	b/d	3 000
					Profit and Loss		3 000
			6 000				6 000
Year 3	Balance	c/d	9 000	Year 3	Balance	b/d	6 000
					Profit and Loss		3 000
			9 000				9 000
Year 4	Balance	c/d	12 000	Year 4	Balance	b/d	9 000
					Profit and Loss		3 000
			12 000				12 000
				Year 5	Balance	b/d	12 000
					Profit and Loss		3 000
							15 000

Notes
- The fixed asset account continues to show the machine at cost each year of its life. Fixed asset accounts sometimes include the words 'at cost' in their titles to emphasise this point.
- The balance on the Provision for Depreciation of Machinery account increases each year.
- A provision in accounting is an amount set aside for a particular purpose.

- A separate Provision for Depreciation account must be opened for each *class* of fixed asset.
- The balance on the Provision for Depreciation account is deducted from the cost of the fixed asset in the Balance Sheet:

		Cost	Depreciation	Net book value
		$	$	$
Year 1:	Machinery	20 000	3 000	17 000
Year 2:	Machinery	20 000	6 000	14 000
Year 3:	Machinery	20 000	9 000	11 000
Year 4:	Machinery	20 000	12 000	8 000
Year 5:	Machinery	20 000	15 000	5 000

The balance remaining after depreciation has been deducted from cost is known as the **net book value** (NBV) or **written down value** (WDV) of the asset. It is the amount of the cost of the asset which has not yet been charged against profit in the Profit and Loss Account. The net book values of assets at which the assets are 'carried' in the Balance Sheet are known as **carrying amounts**.

Note. The fixed assets at cost, the balances on the Provisions for Depreciation accounts, and net book values should now be shown in Balance Sheets under headings as shown in the example above.

Exercise 1

A motor vehicle cost $18 000. It is expected to have a useful life of seven years and to be sold for $4000 at the end of that time.

Required
(a) Prepare the Provision for Depreciation of Motor Vehicles account for each year.
(b) Prepare a Balance Sheet extract to show the fixed asset of Motor Vehicles at the end of each year.

Reducing balance depreciation

In this method, depreciation is calculated as a fixed percentage of the written down value of the asset each year.

Example 2

A machine cost $20 000. It is expected to have a useful life of five years. Depreciation is to be calculated at the rate of 25% per annum on the reducing balance.

Calculation:	$
Cost	20 000
Year 1 (25% × 20 000)	(5 000)
	15 000
Year 2 (25% × 15 000)	(3 750)
	11 250
Year 3 (25% × 11 250)	(2 813)
	8 437
Year 4 (25% × 8437)	(2 109)
	6 328
Year 5 (25% × 6328)	(1 582)
	4 746

The bookkeeping entries for the reducing-balance method are similar to those for straight-line; only the amounts differ.

Exercise 2

A machine costing $40 000 and with an expected useful life of five years is to be depreciated by the reducing-balance method. The annual rate of depreciation is 30%.

Required

(a) Prepare the Provision for Depreciation of Machinery account for years 1 to 5.
(b) Prepare a Balance Sheet extract to show the fixed asset of machinery at the end of each of the five years.

Notes

- Always calculate depreciation to the nearest $.
- The percentage used for the reducing-balance method is much higher than that used for straight-line.
- In the early years of an asset's life, the annual charge for depreciation for the reducing-balance method is higher than for straight-line.
  Example: A machine cost $50 000. It is expected to have a useful life of 10 years at the end of which time it will have no residual value. The annual depreciation for each year is compared in the following table.

	Annual charge for depreciation	
	Straight line (10%)	Reducing balance (40%)
	$	$
Year 1	5000	20 000
2	5000	12 000
3	5000	7 200
4	5000	4 320
5	5000	2 592
6	5000	1 555
7	5000	933
8	5000	560
9	5000	336
10	5000	202

A much higher rate of depreciation has had to be used for the reducing-balance method, and the annual depreciation for the first three years is very much higher than under the straight-line method. In fact, using the reducing-balance method, 50% of cost is provided for within the first 18 months but the machine has not been completely depreciated at the end of 10 years – there is still a residual balance of $302.

- The net book values of assets may be reduced to zero if straight-line depreciation is used. They will never be written down to zero with the reducing-balance method unless a small residual value is deliberately transferred to the Profit and Loss Account.
- Provision for depreciation of an asset should cease to be made once it has been completely written off. Assets that have been completely written off in the books may still be of use to the business, but no further depreciation will be provided for them.

11.4 Which assets should be depreciated?

All assets that have finite useful lives should be depreciated. Therefore depreciation should be provided on all assets except freehold land, which does not have a finite useful life. Freehold buildings will eventually need to be replaced and should be depreciated. Land that is used in an extractive industry, such as quarries and mines, will lose value as the mineral etc. is extracted and should be depreciated

11.5 Choice of depreciation method

Providing for depreciation is an application of the matching principle, and the method chosen for any particular type of asset should depend upon the contribution the asset makes towards earning revenue. Some general principles may be explained as follows.

- The **straight-line method** should be used for assets that are expected to earn revenue evenly over their useful working lives. It is also generally used where the pattern of an asset's earning power is uncertain. It should always be used to amortise the cost of assets with fixed lives such as leases.
- The **reducing-balance method** should be used when it is considered that an asset's earning power will diminish as the asset gets older.

A common excuse for using the reducing-balance method rather than straight-line method is that the reducing charges for depreciation compensate for increases in the cost of maintaining and repairing assets as they get older. It is highly improbable that the two costs will balance each other out. The proper way of dealing with this situation would be to depreciate the asset on the straight-line method and to create a Provision for Repairs and Maintenance by equal transfers annually from the Profit and Loss Account. The costs of repairs are debited to this provision as and when they arise.

11.6 More important points about depreciation

Provision for depreciation in year of acquisition of an asset

Businesses vary in the way they depreciate fixed assets in the year in which they are acquired. The two possibilities are:

- a full year's depreciation is taken in the year of acquisition, but none in the year of disposal
- depreciation is calculated from the date of acquisition; in the year of disposal, depreciation is calculated from the commencement of the year to the date of disposal, that is, only a proportion of the annual depreciation will be provided.

In an examination, follow the instructions given in the question. If the question gives the dates of acquisition and disposal, calculate depreciation on a time basis for the years of acquisition and disposal. Otherwise, calculate depreciation for a full year in the year of acquisition, but not for the year of disposal.

Consistency

The chosen method of depreciating an asset should be used consistently to ensure that the profits or losses of different periods of account can be compared on a like-for-like basis.

A change in the method of calculating depreciation should only be made if it will result in the financial results and position of the business being stated more fairly. A change should never be made in order to manipulate profit.

Exceptional depreciation

An event may occur that causes the amount that may be recovered on the disposal of an asset to fall significantly below its net book value (carrying amount). The asset is said to be **impaired**. When this happens, the asset should immediately be written down to its recoverable amount and the loss charged in the Profit and Loss Account. The remaining useful life of the asset should be reviewed. Depreciation should then be recalculated by dividing the new carrying amount by the number of years of useful life remaining.

Example

A machine was purchased in 1998 at a cost of $30 000. It had an estimated useful life of 10 years and a residual value of $2000. Straight-line depreciation of $2800 was provided each year until 31 December 2002 when the machine had a written down value of $16 000. At 31 December 2003 it was then found that the recoverable amount of the machine was only $9000 and that it had only three years' useful life left and no residual value.

In the year ended 31 December 2003, the Profit and Loss Account should be debited with $7000, $(16 000 – 9000), and the annual depreciation for the next three years should be $9000 ÷ 3 = $3000.

11.7 How to account for the disposals of fixed assets

When a fixed asset is sold, the difference between its net book value and the proceeds of sale represents a profit or loss on disposal, which is transferred to the Profit and Loss Account. The profit or loss is calculated in a Disposal account. The bookkeeping entries are as follows:

Debit the Disposal account and **credit** the fixed asset account with the original cost of the asset.

Debit the Provision for Depreciation account and **credit** the Disposal account with the depreciation provided to date on the asset.

Debit the Bank account and **credit** the Disposal account with the proceeds (if any) of the disposal.

A debit balance remaining on the Disposal account is a loss on disposal. A credit balance is a profit on disposal. The balance is transferred to the Profit and Loss Account.

Example 1

At 1 December 2003, a machine which had cost $20 000 was sold for $500. A total of $18 000 had been provided for depreciation on the machine. The bookkeeping is as follows.

Machinery at Cost

2003	$	2003	$
Jan 1 Balance b/d	20 000	Dec 1 Machinery Disposal	20 000

Provision for Depreciation of Machinery

2003	$	2003	$
Dec 1 Machinery Disposal	18 000	Jan 1 Balance b/d	18 000

Machinery Disposal

2003	$	2003	$
Dec 1 Machinery at Cost	20 000	Dec 1 Provision for Depreciation	18 000
		Bank	500
		31 Profit and Loss A/c (loss on disposal)	1 500
	20 000		20 000

Notes

- The cost of the machine exceeds the accumulated depreciation + the sale proceeds; there is a loss on disposal.
- The debit entry in the Profit and Loss Account is really an adjustment to previous years' depreciation charges, which have proved to be insufficient.

Part exchange

A new asset may be acquired in part exchange for one that is being disposed of. The part exchange value of the asset being disposed of is debited to the fixed asset account and credited to the Disposal account as the proceeds of disposal.

Example 2

On 5 March 2004 a motor vehicle X100 was purchased for $15 000. The cost was settled by a payment of $13 000 and the part exchange of motor vehicle Z23 for the balance.

Motor vehicle Z23 cost $11 000 and had a net book value of $800 at 5 March 2004.

Motor Vehicles at Cost

2004	$	2004	$
Jan 1 Balance b/d (Z23)	11 000	Mar 5 Motor Vehicles Disposal A/c	11 000
Mar 5 Bank (X100)	13 000		
Motor Vehicles Disposal A/c	2 000		
	15 000		

Provision for the Depreciation of Motor Vehicles

2004	$	2004	$
Mar 5 Motor Vehicles Disposal A/c	10 200	Jan 1 Balance b/d	10 200

Motor Vehicles Disposal

2004	$	2004	$
Mar 5 Motor Vehicles at Cost	11 000	Mar 5 Provision for Depreciation of Motor Vehicles (see note below)	10 200
Profit and Loss Account (Profit on disposal)	1 200	Motor Vehicles at Cost	2 000
	12 200		12 200

Notes

- No depreciation has been charged in the year of disposal.
- The profit of $1200 is credited in the Profit and Loss Account and is, in effect, an adjustment of over-depreciation of the motor vehicle in previous years.

Exercise 3

The following balances have been extracted from Joel's books at 31 December 2003. Machinery at Cost $18 000; Provision for Depreciation of Machinery $9600.

Joel's transactions in 2004 included the following.

May 7	Sold machine No. 1 for $1500. This machine cost $6000 when purchased in 2000.
June 3	Purchased machine No. 3 which was priced at $10 000. Joel paid $7000 and gave machine No. 2 in part exchange. Machine No. 2 cost $12 000 when purchased in 1998.

Joel depreciates his machinery using the straight-line method and the rate of 10% per annum. He provides for a full year's depreciation in the year of purchase, but none in the year of disposal.

Required

Prepare the following accounts to show the transactions on 7 May and 3 June:

(a) Machinery at Cost
(b) Provision for Depreciation of Machinery
(c) Machinery Disposal.

11.8 How to adjust a trial balance for depreciation

Examination questions frequently provide a trial balance that has to be adjusted to provide for a further year's depreciation of the fixed assets. The amount that has to be debited in the Profit and Loss Account should be inserted in the debit column of the trial balance and added to the credit side.

Example

The following extract is taken from a trial balance.

	$	$
Leasehold Premises	30 000	
Provision for Depreciation of Leasehold Premises		6 000
Plant and Machinery	40 000	
Provision for Depreciation of Plant and Machinery		23 125

Further information

1. Leasehold premises are to be amortised over the term of the lease of 10 years on the straight-line basis.

2. Plant and machinery is to be depreciated at the rate of 25% per annum on the reducing-balance method.

Adjust the trial balance as follows (adjustments shown in *italics*):

	$	$
Leasehold Premises	30 000	
Provision for Depreciation of Leasehold Premises	*3 000*	*6 000 + 3 000*
Plant and Machinery	40 000	
Provision for Depreciation of Plant and Machinery	*4 219**	*23 125 + 4 219*
* 25% of (40 000 − 23 125)		

11.9 Provisions for depreciation and the accounting concepts

Provisions for depreciation are made to comply with the following concepts.

Matching The cost of using assets to earn revenue should be matched in the Profit and Loss Account to the revenue earned.

Prudence If the cost of using fixed assets was not included in the Profit and Loss Account, profit would be overstated.

11.10 Examination hints

- Read questions carefully to make sure you understand which method of depreciation you should use.
- If required to prepare ledger accounts for depreciation or disposals of fixed assets, be sure to include in each posting the name of the other account in which the double entry is completed. The examiner needs to see that you understand the double entry involved.
- When calculating straight-line depreciation, include any residual value in your calculation.
- Be sure to complete the double entry for each adjustment on the trial balance.
- Show all workings on your answer paper.
- As you make the adjustments to the trial balance, tick the instructions on the question paper. Check that all instructions are ticked before copying out your answer.
- Show fixed assets in Balance Sheets with cost, depreciation and net book value presented in columnar form

11.11 Multiple-choice questions

1 Why is depreciation on fixed assets charged in the accounts of a business?

   A to ensure that assets are replaced when they are worn out

   B to make sure that cash is available to replace assets when they are worn out

   C to show what assets are worth in the Balance Sheet

   D to spread the cost of assets over their useful lives

2 A business purchased a crane for $40 000 on 1 January 2001. The crane was depreciated at the rate of 30% per annum using the reducing-balance method. The crane was sold on 31 December 2003 for $7750.

   What was the profit or loss on disposal?

   A $3750 loss   **B** $3750 profit   **C** $5970 loss
   D $5970 profit

3 The following information relates to the fixed assets of a business.

	$
Cost at 1 April 2002	32 000
Accumulated depreciation at 1 April 2002	13 600
Fixed assets purchased in year ended 31 March 2003	7 000
Depreciation charged for the year ended 31 March 2003	4 200

Depreciation is calculated on the reducing balance basis at the rate of 30%. What was the net book value of the assets that were disposed of in the year ended 31 March 2003?

A $11 400   **B** $16 800   **C** $18 400   **D** $25 400

4 The following information is extracted from the books of a business.

	At 31.12.02	At 31.12.03
	$	$
Fixed assets (at cost)	230 000	275 000
Less accumulated depreciation	85 000	98 000

Further information for the year ended 31 December 2003 is as follows.

	$
Depreciation charged in the Profit and Loss Account	25 000
Additions to fixed assets (at cost)	60 000
Loss on sale of fixed assets	1 000

How much was received from the sales of fixed assets?

A $2000   **B** $3000   **C** $4000   **D** $5000

11.12 Additional exercises

1 The following trial balance was extracted from the books of Piccolo at 31 May 2004.

	$	$
Freehold Land and Buildings at cost	100 000	
Provision for Depreciation of Freehold Buildings		40 000
Plant and Machinery at cost	76 000	
Provision for Depreciation of Plant and Machinery		32 000
Trade debtors	14 000	
Trade creditors		6 300
Bank	5 500	
Sales		300 000
Purchases	190 000	
Stock	30 000	
Wages	56 000	
Heating and Lighting	17 600	
Repairs to Plant and Machinery	5 100	
Advertising	7 000	
Drawings	27 100	
Capital		150 000
	528 300	528 300

Further information

1. Stock at 31 May 2004: $42 000.

2. Freehold land and buildings at cost is made up as follows: land $20 000; buildings $80 000.

3. Freehold buildings are depreciated at 4% per annum on the straight-line basis.

4. Plant and machinery are depreciated at 25% per annum on the reducing-balance basis.

5. At 31 May 2004, $1800 was owing for heating and lighting. $6000 of the cost of advertising related to the year beginning 1 June 2004.

6. In the year ended 31 May 2004, Piccolo had taken stock costing $4000 for his personal use. No entry had been made in the books for this.

Required

(a) Prepare Piccolo's Profit and Loss Account for the year ended 31 May 2004.

(b) Prepare the Balance Sheet at 31 May 2004.

2 Wilhelmina is a trader whose financial year ends on 31 March. Her trial balance at 31 March 2004 was as follows.

	$	$
Leasehold Property at cost	45 000	
Provision for Depreciation of Leasehold Property		13 500
Plant and Machinery at cost	21 000	
Provision for Depreciation of Plant and Machinery		9 200
Office Equipment at cost	7 000	
Provision for Depreciation of Office Equipment		2 400
Trade debtors	1 526	
Trade creditors		973
Stock	13 000	
Bank	1 964	
Wages	13 017	
Electricity	1 012	
Repairs to Machinery	643	
Sundry Expenses	1 234	
Interest on Loan	1 000	
Sales		80 600
Sales Returns	1 590	
Purchases	50 914	
Purchases Returns		825
Long-term Loan		20 000
Drawings	18 598	
Capital		50 000
	177 498	177 498

Further information

1. Stock at 31 March 2004 cost $16 000.

2. The loan was received in 2001 and is repayable in 2006. Interest on the loan is at the rate of 10% per annum.

3. Plant and machinery includes $6000 for a machine bought on hire purchase on 1 January 2004. The cash price of the machine is $30 000. The balance is payable in four quarterly instalments of $6200, including interest, on 1 April 2004, 1 July 2004, 1 October 2004 and 1 January 2005.

4. The leasehold property was acquired on 1 October 1998 for a period of 15 years. It is being amortised on the straight-line basis.

5. Plant and machinery are depreciated on the reducing-balance method using the annual rate of 25%.

6. Office equipment is depreciated at 15% per annum on the straight-line basis.

7. At 31 March 2004, $300 was owing for electricity, and sundry expenses of $180 had been prepaid.

Required

(a) Prepare Wilhelmina's Trading and Profit and Loss Account for the year ended 31 March 2004.

(b) Prepare the Balance Sheet at 31 March 2004.

12 Bad and doubtful debts

> **In this chapter you will learn:**
> - the difference between bad debts and doubtful debts
> - how to account for bad debts and bad debts recovered
> - how to provide for doubtful debts.

12.1 Bad debts

When somebody owes money but is unable to pay, the debt is a bad one. As soon as debts are known to be bad, they should be cleared from the sales ledger by transferring them by journal entry to a Bad Debts account.

Example

Samuel is owed $1200 by H. Ardup and $850 by Tony Broke. Both of these debtors have become bankrupt on 1 November 2003 and are unable to pay their debts. Samuel writes the debts off as bad.

Journal entries:

2003		$	$
Nov 1	Bad Debts account	1200	
	H. Ardup		1200
H. Ardup has become bankrupt and unable to pay amount due.			
Nov 1	Bad Debts account	850	
	Tony Broke		850
T. Broke has become bankrupt and unable to pay amount due.			

Sales ledger accounts:

H. Ardup

2003			$	2003		$
Nov 1	Balance	b/d	1200	Nov 1	Bad Debts	1200

Tony Broke

2003			$	2003		$
Nov 1	Balance	b/d	850	Nov 1	Bad Debts	850

General ledger:	**Bad debts**		

2003		$	2003	$
Nov 1	H. Ardup	1200	2003	
	Tony Broke	850		

When Samuel prepares his annual accounts, he will transfer the balance on the Bad Debts account to the Profit and Loss Account as an expense.

12.2 Bad debts recovered

A debt that has been written off as bad may be recovered at a later date if the debtor becomes able to pay. The debt must be recorded once more on the sales ledger account by a journal entry. The debtor's account will be debited and a Bad Debts Recovered account credited with the amount recovered. The amount received from the debtor may then be credited to his account and debited in the cash book.

Example

On 6 January 2004, Tony Broke had sufficient funds to enable him to pay Samuel and sent him a cheque for $850.

Journal entry:

2004		$	$
Jan 6	Tony Broke	850	
	Bad Debts Recovered		850
An amount of $850 received from Tony Broke. This debt was previously written off as a bad debt on 1 November 2003.			

On 8 January 2004, Samuel received a cheque for $300 being a dividend (or part payment) of 25% of H. Ardup's debt.

Journal entry:

2004		$	$
Jan 8	H. Ardup	300	
	Bad Debts Recovered		300
$300 received in respect of a dividend of 25% of H. Ardup's debt of $1200, which was written off as a bad debt on 1 November 2003.			

Sales ledger accounts:

H. Ardup

2003			$	2003			$
Nov 1	Balance	b/d	1200	Nov 1	Bad Debts		1200
2004				2004			
Jan 8	Bad Debts Recovered		300	Jan 8	Bank		300

Tony Broke

2003			$	2003			$
Nov 1	Balance	b/d	850	Nov 1	Bad Debts		850
2004				2004			
Jan 6	Bad Debts Recovered		850	Jan 6	Bank		850

General ledger account:

Bad Debts Recovered

2004		$	2004		$
			Jan 6	Tony Broke	850
			8	H. Ardup	300

The balance on Bad Debts Recovered account will be credited to the Profit and Loss Account.

Sometimes, only the difference between the balances on the Bad Debts account and the Bad Debts Recovered account will be included in the Profit and Loss Account.

12.3 Provisions for doubtful debts

Although a debt may not actually have become bad, there may be doubt as to whether it will be paid; it may turn out eventually to be a bad debt. It would be misleading to include that debt as an asset in the Balance Sheet pretending that the amount is not in doubt. On the other hand, since it has not yet become bad, it would be wrong to write it off. A provision is made to cover that and other doubtful debts.

12.4 How to create and maintain a provision for doubtful debts

When the provision is first created, debit the Profit and Loss Account and credit a Provision for Doubtful Debts account with the full amount of the provision.

In the years that follow, the entries in the accounts will be for increases or decreases in the amounts required for the provision:

Debit the Profit and Loss Account and credit the Provision for Doubtful Debts with increases in the provision.

Debit the Provision for Doubtful Debts and credit the Profit and Loss Account with decreases in the provision.

The Provision for Doubtful Debts is deducted from debtors in the Balance Sheet.

Example

The following information is extracted from Jonah's accounts.

	Total of all debtors	Doubtful debts
	$	$
At 31 December: 2001	12 000	900
2002	14 000	1100
2003	10 000	800

Jonah had not previously made a provision for doubtful debts. The following entries will be made in his accounts.

Profit and Loss Account (extracts) for the years ended 31 December

	Debit	Credit
	$	$
2001 Provision for Doubtful Debts	900	
2002 Provision for Doubtful Debts	200	
2003 Provision for Doubtful Debts		300

Provision for Doubtful Debts (3 years ended 31 December 2001/2002/2003)

2001			$	2001			$
Dec 31	Balance	c/d	900	Dec 31 Profit and Loss A/c			900
2002				2002			
Dec 31	Balance	c/d	1100	Jan 1 Balance		b/d	900
			___	Dec 31 Profit and Loss A/c			200
			1100				1100
2003			$	2003			$
Dec 31 Profit and Loss A/c			300	Jan 1 Balance b/d			1100
Balance		c/d	800				___
			1100				1100
				2004			
				Jan 1 Balance		b/d	800

Jonah's Balance Sheets at 31 December (extracts)

		$	$
2001	Trade debtors	12 000	
	Less Provision for Doubtful Debts	900	11 100
2002	Trade debtors	14 000	
	Less Provision for Doubtful Debts	1 100	12 900
2003	Trade debtors	10 000	
	Less Provision for Doubtful Debts	800	9 200

12.5 How to calculate the amount of a provision for doubtful debts

The calculation of a provision for doubtful debts depends upon the type of provision required. There are three kinds of provision:

- specific
- general
- specific and general.

Specific Certain debts are selected from the sales ledger as doubtful. The provision will be equal to the total of those debts.

General The provision is calculated as a percentage of the total debtors. The average percentage of debts by amount that prove to be bad is usually taken for this purpose.

Specific and general The provision is made up of the debts that are thought to be doubtful plus a percentage of the remainder.

Example

Job maintains a specific and general provision for doubtful debts. The general provision is based on 4% of debtors after deducting doubtful debts.

At 31 December	Total debtors (a) $	Doubtful debts (b) $	Provision Specific (c) $	Provision General (c) $	Total $
2000	31 000	4500	4500	1060	5560
2001	37 000	5000	5000	1280	6280
2002	34 200	3700	3700	1220	4920
2003	35 640	4090	4090	1262	5352

Notes

- Specific provisions must be deducted from debtors before the general provision is calculated. In the above example: [column (a) – column (b)] × 4% = column (c).
- Never refer to a Provision for Bad debts. Bad debts are never provided for; they should always be written off as soon as they become bad.

Exercise 1

Saul maintains a provision for doubtful debts in his books. It is made up of a specific provision for doubtful debts and a general provision equal to 5% of the remainder. The following information is extracted from Saul's books.

At 31 March	Total debtors	Doubtful debts (included in total debtors)
	$	$
2000	27 000	4000
2001	33 900	6400
2002	30 000	7500
2003	28 000	3000
2004	36 700	8300

Required

(a) Calculate the total provision for doubtful debts for each of the above years.

(b) Prepare the Provision for Doubtful Debts account for each of the years. (Assume that Saul had not made a provision for doubtful debts before 31 March 2000.)

12.6 How to adjust a trial balance for bad and doubtful debts

The adjustments to a trial balance for bad and doubtful debts are demonstrated in the following example.

Example

A trial balance includes: Trade debtors $40 650 (including $400 which are bad debts), and a Provision for Doubtful Debts of $1900. A provision of 8% is to be made for doubtful debts. (The adjustments are shown in *italics*.)

	Trial balance	
	$	$
Trade debtors	40 650 – *400*	
Bad debts	*400*	
Provision for Doubtful Debts	*1 320*	1900 + *1320*

Step 1 Deduct the bad debts, $400, from Trade debtors. Insert 'Bad debts 400' as a new debit balance; this will be debited in the Profit and Loss Account.

Step 2 Calculate the new provision for doubtful debts and deduct the provision brought forward: $(40 650 – 400) \times 8\% - \$1900 = \$1320$. Add the result to both sides of the trial balance.

12.7 Provisions for doubtful debts and the concepts

A provision for doubtful debts complies with the following accounting concepts.

Prudence Amounts expected to be received from debtors should not be overstated in Balance Sheets. The Profit and Loss Account should provide for the loss of revenue and not overstate profit.

Matching The possible loss of revenue should be provided for in the period in which the revenue was earned, not in a later period when the debt becomes bad.

12.8 Examination hints

- Read questions carefully and make sure you know exactly what you are required to do.
- Make sure you calculate doubtful debt provisions on debtors after you have deducted any bad debts.
- Debit an increase, but credit a decrease, in a provision to the Profit and Loss Account.
- Be sure to complete the double entry for each adjustment.
- Show your workings with your answer.
- Tick the adjustments on the question paper. This will ensure you do not overlook them.
- Deduct the new balance on the Provision for Doubtful Debts account from the debtors in the Balance Sheet.

12.9 Multiple-choice questions

1 Kapil has decided to maintain a Provision for Doubtful Debts.

Which of the following concepts should he apply in his accounts?

1 going concern

2 matching

3 prudence

4 realisation

A 1 and 3

B 1 and 4

C 2 and 3

D 2 and 4

2 The following information is available about a business.

	$
Provision for Doubtful Debts at 1 April 2003	1 100
Debtors at 31 March 2004	24 800
Bad debt included in debtors at 31 March 2004	600
Charge to Profit and Loss Account for bad and doubtful debts, including bad debt of $600	1 194

Which percentage was used to calculate the Provision for Doubtful Debts at 31 March 2004?

A 6.8

B 7

C 9.3

D 9.5

3 At 31 December 2002 a business had a Provision for Doubtful Debts of $1200. At 31 December 2003 the provision was adjusted to $900.

How did this affect the final accounts?

	Net profit	Net debtors
A	decrease by $300	decrease by $300
B	decrease by $300	increase by $300
C	increase by $300	decrease by $300
D	increase by $300	increase by $300

4 Before any end-of-year adjustments had been made, the trial balance of a business at 31 May 2004 included the following.

	Debit $	Credit $
Trade debtors	13 400	
Provision for Doubtful Debts		730

At 31 May 2004 it was found that debtors included a bad debt of $650. It was decided to adjust the Provision for Doubtful Debts to 4% of debtors. A debt of $420, which had been written off as bad in January 2003, was recovered in January 2004.

What was the effect of these events on the Profit and Loss Account for the year ended 31 May 2004?

A Credit $10

B Debit $10

C Credit $36

D Debit $36

12.10 Additional exercises

1 David's trial balance at 31 March 2004 was as follows.

Account	$	$
Sales		210 000
Sales Returns	9 240	
Purchases	84 000	
Purchases Returns		5 112
Wages	37 000	
Rent	7 600	
Electricity	1 027	
Telephone	900	
Postage and Stationery	359	
Carriage Inwards	1 840	
Carriage Outwards	1 220	
Discounts Allowed	6 015	
Discounts Received		2 480
Leasehold Premises at cost	70 000	
Provision for Depreciation of Leasehold Premises		5 000
Delivery Vans at cost	18 000	
Provision for Depreciation of Delivery vans		3 600
Office Furniture at cost	3 000	
Provision for Depreciation of Office Furniture		1 500
Stock	4 000	
Bank	1 245	
Trade debtors	19 800	
Provision for Doubtful Debts		800
Trade creditors		7 200
Drawings	20 446	
Capital		50 000
	285 692	285 692

Further information

1. Stock at 31 March 2004: $5000.

2. Sales include goods sent on sale or return to a customer who has not yet indicated acceptance of the goods. The goods cost $3000 and the customer has been invoiced for $4000.

3. Trade debtors includes debts totalling $1700 which are known to be bad. The Provision for Doubtful Debts is to be adjusted to include a specific provision of $3100 and a general provision of 5%.

4. The following expenses are to be accrued: wages $400, electricity $360 and telephones $100.

5. Rent of $1600 has been prepaid.

6. Depreciation is to be provided on the following bases: leasehold premises at 5% straight line; delivery vans at 25% reducing balance; office furniture at 10% straight line.

Required

(a) Prepare David's Trading and Profit and Loss Account for the year ended 31 March 2004.

(b) Prepare the Balance Sheet at 31 March 2004.

2 Saul is a trader and his trial balance at 31 May 2004 was as follows.

Account	$	$
Freehold Property at cost	180 000	
Provision for Depreciation of Freehold Property		45 000
Plant and Machinery at cost	97 000	
Provision for Depreciation of Plant and Machinery		53 000
Motor Vehicles at cost	41 000	
Provision for Depreciation of Motor Vehicles		27 000
Trade debtors	34 600	
Provision for Doubtful Debts		1 200
Trade creditors		5 720
Bank	11 374	
Sales		700 000
Sales Returns	6 670	
Purchases	410 890	
Purchases Returns		3 112
Wages	137 652	
Rent Payable	10 000	
Rent Receivable		1 020
Heating and Lighting	4 720	
Telephone and Postage	3 217	
Stationery	6 195	
Repairs to Machinery	17 600	
Discounts Allowed	3 220	
Discounts Received		2 942
Carriage Inwards	4 240	
Carriage Outwards	1 819	
Stock	40 000	
Drawings	28 797	
Capital		200 000
	1 038 994	1 038 994

Further information

1. Stock at 31 May 2004 cost $58 000.

2. Depreciation is to be calculated as follows: freehold property at 4% per annum, straight line; plant and machinery at 15% per annum; motor vehicles at 30% per annum on the reducing balance.

3. Included in trade debtors is a bad debt of $1800; the provision for doubtful debts is to be 5% of trade debtors.

4. $400 was owing for heating and lighting, and $220 for stationery. The stock of stationery at 31 May 2004 had cost $450.

5. Rent paid in advance was $2000; rent receivable was owing in the sum of $280.

6. Saul had taken goods for his own use. The goods had cost $2400. No entries for this had been made in the books.

Required

(a) Prepare Saul's Trading and Profit and Loss Account for the year ended 31 May 2004.

(b) Prepare the Balance Sheet at 31 May 2004.

13 Bank reconciliation statements

In this chapter you will learn:
- what a bank reconciliation statement is
- how to ensure that the bank balance in the cash book equals the correct balance of cash at bank
- how to adjust a trial balance after the cash book has been reconciled to the bank statement.

13.1 What is a bank reconciliation statement?

A **bank reconciliation statement** shows the correct balance on a bank account. The balance on the bank account in a cash book may not agree with the balance on the bank statement at any particular date. This may be because of

- timing differences (the delay between items being entered in the cash book and their entry on the bank statement)
- items on the bank statement that have not been entered in the cash book (for example, bank charges and interest, direct debits and other items).

Note. A bank statement is a copy of a customer's account in the books of a bank. Consequently items debited in the customer's own cash book appear as credits in the bank statement, and items credited in the cash book are debited in the bank statement. A debit balance in the cash book will appear as a credit balance in the bank statement. If a bank account is overdrawn the customer owes the bank money. The bank is now a creditor represented by a credit balance in the cash book; the customer is the bank's debtor and is shown as a debit balance on the bank statement.

When the balances in the cash book and bank statement do not agree, the correct balance must be found by preparing a bank reconciliation statement.

13.2 How to prepare a bank reconciliation statement

Follow these three steps.

1. Compare the entries in the cash book with the bank statements. Tick items that appear in both the cash book *and* the bank statement. Be sure to tick them in both places.

2. Enter in the cash book any items that remain unticked in the bank statement. Then tick those in both places. Calculate the new cash book balance.

3. Prepare the reconciliation statement. Begin with the final balance shown on the bank statement and adjust it for any items that remain unticked in the cash book. The result should equal the balance in the cash book.

The cash book balance will now be the correct balance of cash at bank.

Example 1

After step 1 has been completed, A.J. Belstrode's cash book and bank statement appear as follows at 31 March 2004. (Note the items which have been ticked.)

Cash book Bank account						
2004		$	2004	Cheque no.		$
Mar 1	Balance brought forward	1250	Mar 8	1022	Electricity	300 ✓
7	Cash banked	700 ✓	10	1023	Wages	600 ✓
12	P. Witte	200 ✓	11	1024	Rent	400 ✓
15	Cash banked	600 ✓	14	1025	T. Bone	920 ✓
20	T. Bagge	430 ✓	15	1026	Wages	440 ✓
31	T. Cake	594	28	1027	A. Cape	120
			29	1028	F. Goode	96
			31	1029	H. Ope	300
			31		Balance c/d	598
		3774				3774
April 1	Balance b/d	598				

Bank statement

THE REDDYPAY BANK

Account: A.J. Belstrode

			Money out $	Money in $	$
March	1	Balance brought forward			1250 Cr
	7	Paid in		700 ✓	1950 Cr
	10	Paid by cheque 1023	600 ✓		1350 Cr
	11	Paid by cheque 1022	300 ✓		1050 Cr
	12	Paid in		200 ✓	1250 Cr
	14	Direct debit: I. Taikeit	227		1023 Cr
	15	Paid in		600 ✓	1623 Cr
		Paid by cheque 1026	440 ✓		1183 Cr
	6	Paid by cheque 1024	400 ✓		783 Cr
		Paid by cheque 1025	920 ✓		137 Dr
	20	Paid in		430 ✓	293 Cr
	25	Bank Giro credit – Invest dividend		200	493 Cr
	31	Bank charges	112		381 Cr

Step 2 The unticked items in the bank statement are entered in the cash book and ticked.

Cash book
Bank account

2004		$	2004		$
Apr 1	Balance b/d	598	Mar 14	D/d I. Taikeit	227 ✓
Mar 25	Invest – dividend	200 ✓	Mar 31	Bank charges	112 ✓
		____	Mar 31	Balance c/d	459
		798			798
April 1	Balance b/d	459			

Note. Do not re-write the whole cash book to enter the new items.

Step 3 A bank reconciliation statement is prepared commencing with the bank statement balance which is adjusted for the items remaining unticked in the cash book.

Bank reconciliation statement at 31 March 2004

		$	$
Balance per bank statement			381
Add: Item not credited in bank statement			594
			975
Deduct cheques not presented:	1027	120	
	1028	96	
	1029	300	516
Balance per cash book			459

The correct bank balance, $459, has been calculated and, if a Balance Sheet at 31 March 2004 is prepared, $459 will be the amount included in it as the bank balance.

Example 2

At 30 June 2004 Eliza's bank statement shows a balance at bank of $1000. When Eliza checks her cash book she finds the following.

- A payment of $200 into the bank on 30 June does not appear in the bank statement.
- Cheques totalling $325 sent to customers on 29 June do not appear in the bank statement.

- The bank statement shows that Eliza's account has been debited with bank charges of $40. These have not been recorded in the cash book.

Required

(a) Prepare Eliza's bank reconciliation at 30 June 2004.

(b) Calculate Eliza's cash book balance at 30 June 2004 before it was corrected.

Answer

(a)	Bank reconciliation statement at 30 June 2004	
		$
	Balance per bank statement	1000
	Add amount paid in not credited	200
		1200
	Deduct cheques not presented	325
	Balance at 30 June 2004	875
(b)	Cash book balance before correction	
	Correct balance at bank at 30 June 2004	875
	Add bank charges not debited in cash book	40
	Cash book balance before it was corrected	915

13.3 Uses of bank reconciliation statements

- They reveal the correct amount of the cash at bank. Without a reconciliation, the cash book and bank statement balances may be misleading.
- They ensure that the correct bank balance is shown in the Balance Sheet.
- They are an important system of control:
  - unintended overdrawing on the bank account can be avoided
  - a surplus of cash at bank can be highlighted and invested to earn interest
  - if reconciliations are prepared regularly, errors are discovered early
  - if the reconciliation is prepared by somebody other than the cashier, the risk of fraud or embezzlement of funds is reduced. This division of duties is called **internal check**.

Exercise 1

The balance on a bank statement at 31 January 2004 was $1220 Credit. The following items had been entered in the cash book in January but did not appear on the bank statements:

(i) amount paid into the bank $300

(ii) cheques sent to customers $1045.

Required

Calculate the cash book balance at 31 January 2004.

Exercise 2

The bank balance in a cash book at 31 July 2004 was $310 (debit). The following items did not appear in the bank statement at that date:

(i) cheques totalling $1340 which had been paid into the bank on 31 July 2004

(ii) cheques sent to customers in July, totalling $490.

Required

Calculate the bank statement balance at 31 July 2004.

Exercise 3

At 31 March 2004 a cash book showed a balance of $80 at bank. On the same date the bank statement balance was $650 (credit). When the cash book was compared with the bank statement the following were found:

(i) a cheque sent to a supplier for $1000 had not been presented for payment

(ii) a cheque for $220 paid into the bank had not been credited on the bank statement

(iii) bank charges of $210 were omitted from the cash book.

Required

(a) Calculate the corrected cash book balance at 31 March 2004.

(b) Prepare a bank reconciliation statement at 31 March 2004.

Exercise 4

The following balances were extracted from the trial balance of a business at 31 December 2003.

	$	$
Trade debtors	1055	
Trade creditors		976
Rent	800	
Bank	1245	

When the bank statement for December was received it was discovered that the following items had not been entered in the cash book.

	$
Payment to a supplier by direct debit	360
Amount received from a customer by bank giro	420
Rent paid by standing order	200
Customer's cheque returned, dishonoured	323

Required

Prepare the adjusted trial balance to include the items omitted from the cash book.

13.4 Examination hints

- Remember the three steps required to reconcile a bank account.
- Note carefully if the balances given for the cash book or bank statement are overdrafts.
- Complete the double entry for all items entered in the cash book. Amend the other balances in the trial balance.
- Show bank overdrafts as current liabilities in Balance Sheets, never as current assets.

13.5 Multiple-choice questions

1 At 30 April 2004 the balance in X's cash book was $1740. At the same date the balance on his bank statement was $2240. Comparison of the cash book and bank statement showed the following:

(i) a dividend, $200, credited to X in the bank statement had not been entered in the cash book

(ii) cheques totalling $300 sent to suppliers in April had not been entered in the bank statement.

Which amount should be shown in the Balance Sheet at 30 April 2004?

A $1640 **B** $1740 **C** $1940 **D** $2240

2 A cash book balance at 31 October 2003 was $1600. When the bank statement was received the following were discovered:

(i) a cheque for $425 sent to a customer had been entered in the cash book as $452

(ii) a cheque for $375 sent to a customer had not been presented for payment

(iii) a cheque for $400 paid into the bank had not been credited in the bank statements.

What was the balance on the bank statement at 31 October 2003?

A $1548 **B** $1575 **C** $1602 **D** $1652

3 Y's bank statement showed a credit balance of $2170 at 31 May 2004. An examination of the statement showed the following:

(i) a direct debit for $300 had been debited twice in the bank statement

(ii) a cheque for $1015 sent to a customer had not been presented for payment

(iii) a cheque for $600 paid into the bank had not been credited in the bank statement.

What was the cash book balance at 31 May 2004?

A $1455 **B** $2055 **C** $2285 **D** $2885

4 A bank statement at 31 January 2004 showed a balance of $1000 Dr. The following did not appear on the statement:

(i) cheques not presented for payment, $230

(ii) a cheque for $400 banked on 31 January 2004

(iii) bank charges of $200 had not been entered in the cash book.

What was the original balance in the cash book at 31 January 2004 before it was amended?

A $630 Cr **B** 630 Dr **C** $970 Cr **D** $970 Dr

5 A bank statement showed an overdraft of $360 at 31 July 2004. The following discoveries were made:

(i) cheques totalling $2100 banked in July had not been credited in the bank statement.

(ii) cheques drawn for $875 in the cash book in July had not been entered on the bank statement.

What was the balance in the cash book at 31 July 2004?

A $865 Cr **B** $865 Dr **C** $1585 Cr
D $1585 Dr

13.6 Additional exercise

The following balances have been extracted from a trial balance at 30 June 2004.

	$	$
Trade debtors	400	
Trade creditors		380
Rent receivable		750
Bank charges	100	
Bank	990	

After the preparation of the trial balance a bank statement was received and revealed that the following had not been entered in the cash book.

	$
Bank interest receivable credited to account	10
Bank charges	130
Standing order payment to supplier	298
Amount received from customer by direct debit	78
Rent received by bank giro	150

Required

Prepare an amended trial balance extract at 30 June 2004 to take account of the amounts not entered in the cash book.

14 Control accounts

In this chapter you will learn:
- what Control accounts are and how to prepare them
- how to reconcile Control accounts and ledgers
- how to calculate revised net profit per draft accounts after the Control and ledger accounts have been reconciled
- how to revise the current assets and current liabilities in a draft Balance Sheet.

14.1 What is a Control account?

A **Control account** contains the totals of all postings made to the accounts in a particular ledger.

Control accounts are usually maintained for the sales and purchase ledgers. The totals are the periodic totals of the books of prime entry from which postings are made to the ledger.

The balance on a Control account should equal the total of the balances in the ledger it controls. Because the entries in the Control accounts are the totals of the books of prime entry they are also known as Total accounts. Control (or Total) accounts are kept in the nominal (or general) ledger.

Just as a trial balance acts as a check on the arithmetical accuracy of *all* the ledgers, a Control account checks the arithmetical accuracy of a single ledger. A difference between a Control account balance and the total of the balances in the ledger it controls shows where a cause of a difference on a trial balance may be found. Any difference between the Control account and the total of the balances in the ledger must be found without delay. The Sales Ledger Control account is also known as the Debtors' Control account, and the Purchase Ledger Control account is also known as the Creditors' Control account.

The following examples show how postings are made from the books of prime entry to the ledgers and the Control accounts, and how the balances on the Control accounts should equal the totals of the balances on the accounts in the ledgers.

14.2 The purchase ledger and its Control account

Books of prime entry

Purchases journal		Purchases returns journal		Cash Book		
	$		$		$	$
AB	100	PQ	8		AB	80
PQ	50	XY	10		PQ	40
XY	240		18		XY	200
	390					320

Purchase ledger
AB

		$			$
Cash book		80	Purchases		100
Balance	c/d	20*			—
		100			100
			Balance b/d		20

PQ

		$			$
Purchases returns		8	Purchases		50
Cash book		40			
Balance	c/d	2*			—
		50			50
			Balance b/d		2

XY

		$			$
Purchases returns		10	Purchases		240
Cash book		200			
Balance	c/d	30*			—
		240			240
			Balance b/d		30

Nominal (general) ledger
Purchase Ledger Control account

		$			$
Purchases returns journal		18	Purchases journal		390
Cash Book		320			
Balance	c/d	52 =	*20 + 2 + 30		—
		390			390
			Balance b/d		52

*Balancing figure

14.3 How to prepare a Purchase Ledger Control account

Enter items in the Control account as follows:

Debit side	Credit side
Total of purchase ledger debit balances (if any) brought forward from the previous period	Balance on the account brought forward from the previous period
Total of goods returned to suppliers (from purchases returns journal)	Total of purchases on credit (from purchases journal)
Total of cash paid to suppliers (from cash book)	Refunds from suppliers (from cash book)
Cash discounts received (from discount column in cash book)	Interest charged by suppliers on overdue invoices (from purchases journal)
Purchase ledger balances set against balances in sales ledger (from journal)	Total of debit balances (if any) at end of period in purchase ledger, carried forward
Balance carried forward (to agree with total of credit balances in purchases ledger)	

Note. Debit balances in the purchase ledger must *never* be netted against (deducted from) the credit balances.

❖ Warning. Only credit purchases are entered in the Purchase Ledger Control account. Do not enter cash purchases in it.

14.4 The sales ledger and its Control account

Books of prime entry

Sales journal		Sales returns journal		Cash book		
	$		$		$	$
Bali	300			Bali	180	
Carla	520	Bali	50	Carla	480	
Paula	140	Paula	10	Paula	100	—
	960		60		760	

Sales ledger
Bali

		$				$
Sales		300	Sales returns			50
			Cash book			180
		—	Balance	c/d		70*
		300				300
Balance	b/d	70				

Carla

		$				$
Sales		520	Cash book			480
		—	Balance	c/d		40*
		520				520
Balance	b/d	40				

Paula

		$				$
Sales		140	Sales returns			10
			Cash book			100
		—	Balance	c/d		30*
		140				140
Balance	b/d	30				

*Balancing figure

Nominal (general) ledger
Sales Ledger Control account

		$		$	
Sales journal		960	Sales returns journal	60	
			Cash book	760	
		—	Balance c/d	140	= *70 + 40 + 30
		960		960	
Balance	b/d	140			

14.5 How to prepare a sales ledger Control account

Enter items in the Control account as follows.

Debit side	Credit side
Balance brought forward from previous period	Total of sales ledger credit balances (if any) brought forward from previous period
Credit sales for period (total of sales journal)	Sales returns for the period (total of sales returns journal)
Refunds to credit customers (from cash book)	Cash received from credit customers (from cash book)
Dishonoured cheques (from cash book)	Cash discounts allowed (discount columns in cash book)
Interest charged to customers on overdue accounts (sales journal or cash book)	Bad debts written off (journal)
Bad debts previously written off, now recovered (journal)	Cash from bad debts recovered, previously written off (cash book)
Total of credit balances (if any) in sales ledger at end of period carried forward	Sales ledger balances set against balances in purchase ledger (journal)
	Balance carried forward to agree with total of debit balances in sales ledger

Note. Do not 'net' credit balances in the sales ledger against the debit balances.

14.6 Control accounts and the double-entry model

Control accounts duplicate the information contained in the purchase and sales (personal) ledgers. Control accounts *and* personal ledgers cannot both be part of the double-entry model. It is usual to treat the Control accounts as part of the double entry and to regard the personal ledgers as memorandum records containing the details which support the Control accounts.

Example

The following information has been extracted from the books of Useful Controls Ltd.

		$
At 1 June 2004 Purchase ledger balances brought forward	– debit	900
	– credit	16 340
Sales ledger balances brought forward	– debit	30 580
	– credit	620
Month to 30 June 2004		
Purchases journal total		65 000
Purchases returns journal total		3 150
Sales journal total		96 400
Sales returns journal total		1 980
Cash book: payments to suppliers		59 540
cheques received from customers (see note below)		103 900
discounts received		2 670
discounts allowed		4 520
Dishonoured cheques		3 300
Journal: Bad debts written off		1 220
Sales ledger balances set against purchase ledger balances		4 800
At June 30 Debit balances on purchase ledger accounts		600
Credit balances on sales ledger accounts		325

Note. The cash received from customers includes $800 relating to a bad debt previously written off.

Required

Prepare a Purchase Ledger Control account and a Sales Ledger Control account for Useful Controls, for the month of June 2004.

Answer

Purchase Ledger Control account

2004			$	2004			$
Jun 1	Balance	b/d	900	Jun 1	Balance	b/d	16 340
30	Purchases returns journal		3 150	30	Purchases journal		65 000
	Cash book		59 540	30	Balance	c/d	600
	Discounts received		2 670				
	Sales ledger – contra		4 800				
	Balance c/d						
	(Balancing figure)		10 880				
			81 940				81 940
Jul 1	Balance	b/d	600	Jul 1	Balance	b/d	10 880

Sales Ledger Control account

2004			$	2004			$
Jun 1	Balance	b/d	30 580	Jun 1	Balance	b/d	620
30	Sales journal		96 400	30	Sales returns journal		1 980
	Bad debt recovered		800		Cash book		103 900
	Bank – dishonoured cheques		3 300		Discounts allowed		4 520
	Balance	c/d	325		Bad debts written off		1 220
					Purchase ledger – contra		4 800
				30	Balance c/d (Balancing figure)		14 365
			131 405				131 405
Jul 1	Balance	b/d	14 365	Jul 1	Balance	b/d	325

Exercise 1

The following information has been obtained from the books of Byit Ltd.

	$
At 1 March 2004 Purchase ledger balances brought forward (credit)	10 000
(debit)	16
In the month to 31 March 2004	
Total of invoices received from suppliers	33 700
Goods returned to suppliers	824
Cheques sent to suppliers	27 500
Discounts received	1 300
At 31 March 2004 Debit balances in purchase ledger	156
Credit balances in purchase ledger	?

Required

Prepare the Purchase Ledger Control account for the month of March 2004.

Exercise 2

Information extracted from the books of Soldit Ltd is as follows.

	$
At 1 May 2004 Sales ledger balances brought forward (debit)	27 640
(credit)	545
In the month to 31 May 2004	
Total of invoices sent to customers	109 650
Goods returned by customers	2 220
Cheques received from customers	98 770
Discounts allowed	3 150
Cheque received in respect of bad debt previously written off (not included above)	490
Sales ledger balance set against balance in purchase ledger	2 624
At 31 May 2004 Credit balances in sales ledger	800
Debit balance carried down	?

Required

Prepare the Sales Ledger Control account for the month of May 2004.

14.7 Uses and limitations of Control accounts

Uses

- They are an important system of control on the reliability of ledger accounts.
- They warn of possible errors in the ledgers they control if the totals of the balances in those ledgers do not agree with the balances on the Control accounts.
- They may identify the ledger or ledgers in which errors have been made when there is a difference on a trial balance.
- They provide totals of debtors and creditors quickly when a trial balance is being prepared.
- If a business employs several accounting staff, the Control accounts should be maintained by somebody who is not involved in maintaining the sales or purchase ledgers. This increases the likelihood of errors being discovered and reduces the risk of individuals acting dishonestly. This division of duties is called **internal check**. For this reason Control accounts are kept in the general ledger and not in the sales and purchase ledgers.

Limitations

- Control accounts may themselves contain errors. (See (1) and (2) in §14.8.)

- Control accounts do not guarantee the accuracy of individual ledger accounts, which may contain compensating errors, for example items posted to wrong accounts.

14.8 How to reconcile Control accounts with ledgers

When there is a difference between the balance on a Control account and the total of the balances in the ledger it controls, the cause or causes must be found and the necessary corrections made. This is known as reconciling the Control accounts.

It is helpful to remember the following.

1. If a transaction is omitted from a book of prime entry, it will be omitted from the personal account in the sales or purchase ledger *and* from the Control account. Both records will be wrong and the Control account will not reveal the error.

2. If a transaction is entered incorrectly in a book of prime entry, the error will be repeated in the personal account in the sales or purchase ledger *and* in the Control account. Both records will be wrong and the Control account will not reveal the error.

3. If an item is copied incorrectly from a book of prime entry to a personal account in the sales or purchase ledger, the Control account will *not* be affected, and it will reveal that an error has been made.

4. If a total in a book of prime entry is incorrect, the Control account will be incorrect *but* the sales or purchase ledgers will not be affected. The Control account will reveal that an error has been made.

Example

The following information has been extracted from Duprey's books at 31 December 2003.

	$
Total of sales ledger balances (debit)	17 640
(credit)	110
Balance on Sales Ledger Control account (debit)	18 710
Total of purchase ledger balances (credit)	6 120
(debit)	80
Balance on Purchase Ledger Control account (credit)	6 330

The following errors have been discovered.

1. A sales invoice for $100 has been omitted from the sales journal.

2. A credit balance of $35 in the sales ledger has been extracted as a debit balance in the list of sales ledger balances.

3. The sales journal total for December has been overstated by $1000.

4. A balance of $250 on a customer's account in the sales ledger has been set against the amount owing to him in the purchase ledger but no entries have been made for this in the Sales and Purchase Ledger Control accounts.

5. A supplier's invoice for $940 has been entered in the purchases journal as $490.

6. An item of $340 in the purchases returns journal has been credited in the supplier's account in the purchase ledger. There was a credit balance of $800 on the customer's account at 31 December.

7. Discounts received in December amounting to $360 have been credited to the Purchase Ledger Control account.

Further information
Duprey's draft accounts for the year ended 31 December 2003 show a net profit of $36 000. He makes a provision for doubtful debts of 6%.

Required
(a) Calculate the following at 31 December 2003:
 (i) the revised sales ledger balances
 (ii) the revised purchase ledger balances.
(b) Prepare the amended Sales Ledger and Purchase Ledger Control accounts.
(c) Prepare a statement of the revised net profit for the year ended 31 December 2003.
(d) Prepare an extract from the Balance Sheet at 31 December 2003 to show the trade debtors and trade creditors.

Answer
(a) (i) Revised sales ledger balances

	Debit $	Credit $
Before adjustment	17 640	110
Invoice omitted from sales journal	100	
Credit balance listed as a debit	(35)	35
Revised balances	17 705	145

(ii) Revised purchase ledger balances

	Debit $	Credit $
Before adjustment	80	6120
Error in purchases journal $(940 – 490)		450
Adjustment of return credited to supplier $(340 × 2)*	—	(680)
Revised balances	80	5890

* An adjustment for an item placed on the wrong side of an account must be twice the amount of the item.

(b)

Amended Sales Ledger Control account

2003		$	2003		$
Dec 31	Balance brought forward	18 710	Dec 31	Correction of sales journal total	1 000
	Invoice omitted from S J	100		Contra to purchase ledger ¢	250
	Balance c/d	145		Balance c/d	17 705
		18 955			18 955
2004			2004		
Jan 1	Balance b/d	17 705	Jan 1	Balance b/d	145

Amended Purchase Ledger Control account

2003		$	2003		$
Dec 31	Contra to sales ledger ¢	250	Dec 31	Balance brought forward	6330
	Correction of discounts $(360 × 2)	720		Error in purchase journal	450
	Balance c/d	5890		Balance c/d	80
		6860			6860
	Balance b/d	80		Balance b/d	5890

(c) Revised net profit for the year ended 31 December 2003

	Decrease $	Increase $	$
Net profit per draft accounts			36 000
Sales invoice omitted from sales journal		100	
Overcast of sales journal	1000		
Purchase invoice understated	450		
Increase in provision for doubtful debts			
6% of (17 705 – 17 640)	4		
	1454	100	(1 354)
Revised net profit			34 646

(d) Balance sheet extracts at 31 December 2003

	$	$
Trade debtors		
Sales ledger	17 705	
Deduct provision for doubtful debts	1 062	
	16 643	
Purchase ledger	80	16 723
Trade creditors		
Purchase ledger	5 890	
Sales ledger	145	6 035

Notes

- Debtors should never be deducted from creditors, or creditors from debtors in a Balance Sheet.
- Do not provide for doubtful debts on debit balances in the purchase ledger

Exercise 3

The following information has been extracted from the books of Rorre Ltd at 31 December 2003.

	$
Total of purchase ledger balances	64 (debit)
	7 217 (credit)
Total of sales ledger balances	23 425 (debit)
	390 (credit)
Purchase Ledger Control account	7 847 (credit)
Sales Ledger Control account	22 909 (debit)

Draft accounts show a net profit of $31 000 for the year ended 31 December 2003. The following errors have been discovered.

1. An invoice for $100 has been entered twice in the purchases journal.

2. A total of $84 has been omitted from both the Discounts Received account and the Purchase Ledger Control account.

3. A debit balance of $50 has been entered in the list of purchase ledger balances as a credit balance.

4. An amount of $710 owing to Trazom, a supplier, has been offset against their account in the sales ledger, but no entry has been made in the Control accounts.

5. An invoice in the sales journal for $326 has been entered in the sales ledger as $362.

6. The sales journal total for December has been understated by $800.

Required

(a) Prepare a statement to show the corrected purchase and sales ledger balances.

(b) Prepare corrected Purchase and Sales Ledger Control accounts.

(c) Calculate the amended net profit for the year ended 31 December 2003.

(d) Prepare a Balance Sheet extract at 31 December 2003 to show the debtors and creditors.

14.9 Examination hints

- Give the Control accounts their correct title and head the money columns with $ signs.
- Check carefully that the entries are on the correct sides of the accounts.
- Enter the dates for the entries, distinguishing between the start and end of the period.
- Make sure that you enter the total of any credit balances in the sales ledger into the Sales Ledger Control account and the total of any debit balances in the purchase ledger into the Purchase Ledger Control account.
- Calculate the other closing balances if necessary.
- Bring down the closing balances on the first day of the next period.
- Assume that Control Accounts, when they are kept, are part of the double entry and that the personal ledgers contain memorandum accounts, unless the question indicates otherwise. If Control accounts are not maintained, the double entry is completed in the personal ledger accounts.
- Enter bad debts recovered on the debit side of the Sales Ledger Control account as well as showing the cash received for them on the credit side.
- Enter 'contra' items (balances in the sales ledger set off against balances in the purchase ledger) in *both* Control accounts. The entries will always be credited in the Sales Ledger Control account and debited in the Purchase Ledger Control account.

14.10 Multiple-choice questions

1 The debit balance on a Sales Ledger Control Account at 30 September 2003 is $104 000. The following errors have been discovered.

	$
Total of sales journal overstated	1300
Discounts allowed omitted from Sales Ledger Control account	870
Bad debts written off not recorded in Sales Ledger Control account	240
Increase in provision for doubtful debts	600

What is the total of the balances in the sales ledger?

A $100 990   **B** $101 590   **C** $102 070

D $103 330

2 The credit balance on a Purchase Ledger Control account at 31 October is $28 000. The following errors have been found.

	$
Amount transferred from Calif's account in the sales ledger to his account in the purchase ledger not recorded in the Control accounts	1 400
A debit balance in the purchase ledger at 31 October not carried down in the Purchase Ledger Control account	300
A refund to a cash customer debited in Purchase Ledger Control account	150

What is the total of the credit balances in the purchase ledger?

A $26 450

B $26 750

C $27 050

D $28 950

3 A Purchase Ledger Control account has been reconciled with the purchase ledger balances as shown.

	$
Balance per Control account	76 000
Total of purchases journal for one month not posted to general ledger	4 000
Cash paid to creditors not posted to purchase ledger	5 000
Total of balances in purchase ledger	85 000

Which figure for creditors should be shown in the Balance Sheet?

A $75 000

B $77 000

C $80 000

D $85 000

14.11 Additional exercises

1 The following information was taken from Peter's books.

2004		$	
March 1	Sales Ledger Control account balance	55 650	Dr
	Purchase Ledger Control account balance	34 020	Cr
31	Sales for March	47 700	
	Purchases for March	21 840	
	Cheques received from credit customers	36 900	
	Payments to creditors	24 300	
	Customers' cheques returned unpaid	1 920	
	Bad debts written off	2 250	
	Discounts received	600	
	Discounts allowed	930	
	Returns inwards	580	
	Returns outwards	330	
	Credit balance in purchase ledger transferred from sales ledger	810	

Required

Prepare the Sales Ledger Control account and the Purchase Ledger Control account for the month of March 2004.

2 The following information was extracted from the books of Colombo for the year ended 30 April 2004.

	$
Purchase ledger balances at 1 May 2003	64 680
Credit purchases	1 236 210
Credit purchases returns	18 600
Cheques paid to creditors	1 118 970
Cash purchases	13 410
Discount received on credit purchases	47 100
Credit balances transferred to sales ledger accounts	7 815

Required

(a) Prepare the Purchase Ledger Control account for the year ended 30 April 2004.

The total of the balances extracted from Colombo's purchase ledger amounts to $101 490, which does not agree with the closing balance in the Control account. The following errors were then discovered.

1. The total of discount received had been overstated by $1500.
2. A purchase invoice for $3060 had been completely omitted from the books.

3. A credit balance in the purchase ledger account had been understated by $150.
4. A credit balance of $1275 in the purchase ledger had been set off against a contra entry in the sales ledger, but no entry had been made in either Control account.
5. A payment of $2175 had been debited to the creditor's account but was omitted from the bank account.
6. A credit balance of $4815 had been omitted from the list of creditors.

Required

(b) (i) Extract the necessary information from the above list and draw up an amended Purchase Ledger Control account for the year ended 30 April 2004.
   (ii) Beginning with the given total of $101 490, show the changes to be made in the purchase ledger to reconcile it with the new Control account balance.

3 At 31 December 2003 the balance on Sellit's Sales Ledger Control account was $17 584 (debit). It did not agree with the total of balances extracted from the sales ledger. The following errors have been found.

1. The total of the discount allowed column in the cash book has been overstated by $210.
2. A receipt of $900 from P. Ford, a customer, has been treated as a refund from B. Ford, a supplier.
3. An invoice for $1200 sent to P. Williams, a customer, has been entered in the sales journal as $1020.
4. The total of the sales journal for December has been understated by $600.
5. Goods with a selling price of $578 were sent to Will Dither, a customer, in December, and he has been invoiced for that amount. It has now been discovered that the goods were sent on sale or return and the customer has not yet indicated whether he will purchase the goods.
6. An invoice for $3160 sent to W. Yeo, a customer, has been entered correctly in the sales journal but has been entered in the customer's account as $3610.

Required

(a) Prepare the Sales Ledger Control account showing clearly the amendments to the original balance.
(b) Calculate the total of the balances extracted from the sales ledger before the errors listed above had been corrected.
(c) Prepare the journal entries to correct the sales ledger accounts. Narratives are required.

4 At 31 May 2004 the debit balance on a Sales Ledger Control account was $18 640. This balance did not agree with the total of balances extracted from the sales ledger. The following errors have now been found.

1. Cash received from debtors entered in the Control account included $400 in respect of a debt which had previously been written off. This fact had not been recognised in the Control account.
2. A debit balance of $325 in the sales ledger had been set off against an account in the purchase ledger. This transfer had been debited in the Sales Ledger Control account and credited in the Purchase Ledger Control account.
3. Cash sales of $1760 had been recorded in the cash book as cash received from debtors.
4. Cash received from K. Bali, $244, had been entered in the account of B. Kali in the sales ledger.
5. Credit balances in the sales ledger totalled $436.

Required

Prepare the corrected Sales Ledger Control account at 31 May 2004.

5 (a) Outline *three* reasons for keeping control accounts.
   (b) The following information was extracted from the books of William Noel for the year ended 30 April 2001.

	$
Purchase Ledger Balance at 1 May 2000	43 120
Credit purchases for the year	824 140
Credit purchases returns	12 400
Cheques paid to creditors	745 980
Cash purchases	8 940
Discount received on credit purchases	31 400
Credit balances transferred to sales ledger accounts	5 210

Draw up the Purchase Ledger Control account for the year ended 30 April 2001.

The total of the balances in William Noel's purchase ledger amounts to $67 660, which does not agree with the closing balance in the Control account.

The following errors were then discovered.

1. Discount received had been overstated by $1000.
2. A credit purchases invoice for $2040 had been completely omitted from the books.
3. A purchases ledger account had been understated by $100.
4. A credit balance of $850 in the purchases ledger had been set off against a contra entry in the sales ledger, but no entry had been made in either Control account.
5. A payment of $1450 had been debited to the creditor's account but was omitted from the bank account.

6. A credit balance of $3210 had been omitted from the list of creditors.

(c) (i) Extract the necessary information from the above list and draw up an amended Purchase Ledger Control account for the year ended 30 April 2001.

(ii) Beginning with the given total of $67 660, show the changes to be made in the Purchase Ledger to reconcile it with the new Control account balance.

(UCLES, 2001, AS/A Level Accounting, Syllabus 8706/2, October/November)

15 Suspense accounts

In this chapter you will learn:
- **what the purpose of Suspense accounts is, and how to prepare them**
- **how to prepare journal entries to correct errors**
- **how to revise the net profit per draft accounts after errors have been corrected**
- **how to revise the working capital in a draft Balance Sheet.**

15.1 What is a Suspense account?

Suspense accounts are sometimes used when transactions are recorded in the books before any decision has been made about their proper accounting treatment. For example, an invoice may contain a mixture of capital and revenue expenditure. The expenditure may be recorded in a Suspense account until it is decided how much is capital expenditure and how much revenue.

This chapter is concerned with Suspense accounts that are opened when the causes of differences on trial balances cannot immediately be found and corrected.

15.2 When a Suspense account should be opened

A Suspense account should be opened only when attempts to find the cause of a difference on a trial balance have been unsuccessful. The following checks should be carried out before opening a Suspense account.

1. Check the additions of the trial balance.
2. If the difference is divisible by 2, look for a balance of half the difference which may be on the wrong side of the trial balance. (Example: a difference of $1084 may be caused by 'discounts allowed $542' being entered on the credit side of the trial balance.)
3. If the difference is divisible by 9, look for a balance where digits may have been reversed. (Example: a difference of $18 may be caused by $542 entered in trial balance as $524.)
4. Check the totals of sales ledger balances and purchase ledger balances to the Control accounts, if these have been prepared.

5. Check the extraction of balances from the ledgers.

If the cause of the difference has still not been found, and a Profit and Loss Account and Balance Sheet are required urgently, a Suspense account may be opened.

15.3 How to open a Suspense account

A Suspense account is opened in the general ledger with a balance on whichever side of the account will make the trial balance agree when the balance is inserted in it. For example, if the total of the credit side of a trial balance is $100 less than the total of the debit side, the Suspense account will be opened with a credit balance of $100. When the Suspense account balance is inserted in the trial balance, the latter will balance. A Balance Sheet may then prepared.

15.4 When a Suspense account has been opened

The cause or causes of the difference on the trial balance must be investigated at the earliest opportunity and the errors corrected.

In real life, if there is still a small balance on a Suspense account after all reasonable attempts have been made to find the difference, a business may decide that the amount involved is not material. It will save further time and expense in searching for errors by writing the balance off to the Profit and Loss Account. However, there may be a danger that a small difference hides large errors which do not quite cancel each other out.

15.5 How to correct errors

The correction of errors will require journal entries which will be posted to the Suspense (and other) accounts *unless* they are errors that do *not* affect the trial balance, which are as follows.

- errors of omission
- errors of commission
- errors of principle
- errors of original entry
- errors caused by the complete reversal of entries
- compensating errors.

(These types of error have been explained more fully in §6.3.)

To decide how to correct an error, ask the following three questions.

- (i)   How has the transaction been recorded?
- (ii) How should the transaction have been recorded?
- (iii) What adjustments are required to correct the error?

Remember the following.

- An item on the wrong side of an account must be corrected by an adjustment equal to *twice* the amount of the original error (once to cancel the error and once to place the item on the correct side of the account).
- Some errors do not affect the double entry; an example would be a balance on a sales ledger account copied incorrectly onto a summary of balances for inclusion in the trial balance. The summary of balances should be amended and a one-sided entry in the journal prepared to correct the Suspense account. Such errors do not require to be corrected by debit *and* credit entries

Example

Kadriye extracted a trial balance from her ledgers on 31 December 2003. The trial balance totals were $23 884 (debit) and $24 856 (credit). She placed the difference in a Suspense account so that she could prepare a draft Profit and Loss Account for the year ended 31 December 2003, and a Balance Sheet at that date.

Kadriye then found the following errors.

1. The debit side of the Telephone account had been overstated by $200.
2. An invoice sent to Singh for $240 had been completely omitted from the books.
3. A cheque for $124 received from X and Co. had been posted to the debit of their account.
4. The purchase of some office equipment for $1180 had been debited to Office Expenses account.
5. Discounts received, $90, had been posted to the purchase ledger but not to the Discounts Received account.
6. Rent paid, $800, had been credited to Rent Receivable account.
7. A refund of an insurance premium, $60, had been recorded in the cash book but no other entry had been made.
8. A purchase of office stationery, $220, had been debited to Purchases account in error.
9. A credit balance of $30 in the purchase ledger had been omitted from the list of balances extracted from the ledger. The total of the list had been included in the trial balance.
10. Goods returned to Speedsel had been credited to Speedsel's account and debited to Purchases Returns account. The goods had cost $400.

Required

(a) Prepare journal entries to correct errors 1 to 10. (Narratives are required.)
(b) Prepare the Suspense account showing the opening balance and the correcting entries.

The draft Profit and Loss Account showed a net profit for the year ended 31 December 2003 of $8400 and the Balance Sheet at that date showed working capital (current assets less current liabilities) of $1250.

Required

(c) Calculate the revised net profit for the year ended 31 December 2003.
(d) Calculate the revised working capital at 31 December 2003.

Answer

(a)

<table>
<tr><td colspan="3" style="text-align:center;">Journal entries</td></tr>
<tr><td></td><td>$</td><td>$</td></tr>
<tr><td>1. Note. The debit side of the Telephone account is overstated by $200. Reduce this by crediting the account and debiting the Suspense account with $200</td><td></td><td></td></tr>
<tr><td>Suspense account</td><td>200</td><td></td></tr>
<tr><td>Telephone account</td><td></td><td>200</td></tr>
<tr><td>Correction of the overcast of $200 of the Telephone account.</td><td></td><td></td></tr>
<tr><td>2. Note. This transaction has been omitted from the books entirely. It has not affected the trial balance and the Suspense account is not involved..</td><td></td><td></td></tr>
<tr><td>Singh</td><td>240</td><td></td></tr>
<tr><td>Sales</td><td></td><td>240</td></tr>
<tr><td>Recording invoice for $240 sent to Singh but omitted from books.</td><td></td><td></td></tr>
<tr><td>3. Note. $124 has been posted to the wrong side of X and Co.'s account. This is corrected by crediting their account with double that amount.</td><td></td><td></td></tr>
<tr><td>Suspense account</td><td>248</td><td></td></tr>
<tr><td>X and Co. account</td><td></td><td>248</td></tr>
<tr><td>Correction of $124 received from X and Co. debited to their account in error.</td><td></td><td></td></tr>
<tr><td>4. Note. This is an error of principle; do not adjust through the Suspense account.</td><td></td><td></td></tr>
<tr><td>Office Equipment (asset) account</td><td>1180</td><td></td></tr>
<tr><td>Office Expenses account</td><td></td><td>1180</td></tr>
<tr><td>Purchase of office equipment treated as revenue expense in error.</td><td></td><td></td></tr>
<tr><td>5. Note. This is not an error of complete omission; correct through the Suspense account.</td><td></td><td></td></tr>
<tr><td>Suspense account</td><td>90</td><td></td></tr>
<tr><td>Discounts Received account</td><td></td><td>90</td></tr>
<tr><td>Discounts received, $90, omitted from Discounts Received Account.</td><td></td><td></td></tr>
<tr><td>6. Note. Rent Receivable account must be debited to cancel error; Rent Payable must be debited to record payment correctly. Note separate debit entries must be made.</td><td></td><td></td></tr>
<tr><td>Rent Receivable account</td><td>800</td><td></td></tr>
<tr><td>Rent Payable account</td><td>800</td><td></td></tr>
<tr><td>Suspense account</td><td></td><td>1600</td></tr>
<tr><td>Correction of rent paid incorrectly treated as rent received.</td><td></td><td></td></tr>
<tr><td>7. Note. This refund has not been completely omitted from the books. Adjust through the Suspense account.</td><td></td><td></td></tr>
<tr><td>Suspense account</td><td>60</td><td></td></tr>
<tr><td>Insurance account</td><td></td><td>60</td></tr>
<tr><td>Refund of insurance premium omitted from the Insurance account.</td><td></td><td></td></tr>
</table>

8. *Note. This is an error of commission. Do not adjust through the Suspense account.*

	$	$
Office Stationery account	220	
Purchases account		220

Purchase of office stationery treated as stock for re-sale in error.

9. *Note. This not a double-entry error but it has affected the trial balance. The list of balances must be corrected and a one-sided entry in the Suspense account is required*

Suspense account	30	

10. *Note. This is a complete reversal of entries. The correcting entry is twice the original amount and the Suspense account is not involved.*

Speedsel Ltd	800	
Purchases Returns account		800

Goods returned to Speedsel Ltd, $400, credited to their account and debited to Purchases Returns account in error.

(b)

Suspense account

	$		$
Difference on trial balance	972	Rent receivable	800*
Telephone	200	Rent payable	800*
X and Co.	248		
Discounts received	90		
Insurance	60		
Correction of trade creditors	30		
	1600		1600

*These two entries should be shown separately as the double entry is completed in different accounts.

Note. The Suspense account is opened with the difference on the trial balance and then posted from the journal entries in (a).

(c)

Calculation of corrected net profit for the year ended 31 December

	Decrease (Dr)	Increase (Cr)	
	$	$	$
Net profit per draft Profit and Loss Account			8400
(1) Decrease in telephone expense		200	
(2) Increase in sales		240	
(4) Decrease in office expenses		1180	
(5) Increase in discounts received		90	
(6) Reduction in rent receivable	800		
Increase in rent payable	800		
(7) Reduction in insurance premium		60	
(8) No effect on net profit			
(10) Increase in purchases returns		800	
	1600	2570	
		(1600)	970
Revised net profit			9370

Note. Set the calculation out as shown above. Untidy, 'straggly' calculations do not commend themselves to examiners. Debit entries to nominal accounts in the journal decrease profit, and credit entries to nominal accounts increase profit.

(d)

Calculation of working capital at 31 December			
	Increase (Dr)	Decrease (Cr)	
	$	$	$
Working capital per draft Balance Sheet			1250
(2) Singh invoice omitted	240		
(3) X and Co. $124 cheque misposted		248	
(9) Credit balance omitted		30	
(10) Goods returned to Speedsel	800	—	
	1040	278	
	(278)		762
Revised working capital			2012

Note. The layout of the answer given above is a good one and should be followed whenever possible. Adjust working capital by journal postings to personal accounts and by personal accounts omitted from the trial balance.

Exercise 1

Lee's trial balance at 30 June 2004 fails to agree and he places the difference in a Suspense account. Lee then discovers the following errors.

1. The total of the sales journal for one month was $5430. This had been posted to the Sales account as $5340.

2. An invoice for $150 for the purchase of stock from Bilder had been entirely omitted from the books.

3. A cheque for $75 from Doyle, a customer, had been credited to his account as $57.

4. A debt of $50 in the sales ledger had been written off as bad but no entry had been made in the Bad debts account.

5. An improvement to a machine at a cost of $400 had been debited to Machinery Repairs account. (Lee depreciates machinery by the straight-line method over 10 years; a full year's depreciation is calculated for the year of purchase.)

Required

(a) Prepare the Suspense account in Lee's ledger showing clearly the difference on the trial balance at 30 June as the first entry and the entries required to adjust the errors.

(b) Prepare journal entries for errors 2 and 5. (Narratives are *not* required.)

Lee's draft Profit and Loss Account for the year ended 30 June 2004 showed a net profit of $3775.

Required

(c) Calculate the corrected net profit for the year ended 30 June 2004.

Exercise 2

When Jayesh extracted a trial balance from his books at 31 December 2003 he found that it did not balance. He entered the difference in a Suspense account and then prepared a draft Profit and Loss Account which showed a net profit of $2500. Jayesh later found the following errors.

1. The balance of opening stock $8500 had been entered in the trial balance as $5800.

2. The stock at 31 December 2003 had been understated by $2000.

3. Repairs to a machine, $3500, had been posted to Machinery at Cost account as $5300.

4. An invoice in the sum of $800 for the sale of goods to Bane had been posted to Bane's account but had not been entered in the sales journal.

5. A credit balance of $63 in the sales ledger had been extracted as a debit balance. Jayesh does not maintain Control accounts.

Required

(a) Prepare the journal entries to correct the errors. (Narratives are *not* required.)

(b) Prepare the Suspense account showing the trial balance difference and the correcting entries.

Jayesh's draft Balance Sheet at 31 December 2003 showed working capital of $3200.

Required

(c) Calculate Jayesh's corrected working capital at 31 December 2003.

15.6 Examination hints

- Remember the six types of error that do not affect the trial balance. These are not corrected through the Suspense account.
- Prepare correcting journal entries in proper form. (Revise §3.10.) Note whether narratives are required.
- The first entry in a Suspense account is the difference on the trial balance. Enter it on the same side of the account as it will be entered in the trial balance.
- Post the Suspense account from journal entries. If these have not been required by the question it may be helpful to prepare them in rough.
- The Suspense account should not have a balance on it when you have posted the journal entries to it.
- Calculate revised profit or loss from the nominal account entries in the journal.
- Calculate revised working capital from the journal entries affecting current assets and current liabilities.
- Do not make journal entries to other books of prime entry. Postings from the journal should always be to named accounts in the ledgers.

15.7 Multiple-choice questions

(In each of the following cases, a trial balance has failed to agree and the difference has been entered in a Suspense account.)

1 A credit balance in the sum of $93 has been omitted from the list of balances extracted from the sales ledger.

What is the effect on the trial balance?

A The credit side is understated by $93.

B The credit side is overstated by $93.

C The debit side is understated by $93.

D The debit side is overstated by $93

2 A credit note for $46 sent to A. Moses has been debited to A. Mason's account in the sales ledger.

What effect will this have on the trial balance?

	Debit total	Credit total
A	none	none
B	$46 overstated	$46 understated
C	none	$92 understated
D	$92 overstated	none

3 The total of the sales journal for one month is $9160. It has been entered in the Sales account as $9610. Which entries are required to correct the error?

	Debit		Credit	
A	Sales account	$450	Sales journal	$450
B	Sales journal	$450	Sales account	$450
C	Sales account	$450	Suspense account	$450
D	Suspense account	$450	Sales account	$450

4 An invoice for repairs to machinery, $500, has been entered in the Machinery at Cost account.
Which entries are required to correct the error?

	Debit		Credit	
A	Machinery at Cost account	$500	Repairs to Machinery account	$500
B	Repairs to Machinery account	$500	Machinery at Cost account	$500
C	Repairs to Machinery account	$500	Suspense account	$500
D	Suspense account	$500	Machinery at Cost account	$500

5 Which of the following will cause a difference on a trial balance?

A An invoice omitted from the sales journal

B An invoice for $415 entered in the Sales journal as $451

C An invoice for $600 entered in the sales journal not included in the monthly total

D A credit note entered in the sales journal

6 After which error will a trial balance still balance?

A Wages paid, $1500, was entered correctly in the bank account but debited to the wages account as $2500.

B Rent receivable of $200 was debited to the Rent Payable account.

C Goods returned to supplier, $150, were entered in purchases returns journal as $105.

D The sales journal was undercast by $200.

7 A trial balance failed to agree and a Suspense account was opened. It was then found that rent received of $500 had been debited to the Rent Payable account. Which entries are required to correct this error?

	Rent Received account		Rent Payable account		Suspense account	
		$		$		$
A	credit	500	credit	500	debit	1000
B	credit	500	debit	500	no entry	
C	debit	500	credit	500	debit	1000
D	debit	500	credit	500	no entry	

15.8 Additional exercises

1 Bastien does not maintain Control accounts. His trial balance does not balance and he has opened a Suspense account. The following errors have now been discovered.

1. Discount received from Veeraj, amounting to $70, has been included in the discount column of the cash book but has not been posted to Veeraj's account.

2. Goods have been sold on credit to Bernard for $1400 less 25% trade discount. Correct entries have been made in the sales journal but $1000 has been posted to Bernard's ledger account.

3. A cheque for $400 received from Rodney has been debited in the cash book and also debited in Rodney's ledger account.

4. A motor vehicle costing $12 000 has been bought on credit from Nedof Motors. The Purchases account has been debited and Nedof Motor's account credited.

5. $60 spent by Bastien on his personal expenses has been posted to the Sundry Expenses account.

Required

Prepare the entries in Bastien's journal, with suitable narratives, to correct the above errors.

2 Boulder's trial balance at 31 March 2004 did not balance and the difference was entered in a Suspense account. Boulder does not maintain Control accounts. The following information was later discovered.

1. A receipt of $313 from Head, a customer, has been entered correctly in the cash book but has been debited to Head's account in the sales ledger as $331.

2. Goods sold to Joey for $100 have been returned by him and entered correctly in the Sales Returns account. No entry has been made for the return in Joey's account in the sales ledger.

3. The purchase of a second-hand motor vehicle costing $3000 has been debited to the Motor Vehicle Expenses account.

4. The total of the Discount Allowed column in the cash book has been overcast by $300.

5. A dishonest employee has stolen $700 from the business and the cash will not be recovered. No entry to record the theft has been made in the accounts.

Required

(a) Prepare journal entries to correct errors 1 to 5. Narratives are required.

(b) Prepare a Suspense account commencing with the trial balance difference.

The working capital shown in the Balance Sheet at 31 March 2004 before the errors were corrected was $2400.

Required

(c) Calculate the working capital after the errors have been corrected.

3 Amber's trial balance at 31 December 2003 failed to agree and the difference was entered in a Suspense account. The total of the purchase ledger balances had been entered as creditors in the trial balance but it did not agree with the credit balance of $5419 on the Purchase Ledger Control account. The following errors were found.

1. No entry had been made in the books to record a refund by cheque of $90 from Victor, a supplier.

2. A cheque for $420 sent to Shah, a supplier, had been entered correctly in the cash book but debited to General Expenses account as $240.

3. Goods returned, $900, by Amil, a customer, had been credited in Amil's account and debited in the Purchases account.

4. Goods which cost $350 had been returned to Hussein, a supplier. No entry had been made in the books for this.

5. The discount received column in the cash book had been undercast by $600.

Required

(a) Prepare journal entries to correct errors 1 to 5. Narratives are *not* required.

(b) Prepare the Suspense account commencing with the difference on the trial balance.

(c) Explain how a balance which is not considered material in amount may be treated in the accounts.

4 Logan has prepared the following trial balance at 31 March 2004.

	$	$
Sales		131 940
Purchases	33 000	
Sales returns	260	
Purchase returns		315
Opening stock	6 900	
Debtors Control	14 125	
Creditors Control		16 070
Discount allowed	700	
Discount received		614
Wages and salaries	20 600	
Advertising	1 000	
General expenses	2 340	
Bank	13 710	
Premises	70 000	
Motor vehicles	5 000	
Equipment	3 500	
Capital		25 000
Drawings	3 000	
Suspense		196
	174 135	174 135

Logan is unable to find the difference on the trial balance and has entered the difference in the Suspense Account. The following errors have been made in the accounts.

1. Discount allowed of $55 has been posted to the credit of Discount received.

2. Purchase returns of $108 have been posted to the debit of Sales returns.

3. A cheque for $400 from a debtor has been dishonoured, but no record has been made of this in the accounts. There is no reason to believe that payment will not be made in April 2004.

4. Equipment bought during the year for $4400 has been debited to Purchases account.

5. During the year Logan had taken stock which cost $800 for his own personal use.

6. $90 of the general expenses related to an amount paid out of the business bank account for one of Logan's private expenses. In his attempt to correct the accounts, Logan made another debit entry of $90 in the General Expenses account, with no other entry being made.

Required

(a) Prepare journal entries to correct errors 1 to 6 (narratives are not required).

(b) Prepare the Suspense account to show the correcting entries.

(c) Prepare a corrected trial balance at 31 March 2004.

The net profit per the draft accounts, prepared before the above errors were corrected, was $25 000.

Required

(d) Prepare a statement of corrected net profit showing the effect of each error on the net profit per the draft accounts.

16 Incomplete records

In this chapter you will learn:
- how to calculate profit or loss from statements of affairs
- how to prepare Trading and Profit and Loss Accounts and Balance Sheets from incomplete records
- the relationship between mark-up and margin
- how to calculate the cost of stock lost by fire or theft.

16.1 What are incomplete records?

The term **incomplete records** describes any method of recording transactions that is not based on the double-entry model. Often, only a cash book, or only records of debtors and creditors, are kept, so that only one aspect of each transaction is recorded. This is **single-entry bookkeeping**. Incomplete records also describes situations where the only records kept may be invoices for purchases, copies of sales invoices, cheque counterfoils and bank statements. In all these cases, Profit and Loss Accounts and Balance Sheets cannot be prepared in the normal way.

16.2 How to calculate profit or loss from statements of affairs

When records of transactions are insufficient to enable a Trading and Profit and Loss Account to be prepared, the profit or loss of a business for a given period may be calculated if the assets and liabilities of the business at both the start and end of the period are known. The method is based upon two principles:

1. the accounting equation, capital = assets − liabilities
2. profit increases capital; losses reduce capital.

The difference between the opening and closing capitals, after making adjustments for new capital introduced and the owner's drawings in the period, will reveal the profit or loss. Capital is calculated by listing the assets and liabilities in a **statement of affairs**.

Example

Fatima is a hair stylist who has been in business for some time. She has never kept records of her takings and payments. She wishes to know how much profit or loss she has made in the year ended 31 December 2003. Her assets and liabilities at 1 January and 31 December 2003 were as follows.

	1 January 2003	31 December 2003
	$	$
Equipment	800	1000
Stock of hair styling sundries	70	45
Amounts owing from clients	50	70
Rent paid in advance	100	120
Balance at bank	150	160
Creditors for supplies	25	30
Electricity owing	40	50

Fatima has drawn $100 per week from the business for personal expenses.

Required

Calculate Fatima's profit for the year ended 31 December 2003.

Answer

	Statements of affairs at	
	1 January 2003	31 December 2003
	$	$
Equipment	800	1000
Stock of hair styling sundries	70	45
Amounts owing from clients	50	70
Rent paid in advance	100	120
Balance at bank	150	160
	1170	1395
Less		
Creditors for supplies	25	30
Electricity owing	40 65	50 80
Net assets (= capital)	1105	1315
Add drawings in year to 31 December 2003		
(52 × $100)		5200*
		6515
Deduct capital at beginning of year		1105
Profit for the year ended 31 December 2003		5410

* Drawings have been added back as the capital at 31 December 2003 would have been greater if Fatima had not taken this money out of the business.

Note. When an asset is valued at more or less than cost, it should be included in a statement of affairs at valuation.

Exercise 1

Lian has run a business repairing motor vehicles for some years but has not kept proper accounting records. However, the following information is available.

	at 1 January 2003	at 31 December 2003
	$	$
Premises at cost	4000	4000
Motor van at cost	5000	5000
Motor car at cost	—	3000
Plant and equipment	1100	1300
Stock of parts	400	200
Debtors for work done	700	800
Balance at bank	1300	900
Owing to suppliers for parts	170	340

The premises were bought some years ago and were valued at $9000 at 31 December 2003. At the same date, the motor van was valued at $4000. The motor car was Lian's own car, which he brought into the business at its original cost. Lian's weekly drawings were $120.

Required

Calculate Lian's profit or loss for the year ended 31 December 2003.

16.3 How to prepare a Profit and Loss Account and Balance Sheet from incomplete records

Most businesses keep records of receipts and payments. The records may consist of bank paying-in-book counterfoils, cheque-book counterfoils and bank statements in addition to suppliers' invoices and copies of sales invoices. From these records it may be possible to prepare a Profit and Loss Account and Balance Sheet. The steps are as follows.

Step 1	Prepare an opening statement of affairs. (This calculates opening capital.)
Step 2	Prepare a Receipts and Payments account.
Step 3	Prepare Control accounts for debtors and creditors, if necessary, to calculate sales and purchases. These will be the amounts required to make the Control accounts balance.
Step 4	Adjust the receipts and payments for accruals and prepayments at beginning and end of the period.
Step 5	Calculate provisions for doubtful debts, depreciation and any other matters not mentioned above.
Step 6	Prepare the Profit and Loss Account and Balance Sheet from the information now available.

Example

The only records that Aasim has kept for his business are bank paying-in-book counterfoils, cheque-book counterfoils and records of debtors and creditors. From these it is possible to summarise his transactions with the bank in the year ended 31 December 2003 as follows.

Takings paid into the bank: $8000.

Cheques drawn: payments to suppliers $2430; rent $600; electricity $320; postage and stationery $80; purchase of shop fittings $480; cheques drawn for personal expenses $2700.

Aasim banked all his takings after paying the following in cash: creditors for supplies $400 and sundry expenses $115.

Aasim estimated his assets and liabilities at 1 January 2003 to be: shop fittings $1600; stock $1960; debtors $240; rent prepaid $80; bank balance $1500; cash in hand $50; creditors for goods $420; electricity owing $130.

At 31 December 2003 Aasim listed his assets and liabilities as follows: shop fittings $1800; stock $1520; debtors $380; rent prepaid $50; bank balance $2640; cash in hand $50; creditors for goods $390; electricity owing $225.

Required

Prepare Aasim's Profit and Loss Account for the year ended 31 December 2003 and his Balance Sheet at that date.

Answer

Step 1 Opening statement of affairs

	$	$
Assets		
Shop fittings		1600
Stock		1960
Debtors		240
Rent prepaid		80
Bank		1500
Cash in hand		50
		5430
Less Liabilities		
Creditors for goods	420	
Electricity owing	130	550
Capital at 1 January		4880

Step 2 Receipts and Payments account. This includes only those amounts actually received and spent. It is a cash book summary with columns for cash and bank.

	Cash $	Bank $		Cash $	Bank $
Jan 1 Balance b/f	50	1500	Trade creditors	400	2430
Takings			Rent		600
(8000 + 400 + 115)	8515		Electricity		320
Cash	¢	8000	Postage and stationery		80
			Shop fittings		480
			Sundry expenses	115	
			Drawings		
			(2700 + 250†)		2950
			Bank ¢	8000	
			Balance c/f	50	2640
	8565	9500		8565	9500

† $250 is money not accounted for and is treated as Aasim's drawings.

Step 3 Debtors and Creditors Control accounts

Debtors Control				**Creditors Control**			
	$		$		$		$
Jan 1 Balance b/f	240	Dec 31 Takings[1]	8515	Dec 31 Bank and cash[2]	2830	Jan 1 Balance b/f	420
Dec 31 Sales[3]	8655	Balance c/f	380	Balance c/f	390	Dec31 Purchases[3]	2800
	8895		8895		3220		3220

1 From Receipts and Payments account.

2 From Receipts and Payments account.

3 Balancing figures.

Step 4 Adjust for prepayment and accruals.

	$		$
Rent paid	600	Electricity paid	320
Add prepaid at 1 Jan	80	Less owing at 1 Jan	(130)
Deduct prepaid at 31 Dec	(50)	Add owing at 31 Dec	225
Rent payable for the year	630	Electricity payable for the year	415

Step 5 Calculate depreciation of shop fittings.

	$
Shop fittings at valuation at 1 Jan	1600
Add fittings purchased in year	480
	2080
Shop fittings at valuation at 31 Dec	1800
Depreciation for the year	280

Step 6

Aasim
Trading and Profit and Loss Account for the year ended 31 December 2003

	$	$
Sales		8655
Less cost of sales		
Stock at 1 January	1960	
Purchases	2800	
	4760	
Less stock at 31 December	1520	3240
Gross profit		5415
Less		
Rent	630	
Electricity	415	
Postage and stationery	80	
Sundry expenses	115	
Depreciation of shop fittings	280	1520
Net profit		3895

Balance Sheet at 31 December 2003

	$	$	$
Fixed assets: Shop fittings			1800
Current assets			
Stock		1520	
Trade debtors		380	
Rent prepaid		50	
Bank		2640	
Cash		50	
		4640	
Current liabilities			
Trade creditors	390		
Electricity owing	225	615	4025
			5825
Capital at 1 Jan			4880
Profit for the year			3895
			8775
Less Drawings			2950
			5825

16.4 Margin and mark-up

Ability to calculate margin and mark-up may be necessary to solve some incomplete record problems. **Margin** is gross profit expressed as a percentage or fraction of selling price.

Example

	$
Cost price of goods	100
Profit	25
Selling price	125

The margin is profit/selling price $\times 100 = \frac{25}{125} \times 100 = 20\% = \frac{1}{5}$.

Mark-up is gross profit expressed as a percentage or fraction of cost of sales.

In the above example, mark-up is profit/cost price of goods $\times 100 = \frac{25}{100} \times 100 = 25\% = \frac{1}{4}$.

There is a close relationship between margin and mark-up. In the above examples:

$$\text{margin} = \frac{1}{5} \ (\text{or } \frac{1}{4+1}); \text{mark-up} = \frac{1}{4} \text{ or } (\frac{1}{5-1}).$$

From this, a general rule will be observed:

When margin is $\frac{a}{b}$, mark-up is $\frac{a}{b-a}$ and, when mark-up is $\frac{a}{b}$, margin is $\frac{a}{b+a}$.

Examples

If margin is $\frac{1}{3}$, mark-up is $\frac{1}{3-1} = \frac{1}{2}$; if mark-up is $\frac{1}{6}$, margin is $\frac{1}{6+1} = \frac{1}{7}$.

If margin is $\frac{2}{5}$, mark-up is $\frac{2}{5-2} = \frac{2}{3}$; if mark-up is $\frac{2}{5}$, margin is $\frac{2}{5+2} = \frac{2}{7}$.

Conversion of percentages to fractions Enter the *rate* percentage as the numerator of the fraction and 100 as the denominator, and reduce to a common fraction, for example $25\% = \frac{25}{100} = \frac{1}{4}$.

Conversion of fraction to a percentage Multiply the numerator of the fraction by 100, cancel top and bottom of the fraction and add 'per cent' or % sign, for example $\frac{2}{5} = \frac{200}{5} = 40\%$.

Most useful examples to remember $12\frac{1}{2}\% = \frac{1}{8}$; $20\% = \frac{1}{5}$;

$25\% = \frac{1}{4}$; $33.3\% = \frac{1}{3}$; $40\% = \frac{2}{5}$; $50\% = \frac{1}{2}$; $66.7\% = \frac{2}{3}$;

$75\% = \frac{3}{4}$; $80\% = \frac{4}{5}$

Examples

1 Cost of sales: $3000. Margin is 25%. Calculate the sales revenue.

> *Answer* Margin is $\frac{1}{4}$, mark-up is $\frac{1}{3}$, i.e. $3000 \times \frac{1}{3} = \$1000$.
> Therefore sales revenue = $(3000 + 1000) = \$4000$.

2 Sales revenue: $7000. Mark-up is 40%. Calculate the gross profit.

> *Answer* Mark-up is $\frac{2}{5}$; margin is $\frac{2}{7}$.
> Therefore gross profit = $\frac{2}{7} \times \$7000 = \$2000$.

3 Maheen provides the following information for the year ended 31 December 2003.

	$
Stock at 1 January 2003	9 000
Stock at 31 December 2003	11 000
Sales in the year ended 31 December 2003	84 000

Maheen sells her goods at a mark-up of $33\frac{1}{3}\%$.

Prepare Maheen's Trading Account for the year ended 31 December 2003 in as much detail as possible.

> *Answer* This a typical example of a problem that is solved by working backwards.
>
> Maheen: Trading account for the year ended 31 December 2003
>
> | | | $ | $ |
> |---|---|---|---|
> | | Sales *(given)* | | 84 000 |
> | | Less | | |
> | | Stock at 1 January *(given)* | 9 000 | |
> | Step 4 | Purchases (balancing figure 3) | 65 000 | |
> | Step 3 | (balancing figure 2) | 74 000 | |
> | | Stock at 31 December *(given)* | 11 000 | |
> | Step 2 | Cost of sales (balancing figure 1) | | 63 000 |
> | Step 1 | Gross profit $\frac{1}{4} \times \$84\,000$ | | 21 000 |

Exercise 2

Ammar provides the following information for the year ended 30 June 2004.

	$
Opening stock	4 000
Closing stock	7 000
Cost of goods sold	28 000

Ammar's margin on all sales is 20%.

Required

Prepare Ammar's Trading Account for the year ended 30 June 2004 in as much detail as possible.

16.5 Stock lost in fire or by theft

The methods used for preparing accounts from incomplete records are also used to calculate the value of stock lost in a fire or by theft when detailed stock records have not been kept, or have been destroyed by fire.

Solve this type of problem by preparing a 'pro forma' Trading Account. (It is described as 'pro forma' because it is not prepared like a normal Trading Account by transferring balances from ledger accounts.)

Example

Shahmir's warehouse was burgled on 10 April 2004. The thieves stole most of the stock but left goods worth $1250. Shahmir supplies the following information.

Extracts from Shahmir's Balance Sheet at 31 December 2003:

	$
Stock	30 000
Debtors	40 000
Creditors	20 000

Extracts from cash book, 31 December 2003 to 10 April 2004:

	$
Receipts from debtors	176 000
Payments to suppliers	120 000

Other information:

	$
Debtors at 10 April 2004	24 000
Creditors at 10 April 2004	26 000

Shahmir sells his goods at a mark-up of 25%.

Required
Calculate of the cost of the stolen goods.

Answer

Shahmir
Proforma Trading Account for the period
1 January to 10 April

	$	$
Sales (see working 1 below)		160 000
Cost of sales: Stock at 1 January 2004	30 000	
Purchases (see working 2 below)	126 000	
	156 000	
Stock at 10 April 2004		
(balancing figure)	28 000	128 000
Gross profit (mark-up is 25% so margin is 20%; $160 000 × 20%)		32 000

Cost of stock stolen: $(28 000 − 1250) = $26 750

Working 1		Debtors Total account		
		$		$
1 January Debtors	b/f 40 000	10 April Cash	176 000
10 April Sales (balancing figure)	160 000	Debtors o/s	24 000
	200 000		200 000

Working 2		Creditors Total account		
	$			$
10 April Cash	120 000	1 January Creditors	b/f	20 000
Creditors c/d	26 000	10 April Purchases (balancing figure)	126 000
	146 000			146 000

Exercise 3

Neha's warehouse was damaged by fire on 5 November 2003 and most of the stock was destroyed. The stock that was salvaged was valued at $12 000.

Neha has provided the following information to enable the cost of the stock lost to be calculated.

Extracts from Balance Sheet at 30 June 2003:

	$
Stock	47 000
Debtors	16 000
Creditors	23 000

Further information for the period 30 June 2003 to 5 November 2003:

	$
Receipts from debtors	122 000
Cash sales	17 000
Payments to suppliers	138 000
At 5 November: Debtors	37 000
Creditors	28 000

Neha's mark-up on goods sold is $33\frac{1}{3}$%.

Required
Calculate the cost of the stock lost in Neha's fire.

16.6 Examination hints

- A question that gives only assets and liabilities requires the preparation of statements of affairs to find the profit or loss of the business. The 'requirement' usually begins with 'calculate'.
- If required to prepare a Trading and Profit and Loss Account and Balance Sheet, prepare them in as much detail as possible.
- Be careful to distinguish between 'mark-up' and 'margin'. Learn how to convert mark-up to margin, and vice versa.

- Include all your workings with your answer. If your workings are not quite right, you may still gain some marks; but 'no workings – no marks' for a wrong answer.
- Tick each item in the question as you deal with it; check that everything has been ticked before writing your answer to ensure you have not missed anything.
- Incomplete records questions test a whole range of candidates' accounting knowledge and skills. For that reason they are frequently set in examinations. Some candidates fear these questions unnecessarily. Keep calm and follow the steps taught in this chapter carefully. If your Balance Sheet does not balance first time, don't panic. Do not spend valuable time looking for the difference if this time is better spent answering the next question. You have probably done enough to gain useful marks, anyway.

16.7 Multiple-choice questions

1 Jackson commenced business with $10 000 that he had received as a gift from his aunt and $8000 that he had received as a loan from his father. He used some of this money to purchase a machine for $15 000. He obtained a mortgage for $20 000 to purchase a workshop.

How much was Jackson's capital?

A $3000 **B** $10 000 **C** $18 000 **D** $38 000

2 At 1 January 2003 Robert's business assets were valued at $36 000 and his liabilities amounted to $2000. At 31 December 2003 Robert's assets amounted to $57 000 and included his private car which he had brought into the business on 1 November 2003 when it was valued at $9000. His creditors at 31 December 2003 totalled $17 000 and his drawings during the year

What was Robert's profit for the year ended 31 December 2003?

A $6000 **B** $14 000 **C** $ 24 000 **D** $33 000

3 At 1 April 2002 Tonkin's business assets were: motor van valued at $5000 (cost $8000), tools $1600, stock $700, debtors $168, cash $400. His creditors totalled $1120. At 31 March 2003 his assets were: workshop which had cost $20 000 and on which a mortgage of $16 000 was still outstanding, motor van $4000, tools $1900, stock $1000, debtors $240 (of which $70 were known to be bad), cash $500. His creditors amounted to $800. During the year Tonkin's drawings amounted to $5200.

What was Tonkin's profit for the year ended 31 March 2003?

A $6222 **B** $6292 **C** $9222 **D** $9292

4 At 1 March 2003 Allen's debtors amounted to $12 100. In the year ended 28 February 2004 he received $63 500 from debtors and allowed them cash discounts of $3426. At 28 February 2004 his debtors totalled $14 625.

How much were Allen's sales for the year ended 28 February 2004?

A $62 599 **B** $64 401 **C** $66 025
D $69 451

5 At 1 October 2003 Maria's debtors amounted to $7440. Of this amount $384 is known to be bad. In the year to 30 September 2004 she received $61 080 from debtors. Her debtors at 30 September 2004 were $8163. How much were Maria's sales for year ended 30 September 2004?

A $60 741 **B** $61 419 **C** $61 803
D $62 187

6 All of Grayson's stock was stolen when his business was burgled on 4 March 2004. His stock at 31 December 2003 was $23 000. From 1 January to 4 March 2004 sales totalled $42 000 and purchases were $38 000. Grayson's mark-up on goods is $33\frac{1}{3}$% to arrive at selling price.

What was the cost of the stock that was stolen?

A $28 000 **B** $29 500 **C** $33 000
D $40 000

16.8 Additional exercises

1 Seng commenced business on 1 January 2003 when he paid $40 000 into the bank together with $20 000 which he had received as a loan from his brother. At 31 December 2003 Seng's assets and liabilities were as follows.

	$
Shop premises	20 000
Motor van	8 000
Shop fittings	3 000
Stock	4 000
Debtors	1 000
Bank balance	5 000
Creditors	6 000
Loan from brother	16 000

Seng's drawings were $100 per week.

Required
(a) Prepare Seng's statements of affairs at (i) 1 January 2003 and (ii) 31 December 2003.
(b) Calculate Seng's profit or loss for the year ended 31 December 2003.

2 Saeed does not keep proper books of account for his business but he has provided the following details of his assets and liabilities.

	At 1 July 2003	At 30 June 2004
	$	$
Land and buildings at cost	60 000	60 000
Fixtures and fittings	10 000	12 000
Office machinery	8 000	7 000
Stock	17 000	21 000
Trade debtors	4 000	5 000
Rent prepaid	1 000	600
Bank balance	14 000	16 000
Trade creditors	3 000	1 600
Wages owing	2 000	1 000

Further information

1. Land and buildings have been revalued at $90 000 at 30 June 2004.

2. Office machinery at 30 June 2004 included a computer costing $1400, which Saeed had paid for from his personal bank account.

3. Saeed had withdrawn $200 per week from the business in cash, and a total of $2000 of goods for his own use during the year to 30 June 2004.

Required

Calculate Saeed's profit or loss for the year ended 30 June 2004.

3 Ahmed carries on business as a general trader. He has not kept proper accounting records and he asks you to help him prepare his Trading and Profit and Loss Account for the year ended 30 September 2004 and his Balance Sheet at that date. Ahmed's assets and liabilities at 30 September 2003 were as follows.

	$
Premises	60 000
Motor van	8 000
Stock	6 250
Trade debtors	3 200
Rent paid in advance	400
Balance at bank	9 450
Cash in hand	50
Trade creditors	1 800
Electricity owing	600
Interest on loan owing	150
Loan from brother	2 000

The loan carries interest at 10% per annum payable in arrears annually on 31 December each year.

Ahmed's transactions in the year ended 30 September 2004 were as follows.

Bank summary

	$
Receipts	
Receipts from debtors	29 400
Cash banked	17 000
Payments	
Suppliers	23 000
Electricity	2 200
Rent	4 000
Motor van expenses	1 800
Interest on loan	200
Wages	7 400
Telephone and stationery	1 650
Purchase of fixtures and fittings	3 000
Drawings	11 800

Cash summary

	$
Receipts	
Cash sales	21 750
Payments	
Goods for resale	3 140
Stationery	300
Motor van expenses	600
Sundry expenses	400

Further information

1. The balance of cash in hand has been maintained at $50.

2. At 30 September 2004, the closing stock was $8000. Trade debtors were $1600 and trade creditors for supplies were $1300.

3. Bad debts written off in the year were $250.

4. Discounts received from suppliers in the year were $420.

5. At 30 September 2004 electricity owing was $320 and rent of $450 had been prepaid.

6. At 30 September 2004 the motor van was valued at $6000.

7. Fixtures and fittings are to be depreciated on the reducing balance method using the rate of 25% per annum. A full year's depreciation is to be taken in the year ended 30 September 2004.

8. Ahmed does not provide for depreciation on the premises.

9. Ahmed has taken goods costing $800 from the business for his own use during the year.

10. Ahmed states that he paid some private bills out of the cash takings, but cannot remember how much is involved.

Required

(a) Prepare Ahmed's Trading and Profit and Loss Account for the year ended 30 September 2004.

(b) Prepare Ahmed's Balance Sheet at 30 September 2004.

4 Nurvish, who does not keep proper records for his business, supplies the following information.

	1 July 2003	30 June 2004
	$	$
Stock of goods	16 000	11 000
Creditors for goods	3 600	5 200

In the year ended 30 June 2004, Nurvish paid suppliers $54 000.

Nurvish sells his goods at a gross profit margin of 40%.

On 17 January 2004, Nurvish's premises were flooded and stock that cost $5000 was damaged and could only be sold at half cost price.

In the year ended 30 June 2004, Nurvish took goods which cost $1300 for his personal use.

Required

Prepare Nurvish's Trading Account for the year ended 30 June 2004.

5 Nadia was ill when her stock should have been counted on 31 December 2003. The stock count did not take place until 8 January 2004 when it was carried out by an inexperienced member of staff. The stock was valued at $62 040 at 8 January 2004.

Nadia was sure that the stock had been overvalued and discovered the following errors.

1. The stock had been valued at selling price instead of at cost. The gross profit margin on all goods sold is 20%.

2. Goods had been sent on sale or return to a customer who had not yet accepted the goods. The customer had been sent an invoice for $2000. This had been treated as a sale.

3. Goods sold to a customer on 3 January 2004 had been overcharged by $240.

4. The following transactions had taken place between 1 January and 8 January 2004 but had not been taken into account in the stock taking:

   (i) goods costing $4400 had been received from suppliers

(ii) sales of goods for $12 000 (not including goods sent on sale or return).

Required

Calculate the value of stock at cost at 31 December 2003.

6 Korn, a retailer, does not keep proper books of account but he has provided the following information about his business.

Balances at	30 April 2003	30 April 2004
	$	$
Land and buildings at cost	60 000	70 000
Fixtures and fittings	8 000	10 000
Motor vehicles	10 000	8 000
Trade creditors	7 500	6 900
Trade debtors	20 400	32 000
Rent owing	800	1 000
Wages and salaries owing	800	600
Stock	22 400	21 923
Bank	39 000	To be calculated

Korn's bank account transactions for the year ended 30 April 2004 were as follows.

	$
Receipts	
Trade debtors	170 430
Cash sales	103 000
Sales of fixed assets (see note (4) below)	2 400
Payments	
Trade creditors	227 668
Wages	17 200
Rent	8 000
Electricity	9 670
General expenses	5 150
Purchases of fixed assets (see point 4 below)	27 000

Further information

1. Korn banks his receipts from cash sales after taking $300 each week as drawings.

2. During the year ended 30 April 2004, Korn had taken goods costing $1350 for his own use.

3. Korn normally valued his stock at cost but on the advice of a friend he decided to value his stock at 30 April 2004 at selling price. His normal mark-up on stock was 30%.

4. Korn had borrowed $30 000 from his brother on a long-term basis on 1 May 2003. He had not recorded this transaction. Interest on the loan at 10% per annum is payable on 1 May each year.

During the financial year ended 30 April 2004 the following transactions had taken place.

	$	
Purchases		
Freehold land and buildings	10 000	
Motor vehicles	10 000	
Fixtures and fittings	7 000	
Sales		
Motor vehicles	2 000	(net book value at 30 April 2003 $3500)
Fixtures and fittings	400	(net book value at 30 April 2003 $800)

Required

(a) Prepare Korn's Trading and Profit and Loss Account for the year ended 30 April 2004.
(b) Prepare the Balance Sheet at 30 April 2004.
(c) Comment on the suggestion by Korn's friend that stock should be valued at selling price, and refer to any relevant accounting principle.

7 Cornelius commenced business on 1 April 2002. He has not kept complete records of his transactions but he supplies the following information.

	1 April 2002	31 March 2003	31 March 2004
	$	$	$
Balance at bank	30 000	116 000	111 110
Equipment	15 000	28 000	45 900
Stock of goods at cost	37 500	52 000	74 250
Long-term loan from father	20 000	20 000	20 000
Premises		80 000	80 000
Trade debtors		22 400	34 200
Trade creditors		56 000	67 410
Sundry expenses in arrears		2 280	875
Sundry expenses in advance		700	4 050

Further information

1. Cornelius made payments of $371 340 to suppliers in the year ended 31 March 2004.

2. Complete records of takings are not available but goods are sold at a mark-up of 30%.

3. Takings were banked after deduction of the following.

   (i) From 1 April 2002 to 31 March 2003, Cornelius drew $400 per week from takings for his personal expenses. From 1 April 2003 the weekly amounts drawn were increased to $500.

   (ii) On 1 July 2003, Cornelius paid $5000 out of takings to pay for a family holiday.

   (iii) Cornelius has taken various other amounts from takings for personal expenses, but he has not kept a record of these.

4. Cornelius purchased the business premises on 1 October 2002. He paid $40 000 for these from his own private bank account. The balance was obtained as a bank loan on which interest is payable at 15% per annum on 31 December each year.

5. Cornelius' father has agreed that his loan to the business will be free of interest for the first year. After that, interest will be at the rate of 8% per annum, payable annually on 31 March.

6. Cornelius purchased additional equipment costing $24 000 in the year ended 31 March 2004.

7. Sundry expenses paid in the year ended 31 March 2004 amounted to $27 000.

Required

(a) Calculate Cornelius' profit or loss for the year ended 31 March 2003.

(b) Prepare in as much detail as possible a Trading and Profit and Loss Account for the year ended 31 March 2004.

(c) Prepare a Balance Sheet as at 31 March 2004.

17 Non-profit-making organisations (clubs and societies)

> *In this chapter you will learn:*
> - new terms used for non-profit-making organisations
> - new forms of financial statements for non-profit-making organisations
> - how to apply the techniques used for incomplete records to prepare accounts for non-profit-making organisations.

17.1 What are non-profit-making organisations?

Non-profit-making organisations exist to provide facilities for their members. Examples are: sports and social clubs, dramatic societies, music clubs, etc. Making a profit is not their main purpose, although many carry on fund-raising activities to provide more or better facilities for the members. The organisation is 'owned' by all of its members and not by just one person or partnership. Records of money received and spent are usually kept by a club member who is not a trained bookkeeper or accountant. Usually no other records are kept. This topic is therefore an extension of the work of the previous chapter, which deals with incomplete records.

It follows from the above that a business which is *meant* to make profits is not a non-profit-making organisation, even if it keeps making losses.

17.2 Special features of the accounts of non-profit-making organisations

- An **Income and Expenditure Account** takes the place of the Profit and Loss Account.
- The words **surplus of income over expenditure** are used in place of 'net profit'.
- The words **excess of expenditure over income** are used in place of 'net loss'.
- The term **Accumulated fund** is used in place of 'Capital account'.
- A Trading Account is only prepared for an activity that is in the nature of trading and is carried on to increase the club's funds.

17.3 The treatment of income

Income of a club (which is the term that will be used in the rest of this chapter to cover all non-profit-making organisations) should be treated in the club's accounts as follows.

Subscriptions

The amount credited to the Income and Expenditure Account should equal the annual subscription per member multiplied by the number of members. It may be helpful to prepare a Subscriptions account as workings to decide how much should be credited to the Income and Expenditure Account.

Subscriptions in arrears and **subscriptions in advance** should *normally* be treated as accruals and prepayments. However, each club has its own policy for treating subscriptions in arrears or in advance. The two possible policies are as follows.

- **Cash basis**. The amount actually received in the year is credited to the Income and Expenditure Account. This may include subscriptions for a previous year or paid in advance for the next year.
- **Accruals basis**. All subscriptions due for the year, including those not yet received, are credited to the Income and Expenditure Account. It will usually be the club's policy to write off, as bad debts, subscriptions that are not received in the year after they were due.

Life subscriptions and entry fees

Life subscriptions and entry fees are received as lump sums but should not be credited in full to the Income and Expenditure Account when received. The club should have a policy of spreading this income over a period of, say, five years. The amounts received should be credited to a Deferred Income account and credited to the Income and Expenditure Account in equal annual instalments over a period determined by the club committee.

Donations

Donations and legacies to a club are usually made for particular purposes, for example towards the cost of a new pavilion or a piece of equipment. Such donations should be credited to an account opened for the purpose, and expenditure on it debited to the account. Money received for special purposes should be placed in a separate bank account to ensure that it is not spent on other things.

Ancillary activities

Ancillary activities are incidental to a club's main purpose. They raise money to supplement income from subscriptions. If they involve some sort of trading, a Trading Account should be prepared for them as part of the annual accounts, and the profit or loss should be transferred to the Income and Expenditure Account.

Non-trading activities, such as socials, outings and dinner-dances, may be dealt with in the Income and Expenditure Account with the income and costs being grouped together as follows.

	$	$
Annual dinner-dance		
Sale of tickets	600	
Less: hire of band	(100)	
catering	(240)	
Net receipts		260

17.4 How to prepare club accounts

The preparation of club accounts follows the same procedures as those used for businesses whose records are incomplete (see chapter 16) together with the principles explained in §§17.2 and 17.3.

Example

The Star Sports and Social Club provides recreational activities, refreshments and social events for its members. It sells sports equipment to its members at reduced prices. Its assets and liabilities at 31 December 2003 were as follows.

	$
Fixed assets	
Pavilion	120 000
Club sports equipment	40 000
Motor roller	2 000
Current assets	
Stock of equipment for sale to members	4 000
Annual subscriptions owing	1 200
Bank balance	6 730
Current liabilities	
Creditors for equipment for sale to members	1 300
Annual subscriptions received in advance	800
Life subscriptions fund	1 750

In the year ended 31 December 2003 the club's cash receipts and payments were as follows.

	$
Receipts	
Annual subscriptions	18 000
Proceeds from sale of equipment	12 000
Sale of tickets for dinner-dance	4 400
Refreshment bar takings	2 660
Life member subscriptions	400
Payments	
Caretaker's wages	8 000
Repairs to club equipment	1 700
Purchase of club equipment	2 000
Equipment for sale to members	4 000
Heating and lighting	1 800
Dinner-dance expenses	
Hire of band	200
Catering	1 000
Food for refreshment bar	1 400
Secretary's expenses	840

Further information

1. At 31 December 2004:
   annual subscriptions in arrears were $1400
   annual subscriptions received in advance were $900.
2. Stock of equipment for sale to members: $2000.
3. Creditors for equipment for sale to members: $900.
4. A member donated $5000 to a fund to encourage young people to train for sport. This donation was invested immediately in savings bonds.

5. The club transfers life subscriptions to the Income and Expenditure Account in equal instalments over five years.

6. Depreciation is to be provided on fixed assets by the reducing-balance method as follows.

Pavilion	6%
Sports equipment	20%
Motor roller	20%

Required

(a) Prepare the Star Sports and Social Club's Income and Expenditure Account for the year ended 31 December 2004.

(b) Prepare the club's Balance Sheet as at 31 December 2004.

Note. Often the amount of information given in questions such as this looks terrifying but don't let that worry you. Keep calm. Read the question carefully two or three times, making sure you understand it, and underline important points. Decide what workings are required and which must be shown in your answer. Then proceed as follows.

Step 1 Prepare an opening statement of affairs. This will give the balance on the Accumulated fund at 1 January 2004 and will be the starting point for recording the transactions during the year.

Statement of affairs at 31 December 2003

		$
Fixed assets		
Pavilion		120 000
Club sports equipment		40 000
Motor roller		2 000
Current assets		
Stock of equipment for sale to members		4 000
Annual subscriptions owing		1 200
Bank balance		6 730
Total assets		173 930
Current liabilities		
Creditors for equipment for sale to members	1300	
Annual subscriptions received in advance	800	
Life subscriptions fund	1750	3 850
Accumulated fund at 1 January 2004		170 080

Step 2 Prepare a Receipts and Payment account. This will summarise all the transactions affecting the Income and Expenditure Account and Balance Sheet and calculate the bank balance at 31 December 2004.

Receipts and Payments account for the year ended 31 December 2004

		$			$
1 Jan	Balance brought forward	6 730	31 Dec	Caretaker's wages	8 000
31 Dec	Annual subscriptions	18 000		Repairs: club equipment	1 700
	Sales of equipment	12 000		Purchase: club equipment	2 000
	Sale of tickets			Purchase of equipment	
	Dinner-dance	4 400		for resale	4 000
	Takings – refreshments	2 660		Heating and lighting	1 800
	Life membership			Dinner-dance	
	subscriptions	400		hire of band	200
				catering	1 000
				Food for refreshment bar	1 400
				Secretary's expenses	840
				Balance c/f	23 250
		44 190			44 190

Step 3 Prepare workings to adjust for accruals, prepayments, depreciation and any other items. Show these workings with your answer.

You may show your workings as ledger ('T') accounts or as calculations. Decide which method is best for you and practise it in all your exercises. Both methods will be shown here.

'T' accounts				**Calculations**	

1. Purchase of equipment for resale

	$		$		$
				Cash paid	4 000
Cash paid	4 000	Creditors b/f	1 300	less creditors b/f	(1 300)
Creditors c/f	900	I & E a/c	3 600		2 700
	4 900		4 900	add creditors c/f	900
				Trading a/c	3 600

2. Annual subscriptions

	$		$		$
Owing at 1 Jan	1 200	Prepaid at 1 Jan	800	Received in year	18 000
Prepaid at 31 Dec	900	Cash	18 000	less owing 1 Jan	(1 200)
I & E a/c	18 100	Owing at 31 Dec	1 400	prepaid 31 Dec	(900)
	20 200		20 200		15 900
				add prepaid 1 Jan	800
				owing 31 Dec	1 400
				I & E a/c	18 100

3. Life subscriptions

	$		$		$
I & E a/c $\frac{1}{5} \times 2150$	430	B/f	1 750	Balance b/f	1 750
C/f	1 720	Cash received	400	Cash received	400
	2 150		2 150		2 150
				I & E a/c $\left(\frac{1}{5}\right)$	430

4. Club sports equipment

	$		$		$
B/f	40 000	I & E (20%)	8 400	Balance b/f	40 000
Cash	2 000	c/d	33 600	Cash	2 000
	42 000		42 000		42 000
				I & E a/c (20%)	8 400
				Net book value	33 600

Step 4 The Income and Expenditure Account and Balance Sheet may now be copied out from steps 1, 2 and 3. As the sale of equipment to members is trading, a Trading Account should be prepared even though one is not asked for in the question.

If steps 1, 2 and 3 have been carried out with care, preparing the Income and Expenditure Account and Balance Sheet is now little more than a copying exercise and can be completed in little time.

(a)

Sales of equipment

	$	$
Sales		12 000
Less cost of sales		
Stock at 1 January 2004	4000	
Purchases (working 1)	3600	
	7600	
Less stock at 31 December 2004	2000	5 600
Profit transferred to Income & Expenditure Account		6 400

Star Sports and Social Club
Income and Expenditure Account for the year ended 31 December 2004

	$	$	$
Annual subscriptions (working 2)			18 100
Life subscriptions (working 3)			430
Profit on sale of equipment			6 400
Dinner/dance*			
Sale of tickets		4 400	
less hire of band	200		
catering	1 000	1 200	3 200
Refreshment bar*			
Takings		2 660	
less cost of food		1 400	1 260
			29 390
Less expenses			
Caretaker's wages		8 000	
Repairs to club equipment		1 700	
Heating and lighting		1 800	
Secretary's expenses		840	
Depreciation: Pavilion (6% of $120 000)		7 200	
Equipment (working 4)		8 400	
Motor roller (20% of $2000)		400	28 340
Surplus of income over expenditure			1 050

*Expenses of dinner-dance and refreshment bar are grouped with the income from those activities to help members see how those activities have contributed to the club's funds.

(b)

Balance Sheet at 31 December 2004

	$	$	$
Fixed assets at net book value			
Pavilion			112 800
Club equipment			33 600
Motor roller			1 600
			148 000
Current assets			
Stock of equipment for sale to members		2 000	
Subscriptions owing		1 400	
Bank		23 250	
		26 650	
Less Current liabilities			
Creditors	900		
Subscriptions prepaid	900		
Life subscriptions	1 720	3 520	23 130
			171 130
Represented by			
Accumulated fund at 1 January 2004			170 080
Add surplus of income over expenditure			1 050
Accumulated fund at 31 December 2004			171 130
Fund to encourage young people to train for sport			5 000
Represented by savings bonds			5 000

Exercise 1

The Wellington Drama Club has 120 members. The annual subscription is $20 per member. Subscriptions not paid in one year are written off if not paid by the end of the next year.

The Club presents two plays a year, each play being performed over ten days. The Club hires a local hall for the performances and the dress rehearsals, which take place over three days before the presentation of each play. The Club donates half of its net surpluses to the Actors Benevolent Fund.

The receipts and payments of the Club in the year ended 31 December 2004 were as follows.

Receipts	$
Sales of tickets	20 000
Sales of programmes	3 000
Sales of refreshments	3 500
Subscriptions for the year ended 31 December 2004	2 000
Subscriptions for the year ended 31 December 2003	280
Subscriptions for the year ending 31 December 2005	360
Payments	
Hire of hall	2 600
Printing of posters, tickets and programmes	180
Hire of costumes	4 700
Cost of refreshments	2 200
Payments for copyrights	1 400

At 31 December 2003, members subscriptions of $360 were owing.

Required

(a) Prepare The Wellington Drama Club's Income and Expenditure Account for the year ended 31 December 2004.

(b) Prepare a Balance Sheet extract at 31 December 2004 to show the items for subscriptions.

Exercise 2

The Hutt River Dining Club is funded partly by the members' annual subscriptions ($20 per member), partly by restaurant takings and partly from profits from the sale of books on dieting, healthy eating and cooking.

At 31 December 2003, the club's Balance Sheet showed the following.

	$	$
Catering equipment at cost	11 000	
Depreciation of catering equipment	3 000	8000
Stock of food		200
Stock of books		1100
Subscriptions owing		180
Cash at bank		1520
Creditors for supplies of food		40
Subscriptions in advance		60

Receipts and payments for the year ended 31 December 2004 were as follows.

Receipts	$
Annual subscriptions	5 000
Restaurant takings	73 760
Sales of books	12 150
Payments	
Staff wages	39 000
Cost of food	24 980
Purchase of books	4 840
New catering equipment	3 750
Heating and lighting	8 390
Sundry expenses	2 270

Further information

1. Subscriptions owing at 31 December 2004: $40.

2. Subscriptions paid in advance at 31 December 2004: $140.

3. Stocks at 31 December 2004: food $270; books $965.

4. Creditors at 31 December 2004: for food $360; for books $200.

5. Annual depreciation of catering equipment is 10% on cost.

Required

(a) Calculate the Accumulated fund at 1 January 2004.

(b) Prepare a Receipts and Payments account for the year ended 31 December 2004.

(c) Prepare the Members Subscriptions account for the year ended 31 December 2004.

(d) Prepare a Trading Account for the year ended 31 December 2004 for the sale of books.

(e) Prepare a Restaurant account for the year ended 31 December 2004.

(f) Prepare The Hutt River Dining Club's Income and Expenditure Account for the year ended 31 December 2004.

(g) Prepare the Balance Sheet as at 31 December 2004.

17.5 Examination hints

- Club accounts often look difficult, but they need not be so. Keep calm and follow carefully the steps taught in this and the previous chapter.
- Always follow carefully whatever instructions are given in an examination question.
- Even if your answer is not perfect, you can earn many useful marks if you show the examiner what you can do.

- Include all your workings with your answer.
- Tick each item in the question as you deal with it; check that everything has been ticked to ensure you have not missed anything.

17.6 Multiple-choice questions

1 Which of the following will *not* be found in the accounts of a club?

A Accumulated fund

B Drawings account

C Receipts and Payments account

D Balance Sheet

2 The following information for a year is extracted from a sports club's accounts.

	$
Subscriptions received	10 000
Sales of equipment to members	7 000
Opening stock of equipment	1 300
Closing stock of equipment	800
Purchases of equipment	5 000

What was the club's total income for the year?

A $10 000   **B** $11 500   **C** $12 500

D $17 000

3 The following information relates to a club for a year.

Number of members	60
Annual subscription	$20
Subscriptions owing at beginning of year	$100
Subscriptions owing at end of year	$60

How much should be credited to the club's Income and Expenditure Account for annual subscriptions for the year?

A $1100   **B** $1160   **C** $1200   **D** $1260

4 A club's records provide the following information for a year.

	$
Annual subscriptions received in the year	4000
Annual subscriptions received in advance at end of year	50
Balance on Life Subscriptions account at beginning of year	500
Life subscriptions received during the year	100

The club's policy is to credit life subscriptions to the Income and Expenditure Account over five years.

How much should be credited to the Income and Expenditure Account for subscriptions for the year?

A $4050   **B** $4070   **C** $4150   **D** $4170

17.7 Additional exercises

1 The Civic Athletics Club's Receipts and Payments account for the year ended 31 May 2004 is as follows.

Receipts	$	Payments	$
Balance at bank 1 June 2003	4 650	Refreshment supplies bought	2 654
Subscriptions received	7 970	Wages	4 000
Sales of tickets for dance	1 897	Rent of rooms	540
Refreshment bar takings	4 112	Purchase of new equipment	1 778
Sale of old equipment	94	Teams' travelling expenses	995
Donation	90	Balance at bank at 31 May 2004	8 846
	18 813		18 813

Further information

1. Refreshment bar stocks were valued at $150 at 1 June 2003, and at $180 at 31 May 2004.

2. Creditors for refreshment bar stocks were: at 1 June 2003 $15; at 31 May 2004 $40.

3. At 1 June 2003, subscriptions owing were $330, of which $310 was paid in the year to 31 May 2004. It is club policy to write off subscriptions if they have not been received by the end of the year following their due date. Subscriptions owing at 31 May 2004 were $275.

4. Of the wages paid, $900 was paid to staff serving refreshments.

5. On 1 June 2003 the club's equipment was valued at £4700. The equipment sold during the year had a book value of $70 at the date of sale. At 31 May 2004, the equipment was valued at $6000.

Required

(a) Calculate the Accumulated fund as at 1 June 2003.

(b) Prepare the refreshments Trading Account for the year ended 31 May 2004.

(c) Prepare the Income and Expenditure Account for the year ended 31 May 2004.

(d) Prepare the club's Balance Sheet as at 31 May 2004.

2 The members of The Howzidun Magic Club meet to demonstrate their conjuring skills and to entertain visitors, who pay an entrance fee at the door. The club also has a shop for the sale of conjuring tricks and props.

The club's Bank account for the year ended 30 June 2004 was as follows.

	$		$
Balance at 1 July 2003	16 800	Purchases of tricks and props	8 220
Subscriptions received	10 730	Shop wages	6 000
Cash taken at door	9 456	Cost of annual dance	2 600
Shop takings	12 348	Purchase of equipment	5 000
Annual dance receipts	3 720	Secretary's expenses	2 125
Grant from local council	4 000	Transfer to Deposit account	20 000
Donations to the Disappeared		Balance at 30 June 2001	13 775
Wizards Memorial Fund	666		
	57 720		57 720

The club has 200 members. The annual subscription was $30 until 1 July 2003 when it was increased to $40.

At 1 July 2003, 20 members had not paid their subscriptions for the year ended 30 June 2003 but, of these, 15 had paid their arrears of subscriptions by 30 June 2004. By 30 June 2004, all members had paid their subscriptions for the year up to date and some had paid their subscriptions for the year to 30 June 2005.

Other assets and liabilities were:

	At 1 July 2003	At 30 June 2004
	$	$
Shop stock	1 600	1 850
Creditors for shop purchases	400	210
Equipment at cost	7 000	12 000
Deposit account	10 000	30 000
Disappeared Wizards Memorial Fund	–	666

The equipment at 1 July 2003 had been depreciated for five years by $1400 per annum. The new equipment is to be depreciated at the same annual percentage rate.

The grant from the local council was the first instalment of an annual grant of $8000.

The transfer to the Deposit account was made on 1 January 2004. Interest at 4% per annum is payable on 30 June each year.

Required
(a) Calculate the Accumulated fund at 1 July 2003.
(b) Prepare the Club Shop Trading Account for the year ended 30 June 2004.
(c) Prepare the Club Subscriptions account for the year ended 30 June 2004.
(d) Prepare the Club Income and Expenditure Account for the year ended 30 June 2004.
(e) Prepare the Club Balance Sheet at 30 June 2004.

3 The Taupo Sailing Club provides its members with a number of activities:
(i) hire of boats for members; non-members are charged an extra 20% for boat hire
(ii) yacht racing competitions
(iii) a clubhouse with a refreshment bar which is also used for social functions
(iv) a sailing training school for all age groups.

The following financial information relates to 1 April 2003.

	$
Fixed assets at net book value	
Freehold premises	350 000
Yacht maintenance shop	42 000
Boatyard and launch facilities	74 000
Fixtures and fittings	28 000
Boats and yachts	465 000
Other items	
Members' subscriptions:	
in arrears	3 000
in advance	6 000
Balance at bank	94 000
Stocks of refreshments	1 250
Creditors for refreshments	1 030

The following financial information relates to the year ended 31 March 2004.

(continues)

Receipts	$	Payments	$
Hire of yachts and boats		Repairs and maintenance of yachts	23 400
to members	43 000	Purchase of new boats and yachts	61 000
to non-members	34 000	Wages of training-school staff	16 500
Receipts from training school	34 500	Wages of refreshment-bar staff	14 000
Members' subscriptions	186 000	Purchase of refreshment-bar food	53 000
Refreshments and social events	77 000	Receipts from yacht racing competition	13 000
Expenses of yacht racing competition	28 900	Sundry expenses	26 000

Further information

1. At 31 March 2004, members' subscriptions owing amounted to $2000; members' subscriptions in advance for 2004/2005 were $3400.

2. The club's depreciation policy is as follows.

- Freehold premises, boatyard and launch facilities, and boats and yachts: 5% per annum on net book value

- Fixtures and fittings, and yacht maintenance shop: 10% per annum on net book value.

3. Creditors at 31 March 2004 were as follows.

	$
Repairs and maintenance of yachts	1350
Refreshments	970
Wages: training-school staff	700
refreshment bar staff	400

Refreshment bar stock at 31 March 2004 was valued at $1600.

Required

(a) Prepare Taupo Sailing Club's Income and Expenditure Account for the year ended 31 March 2004 in good format. A Trading Account should be prepared for the refreshment bar.

(b) Prepare the club's Balance Sheet as at 31 March 2004.

4 The Abracamagic Club's Bank Current account for the year ended 30 September 2001 was as follows.

	$		$
Balance at 1.10.2000	8 400	Purchases for shop	3 745
Subscriptions received	6 435	Shop wages	4 000
Donations	600	General expenses	1 500
Cash taken at door	3 500	Cost of Annual Dance	1 490
Grant from local council	6 000	Transfer to Deposit account	16 000
Annual Dance receipts	1 400	New equipment	2 000
Shop takings	7 168	Rent	8 000
Balance at 30.9.2001	3 232		
	36 735		36 735

In order to increase funds the club has a shop which sells magic tricks. In addition to an annual membership subscription, members pay $1 each time they visit the club. This is referred to as 'Cash taken at door'.

The annual membership subscription was $40 until 30 September 2001 when it was raised to $45.

There were 150 members at 1 October 2000.

At that date 15 of them had not paid their subscriptions for the year ended 30 September 2000, and 12 had already paid their subscriptions for the year ended 30 September 2001.

By 30 September 2001, all members had paid their due subscriptions, and some had paid in advance for the year ending 30 September 2002, but the Treasurer had not yet calculated how many.

Other balances were as follows.

	At 1 October 2000	At 30 September 2001
	$	$
Shop stock	500	850
Cash float for shop	50	70
Creditors for shop	1 450	1 260
Deposit account	15 000	31 000
Equipment at cost	8 000	10 000

The equipment at 1 October 2000 had been depreciated by $1600 per annum for five years.

The new equipment is to be depreciated at the same annual percentage rate.

The local council's grant was for $10 000 and the remainder of this has yet to be received. This will be treated as revenue income in the final accounts.

Interest of $800 is due on the deposit account for the year ended 30 September 2001.

At 30 September 2001, general expenses of $65 were due and unpaid.

Required

(a) Calculate the Accumulated fund at 1 October 2000.

(b) Prepare the Club Shop Trading Account for the year ended 30 September 2001.

(c) Prepare the Club Subscriptions account for the year ended 30 September 2001.

(d) Prepare the Club Income and Expenditure Account for the year ended 30 September 2001.

(UCLES, 2001, AS/A Level Accounting, Syllabus 8706/2, October/November)

18 Departmental accounts

In this chapter you will learn:
- how to allocate or apportion expenses to the departments of a business
- how to prepare departmental Trading and Profit and Loss Accounts in columnar form.

18.1 What are departmental accounts?

Departmental accounts are Trading and Profit and Loss Accounts for businesses that have more than one department. A business may sell furniture, electrical appliances and clothing. It may also provide a restaurant for its customers. Each of these activities will be carried on in a separate department and will make its own contribution to the profit of the business. To find the profit of each department, separate Trading and Profit and Loss Accounts are prepared. This will require entries in the books of prime entry to be analysed between the departments, or separate books to be kept for each department.

18.2 How to prepare departmental Trading and Profit and Loss Accounts

Trading Accounts

Trading Accounts should be prepared in columnar form, that is, with a separate column for each department, and one for totals.

Example 1

Omnimart sells furniture, clothing and electrical goods. The following information has been extracted from its books for the year ended 31 December 2003.

		$
Sales:	Furniture	272 000
	Clothing	138 000
	Electrical	110 000
Purchases:	Furniture	112 000
	Clothing	76 000
	Electrical	50 000
Stock at 1 January 2003:		
	Furniture	28 000
	Clothing	19 000
	Electrical	22 000
Stock at 31 December 2003:		
	Furniture	35 000
	Clothing	23 000
	Electrical	26 000

The Trading Account is prepared in columnar form as follows.

Omnimart Trading Account for the year ended 31 December 2003							
	Furniture		Clothing		Electrical		Total
	$	$	$	$	$	$	$	$
Sales		272 000		138 000		110 000		520 000
Less Cost of sales								
Opening stock	28 000		19 000		22 000		69 000	
Purchases	112 000		76 000		50 000		238 000	
	140 000		95 000		72 000		307 000	
Closing stock	35 000	105 000	23 000	72 000	26 000	46 000	84 000	223 000
Gross profit		167 000		66 000		64 000		297 000

Profit and Loss Accounts

Overheads are allocated to departments if the actual amounts to be debited to them are known. Wages and salaries can be allocated to departments if the payroll is analysed. Electricity can be charged to each department if separate meters are provided for each department.

Overheads which cannot be allocated to departments must be apportioned to them on suitable bases. Examples of the ways in which overheads may be apportioned are:

Expense	Basis of apportionment
Heating and lighting (when not separately metered) Rent Insurance of buildings	in proportion to the respective floor areas of the departments
Advertising, distribution	in proportion to departmental sales
Insurance of plant, machinery and other assets	on the replacement values of assets in each department
Depreciation	on the cost of assets in each department
Administration costs	on number of employees in each department, or on departmental turnover

Commission paid to an employee, based on profit The commission is usually calculated as a percentage of the profit after charging the commission. Calculate the commission using the following formula:

$$\frac{\text{percentage of commission}}{100 + \text{percentage of commission}}$$

Example 2

A manager is entitled to 5% commission calculated on profit after charging the commission. The profit before charging commission is $84 000. What is the profit after commission?

The commission is

$$\$\left(84\ 000 \times \frac{5}{105}\right) = \$4000.$$

Profit after commission = $80 000.

Note. Make all calculations of apportionment to the nearest dollar.

Example 3

(Continuing Omnimart as shown above.)
In the year ended 31 December 2003, Omnimart's expenses were as follows.

	$
Salaries and wages: Furniture	35 000
Clothing	28 000
Electrical	25 000
Rent	60 000
Heating and lighting	15 000
Advertising	6 000
Delivery expenses	4 000
Depreciation of fixed assets	10 000
Administration	30 000

Further information

1. Delivery and advertising costs are to be apportioned in proportion to departmental sales.

2. Administration costs are to be divided equally between the three departments.

3. Departmental statistics are:

	Furniture	Clothing	Electrical
Area occupied in metres^2	150	90	60
Fixed assets at cost	$50 000	$30 000	$20 000

4. The manager of each department is entitled to a commission of 5% of his departmental net profit after charging the commission.

Required

Prepare a departmental Trading and Profit and Loss Account for the year ended 31 December 2003.

Answer

Omnimart
Trading and Profit and Loss Account for the year ended 31 December 2003

	Furniture		Clothing		Electrical		Total	
	$	$	$	$	$	$	$	$
Gross profit		167 000		66 000		64 000		297 000
Salaries and wages	35 000		28 000		25 000		88 000	
Rent[1]	30 000		18 000		12 000		60 000	
Heating[1]	7 500		4 500		3 000		15 000	
Advertising[2]	3 139		1 592		1 269		6 000	
Delivery[2]	2 092		1 062		846		4 000	
Depreciation[3]	5 000		3 000		2 000		10 000	
Administration	10 000	92 731	10 000	66 154	10 000	54 115	30 000	213 000
		74 269		(154)		9 885		84 000
Managers' commission ($\frac{5}{105}$)		3 537		–		471		4 008
Net profit/(loss)		70 732		(154)		9 414		79 992

1 Apportioned on basis of area occupied.

2 Apportioned on basis of sales.

3 Apportioned on basis of cost of fixed assets.

Exercise 1

Geeta owns a shoe shop. The shop has three departments: ladies', men's and children's. Information extracted from Geeta's books for the year ended 31 March 2004 is given:

	Ladies'	Men's	Children's
	$	$	$
Sales	100 000	120 000	80 000
Stock at 1 April 2003	14 000	17 000	5 000
Purchases	50 000	63 000	42 000
Stock at 31 March 2004	18 000	22 000	4 000
Wages	20 000	20 000	12 000

Other balances at 31 March 2003:

	$
Rent	28 000
Heating and lighting	6 000
Advertising	5 000
Administration	27 000
Depreciation	7 200

Further information

	Ladies'	Men's	Children's
Area occupied	$\frac{2}{5}$	$\frac{2}{5}$	$\frac{1}{5}$
Cost of fixed assets ($000)	30	25	15
Number of staff	4	3	2

Advertising is to be apportioned on the basis of departmental sales.

Administration is to be apportioned in the ratio of departmental staff numbers.

Managers are entitled to a commission of 5% of their departmental profit after charging the commission.

Required

Prepare Geeta's Departmental Trading and Profit and Loss Account for the year ended 31 March 2004.

18.3 A loss-making department

If a department is unprofitable, there are courses of action that may be taken to make it profitable. These include:

- increase prices, provided this does not adversely affect sales volume
- negotiate cheaper prices with suppliers, or find alternative suppliers
- advertise the department's products in order to increase its sales
- offer discounts or other incentives to increase turnover, provided these do not cancel out the additional revenue
- offer more attractive products
- reduce the department's overheads.

If the loss-making department cannot be made profitable, closure may have to be considered. Two factors should be considered before the department is closed:

(i) the effect of the closure of a department on the fixed overheads

(ii) any other effect of closure on the remaining departments.

Fixed overheads

Some overheads are fixed; that is, they must still be paid even if the business does not trade. Examples are: rent and insurance of premises, depreciation of fixed assets and some other administration expenses. The fixed overheads of a department may still have to be paid even if it is closed; the remaining departments will have to bear additional costs, which will affect their profitabilty.

Example

Hiatus is a retail store with three departments: A, B and C. Its Profit and Loss Account for the year ended 31 January 2004 is as follows.

	Department A		Department B		Department C	
	$	$	$	$	$	$
Gross profit		80 000		48 000		30 000
Wages	24 000		18 000		13 000	
Rent	5 000		6 000		4 000	
Electricity	1 500		1 800		1 200	
Advertising	5 000		3 000		4 000	
Administration	16 000	51 500	16 000	44 800	16 000	38 200
Net profit/(loss)		28 500		3 200		(8 200)

Wages have been allocated on an actual basis. Rent and electricity have been apportioned on the basis of floor areas occupied. Advertising has been apportioned on the basis of relative sales.

Each department is debited with one third of the administration expenses. No administration expenses will be saved if department C is closed.

At present, the business is making a profit of $(28 500 + 3200 − 8200) = $23 500.

Closure of department C would reduce the total profit of the business as departments A and B would have additional administration expenses: $(28 500 + 3200 − 16 000) = $15 700. The business will be worse off by $7800. This is department C's contribution to the overall profit before it has been charged with administration ($30 000 − $22 200). It would be better to keep department C open and to benefit from its contribution to the overall profitability.

The way in which administration costs have been apportioned to the departments should be questioned. The costs have been spread evenly over the three departments, but examination of the apportionment of the other expenses suggests that department C is smaller than the others. It would be more reasonable to reflect the differences in the sizes of the departments in the apportionment of administration costs.

The situation might be different if administration costs could be reduced by the closure of department C.

Other factors

It may sometimes be desirable to keep a loss-making department open regardless of the effect that closure would have on the fixed overheads. Department C in the above example may be necessary for the operations of the other departments. Or it may attract customers if, for example, it is a restaurant situated where customers have to pass through the other departments to get to it. The sales of those departments may benefit as a result.

18.4 Examination hints

- Adjust overhead expenses for accruals and prepayments, if necessary, before apportioning them to departments.
- Apportion expenses as directed by the question. If the question does not give directions, choose suitable bases for apportionment and state what they are.
- Calculate departmental expenses to the nearest $ or $000 (depending on the question).
- Show all workings.
- Prepare the accounts in columnar form and include a total column.

18.5 Multiple-choice questions

1 Which basis is suitable for apportioning advertising cost between departments?

   A departmental cost of goods sold

   B departmental gross profit

   C departmental turnover

   D number of staff in each department

2 Which basis should be used to apportion the cost of insuring plant and machinery between departments?

   A net book value

   B original cost

   C present disposable value

   D replacement cost

3 A manager is paid a commission of 5% based on net profit after charging the commission. The profit before commission is $157 500.

   How much commission is paid to the manager?

   A $1500

   B $1658

   C $7500

   D $7875

4 The administration expenses of a business amount to $30 000. They are apportioned to three departments as follows: department A $\frac{3}{6}$, department B $\frac{2}{6}$, department C $\frac{1}{6}$. It has been decided to close department C but there will not be any reduction in administration costs.

   How will the administration expenses be apportioned to departments A and B after department C has been closed?

	Dept A	Dept B
	$	$
A	15 000	10 000
B	18 000	12 000
C	21 000	14 000
D	22 200	14 800

18.6 Additional exercises

1 Mason is a retailer selling furnishings, kitchen equipment and clothing. The following information has been extracted from his books for the year ended 30 April 2004.

	Furnishings	Kitchen equipment	Clothing
	$000	$000	$000
Sales	912	696	552
Stock at 1 May 2003	350	306	94
Purchases	491	406	402
Stock at 30 April 2004	394	222	65
Salaries for the year ended 30 April 2004	58	42	60
Fixtures and fittings at cost at 30 April 2004	300	200	200

Further information

1. Mason incurred the following expenses for the year ended 30 April 2004.

	$
Rent	94 000
Heating and lighting	75 000
General expenses	62 000

2. The premises cost $800 000.

3. Floor space occupied:

Furnishings	40%
Kitchen equipment	35%
Clothing	25%

4. Depreciation is to be calculated as follows.

Premises 4% per annum on cost.

Fixtures and fittings 15% per annum on cost.

5. General expenses are to be apportioned between the departments in proportion to their respective turnovers.

Required

Prepare departmental Trading and Profit and Loss Accounts for the year ended 30 April 2004. (Where necessary, calculations should be made to the nearest $000.)

2 Spicer sells electrical goods from three departments: Kitchen Equipment, Radios and TVs, and Home Computers. The following is the summarised Trading and Profit and Loss Account for the year ended 30 April 2004.

		Kitchen Equipment			Radios & TVs			Home Computers	
	$000	$000	$000	$000	$000	$000	$000	$000	$000
Sales		200			90			60	
Less Cost of sales		110			40			35	
Gross profit		90			50			25	
Variable expenses	30			25			18		
Fixed expenses	40	70		18	43		12	30	
Net profit		20			7			(5)	

Further information

1. Year-end stock taking reveals that damaged stock has been included in cost of sales as follows.

	$
Kitchen Equipment	4000
Radios and TVs	5000

The goods have no disposable value.

2. Computer equipment sales includes goods which have been sent to a customer on sale or return for $3000. The equipment cost $2000. It is not known if the customer is going to buy the equipment.

3. Administration expenses of $30 000 have been divided equally between the three departments and included in fixed expenses.

4. All other fixed expenses have been allocated as wholly attributable to the departments concerned.

Required

(a) Calculate revised net profit figures for
   (i)   Kitchen Equipment
   (ii) Radios and TVs
   (iii) Home Computers
   (iv) Spicer.
(b) Calculate the contribution which Home Computers has made to Spicer's profit.

Spicer has decided to close the Home Computer department. This will not result in any reduction of administration expenses.

Required

(c) Calculate Spicers' profit for the year ended 30 April 2004 if the Home Computers department had been closed at 30 April **2003**.

19 Manufacturing Accounts

> *In this chapter you will learn:*
> - how to prepare a Manufacturing Account
> - how to calculate manufacturing profit in the Profit and Loss Account
> - how to provide for unrealised profit in stocks of finished goods.

19.1 What is a Manufacturing Account?

Manufacturing Accounts are prepared by manufacturing companies to show the cost of producing goods.

Trading companies purchase finished goods, but a manufacturing company's purchases consist of materials it uses in its manufacturing process. A large part of a manufacturing company's wages will most probably be paid to employees engaged on making goods, and some of the overheads will relate to the manufacturing process. A Manufacturing Account groups all the manufacturing expenses together as factory expenses. If the goods are produced more cheaply than they can be purchased from an outside supplier, the factory may be considered to have made a profit and will be credited with **factory profit**.

Manufacturing companies' stocks include stocks of raw materials, work in progress and finished goods. Any factory profit included in the stock of finished goods must be excluded from the value of the stock shown in the Balance Sheet.

19.2 How to prepare a Manufacturing Account

Select from the trial balance those expenses that relate to the company's manufacturing operation. The expenses are either direct (e.g. the cost of materials from which the goods are made, and the wages of the workers who actually make the goods) or indirect (all other manufacturing expenses).

The following outline shows how expenditure is allocated to Manufacturing Accounts.

Sample Example Ltd
Manufacturing Account for the year ended 31 December 2004

	$000	$000
Direct costs		
Direct material[1]		200
Direct labour[2]		380
Other direct expenses[3]		60
Prime cost[4]		640
Factory overheads		
Indirect materials[5]	95	
Indirect wages[6]	120	
Other overheads[7]	330	545
		1185
Work in progress at 1 January 2004[8]	78	
Work in progress at 31 December 2004[9]	(53)	25
Factory cost of finished goods (or cost of production)[10]		1210
Factory profit[11]		242
Cost of goods transferred to Trading Account[12]		1452

1. **Direct material:** material from which goods are made. The cost includes carriage inwards on raw material.
2. **Direct labour:** the wages of the workers who actually make the goods
3. **Direct expenses:** royalties, licence fees, etc. which have to be paid to other persons for the right to produce their products or to use their processes. The payment is a fixed sum for every unit of good produced.
4. **Prime cost:** the total of the direct costs. This description must *always* be shown.
5. **Indirect materials:** all materials purchased for the factory but which do not form part of the goods being produced, for example cleaning materials, lubricating oil for the machinery.

6 **Indirect wages:** the wages of all factory workers who do not actually make the goods, for example factory managers, supervisors, stores staff, cleaners, etc.

7 **Other overheads:** overheads relating exclusively to the factory and production, for example factory rent, heating and lighting, depreciation of the factory building and machinery, etc.

8 **Work in progress:** goods in the process of being made at the end of the previous year but which were not finished are brought into the current year as an input to this year's production.

9 Goods that are not completely finished at the end of the current year must be deducted from the year's costs in order to arrive at the cost of finished goods.

10 **Factory cost of finished goods:** either these words or the alternative, **cost of production**, should be shown at this point in the account.

11 **Factory profit:** the percentage to be added to cost of production as profit. The amount is decided by management and will always be given in questions if necessary. It is debited in the Manufacturing Account and credited in the Profit and Loss Account (see below).

12 The total of the Manufacturing Account is debited in the Trading Account under the heading 'Cost of Sales'.

Example

The following balances have been extracted from Makeit & Co.'s trial balance at 31 December 2004.

	$000	$000
Stocks at 1 January 2004:		
Direct materials	10	
Work in progress	38	
Finished goods	40	
Purchases (direct materials)	140	
Carriage inwards	24	
Direct wages	222	
Direct expenses (patent royalties)	46	
Indirect materials	45	
Indirect labour	72	
Rent: factory	100	
offices	90	
Heating, lighting and power: factory	45	
offices	35	
Sales		1 300
Administration salaries and wages	173	

Further information

1. Stock at 31 December 2004 was as follows.

	$000
Direct materials	18
Work in progress	20
Finished goods	60

2. Depreciation is to be provided on fixed assets as follows.

	$000
Factory building	20
Factory machinery	36
Office equipment	24

3. Factory profit is to be calculated at 15% on cost of production.

Required

Prepare the Manufacturing, Trading and Profit and Loss Account for the year ended 31 December 2004.

Answer

Makeit & Co.
Manufacturing, Trading and Profit and Loss Account
for the year ended 31 December 2004

		$000	$000
Direct materials	Stock at 1 January 2004	10	
	Purchases	140	
	Carriage inwards	24	
		174	
	Less Stock at 31 December 2004	18	156
Direct labour			222
Direct expenses			46
Prime cost			424
Indirect materials		45	
Indirect labour		72	
Rent of factory		100	
Heating, lighting and power		45	
Depreciation: factory		20	
machinery		36	318
			742
Work in progress 1 January 2004		38	
Work in progress 31 December 2004		(20)	18
Factory cost of finished goods			760
Factory profit (15%)			114
Transferred to Trading Account			874

	$000	$000
Sales		1300
Cost of sales		
Stock of finished goods at 1 January 2004	40	
Transferred from factory	874	
	914	
Stock of finished goods at 31 December 2004	60	854
Gross profit		446
Wages and salaries	173	
Rent of offices	90	
Heating and lighting	35	
Depreciation of office equipment	24	322
Net profit on trading[1]		124
Add factory profit[2]	114	
Less Unrealised profit on closing stock of finished goods[3]	8	106
Net profit		230

1 Net profit on trading is the profit that has been made from the trading activity and does not include factory profit.

2 Factory profit (after deducting unrealised profit) is added to the net profit on trading to show Makeit & Co.'s total profit.

3 See §19.3.

Note. The Trading and Profit and Loss Account follows on from the Manufacturing Account without a break. It is included in the heading to the Manufacturing Account.

19.3 Unrealised profit included in stocks of finished goods

The figure of closing stock in Makeit & Co.'s Trading Account includes factory profit. This profit will not be realised until the stock is sold and must be excluded to arrive at the realised factory profit. (The concept of realisation must be applied.) Makeit & Co's. unrealised profit is calculated as follows. The stock of $60 000 is 115% of the cost of manufacture and the unrealised profit is $60 000 \times \frac{15}{115}$ = $8000 (rounded). The double entry for unrealised profit, $8000, debited in the Profit and Loss Account is completed by a credit to a Provision for Unrealised Profit.

In future years, it will be necessary only to adjust the Provision for Unrealised Profit for increases or decreases in closing stocks. For example, if Makeit & Co.'s finished goods stock one year later, at 31 December 2005, is $85 000, the provision required for unrealised profit will be $85 000 \times \frac{15}{115}$ = $11 000. Only the increase of $3000 in the provision will be debited in the Profit and Loss Account and credited to the Provision for Unrealised Profit.

An increase in the provision is recorded as follows.

> **Debit** Profit and Loss Account
> **Credit** Provision for Unrealised Profit
> with the amount of the increase

A decrease in the provision is recorded as follows.

> **Debit** Provision for Unrealised Profit
> **Credit** Profit and Loss Account
> with the amount of the decrease.

(The accounting for a Provision for Unrealised Profit is similar to that of a Provision for Doubtful Debts; see §12.4.)

19.4 Manufacturing Balance Sheet

The Balance Sheet of a manufacturing business includes the stocks of materials, work in progress and finished goods at cost.

The stocks appear in Makeit & Co.'s Balance Sheet at 31 December 2004 as follows.

Current assets		$000	$000
Stock:	materials		18
	work in progress		20
	finished goods	60	
	Less unrealised profit	8	52
			90

Exercise 1

The Fabricating Company carries on a manufacturing business. Information extracted from its trial balance at 31 March 2004 is as follows.

		$000	$000
Sales			700
Stocks at 1.4.03	Raw materials	10	
	Work in progress	12	
	Finished goods	24	
Purchase of raw materials		130	
Carriage inwards		14	
Direct labour		170	
Other direct expenses		16	
Factory overheads		128	
Office overheads		96	

The following further information is given.

		$000
Stocks at 31.3.04	Raw materials	20
	Work in progress	22
	Finished goods	36
Depreciation charges for the year:		
	Factory	12
	Office	3

Completed production is transferred to the warehouse at a mark-up on factory cost of 20%.

Required

Prepare a Manufacturing, Trading and Profit and Loss Account for the year ended 31 March 2004.

Exercise 2

The following balances have been extracted from the books of Glupersoo at 30 April 2004.

	$
Sales	800 000
Purchase of raw materials	132 000
Direct wages	146 250
Indirect wages	19 500
Rent	45 000
Heating and lighting	42 300
Insurance	3 150
Office salaries	51 450
Carriage inwards	11 505
Carriage outwards	2 520
Advertising	7 000
Motor van expenses	6 000
Stocks at 1 May 2003: Raw materials	11 250
Work in progress	18 000
Finished goods	27 000

Further information

1. Stocks at 30 April 2004:

	$
Raw materials	13 125
Work in progress	15 750
Finished goods	24 000

2. The following expenses must be accrued at 30 April 2004.

	$
Rent	3750
Heating and lighting	2700

3. The following expenses have been prepaid at 3 April 2004.

	$
Insurance	900
Advertising	3500

4. Expenses are to be apportioned as follows.

Rent: Factory 75%; Offices 25%

Heating and lighting: Factory $\frac{2}{3}$, Offices $\frac{1}{3}$

Insurance: Factory $\frac{9}{10}$; Offices $\frac{1}{10}$

Motor costs: Factory 50%

5. Provision for depreciation is to be made as follows.

	$
Factory building	3 000
Factory machinery	10 000
Office machinery and equipment	4 000
Motor vans	8 000

Required

Prepare a Manufacturing, Trading and Profit and Loss Account for the year ended 30 April 2004.
(Make all calculations to the nearest $.)

19.5 Examination hints

- Adjust for accruals and prepayments, where necessary, before apportioning overhead expenses between the Manufacturing Account and the Profit and Loss Account.
- Take care to calculate the provision for unrealised profit, based on closing stock, correctly. The fraction to be used is

$$\frac{\text{percentage of mark-up}}{100 + \text{percentage of mark-up}}$$

(see §16.4).

- The entry in the Profit and Loss Account for unrealised profit is the increase or decrease in the amount of the provision brought forward from the previous year.
- Ensure that the closing stock of finished goods is shown in the Balance Sheet at cost by deducting the balance on the Provision for Unrealised Profit account.

19.6 Multiple-choice questions

1 Goods are transferred from the Manufacturing Account to the Trading Account at factory cost of production plus a mark-up of 20%.

The transfer prices of the closing stocks of finished goods were as follows.

Year 1 $39 600

Year 2 $42 000

Year 3 $45 600

What was the provision for unrealised profit charged against the profit for Year 3?

A $400

B $600

C $720

D $1200

2 Goods are transferred from the factory to the warehouse at a mark-up of $33\frac{1}{3}$ %. At 1 April 2003, the balance on the Provision for Unrealised Profit was $17000. At 31 March 2004, the closing stock of finished goods was $60 000.

What was the effect on profit of the entry in the Provision for Unrealised Profit on 31 March 2004?

A decrease of $2000

B decrease of $3000

C increase of $2000

D increase of $3000

3 The following items appear in the accounts of a manufacturing company:

(i)   carriage inwards

(ii)   carriage outwards

(iii) depreciation of warehouse machinery

(iv) provision for unrealised profit.

Which items will be included in the Manufacturing Account?

A (i) and (ii)

B (i) and (iii)

C (ii) and (iii)

D (ii) and (iv)

4 A manufacturing company adds a factory profit of 25% to its cost of production. The following information is available:

	$
Stock of finished goods at 1 April 2003 (per Balance Sheet at that date)	30 000
Cost of goods produced (per Manufacturing Account for the year ended 31 March 2004)	300 000
Closing stock of finished goods (per Trading Account for the year end 31 March 2004)	60 000

How much will be credited as factory profit in the Profit and Loss Account for the year ended 31 March 2004?

A $67 500

B $69 000

C $70 500

D $71 500

19.7 Additional exercises

1 The following balances have been extracted from the books of Spinners & Co. at 31 December 2003.

	$
Stocks at 1 January 2003:	
Raw materials	8 000
Work in progress	12 000
Factory expenses	
Direct wages	40 000
Indirect wages	28 000
Patent fees paid to patent holder	16 000
Heating and lighting	5 000
General factory expenses	14 000
Insurance of plant and machinery	6 000
Purchases of raw materials	140 000
Plant and machinery at cost	70 000

Further information

1. Stocks at 31 December 2003:

	$
Raw materials	10 000
Work in progress	9 700

2. Expenses owing at 31 December 2003:

	$
Direct wages	600
Indirect wages	400
General expenses	300

3. Expenses prepaid at 31 December 2003:

	$
Insurance	400
Heating and lighting	180

4. Plant and machinery are to be depreciated at the rate of 10% on cost.

5. A factory profit of 10% is added to the factory cost of goods produced.

Required

Prepare the Manufacturing Account for the year ended 31 December 2003.

2 The following balances have been extracted from the books of the Uggle Box Manufacturing Company at 30 April 2004.

	$
Premises at cost	250 000
Plant and machinery (net book value)	70 000
Motor vehicles at cost	40 000
Stocks at 1 May 2003	
Raw materials	42 000
Work in progress	50 000
Finished goods	48 000
Factory wages (direct)	280 000
Royalties based on production	40 000
Factory expenses	20 000
Selling expenses	42 000
Administrative expenses	62 000
Sales	1 240 000
Purchases of raw materials	390 000
Carriage inwards	26 000

Further information

1. Stocks at 30 April 2004:

	$
Raw materials	36 000
Work in progress	46 000
Finished goods	62 400

2. Finished goods are transferred to the Trading Account at factory cost plus a mark-up of 20%.

3. Depreciation is to be provided as follows.

Premises: 5% per annum on cost
Plant and machinery: 20% per annum on the written down value
Motor vehicles: 20% per annum on cost

4. Depreciation charges are to be apportioned as follows.

Premises:	Factory	50%
	Administration	50%
Plant and machinery:	Factory	80%
	Administration	20%
Motor vehicles:	Factory	90%
	Administration	10%

Required

Prepare a Manufacturing, Trading and Profit and Loss Account for the year ended 30 April 2004.

3 The following balances have been extracted from Yendor's books at 31 March 2004.

		$000	$000
Stocks at 1 April 2003:	Raw materials	450	
	Work in progress	375	
	Finished goods	390	
Factory wages	Direct	900	
	Indirect	90	
Purchases	Direct materials	2250	
	Indirect materials	45	
Carriage inwards		162	
Other factory overheads		245	
Sales			6075
Office salaries		391	
Other administration expenses		675	
Provision for Unrealised Profit			65
Freehold premises at cost		1000	
Provision for Depreciation of Freehold Premises			160
Manufacturing Plant and Machinery at cost		600	
Provision for Depreciation of Manufacturing Plant and Machinery at 31 March 2003			350
Office equipment at cost		300	
Provision for Depreciation of Office Equipment at 31 March 2003			100

Further information

1. Stocks at 31 March 2004 were as follows (in $000s): raw materials $440; work in progress $562; finished goods $594.

2. Carriage inwards relates wholly to the purchase of raw materials.

3. Finished goods are transferred from the factory to the warehouse at a mark-up of 20%.

4. The factory occupies $\frac{3}{4}$ of the freehold premises; the administrative offices occupy the remainder.

5. Depreciation should be provided as follows.

> Freehold premises 4% per annum on cost
>
> Plant and machinery 30% per annum on net book value
>
> Office equipment 15% per annum on net book value

Required

Prepare Yendor's Manufacturing, Trading and Profit and Loss Account for the year ended 31 March 2004.

20 Valuation of stock

In this chapter you will learn:
- the importance of valuing stock in accordance with recognised accounting principles
- valuation of stock on the First In, First Out (FIFO) basis
- valuation of stock on the Last In, Last Out (LIFO) basis
- valuation of stock on Weighted Average Cost (AVCO) basis
- the merits and defects of each method
- what continuous and periodic inventories are.

20.1 The importance of valuing stock in accordance with recognised accounting principles

Opening and closing stocks are included in Trading Accounts to calculate cost of sales and gross profit. Closing stock is included as a current asset in Balance Sheets as part of working capital. The value placed upon stock is therefore of very great importance. Three possible ways in which stock may be valued are

- at its cost price
- at its selling price
- at what it is considered to be worth.

The third way, at the stock's worth, should be ruled out immediately because 'worth' is a very subjective term; it can mean different things to different people, and even different things to the same person at different times and in different circumstances. This aspect has already been discussed in §9.4. Obviously 'profit' and 'working capital' should not mean different things at different times.

Selling price is also an unsatisfactory way of valuing stock as the following example shows.

Aykbourne makes up his accounts to 31 December each year and values his closing stock at selling price. He purchased goods for $800 on 30 November 2004. He sold the goods on 30 January 2005 for $1000. If these were Aykbourne's only transactions, his Trading Accounts for the years ended 31 December 2004 and 2005 would be as follows.

Year ended 31 December 2004			Year ended 31 December 2005		
	$	$		$	$
Sales		0	Sales		1000
Cost of sales			Cost of sales		
Opening stock	0		Opening stock	1000	
Purchases	800		Purchases	0	
	800			1000	
Less closing stock	1000	(200)		0	(1000)
Net profit		200	Net profit		0

This example shows Aykbourne making a profit of $200 in the year ended 31 December 2004 although he had not sold the goods, but not making any profit in the next year when he sold them. Valuing the stock at selling price has offended against three important accounting principles:

- realisation – no profit was realised in the year ended 31 December 2004 because no sale had taken place
- matching – the profit has not been matched to the time the sale took place
- prudence – the profit was overstated in 2004; it was not even certain then that the goods could be sold at a profit.

It is an important principle that stock should never be valued at more than cost. Valuing stock at historic cost observes the principles of realisation, matching and prudence.

Another important principle is that the method used to value stock should be used consistently from one accounting period to the next. The methods are considered next.

20.2 Three methods of valuing stock at cost

In a very few cases, it may be possible to value goods at the price actually paid for them. For example, the owner of an art gallery may be able to say from whom she bought each of the pictures in her gallery and how much she paid for them because there would probably be a limited number of paintings and she would be able to recall how much she paid for them.

A manufacturer of computers, however, would not find it easy to say how much he paid for the stocks of parts he needed for the computers. Purchases of hard drives, for example, would be in bulk and made at different times and at different prices. It would be impossible to say at the year-end how much had been paid for any particular hard drive still in stock. The problem is solved by assuming that stock movements occur in a particular pattern, even if that is not strictly so. This is often called a convention: something that is assumed to happen even if it is not strictly true, at least all the time. The three methods considered here are:

- **First In, First Out (FIFO)**, which assumes that stock is used or sold in the same order in which it was received

- **Last In, First Out (LIFO)**, which assumes that the latest delivery of stock is used or sold before stock received earlier

- **Weighted average cost (AVCO)**, which involves calculating the weighted average cost of stock-on-hand after every delivery to the business. Stock-on-hand at any given time, and stock sold or issued, is valued at weighted average cost.

Each of these methods will now be considered.

20.3 How to value stock

FIFO

Stock is assumed to be used in the order in which it is received from the supplier.

Example 1

At 31 May the stock of a certain material consisted of 80 kilograms which had cost $0.60 per kilogram. The receipts and issues of the material in June were as follows.

		Receipts		Issues
		Quantity	Price per kg	Quantity
		kg	$	kg
June 1	Stock brought forward from May 31	80	0.60	
3		100	1.00	
7				70
16		200	1.20	
23				200
25		50	1.40	
30				80

Required

Calculate the value of stock at 30 June based on FIFO.

Answer

June		1	3	16	25	
	Price per kg	$0.60	$1.00	$1.20	$1.40	
	Stock (kg)	80				
	Receipts (kg)		100	200	50	
7	Issued	(70)				
		10				
23	Issued	(10)	(100)	(90)		
		–	–	110		
30	Issued			(80)	—	
	Closing stock			30	50	
	Valuation at cost			$36	$70	Total $106

This example shows how FIFO works. The same result can be quickly calculated as follows.

Units available (80 + 100 + 200 + 50)	430	
Units issued (70 + 200 + 80)	350	
Balance of units		80
Valuation: 50 at latest price $1.40	$70	
30 at previous price $1.20	$36	$106

Exercise 1

At 30 September Fiford Ltd had a stock of 100 kg of fifolium, which had cost $5 per kilogram. In October, it made the following purchases and sales of fifolium.

	Purchases kg	Price per kg $	Sales kg
October 3			40
10	80	5.20	
12			75
14			50
15	50	5.24	
17			45
22	70	5.28	
29	100	5.32	
30			70

Required

Calculate the quantity and value of the stock of fifolium at 31 October using the FIFO method.

LIFO

By this method, stock is valued on the assumption that all issues or sales of goods are made from the items most recently received.

Example 2

(Data as for example 1, FIFO)

Answer

June		1	3	16	25
Price per kg		$0.60	$1.00	$1.20	$1.40
Stock (kg)		80			
Receipts (kg)			100	200	50
7	Issued		(70)		
			30		
23	Issued			(200)	
				-	
30	Issued		(30)		(50)
Closing stock		80	-	-	-
Valuation at cost		$48			

Note. It is not safe to calculate the value by LIFO using the same quick method shown for FIFO above.

Exercise 2

At 31 July, L.I. Fortune Ltd had a stock of 40 litres of lifoxium, which had cost $1.50 per litre. The purchases and sales of lifoxium in August were as follows.

	Purchases litres	Price per litre $	Sales litres
August 5			20
12	100	1.75	
14			60
18	75	1.90	
19			80
23			25
25	120	2.00	
27			65
30	90	2.15	
31			60

Required

Calculate L.I. Fortune Ltd's stock of lifoxium at 31 August in quantity and value using the LIFO method.

AVCO

The weighted average cost of stock is calculated every time new goods are received.

Example 3

(Data as for example 1, FIFO)

June		Units	Price ($)	Weighted average cost ($)	Balance ($)
1	Balance b/f	80	0.60	0.60	48
3	Received	100	1.00		100
	Balance	180		0.822	148
7	Issued	(70)			58
	Balance	110			90
16	Received	200	1.20		240
	Balance	310		1.065	330
23	Issued	(200)			213
	Balance	110			117
25	Received	50	1.40		70
	Balance	160		1.169	187
30	Issued	(80)			(94)
	Balance	80		1.163*	93

* Rounded calculations may result in an adjustment being made to the average price of closing stock.

The value of stock based on AVCO lies between the values based on FIFO and LIFO.

Exercise 3

A.V. Co. had a stock of 200 digital hammers at 31 May. The hammers were valued at $5 each.

Transactions in digital hammers in the month of June were as follows.

Date received		Quantity	Price per hammer ($)	Sold Quantity
June	4	100	5.20	
	10			75
	13	100	5.35	
	20			150
	26	80	5.40	
	30			90

Required

Calculate the closing stock of digital hammers at 30 June showing quantity and total value based on weighted average cost.

20.4 Perpetual and periodic inventories

A **stock inventory** is a record of goods received by, and used or sold by, a business. A **perpetual inventory** maintains a running balance of stock-on-hand after each transaction. The example given above for AVCO is a typical perpetual inventory.

A periodic inventory shows the balance of stock-on-hand only at intervals, for example at the end of each month. The total of items used in the period is deducted from the total of items received to give the balance of items in stock. The 'quick' method, shown above, of calculating the value of closing stock on the FIFO basis is an example of a periodic inventory.

20.5 The effect of the methods of stock valuation on profits over the whole life of a business

The profit made over the whole life of a business is not affected by the choice of method of valuing stock. This is demonstrated in the following examples.

Quad Ltd began business in year 1 and stopped trading at the end of year 4. The following information is given for each of the four years.

	Year 1 $	Year 2 $	Year 3 $	Year 4 $
Sales	1000	1400	1600	800
Purchases	600	800	700	400
Closing stock:				
FIFO	80	100	90	–
LIFO	60	80	50	–
AVCO	70	90	80	–

Trading Accounts (using FIFO for valuing stock)								
	Year 1 $	$	Year 2 $	$	Year 3 $	$	Year 4 $	$
Sales		1000		1400		1600		800
Opening stock	–		80		100		90	
Purchases	600		800		700		400	
Closing stock (FIFO)	(80)	(520)	(100)	(780)	(90)	(710)	–	(490)
Gross profit		480		620		890		310
							Total gross profit	$2300

Trading Accounts (using LIFO to value stock)

	Year 1 $	Year 1 $	Year 2 $	Year 2 $	Year 3 $	Year 3 $	Year 4 $	Year 4 $
Sales		1000		1400		1600		800
Opening stock	–		60		80		50	
Purchases	600		800		700		400	
Closing stock (LIFO)	(60)	(540)	(80)	(780)	(50)	(730)	–	(450)
Gross profit		460		620		870		350
							Total gross profit $2300	

Trading Accounts (AVCO)

	Year 1 $	Year 1 $	Year 2 $	Year 2 $	Year 3 $	Year 3 $	Year 4 $	Year 4 $
Sales		1000		1400		1600		800
Opening stock	–		70		90		80	
Purchases	600		800		700		400	
Closing stock (AVCO)	(70)	(530)	(90)	(780)	(80)	(710)	–	(480)
Gross profit		470		620		890		320
							Total gross profit $2300	

20.6 FIFO, LIFO and AVCO compared

It is important to compare the advantages and disadvantages of FIFO, LIFO and AVCO in order to decide which method is the right one to use in particular circumstances.

FIFO

Advantages

1. It is a relatively simple system to use.
2. It is generally realistic. Materials are normally used in FIFO order, and goods will be sold in that order, especially if they are perishable.
3. Prices used are those that have actually been paid for goods.
4. Closing stock is valued on current price levels.
5. FIFO is an acceptable method of stock valuation for the purposes of the Companies Act 1985 and Accounting Standards (Statement of Standard Accounting Practice, SSAP 9).

Disadvantages

1. Manufacturing businesses usually prefer to charge materials to production at current prices to enable them to fix realistic selling prices. They may use LIFO for that purpose (or even AVCO) but use FIFO to value stocks for their financial accounts.
2. Identical items of stock from batches bought at different times may be used for similar jobs with the result that job A may be charged for the item at a different price from job B. The customer for job B may be unfairly treated as a result. Quotations for jobs when materials are based on FIFO may be unreliable.
3. In times of rising prices, the closing stock in the financial accounts will be priced at the latest (high) prices. This results in lowering cost of sales and increasing gross profit. It may be considered that this is not consistent with the concept of prudence. However, as stated above, the method is acceptable under SSAP 9.

LIFO

Advantages

1. It is a relatively simple system to operate.
2. Prices used to value stock are prices that have actually been paid.
3. Raw materials are issued to production at the most recent prices paid.

Disadvantages

1. Stocks are not usually used or sold in the reverse order in which they were received.
2. Like FIFO, difficulties may arise from identical items being charged to similar jobs at different prices.
3. Closing stock is not valued at the most recent prices. In times of rising prices, the stock will be valued at out-of-date low prices. Cost of sales will be increased and gross profit will be reduced. Accounting standards warn against profits being artificially understated.
4. LIFO is not an acceptable basis under SSAP 9 or the Companies Act 1985 for valuing stock because it is based on prices that are not current.

AVCO

Advantages

1. The use of average prices avoids the inequality of identical items being charged to different jobs at different prices.
2. AVCO recognises that identical items purchased at different times and prices have identical values. Averaged prices are truer to this concept than actual prices used for FIFO and LIFO.
3. Averaging costs may smooth variations in production costs, and comparisons between the results of different periods more meaningful.
4. Averaged prices used to value closing stock may be fairly close to the latest prices.
5. AVCO is acceptable for the purposes of SSAP 9 and the Companies Act 1985.

Disadvantages

1. The average price must be re-calculated after every purchase of stock.
2. The average price does not represent any price actually paid for stock.

20.7 Net realisable value

Net realisable value is the price that may be expected to be received from the sale of goods, less the cost of putting them into a saleable condition. The costs involved include completion of the goods (if they are being manufactured), and marketing, selling and distribution costs.

Example 1

Some bales of fabric that cost $800 have become damaged by flood water entering the warehouse. If they are cleaned and treated for the damage at a cost of $300, they can be sold for $1000. The net realisable value is what the trader will be left with after they have been sold, which is $(1000 – 300) = $700.

Valuation of stock at the lower of cost and net realisable value

SSAP 9 requires stock to be valued at the lower of cost and net realisable value.

Example 2

Goods were bought at a cost of $1300. They have become damaged and will cost $400 to be put into a saleable condition. They can then be sold for £1900. Net realisable value is $(1900 – 400) = $1500. As this is more than cost, the goods should be valued for stock at cost ($1300).

Example 3

Details as in example 2 but, after repair, the goods can be sold for only $1500. The net realisable value is $(1500 – 400) = $1100. This is less than cost and is the value to be placed upon the goods.

20.8 The valuation of individual items of stock or groups of similar items

Individual items or groups of items of stock should be considered separately when deciding whether they should be valued at cost or net realisable value. This is to ensure that losses on individual items or groups of items are not 'hidden'.

Example

A company sells six different grades of compact discs for computers. The following are the cost to the company and the net realisable values (NRVs) of the stocks of the six grades of discs.

	Cost	NRV	Value to be used for stock valuation
	$	$	$
Grade 1	2 000	2 400	2 000
Grade 2	4 500	3 800	3 800
Grade 3	3 000	3 100	3 000
Grade 4	5 750	5 000	5 000
Grade 5	1 250	2 000	1 250
Grade 6	2 500	2 200	2 200
	19 000	18 500	17 250

If the stock were valued as a whole without taking the individual items into consideration, it would be valued at NRV ($18 500) as this is less than cost; but the items where NRV is more than cost are hiding the losses made on grades 2, 4 and 6. The items must be valued separately at $17 250 as this recognises the losses.

20.9 Stocks of work in progress

A manufacturing company must value work in progress in accordance with SSAP 9. The Standard requires work in progress to be valued at prime cost (see §19.2) plus an appropriate proportion of manufacturing overheads. Selling and distribution costs, administration expenses and any element of profit (see §19.2) are not to be included in the valuation of work in progress.

20.10 Replacement cost

Replacement cost is the price that will have to be paid to replace goods used or sold. The replacement cost may be the latest price of the good, or an estimate of what the price will be at some future date.

Replacement cost is not acceptable as a basis for valuing stock under accounting standards (SSAP 9). However, replacement cost may be used to estimate the cost of a particular job when quoting for an order; a quotation for the job based on historic cost using LIFO (or even FIFO) could lead to an underestimate of the price for the job and low profit. Replacement cost is usually more realistic for this purpose.

Replacement cost should also be used when preparing budgets (see chapter 34).

20.11 Examination hints

- Read questions carefully to see which method or methods of stock valuation are required.
- Some questions are about the value of stock-on-hand, but others are concerned with the cost of stock issued to production or sold. Make sure you understand the point of the question or you may provide the wrong answer.
- Perform all calculations with the utmost care.
- Be prepared to answer questions on the principles governing stock valuation and the advantages and disadvantages of each method.
- Questions on stock valuation may require you to use techniques and knowledge gained from your studies on any part of the syllabus.

20.12 Multiple-choice questions

1 How should stock be valued in a balance sheet?

    A at the lower of net realisable value and selling price

    B at the lower of replacement cost and net realisable value

    C at lower of cost and replacement cost

    D at lower of cost and net realisable value

2 A company bought and sold goods as follows.

	Bought		Sold
	Units	Unit price ($)	Units
March 1	20	2.00	
3	10	2.50	
4			12
5	20	3.00	
6			16

What is the value of the stock at 6 March based on FIFO?

    A $44

    B $45

    C $65

    D $66

3 A company had the following stock transactions in June.

June	1	Purchased 50 units of stock at $3 per unit
	14	Purchased 100 units at $4.50 per unit
	23	Sold 70 units
	30	Purchased 62 units at $5 per unit

What is the value of stock at 30 June based on AVCO?

    A $4.292

    B $4.437

    C $4.50

    D $5.00

4 A trader has valued his opening and closing stocks using LIFO. He has now heard that LIFO is not acceptable under current accounting standards and has amended his accounts to value the stocks on FIFO. His stocks valued at FIFO and LIFO are as follows.

	FIFO	LIFO
Opening stock	$2000	$1500
Closing stock	$4000	$3200

What effect will this amendment make to the trader's gross and net profits?

	Gross profit	Net profit
A	decrease $300	decrease $300
B	decrease $300	no change
C	increase $300	increase $300
D	increase $300	no change

20.13 Additional exercises

1 Discuss how the concept of prudence might be relevant when considering the valuation of Stock in Trade. (UCLES, 2001, AS/A Level Accounting, Syllabus 8706/2, October/November)

2 Janice Jersey's first 6 months of trading showed the following purchases and sales of stock.

1990	Purchases	Sales
January	280 @ $65 each	
February		140 @ $82 each
March	100 @ $69 each	
April		190 @ $85 each
May	220 @ $72 each	
June		200 @ $90 each

Calculate Janice's profit for the 6 months ended 30 June 1990 using the following methods of stock valuation:

(a) FIFO (First In First Out)

(b) LIFO (Last In First Out)

(c) AVCO (Weighted Average Cost). Calculate to 2 decimal places.

(UCLES, 2002, AS/A Level Accounting, Syllabus 9706/2, May/June)

3 Because of illness, Achmed's annual stocktaking, which should have taken place on 31 March 2001, was not completed until 7 April 2001, and was undertaken by an inexperienced member of the staff. Achmed felt that the stock figure of $92050 was too low and ordered an investigation. It was discovered that the following had occurred during the week ended 7 April 2001 and had not been accounted for in the closing stock calculation:

1. Goods with a selling price of $1040 had been sent to a customer on approval.

2. Goods costing $9400 were received and invoiced.

3. Sales of $18760 had been made and invoiced to customers.

   These sales included

   (i)   an overcharge of $160;

   (ii) sales of $6000 on special offer at a margin of 10%;

   (iii) damaged goods which had cost $2500 and were sold for $2800.

Achmed's standard rate of gross profit is 25% of sales.

Calculate the correct value of closing stock at 31 March 2001.

(UCLES, 2001, AS/A Level Accounting, Syllabus 9366/2, May/June)

21 Partnership accounts

In this chapter you will learn:
- what a partnership is
- how profits are shared when there is a partnership agreement
- how to apply the Partnership Act of 1890 when there is no partnership agreement
- how to prepare partnership accounts
- the advantages and disadvantages of partnerships.

21.1 What are partnerships?

A partnership is formed when two or more people carry on business together with the intention of making profit.

Partners must agree on how the partnership is to be carried on, including how much capital each partner is to contribute to the firm and how profits and losses are to be shared. These, and other important matters, are decided in a **partnership agreement**. The agreement will usually be in writing, possibly by deed (a formal legal document), or verbally. If the partners do not make an agreement and a dispute arises regarding their rights and duties as partners, the Court may assume that past practice constitutes an 'implied' agreement, and resolve the dispute according to what the partners have done previously.

The **Partnership Act 1890** governs partnerships and states the rights and duties of partners. The Act includes the following provisions, which are important and apply to partnerships *unless* the partners have agreed to vary the terms.

- All partners are entitled to contribute equally to the capital of the partnership.
- Partners are not entitled to interest on the capital they have contributed.
- Partners are not entitled to salaries.
- Partners are not to be charged interest on their drawings.
- Partners will share profits and losses equally.
- Partners are entitled to interest at 5% per annum on loans they make to the partnership.

The Appropriation Account

The Appropriation Account is a continuation of the Profit and Loss Account. It begins with the net profit or loss brought down from the Profit and Loss Account. The following methods of dividing profits between partners must be treated as appropriations of profit in the Appropriation Account.

Partners' salaries A partnership agreement may entitle one or more partners to be paid a salary. This may be paid in addition to a further share of profit. A salary guarantees a partner an income, even if the firm does not make a profit. Partners' salaries are never debited in the Profit and Loss Account.

Interest on capital and drawings Interest on capital recognises that if partners do not invest their capital in the partnership, their money could earn interest in some other form of investment. The partnership agreement should state the rate of interest to be paid. Interest on capital is payable even if the firm does not make a profit.

Interest charged to partners on their drawings is intended to encourage the partners to leave their shares of profit in the business as additional temporary capital.

Interest on partners' loans to the firm

Interest on a loan made by a partner to a firm is *not* an appropriation of profit – it is an expense to be debited in the Profit and Loss Account, *not in the Appropriation Account*.

Profit/loss sharing

Any balance of profit or loss on the Appropriation Account after charging interest on capitals and partners' salaries is shared between the partners in their agreed profit-sharing ratios. If there is no partnership agreement, the profit or loss will be shared equally.

It is important to remember that interest on capitals and partners' salaries is a method of sharing profit so that a partner's total share of profit includes these items.

Read questions carefully and note what the partners have agreed. If a question does not state what the partners have agreed about any of the matters in the Partnership Act listed above, apply the terms of the Act in your answer to the question.

21.2 How to prepare partnership accounts

Open the following accounts for each partner:

Capital
Drawings
Current

The Current account is used to complete the double entry from the partnership Profit and Loss and Appropriation Account for the partner's share of profits, losses, interest and salary. It is also credited with interest on a partner's loan to the firm, if any, from the Profit and Loss Account. At the end of the year, the balance on the partner's Drawings account is transferred to the debit of his Current account.

Note. If partners do not maintain Current accounts, the double entry for interest, their salaries and shares of profit must be completed in their Capital accounts.

Example 1

(No partnership agreement regarding interest, partners' salaries or sharing of profits/losses)

Michael and Charles began to trade as partners on 1 January 2003. Michael introduced $60 000 into the business as capital, and Charles contributed $40 000.

On 1 July 2003, Charles lent $10 000 to the business. The partnership trial balance at 31 December 2003 was as follows.

	$	$
Sales		300 000
Purchases	120 000	
Staff wages	42 000	
Rent	10 000	
Electricity	7 000	
Sundry expenses	5 400	
Premises at cost	60 000	
Fixtures and fittings at cost	28 000	
Trade debtors	5 460	
Trade creditors		2 860
Bank balance	94 000	
Capital accounts: Michael		60 000
Charles		40 000
Drawings Michael	24 000	
Charles	17 000	
Loan from Charles		10 000
	412 860	412 860

Further information

1. Stock at 31 December 2003: $18 000.
2. Depreciation is to be provided as follows.

   Premises: 5% per annum on cost

   Fixtures and fittings: $12\frac{1}{2}$% per annum on cost.

3. The partners had not made any agreement regarding interest on capital and drawings, salaries or sharing of profits and losses.

Required

(a) Prepare the Trading and Profit and Loss and Appropriation Account for the year ended 31 December 2003.

(b) Prepare the partners' Current accounts at 31 December 2003.

(c) Prepare the Balance Sheet at 31 December 2003.

Answer

(a)

Michael and Charles
Trading and Profit and Loss and Appropriation Account for the year ended 31 December 2003

	$	$	$
Sales			300 000
Less Cost of sales			
Purchases		120 000	
Less Stock at 31 December 2003		18 000	102 000
Gross profit			198 000
Staff wages		42 000	
Rent		10 000	
Electricity		7 000	
Sundry expenses		5 400	
Depreciation: Premises	3000		
Fixtures and fittings	3500	6 500	
Interest on loan (6 months at 5% p.a.)		250	71 150
Net profit			126 850
Shares of profit Michael ($\frac{1}{2}$)		63 425	
Charles ($\frac{1}{2}$)		63 425	126 850

(b)

Partners' Current accounts

		Michael	Charles			Michael	Charles
2003		$	$	2003		$	$
Dec 31	Drawings	24 000	17 000	Dec 31	Interest on loan	–	250
	Balances c/d	39 425	46 675		Share of profit	63 425	63 425
		63 425	63 675			63 425	63 675
				2004			
				Jan 1	Balance b/d	39 425	46 675

(c)

Balance Sheet at 31 December 2003

	Cost $	Dep. $	NBV $
Fixed assets			
Premises	60 000	3 000	57 000
Fixtures and fittings	28 000	3 500	24 500
	88 000	6 500	81 500
Current assets			
Stock		18 000	
Trade debtors		5 460	
Bank		94 000	
		117 460	
Current liabilities: Trade creditors		2 860	114 600
			196 100
Long-term liability: Loan from Charles			10 000
			186 100
Capital accounts: Michael		60 000	
Charles		40 000	100 000
Current accounts: Michael		39 425	
Charles		46 675	86 100
			186 100

Example 2

(Partnership agreement in place)

Data as in example 1 above, with the following additional information.

The partnership agreement includes the following terms.

- Interest on capitals and drawings: 5% per annum.
- Partnership salaries (per annum): Michael $20 000; Charles $10 000.
- The balance of profits and losses is to be shared as follows: Michael $\frac{2}{3}$; Charles $\frac{1}{3}$.
- Charles is to be credited with interest on his loan to the partnership at a rate of 8% per annum.

Required

(a) Prepare the Trading and Profit and Loss and Appropriation Account for the year ended 31 December 2003.

(b) Prepare the partners' Current accounts at 31 December 2003.

Answer

(a)

Michael and Charles
Trading and Profit and Loss and Appropriation Account for the year ended 31 December 2003

		$	$	$
Sales				300 000
Less Cost of sales				
Purchases			120 000	
Less Stock at 31 December 2003			18 000	102 000
Gross profit				198 000
Staff wages			42 000	
Rent			10 000	
Electricity			7 000	
Sundry expenses			5 400	
Depreciation: Premises		3 000		
Fixtures and fittings		3 500	6 500	
Interest on loan (6 months)			400	71 300
Net profit				126 700
Add Interest on drawings:	Michael		1 200	
	Charles		850	2 050
				128 750
Less Interest on capitals:	Michael		3 000	
	Charles		2 000	
			5 000	
Partners' salaries:	Michael		20 000	
	Charles		10 000	35 000
				93 750
Shares of profit	Michael ($\frac{2}{3}$)		62 500	
	Charles ($\frac{1}{3}$)		31 250	93 750

(b)

Partners' Current accounts

		Michael	Charles				Michael	Charles
2003		$	$	2003			$	$
Dec 31	Drawings	24 000	17 000	Dec 31	Interest on capital		3 000	2 000
	Interest on drawings	1 200	850		Interest on loan		–	400
					Salary		20 000	10 000
	Balance c/d	60 300	25 800		Share of profit		62 500	31 250
		85 500	43 650				85 500	43 650
				2004				
				Jan 1	Balance	b/d	60 300	25 800

Exercise 1

(No partnership agreement)
Tee and Leef are trading in partnership. Their trial balance at 31 March 2004 is as follows.

		$	$
Capital accounts at 1 April 2003:	Tee		100 000
	Leef		50 000
Current accounts at 1 April 2003:	Tee		5 000
	Leef		10 000
Drawing accounts:	Tee	29 000	
	Leef	31 000	
Sales			215 000
Purchases		84 000	
Stock at 1 April 2003		16 000	
Selling expenses		30 000	
Administration expenses		42 000	
Fixtures and fittings at cost		48 000	
Provision for depreciation of fixtures and fittings			8 000
Office equipment at cost		27 000	
Provision for depreciation of office equipment			5 000
Trade debtors		24 000	
Trade creditors			11 000
Bank balance		85 000	
Loan from Leef			12 000
		416 000	416 000

Further information

1. Stock at 31 March 2004: $20 000.
2. Selling expenses prepaid at 31 March 2004: $6000.
3. Administration expenses accrued at 31 March 2004: $4000.
4. Depreciation is to be provided as follows: on fixtures and fittings 10% of cost; on office equipment 20% of cost.
5. Leef made the loan to the business on 1 April 2003.
6. The partners had not made any agreement regarding interest, salaries or profit sharing.

Required
(a) Prepare the partnership Trading, Profit and Loss and Appropriation Account for the year ended 31 March 2004.
(b) Prepare partners' Current accounts at 31 March 2004 in columnar form.
(c) Prepare the partnership Balance Sheet at 31 March 2004.

Exercise 2

(Partnership agreement in place)
The facts are as in exercise 1, but Tee and Leaf have a partnership agreement which includes the following terms.

1. Leef is to be credited with interest on his loan to the partnership at the rate of 10% per annum.
2. The partners are allowed interest at 10% per annum on capitals and are charged interest at 10% per annum on drawings.
3. Leef is entitled to a salary of $4000 per annum.
4. The balance of profit/loss is to be shared as follows: Tee $\frac{3}{5}$; Leef $\frac{2}{5}$.

Required
(a) Prepare the partnership Trading, Profit and Loss and Appropriation Account for the year ended 31 March 2004.
(b) Prepare the partners' Current accounts at 31 March 2004 in columnar form.
(c) Prepare the partnership Balance Sheet at 31 March 2004.

21.3 Advantages and disadvantages of partnerships

Advantages

- The capital invested by partners is often more than can be raised by a sole trader.
- A greater fund of knowledge, experience and expertise in running a business is available to a partnership.
- A partnership may be able to offer a greater range of services to its customers (or clients).
- The business does not have to close down or be run by inexperienced staff in the absence of one of the partners; the other partner(s) will provide cover.
- Losses are shared by all partners

Disadvantages

- A partner has not the same freedom to act independently as a sole trader has.
- A partner may be frustrated by the other partner(s) in his or her plans for the direction and development of the business.
- Profits have to be shared by all partners.
- A partner may be legally liable for acts of the other partner(s).

21.4 Examination hints

- Learn the provisions of the Partnership Act 1890 as they affect partners' rights to salaries, interest and sharing of profits and losses.
- Read each question carefully to see if you have to apply the terms of a partnership agreement or the provisions of the Partnership Act 1890.
- Debit interest on a partner's loan to the firm in the Profit and Loss Account and credit it to the partner's Current account.
- Do not debit partners' drawings to the Appropriation Account.
- Complete the double entries from the Appropriation Account to the partners' Current accounts.
- Transfer the end-of-year balances on the partners' Drawings accounts to their Current accounts.
- If partners do not maintain Current accounts, the entries to Current accounts referred to above must be made in their Capital accounts instead.
- Tick every item in the question as you give effect to it. Check that all items are ticked before copying out your answer.

21.5 Multiple-choice questions

1 Cue and Rest are partners sharing profits and losses in the ratio of 2 : 1. They are allowed interest at 10% per annum on capitals and loans to the partnership.
   Other information is as follows.

	Cue		Rest
	$		$
Capitals	20 000		8000
Loan to firm	3 000	–	

The partnership has made a net profit for the year of $40 000.

How much is Cue's total share of the profit?

A $24 800

B $25 100

C $26 800

D $27 100

2 Stump and Bail are in partnership. Stump has lent the partnership $10 000 on which he is entitled to interest at 10%. He is also entitled to a salary of $12 000 per annum. Profits and losses are shared equally. The partnership has made a net loss of $25 000.

How much is Stump's share of the loss?

A $500

B $5500

C $6000

D $6500

3 Gohl and Poast are partners sharing profits and losses equally. Gohl has lent the partnership $8000 on which he is entitled to interest at 10% per annum. The partners are entitled to annual salaries as follows: Gohl $6000; Poast $4000. The partnership has made a profit of $5000. How much is Gohl's share of the profit?

A $3500

B $3900

C $8500

D $9300

21.6 Additional exercises

1 The following trial balance has been extracted from the books of Bell and Binn at 30 April 2004.

	$	$
Sales		425 000
Purchases	200 000	
Stock at 1 May 2003	30 000	
Wages	98 000	
Rent	25 000	
Heating and lighting	16 000	
Office expenses	12 600	
Vehicle expenses	5 510	
Advertising	3 500	
Bad debts written off	416	
Plant and machinery at cost	125 000	
Provision for Depreciation of Plant and Machinery		36 000
Motor vehicles at cost	41 000	
Provision for Depreciation of Motor Vehicles		22 000
Trade debtors and creditors	45 750	18 000
Provision for Doubtful Debts		1 000
Bank balance	15 724	
Loan from Bell		60 000
Capital accounts: Bell		50 000
Binn		40 000
Current accounts: Bell		7 000
Binn		3 000
Drawing accounts: Bell	30 000	
Binn	13 500	
	662 000	662 000

Further information

1. Stock at 30 April 2004 is valued at $27 000.

2. Bell is to be credited with interest on the loan at a rate of 10% per annum.

3. The bank reconciliation shows that bank interest of $314 and bank charges of $860 have been debited in the bank statements. These amounts have not been entered in the cash book.

4. At 30 April 2004, rent of $1500 and advertising of $2000 have been paid in advance.

5. Depreciation is to be provided as follows.
   (i) Plant and machinery: 10% per annum on cost
   (ii) Motor vehicles: 20% per annum on their written down values

6. The partners are to be charged interest on drawings and allowed interest on capitals at a rate of 10% per annum.

7. Partnership salaries are to be allowed as follows: Bell $10 000 per annum; Binn $8000 per annum.

8. The balance of profits and losses is to be shared as follows: Bell $\frac{3}{5}$; Binn $\frac{2}{5}$.

Required

(a) Prepare the partnership Trading, Profit and Loss and Appropriation Accounts for the year ended 30 April 2004

(b) Prepare the partners' Current accounts for the year ended 30 April 2004.

(c) Prepare the Balance Sheet at 30 April 2004.

2 Mill has been a second-hand car dealer for some years. His Trading and Profit and Loss Account for the year ended 31 December 2003 was as follows.

	$	$
Sales		160 000
Less Cost of sales		95 000
Gross profit		65 000
Wages	31 000	
Rent	7 000	
Heating and lighting	4 000	
Advertising	1 000	
Sundry expenses	2 400	45 400
Net profit		19 600

Mill's net profits for the previous two years were as follows.

		$
Year ended:	31 December 2001	30 000
	31 December 2002	24 000

Mill's friend, Grist, has also been trading for some years repairing and servicing motor vehicles. Grist's net profits for the past three years have been as follows.

		$
Year ended:	31 December 2001	11 600
	31 December 2002	14 500
	31 December 2003	18 000

The lease on Grist's premises is about to expire, and Grist has suggested to Mill that the two businesses should be combined and that he and Mill should become partners.

Mill estimates that combining the businesses will immediately improve his net profit by 10% and that the improvement will be maintained in future years. Grist estimates that his net profit will be increased by 20% and that this increase will also be maintained in the future.

The proposed partnership agreement would provide as follows.

> Capitals: Mill $20 000; Grist $30 000
>
> Interest on capitals to be allowed at 10% per annum.
>
> The balance of profits and losses to be shared equally.

Required

(a) Prepare a forecast Profit and Loss Appropriation Account of the partnership for the year ending 31 December 2004, assuming the partnership is formed on 1 January 2004.

(b) State, with reasons, whether Mill should agree to Grist becoming a partner in the combined businesses.

3 Senter and Harf have prepared their draft Balance Sheet as at 30 June 2004 as follows.

	$	$
Fixed assets		
Fixtures and fittings at cost	45 000	
Less Depreciation to date	34 500	10 500
Current assets		
Stock	28 500	
Debtors	24 000	
Bank	9 000	
	61 500	
Less Current liabilities		
Creditors	12 000	49 500
		60 000
Less Long-term loan – Senter		15 000
		45 000
Capital accounts: Senter	22 000	
Harf	14 000	36 000
Current accounts: Senter	7 500	
Harf	1 500	9 000
		45 000

It has now been discovered that the following errors and omissions have been made.

1. Some fixtures and fittings were sold for $3500 in January 2004. These items had cost $15 000 and their net book value at 30 June 2003 was $4500. The sale proceeds were credited to the Fixtures and Fittings at Cost account. No further entries had been made in the books for this sale.

   (The partnership provides for depreciation on the straight-line basis at a rate of 10% on the balance on the Fixtures and Fittings account at the end of each financial year.)

2. Interest at the rate of 10% per annum is to be provided on the long-term loan from Senter for the year ended 30 June 2004.

3. The accounts for the year ended 30 June 2003 included stock-in-trade at 30 June 2003 in the sum of $20 000. The correct value of the stock should have been $30 000. The partners have agreed that this error should be corrected in the partnership accounts.

4. The partners have decided that a provision for doubtful debts equal to 4% of the debtors should be provided in the accounts.

5. An adjustment should be made for the prepaid rent at 30 June 2004 in the sum of $750.

6. During the year ended 30 June 2004, Harf had taken goods costing $1075 for his personal use.

Further information

In addition to the interest allowed on Senter's loan, the partners are allowed interest at 10% per annum on their Capital account balances. The balance of profits and losses are divided between Senter and Harf in the ratio of 3 : 2.

Required

Prepare a corrected Balance Sheet as at 30 June 2004 for the partnership.

22 Partnership changes

22.1 What is a partnership change?

A change in a partnership occurs:

- when partners agree to change the way in which profits and losses are to be shared
- when a new partner joins a firm, or an existing partner leaves.

22.2 How to account for changes in the allocation of profits or losses between partners

Partners may change the way in which profits and losses are to be shared. The change may occur at any date, and the partnership continues whether the change takes place at the start of a new financial year or during the year.

All profits that have been earned and losses that have been incurred before the change must be shared in the old profit/loss-sharing ratio. Subsequent profits and losses must be shared in the new profit/loss-sharing ratio. In each case, profits and losses include realised *and* unrealised profits and losses.

Realised profits and losses are those that are recognised in the Profit and Loss Account. They are usually apportioned on a time basis, but there may be exceptional circumstances. For example, the new partnership agreement may provide for the rate of interest on a partner's loan to be changed; or for a partner to make a loan to the firm; or for the repayment of a loan. The interest on the loan, in these cases, must be apportioned on an actual and not on a time basis.

Unrealised profits and losses are gains and losses arising from the revaluation of assets and liabilities at the date of the change in the profit/loss-sharing agreement and will result in adjustments to the partners' capitals.

Assets and liabilities may have different values at the date of a change in the profit/loss-sharing ratio from the values shown in the last available Balance Sheet. Some assets may not even be shown in the Balance Sheet; an example is **Goodwill** (see §22.4). The partners' Capital accounts will not show their actual interest in the firm unless they are adjusted to reflect the real net asset value of the business. This is a matter of importance when the partnership is dissolved or there is a change in the composition of the partnership.

Unrealised profits and losses must be attributed to the period in which they arose (matching concept). In what follows, the accounting procedures will be explained for:

- adjusting partners' Capital accounts for unrealised profits and losses
- apportioning realised profit and losses in Profit and Loss Accounts.

22.3 How to amend a Balance Sheet following a revaluation of net assets

Revaluation of net assets

Net assets are assets less liabilities. The values of the assets and liabilities must be considered and revalued, if necessary, at the date of a partnership change. Any increase or decrease in values is adjusted through a Revaluation account to the partners' Capital accounts. The adjustments must be made in their old profit-sharing ratios because any gain or loss in values has occurred before the ratios were changed.

Example

Grace and Grant are in partnership, sharing profits and losses in the ratio of 2 : 1. On 1 July 2004 they agree to change the profit-sharing ratio so that they will share profits and losses equally in future. The partnership Balance Sheet at 31 December 2003 was as follows.

	$	$
Fixed assets at net book values		
Freehold premises		60 000
Plant and machinery		35 000
Motor vehicles		23 000
		118 000
Current assets		
Stock	29 000	
Debtors	13 000	
Bank	8 000	
	50 000	
Current liabilities		
Creditors	7 000	43 000
		161 000
Capitals		
Grace		90 000
Grant		71 000
		161 000

The partners agree that the assets shall be revalued at 30 June 2004 as follows.

	$
Freehold premises	100 000
Plant and machinery	30 000
Motor vehicles	20 000
Stock	25 000
Debtors	12 000

Required

(a) Prepare the journal entries to give effect to the revaluation of the assets in the partnership books.

(b) Prepare a redrafted Balance Sheet as at 30 June 2004 after the assets have been revalued.

Answer

(a)

Journal	$	$
Freehold premises	40 000	
Plant and machinery		5 000
Motor vehicles		3 000
Stock		4 000
Debtors control		1 000
Revaluation account		27 000

Revaluation of assets at 30 June 2004

Revaluation account	27 000	
Capital accounts: Grace		18 000
Grant		9 000

Profit on revaluation of assets credited to the partners' Capital accounts in their former profit sharing ratios: Grace $\frac{2}{3}$, Grant $\frac{1}{3}$.

(b)

Grace and Grant
Balance Sheet at 30 June 2004

	$	$
Fixed assets at net book values		
Freehold premises (60 000 + 40 000)		100 000
Plant and machinery (35 000 – 5000)		30 000
Motor vehicles (23 000 – 3000)		20 000
		150 000
Current assets		
Stock (29 000 – 4000)	25 000	
Debtors (13 000 – 1000)	12 000	
Bank	8 000	
	45 000	
Current liabilities		
Creditors	7 000	38 000
		188 000
Capitals		
Grace (90 000 + 18 000)		108 000
Grant (71 000 + 9000)		80 000
		188 000

Exercise 1

Tom and Tilly shared profits and losses equally until 1 September 2004 when they agreed that Tilly would be entitled to a salary of $10 000 per annum from that date. Profits and losses would continue to be shared equally.

The partnership Balance Sheet at 31 March 2004 was as follows.

	$	$
Fixed assets at net book values		
Freehold premises		40 000
Fixtures and fittings		18 000
Office equipment		7 000
		65 000
Current liabilities		
Stock	17 000	
Debtors	4 000	
Bank	6 000	
	27 000	
Current liabilities		
Creditors	3 000	24 000
		89 000
Capital accounts		
Tom		48 000
Tilley		41 000
		89 000

The partners agreed that the assets should be revalued at 1 September 2004 as follows.

	$
Freehold premises	65 000
Fixtures and fittings	15 000
Office equipment	5 000
Stock	14 000
Debtors	3 000

Required

(a) Prepare journal entries to give effect to the revaluation of the partnership assets at 1 September 2004.

(b) Prepare the partnership Balance Sheet as at 1 September 2004 to include the effects of revaluation of the assets.

22.4 How to account for Goodwill

Goodwill is the amount by which the value of a business as a going concern exceeds the value its net assets would realise if they were sold separately. It is an intangible asset; that is, it cannot be touched and felt as buildings, plant and machinery and other 'tangible' assets can be touched and felt.

Goodwill may not be shown in a Balance Sheet for reasons that will be explained later. Nevertheless it must be considered when a partnership change occurs.

Example

Will and Wendy are partners who have shared profits and losses in the ratio of Will $\frac{2}{3}$ and Wendy $\frac{1}{3}$. On 1 January 2005 they agree to share profits and losses equally in future. At that date the partnership assets and liabilities are recorded in the books at the following valuations.

	$
Premises	100 000
Fixtures and fittings	48 000
Motor vehicles	35 000
Stock	12 000
Debtors	6 000
	201 000
Less Creditors	3 250
Net assets	197 750

Will and Wendy have recently been informed that they can expect to receive $230 000 for their business if they decide to sell it. They have agreed to record Goodwill in the partnership books as from 1 January 2005, and to value the business at $230 000 for the purpose of valuing Goodwill. Goodwill is valued at $230 000 – 197 750) = $32 250. The journal entry to record the Goodwill is:

	$	$
Goodwill account	32 250	
Capital accounts: Will ($\frac{2}{3}$)		21 500
Wendy ($\frac{1}{3}$)		10 750

Goodwill recorded at valuation and credited to partners in their old profit-sharing ratios.

An account for Goodwill is opened in the partnership books.

Exercise 2

Vera and Ken are partners who have shared profits and losses equally. On 1 July 2005 they decide to change the profit-sharing ratio to: Vera $\frac{3}{5}$ and Ken $\frac{2}{5}$. The partnership assets and liabilities at book values at 1 July 2005 are as follows.

	$
Premises	140 000
Fixtures and fittings	65 000
Motor vehicles	35 000
Office equipment	15 000
Stock	6 500
Debtors	11 800
Bank	3 620
Creditors	5 830

The partners have been informed that the value of the business as a going concern is $300 000 and have decided to value Goodwill on this figure.

Required

(a) Calculate the value of Goodwill.
(b) Calculate the amounts to be credited to the partners' Capital accounts for Goodwill.

22.5 How to account for Goodwill when no Goodwill account is opened

Partners often do not wish to record Goodwill in their books for two reasons:

- the value placed on Goodwill is usually very difficult to justify, being a matter of opinion; it may not even exist
- if Goodwill is shown in a Balance Sheet at, say, $20 000 it would be very difficult to persuade a prospective purchaser of the business to pay more, even if the value had increased since Goodwill was first introduced into the books.

When there is a partnership change and the partners decide not to open a Goodwill account, the procedure to be followed is as follows.

Step 1 Credit the partners' Capital accounts with their share of Goodwill *in their old profit-sharing ratio*.

Step 2 Debit the partners' capital accounts with their share of the Goodwill *in their new profit-sharing ratio*.

Steps 1 and 2 can be combined in a single operation, as shown in the following example.

Example

Noat and Koyn have shared profits and losses in the ratio of 2 : 1 but have now agreed they will share profits and losses equally in future. Goodwill is valued at $30 000, and the partners' Capital accounts will be adjusted as follows.

Working:	Column A Goodwill shared in *old* profit-sharing ratio (credit Capital accounts)	Column B Goodwill shared in *new* profit-sharing ratio (debit Capital accounts)	Adjustment to Capital accounts (column A − column B)
	$	$	$
Noat	20 000	15 000	5000 Credit
Koyn	10 000	15 000	5000 Debit
	30 000	30 000	

The Capital account of a partner who loses a share of Goodwill is credited with the amount of the loss. The Capital account of a partner who gains a share of Goodwill is debited with the amount of the gain.

Thus, a partner who loses a share of Goodwill is compensated by a partner who gains a share.

In the example, Koyn has 'purchased' his increased share of Goodwill from Noat. A Goodwill account has not been opened.

Exercise 3

Punch and Judy have shared profits and losses in the ratio of 2 : 1. On 1 October 2004 they agree to share profits and losses as follows in future: Punch $\frac{3}{5}$, Judy $\frac{2}{5}$. Goodwill is valued at $18 000. The balances on their Capital accounts before the change in the profit/loss-sharing ratio are: Punch $36 000; Judy $14 000. A Goodwill account is *not* to be opened in the books.

Required

(a) Calculate the adjustments to be made to the Capital accounts.
(b) Prepare the partners' Capital accounts to show the adjustments for Goodwill.

22.6 Apportionment of profit

Partnership changes often occur in the middle of a firm's financial year. If a Profit and Loss Account is not prepared at the time of the change, the profit or loss for the financial year must be apportioned between the periods before and after the change.

If the profit is assumed to have been earned evenly throughout the year, it should be divided between the old and new partnerships on a time basis. However, some expenses may not have been incurred on a time basis and these must be allocated to the period to which they belong. Such expenses will be specified in a question. Apportionment of profit or loss is shown in a Profit and Loss Account prepared in columnar form as in the following example.

Example

Old and New are partners sharing profits and losses equally after allowing Old a salary of $10 000 per annum. On 1 January 2004 their Capital and Current account balances were as follows.

	Old	New
	$	$
Capital accounts	25 000	20 000
Current accounts	7 500	5 000

On 1 July 2004, the partners agree to the following revised terms of partnership.

1. Old to transfer $5000 from his Capital account to a Loan account on which he would be entitled to interest at 10% per annum.
2. New to bring his private car into the firm at a valuation of $12 000.
3. New to receive a salary of $5000 per annum.
4. Profits and losses to be shared: Old $\frac{3}{5}$, New $\frac{2}{5}$

Further information for the year ended 31 December 2004 is as follows.

	$
Sales (spread evenly throughout the year)	200 000
Cost of sales	87 500
Rent	25 000
Wages	35 000
General expenses	15 000

Of the general expenses, $5000 was incurred in the six months to 30 June 2004.

New's car is to be depreciated over four years on the straight-line basis and is assumed to have no value at the end of that time.

All sales produce a uniform rate of gross profit.

Required

(a) Prepare the Trading and Profit and Loss and Appropriation Accounts for the year ended 31 December 2004.
(b) Prepare the partners' Current accounts for the year ended 31 December 2004.

Answer

Old and New
Trading and Profit and Loss and Appropriation Account for the year ended 31 December 2004

	$
Sales	200 000
Less Cost of sales	87 500
Gross profit carried down	112 500

	6 months to 30 June 2004		6 months to 31 December 2004		Year to 31 December 2004	
	$	$	$	$	$	$
Gross profit brought down		56 250		56 250		112 500
Rent	12 500		12 500		25 000	
Wages	17 500		17 500		35 000	
General expenses	5 000		10 000		15 000	
Interest on loan	–		250		250	
Depreciation – car	–		1 500		1 500	
		35 000		41 750		76 750
Net profit		21 250		14 500		35 750
Less						
Salary: Old		5 000		–	5 000	
New		–		2 500	2 500	7 500
		16 250		12 000		28 250
Share of profit: Old ($\frac{1}{2}$) 8 125			($\frac{3}{5}$) 7 200		15 325	
New ($\frac{1}{2}$) 8 125	16 250		($\frac{2}{5}$) 4 800	12 000	12 925	28 250

(b)

	Old	New			Old	New
2004	$	$	2004		$	$
Dec 31 Balance c/d	27 825	20 425	Jan 1 Balance b/d		7 500	5 000
			Dec 31 Salary		5 000	2 500
			Share of profit		15 325	12 925
	27 825	20 425			27 825	20 425
			2005			
			Jan 1 Balance b/d		27 825	20 425

Exercise 4

Hook, Line and Sinker have shared profits and losses in the ratio 3 : 2 : 1 for a number of years. On 1 July 2004, the partners agreed that, from that date,

1. Hook will be entitled to a salary of $6000 per annum

2. profits and losses will be shared equally.

Information extracted from their books for the year ended 31 December 2004 was as follows.

	$
Sales	129 500
Cost of sales	66 500
Wages	14 000
General expenses	5 250
Depreciation of fixed assets	1 750

Two thirds of the General expenses were incurred in the six months ended 31 December 2004.

On 1 April 2004, Hook made a loan of $8000 to the partnership. Interest on the loan is at a rate of 10% per annum.

Sales have accrued evenly throughout the year and all sales have earned a uniform rate of gross profit.

Required

Prepare a Trading and Profit and Loss Account for the year ended 31 December 2004 in columnar form to show the appropriation of profit before and after the change.

22.7 How to account for the introduction of a new, or the retirement of an existing, partner

When a partner leaves a firm, or a new partner joins, it marks the end of one partnership and the beginning of a new one. As in the case of a simple change in profit-sharing ratios, a change in partners may occur at any time in a firm's financial year, and no entries may be made in the books to record the change until the end of the year.

The procedures are similar to those already described in §22.2. Account must be taken of:

- asset revaluation
- Goodwill
- changes in the profit/loss-sharing ratios.

If a partnership change occurs on the first day of a firm's financial year, the procedure is so straightforward that it is unlikely to form the basis of an examination question. There is no reason why partners should join on the first day of a firm's financial year, or why one should leave on the last day of the financial year. In practice, changes usually occur during a financial year and the accounting records are continued without interruption; final accounts are not produced until the end of the year.

Example 1

(Admission of new partner)
Grey and Green have shared profits and losses in the ratio of 3 : 2. On 1 October 2004 they decided to admit Blue as a partner. No entries to record Blue's admittance as a partner were made in the books before the end of the financial year on 31 December 2004.

Information extracted from the books for the year ended 31 December 2004 included the following.

	$	
Turnover	400 000	
Cost of sales	240 000	
Wages	40 000	
Rent	8 000	
General expenses	9 600	
Depreciation of fixed assets:		
1 January to 30 September 2004	6 000	
1 October to 31 December 2004	4 350	(based on asset revaluation as shown below)

At 31 December 2003 the balances on Grey and Green's Capital and Current accounts were as follows.

	Capital accounts	Current accounts
	$	$
Grey	50 000	2000
Green	30 000	3000

On 1 October 2004, the partnership assets were revalued as follows.

	$	
Freehold premises	50 000	increase
Other fixed assets	14 000	decrease
Current assets	3 000	decrease

The partners agreed the value of Goodwill at 1 October 2004 at $40 000 and decided that no Goodwill account should be opened in the books.

On 1 October 2004 Blue paid $20 000 into the firm's bank account as capital. On the same day, Grey lent the partnership $20 000. He is entitled to interest at a rate of 10% per annum on the loan.

The balances on the partners' Drawings account at 31 December 2004 were as follows.

	$
Grey	23 000
Green	17 000
Blue	3 000

The new partnership agreement provided for the following as from 1 October 2004.

(i) Interest was allowed on the balances on Capital accounts at 31 December each year at a rate of 5% per annum.
(ii) Green was entitled to a salary of $12 000 per annum.
(iii) The balance of profits and losses were to be shared: Grey $\frac{2}{5}$; Green $\frac{2}{5}$: Blue $\frac{1}{5}$.

Required

(a) Prepare the Capital accounts of Grey, Green and Blue at 31 December 2004.
(b) Prepare the Partnership Trading, Profit and Loss and Appropriation Account for the year ended 31 December 2004.
(c) Prepare the partners' Current accounts at 31 December 2004.

Answer

Working: Goodwill		Before 1.10.04		After 1.10.04	Capital accounts
		$		$	$
Grey $(\frac{3}{5})$		24 000	$(\frac{2}{5})$	16 000	8000 credit
Green $(\frac{2}{5})$		16 000	$(\frac{2}{5})$	16 000	no change
Blue		–	$(\frac{1}{5})$	8 000	8000 debit

(a)

Partners' Capital accounts

2004		Grey $	Green $	Blue $	2004		Grey $	Green $	Blue $
Oct 1	Green – Goodwill			8 000	Jan 1	Balance b/d	50 000	30 000	–
Dec 31	Balance c/d	77 800	43 200	12 000	Oct 1	Bank	–	–	20 000
						Profit on revaluation	19 800	13 200	–
						Goodwill	8 000		
		77 800	43 200	20 000			77 800	43 200	20 000
					2005				
					Jan 1	Balance b/d	77 800	43 200	12 000

(b)

Grey, Green and Blue
Trading and Profit and Loss and Appropriation Accounts for the year ended 31 December 2004

	$
Turnover	400 000
Less Cost of sales	240 000
Gross profit carried down	160 000

		9 months to 30 June 2004		3 months to 31 December 2004		Year to 31 December 2004	
		$	$	$	$	$	$
Gross profit brought down			120 000		40 000		160 000
Wages		30 000		10 000		40 000	
Rent		6 000		2 000		8 000	
General expenses		7 200		2 400		9 600	
Interest on loan		–		500		500	
Depreciation		6 000	49 200	4 350	19 250	10 350	68 450
Net profit			70 800		20 750		91 550
Interest on capitals:	Grey			973			
	Green			540			
	Blue			150			
				1 663			
Salary: Green				3 000	4 663		4 663
					16 087		86 887
Profit shares:	Grey	$(\frac{3}{5})$ 42 480		$(\frac{2}{5})$ 6 435		48 915	
	Green	$(\frac{2}{5})$ 28 320		$(\frac{2}{5})$ 6 435		34 755	
	Blue	–	70 800	$(\frac{1}{5})$ 3 217	16 087	3 217	86 887

(c)

Partners' Current accounts

2004			Grey $	Green $	Blue $	2004			Grey $	Green $	Blue $
Dec 31	Drawings		23 000	17 000	3 000	Jan 1	Balance	b/d	2 000	3 000	–
Dec 31	Balance	c/d	29 388	24 295	367	Dec 31	Loan interest		500	–	–
							Interest on				
							capital		973	540	150
							Salary		–	3 000	–
							Profit		48 915	34 755	3 217
			52 388	41 295	3 367				52 388	41 295	3 367
2005						Jan 1	Balance	b/d	29 388	24 295	367

Exercise 5

Bell and Booker have been partners for some years, making up their accounts annually to 31 December. The partnership agreement contained the following provisions.

- Interest was allowed on capitals at 10% per annum.
- Booker was entitled to a salary of $15 000 per annum.
- Profits and losses were to be shared: Bell $\frac{2}{3}$; Booker $\frac{1}{3}$.

At 31 December 2003 the partners' Capital and Current account balances were as follows.

	Capitals $	Current accounts $
Bell	100 000	16 000
Booker	60 000	12 000

On 1 September 2004, Bell and Booker admitted their manager, Candell, as a partner. Candell had been receiving a salary of $24 000.

The revised partnership agreement provided as follows.

- Partner's salary: Booker $18 000 per annum.
- Interest on capitals at 10% per annum.
- Profits and losses shared: Bell $\frac{2}{5}$, Booker $\frac{2}{5}$, Candell $\frac{1}{5}$.

The partnership's fixed assets at cost at 31 December 2003 were as follows.

	At cost $	Depreciation to date $	Net book value $
Freehold premises	180 000	45 000	135 000
Plant and machinery	90 000	60 000	30 000
Motor cars	30 000	27 000	3 000
Office equipment	21 000	14 000	7 000

No additions to, or disposals of, fixed assets had taken place between 31 December 2003 and 31 August 2004.

The assets were revalued at 1 September as follows.

	$
Freehold premises	210 000
Plant and machinery	27 000
Motor cars	3 000
Office equipment	6 000

Depreciation of fixed assets is calculated on cost and is provided as follows: freehold premises 4% per annum; plant and machinery 20% per annum; motor cars 25% per annum; office equipment 10% per annum.

Goodwill was valued at $60 000, but no Goodwill account was to be opened in the books.

On 1 September 2004, Candell paid $50 000 into the firm's bank account as capital, and also brought his private car, valued at $9000, into the business. On the same day, Bell transferred $20 000 from his Capital account to a loan account on which interest is to be paid at a rate of 12% per annum.

The following information is available from the partnership books for the year ended 31 December 2004.

	$
Turnover	600 000
Cost of sales	330 000
Wages and salaries	106 000
Rent	42 000
Heating and lighting	6 000
Sundry expenses	12 000

Note. Sales were spread evenly throughout the year and earned a uniform rate of gross profit.

Drawings in the year ended 31 December 2004 were: Bell $30 000; Booker $40 000; Candell $4000.

Required

(a) Prepare a Trading, Profit and Loss and Appropriation Account for the year ended 31 December 2004.

(b) Prepare the partners' Capital and Current accounts for the year ended 31 December 2004.

Example 2

(Partner retires)

Norman, Beard and David have traded in partnership for some years. Norman decided to retire on 30 September 2004 but no accounts were prepared for the partnership until the end of the financial year on 31 December 2004.

The following balances have been extracted from the trial balance at 31 December 2004.

	$	$
Sales		720 000
Purchases	400 000	
Stock at 1 January 2004	20 000	
Wages	100 000	
Rent	26 000	
Heating and lighting	21 000	
Sundry expenses	120 000	

Further information

1. Stock at 31 December 2004 cost $24 000.

2. At 31 December 2004 rent of $2000 had been prepaid and $1200 had accrued for heating and lighting.

3. Fixed assets at 1 January 2004 at cost were as follows.

	$
Plant and machinery	80 000
Office equipment	10 000

Additional machinery was purchased on 1 October 2004 for $12 000.

4. Depreciation of fixed assets is to be provided at 10% per annum on cost.

5. Goodwill was valued at $45 000, but no Goodwill was to be recorded in the books.

6. The partners' Capital and Current account balances at 1 January 2004 were as follows.

	Capital accounts	Current accounts
	$	$
Norman	50 000	8 000 (Cr)
Beard	40 000	9 000 (Cr)
David	20 000	3 000 (Cr)

7. The partners' drawings were as follows.

	$
Norman (up to 30 September 2004)	30 000
Up to 31 December 2004:	
Beard	50 000
David	32 000

8. Norman left $60 000 of his capital in the business as a loan with interest at 10% per annum. The interest was payable on 30 June and 31 December each year.

9. The partnership agreement up to 30 September 2004 allowed for the following.

Interest on capitals: 8% per annum (based on balances on Capital accounts at 1 January 2004).

Salary: David $6000 per annum.

Profit and losses to be shared: Norman $\left(\frac{1}{2}\right)$, Beard $\left(\frac{1}{3}\right)$, David $\left(\frac{1}{6}\right)$.

The agreement was amended on 1 October 2004 as follows.

Interest on capitals: 10% per annum (based on balances on Capital accounts at 1 October 2003).

Salary: David $10 000 per annum.

Profits and losses to be shared: Beard $\left(\frac{3}{5}\right)$, David $\left(\frac{2}{5}\right)$.

10. The assets were not revalued at 30 September 2004.

11. It is assumed that gross profit has been earned evenly throughout the year.

Required

(a) Prepare the partners' Capital accounts.

(b) Prepare the partnership's Trading, Profit and Loss and Appropriation Accounts for the year ended 31 December 2004.

(c) Prepare the partners' Current accounts for the year ended 31 December 2004.

Answer
(a)

Partners' Capital accounts

	Norman $	Beard $	David $				Norman $	Beard $	David $
2004					**2004**				
Sep 30 Goodwill		12 000	10 500		Jan 1	Balance b/d	50 000	40 000	20 000
Loan a/c	60 000				Sep 30	Goodwill	22 500		
Bank	46 750					Current a/c	34 250*		
Dec 31 Balance c/d		28 000	9 500						
	106 750	40 000	20 000				106 750	40 000	20 000
2005									
					Jan 1	Balance b/d		28 000	9 500

* The balance on the outgoing partner's Current account is transferred to Capital account.

(b)

Norman, Beard and David
Trading and Profit and Loss and Appropriation Accounts for the year ended 31 December 2004

	$	$
Sales		720 000
Less Cost of sales		
Stock at 1.1.04	20 000	
Purchases	400 000	
	420 000	
Less Stock at 31.12.04	24 000	396 000
Gross profit		324 000

	9 months to 30.9.04		3 months to 31.12.04		Total	
	$	$	$	$	$	$
Gross profit		243 000		81 000		324 000
Wages	75 000		25 000		100 000	
Rent (26 000 – 2000)	18 000		6 000		24 000	
Heating and lighting (21 000 + 1200)	16 650		5 550		22 200	
Sundry expenses	9 000		3 000		12 000	
Depreciation: Plant and machinery	6 000		2 300		8 300	
Office equipment	750		250		1 000	
Interest on loan	–	125 400	1 500	43 600	1 500	169 000
Net profit		117 600		37 400		155 000
Interest on capital: Norman	3 000		–		3 000	
Beard	2 400		700†		3 100	
David	1 200		238†	–	1 438	
	6 600		938		7 538	
Salary David	4 500	11 100	2 500	3 438	7 000	14 538
		106 500		33 962		140 462
Shares of profit Norman	53 250		–		53 250	
Beard	35 500		20 377		55 877	
David	17 750	106 500	13 585	33 962	31 335	140 462

† On capitals of $28 000 and $9500 respectively.

(c)

Partner's Current accounts

		Norman	Beard	David			Norman	Beard	David
2004		$	$	$	2004		$	$	$
Sep 30	Drawings	30 000			Jan 1	Balance b/d	8 000	9 000	3 000
	Capital a/c	34 250*			Sep 30	Int. on Capital	3 000		
						Profit	53 250		
Dec 31	Drawings		50 000	32 000	Dec 31	Int. on Capital		3 100	1 438
	Balance c/d		17 977	10 773		Salary			7 000
			———	———		Profit	———	55 877	31 335
		64 250	67 977	42 773			64 250	67 977	42 773
					2005				
					Jan 1	Balance b/d		17 977	10 773

* The balance on the outgoing partner's Current account is transferred to Capital account.

Exercise 6

Wilfrid, Hide and Wyte were partners sharing profits and losses in the ratio of 3 : 2 : 1 after charging interest on capitals at 10% per annum. Their Capital and Current account balances at 1 July 2003 were as follows.

	Capital a/cs	Current a/cs
	$	$
Wilfrid	80 000	12 000
Hide	50 000	3 000
Wyte	30 000	4 000

Wilfrid decided to retire on 31 December 2003. He left $75 000 of the balance on his Capital account as a loan to the firm, with interest at 10% per annum. The balance on his Capital account was paid to him by cheque.

At 31 December 2003, Goodwill was valued at $60 000 but Goodwill was not to be shown in the books. It was also agreed that the partnership assets should be revalued at $21 000 less than their current book values.

Hide and Wyte continued in partnership from 1 January 2004, with interest allowed on capitals at 10% per annum and with profits and losses being shared equally.

The partners' drawings in the year ended 30 June 2004 were as follows.

	$
Wilfrid (6 months to 31 December 2003)	23 000
Hide (12 months to 30 June 2004)	28 000
Wyte (12 months to 30 June 2004)	18 000

Further information

1.

		$
Gross profit for the year ended 30 June 2004		187 000 (assumed to have been earned evenly throughout the year.)
Expenditure for the year ended 30 June 2004:		
	Wages	91 000
	Rent paid	14 000
	Electricity paid	7 000
	Sundry expenses	9 000

2. At 30 June 2004, rent of $2000 had been paid in advance, and electricity in the amount of $1400 had accrued.

Required

(a) Prepare the partnership Profit and Loss and Appropriation Account for the year ended 30 June 2004.

(b) Prepare the Capital and Current accounts of the partnership for the year ended 30 June 2004.

22.8 Examination hints

- Read questions involving partnership changes very carefully two or three times before starting to answer them. Highlight or underline important information and instructions. Tick every item as you give effect to it in your answer.

- Treat partnership changes as the ending of one partnership and the commencement of a new one.
- A partnership change requires separate Profit and Loss accounts to be prepared for the old and new firms. It will normally be assumed that revenue has been earned evenly over the whole period before and after the change. Apportion expenses in the Profit and Loss Account on a time basis unless any expense has to be apportioned on some other basis. Perform your arithmetical calculations carefully and show your workings
- Adjust for accrued and prepaid expenses before apportioning them.
- Partners' salaries, interest on drawings and capital will be stated in the question on an annual basis. These must be apportioned on a time basis.
- Read partnership questions very carefully to see whether or not a Goodwill account is to be opened when there is a partnership change.
- If a Goodwill account is not to be opened, Goodwill is credited to the partners' Capital accounts before the change in their old profit-sharing ratio, and debited after the change to the partners' Capital accounts in their new profit-sharing ratio.
- When assets are revalued on a partnership change, they are retained in the books of the new partnership at their new values.
- The balances on an outgoing partner's Current and Drawings accounts must be transferred to his Capital account. Make sure you treat the final balance on his Capital account exactly as required by the question.
- If partners do not maintain Current accounts in their books, the entries that would normally be posted to the Current accounts must be posted to the Capital accounts.
- Before beginning to copy out your answer, make sure that you have ticked every piece of information and every instruction on the question paper

22.9 Multiple-choice questions

1 The summarised Balance Sheet for F and G in partnership is given.

	$		$
Goodwill	12 000	Capital accounts	
Net assets	28 800	Partner F	24 000
		Partner Y	16 800
	40 800		40 800

F and G have previously shared profits and losses in the ratio of 2 : 1 but have now decided to change the ratio to 3 : 2.

Goodwill is to be revalued and shown in the Balance Sheet at £30 000.

What is the new balance on F's Capital account?

A $23 800

B $24 000

C $34 800

D $36 000

2 J and K are partners sharing profits and losses equally. They do not record Goodwill in the firm's books.

L joins the partnership, paying $24 000 for his share of the Goodwill. Profits and losses are to be shared equally between J, K and L.

Which of the following shows the increases in the partners' accounts on the admission of L as a partner?

	Goodwill	Cash	Capital accounts		
			J	K	L
	$	$	$	$	$
A	–	24 000	8 000	8 000	8 000
B	–	24 000	–	–	–
C	–	24 000	12 000	12 000	–
D	24 000	24 000	12 000	12 000	–

3 L and M are in partnership sharing profits and losses in the ratio of 3 : 2. They admit N as a partner on 1 January. On the same date the partnership net assets are revalued and show a loss on revaluation of $40 000. The new profit/loss-sharing ratio is: L $\frac{2}{5}$, M $\frac{2}{5}$, N $\frac{1}{5}$.

How will the revaluation of the net assets be recorded in the partners' Capital accounts?

	Capital accounts		
	L	M	N
	$	$	$
A	Credit 16 000	Credit 16 000	Credit 8000
B	Debit 16 000	Debit 16 000	Debit 8000
C	Credit 24 000	Credit 16 000	–
D	Debit 24 000	Debit 16 000	–

4 P, Q and R were partners, sharing profits and losses equally. P retired and Q and R continued in partnership sharing profits and losses equally. Goodwill was valued at $60 000 but was not shown in the books.

Which entries will record the adjustments for P's retirement in the books?

	Capital accounts		
	P	Q	R
	$	$	$
A	–	Credit 10 000	Credit 10 000
B	Credit 20 000	Debit 10 000	Debit 10 000
C	Debit 20 000	Credit 10 000	Credit 10 000
D	–	Credit 30 000	Credit 30 000

5 S and T are partners sharing profits and losses in the ratio of 1 : 2. They admit V as a partner and revise the profit-sharing ratio to: $S \frac{2}{5}$; $T \frac{2}{5}$; $V \frac{1}{5}$.

Goodwill is valued at $60 000 but no Goodwill is to be recorded in the books.

Which entries will be made in the partners' Capital accounts?

	Capital accounts		
	S	T	V
	$	$	$
A	Debit 4 000	Credit 16 000	Debit 12 000
B	Credit 24 000	Credit 24 000	Debit 48 000
C	Credit 4 000	Debit 16 000	Credit 12 000
D	Debit 24 000	Debit 24 000	Credit 48 000

22.10 Additional exercises

1 Wilson, Keppel and Betty were in partnership and shared profits and losses equally. They did not operate Current accounts and on 30 April 1998 their Capital accounts showed the following balances.

Wilson	$40 000
Keppel	$30 000
Betty	$15 000

(a) Keppel retired from the partnership on 1 May 1998 and at that time Goodwill was valued at $24 000. Fixed assets were revalued as follows.

Premises increased in value by $10 000
Fixtures increased in value by $4000
Vehicles decreased in value by $2000

It was agreed that neither a Goodwill account nor a Revaluation account would be shown in the partnership books. Keppel received cash for his share of the partnership and Wilson and Betty continued to run the partnership still sharing the profits equally. Drawings during the year ended 30 April 1999 were Wilson $46 000 and Betty $45 000. Net profit for that year was $120 000.

Required

Draw up the partners' Capital accounts for the year ended 30 April 1999 in columnar form.

(b) Imogen joined the partnership on 1 November 1999, bringing in capital of $12 000 and $8000 as her share of Goodwill. No Goodwill account was opened. Profits were now to be shared on the following basis:

Wilson $\frac{3}{7}$
Betty $\frac{3}{7}$
Imogen $\frac{1}{7}$

During the year ended 30 April 2000 profits amounted to $140 000 and partners' drawings were Wilson $52 000, Betty $48 000 and Imogen $20 000. Profits accumulated at a regular rate throughout the year. The partnership was sold on 1 May 2000 for $126 000. The partnership was dissolved and all of the partners took the money due to them.

Draw up the partners' Capital accounts for the period 1 May 1999 to 1 May 2000, in columnar form.

(UCLES, 2001, AS/A Level Accounting, Syllabus 8706/2, May/June)

2 Dellow and Coucom are in partnership in a business which has three retail departments, Television, Computing and Telephones. The following balances were extracted from the business accounts at 30 April 2002.

		Dr	Cr
		$	$
Purchases and Sales	Television	120 000	214 000
	Computing	220 000	428 000
.	Telephones	40 000	107 000
Wages		56 000	
Stocks at 1 May 2001	Television	8 000	
	Computing	19 000	
	Telephones	3 000	
Sales staff salaries		147 000	
General expenses		5 000	
Office salaries		35 000	
Advertising		14 000	
Rent		40 000	
Electricity		9 000	
Insurance		5 000	
Motor Vehicles at cost		45 000	
Furniture & Fittings at cost		30 000	

Notes

The following must now be taken into consideration.
Stocks at 30 April 2002:

Television	$17 000
Computing	$40 000
Telephones	$5 000

Stock taking is computerised and is based solely on sales and purchases – no physical stock check has been taken.

Accruals at 30 April 2002:

General expenses	$2000
Electricity	$1000
Rent	$2000

Number of sales staff employed:

Television	3
Computing	4
Telephones	1

Commission is paid to sales staff at 1% of Sales.
Depreciation is charged to Motor Vehicles and Furniture & Fittings at 20% per annum on cost.
Floor space (square metres):

Television	2000
Computing	2500
Telephones	500

Expenses are apportioned as follows:

Expense	Basis of apportionment
Wages	Sales
General expenses	Sales
Office salaries	Sales
Sales staff salaries	Number of sales staff
Advertising	Sales
Rent and rates	Floor area
Electricity	Floor area
Insurance	Floor area
Depreciation	Equally between departments

Dellow and Coucom share profits in the ratio of their Capital accounts, which at 1 May 2001 were: Dellow $60 000, Coucom $40 000.
Interest on capital is payable at 1% of opening capital.
Cash drawings for the year were Dellow, $15 000 and Coucom, $4000.
Interest is chargeable on drawings at 2% of total drawings for the year.
Coucom is paid a Partnership salary of $7600.
During the year Coucom took from stock for her own use a Television costing $1000. No entries were made for this in the accounts.

(a) Prepare, in columnar format, Departmental Trading and Profit and Loss Accounts for the year ended 30 April 2002.
(b) Prepare the Partnership Appropriation Account for the year ended 30 April 2002.
(c) It has been suggested that any department that is making a loss should be closed. Comment on this suggestion
(UCLES, 2002, AS/A Level Accounting, Syllabus 9706/2, October/November)

23 An introduction to the accounts of limited companies

> *In this chapter you will learn:*
> - what limited companies are and how they differ from partnerships
> - the Companies Acts 1985 and 1989 and some of the legal requirements for companies
> - the format of company Profit and Loss Accounts and Balance Sheets
> - types of share capital and reserves
> - which profits are distributable in cash as dividends and how the dividends are calculated
> - what debentures are and how they differ from shares.

23.1 What is a limited company?

A limited company differs from other organisations because it is a *separate legal entity*; its existence is separate from that of its shareholders (the people who own it). It is important to distinguish between the *accounting concept of entity*, which, as explained in §9.2, applies to every business for the purposes of bookkeeping and accounting, and the concept of *legal entity*, which applies only to limited companies. If Mr S. Ossidge, a sole trader, is a butcher, a customer who wishes to sue him for food poisoning will be able to sue him as a person; the *accounting concept* will not protect Mr Ossidge from a legal action. But, if Mr Ossidge has formed his business into a limited company, S. Ossidge Limited, the concept of *separate legal entity* applies and the customer must sue the company and not Mr Ossidge because the goods were purchased from the company and not from Mr Ossidge!

23.2 The growth of limited companies

The concept of limited liability goes back to the sixteenth century but it became important in the eighteenth. century because of the Industrial Revolution. Before that, people earned their living by farming, or from cottage industries that did not require large sums of capital. With the invention of machinery powered by steam engines, increased productivity led to manufacturing being concentrated in factories. Larger amounts of capital were needed to construct the factories and equip them with machinery. This capital could be raised by inviting people to buy shares (or invest) in the business without taking part in its management. These investors were the **shareholders** or members of the companies. By the middle of the nineteenth century, limited companies had become very important as business organisations.

Limited companies are sometimes known as **limited liability companies** because the liability of their shareholders is limited to the amounts they have paid, or have agreed to pay, for their shares. For example, a shareholder owning 100 shares of $1 each cannot be compelled to pay more than the $100 he has already paid for his shares if the company cannot pay its creditors; the creditors may be the losers. (It is possible to have limited partnerships in which the liability of some, but not all, of the partners for the firm's debts is limited. Limited partnerships are outside the scope of this book.)

23.3 The Companies Acts of 1985 and 1989

Two characteristics of limited companies have now been identified:

1. creditors risk not being paid if a company has insufficient funds, that is, the company is insolvent
2. shareholders are not entitled to help manage a company simply because they own shares in it; they rely on directors to manage the company for them.

The Companies Act 1985, as amended by the Companies Act 1989, is designed to protect the interests of creditors and shareholders, including those who might in future become creditors or shareholders. Some of the provisions of the Companies Act 1985 are as follows.

Formation A company is formed when certain documents are registered by people, known as its 'founders', with the Registrar of Companies and various fees and duties are paid to the Registrar.

Memorandum and Articles of Association These are two of the documents which must be filed with the Registrar of Companies.

The Memorandum defines the relationship of the company to the rest of the world. It contains information about:

1. the name of the company, which must end with the words **Public limited company** or **Plc** if it is a public company, or **Limited** or **Ltd** if it is a private company (the difference between the two types of company will be explained below)

2. a statement that the liability of the company is limited

3. the amount of the **authorised capital**, which is the maximum amount of capital that the company may raise; it may need to raise less, at least in its early years, but the amount of the authorised capital will be stated to cover possible expansion of the company. The company must pay stamp duty on the amount of the registered capital, and the amount of the duty is decided by the amount of the capital.

The Articles of Association is a document that defines the rights and duties of a company's shareholders and directors. It contains regulations for calling meetings of shareholders, members' voting rights, the forfeiture of shares by members who fail to pay the amounts called upon them, and the appointment of directors to manage the company. Another clause fixes the directors' **qualification**, that is the number of shares that directors must hold. This ensures that the directors have a financial stake in the company, giving some sort of insurance that they will manage the company well for the shareholders. It is important to remember that the directors manage the company because they are voted into office by the shareholders, and not simply because they own shares.

Public and private companies Companies register as either public companies or private companies.

Public companies may offer their shares to the public and the shares may be bought and sold on the Stock Exchange. The Companies Act 1985 states that their authorised capital must be at least £50 000 of which one quarter must have been paid by the shareholders. The whole of any premium on the shares must have been paid. The premium on shares is dealt with later in this chapter.

Private companies may have authorised capitals of less than £50 000. They are not allowed to offer their shares to the public and the shares cannot therefore be bought and sold on the Stock Exchange.

The distinction between public and private companies applies in the United Kingdom, but may not apply in all other countries. To cater for this situation, companies will be described as 'Limited' or 'Ltd' in this text, but will be assumed to be public companies unless they are specifically stated to be private companies or the context implies that they are private.

23.4 Partnerships and limited companies compared

	Partnerships	Limited companies
Number of partners/shareholders	Not less than 2. Not more than 20 (except in certain professional firms such as accountants, lawyers, etc.).	Not less than 2. Maximum number depends on the number of shares permitted by the authorised capital.
Liability of partners/shareholders	Unlimited. The private assets of partners may be seized to pay the firm's creditors (except in the case of limited partners in a limited partnership).	Shareholders' liability is limited to the amount they have paid, or agreed to pay on their shares.
Capital	Determined by the partnership agreement.	Limited by the authorised capital stated in the Memorandum of Association (but the authorised capital may be increased by amending the Memorandum and paying additional stamp duty).
Management	All partners (except those with limited liability) may manage the firm's affairs.	Shareholders are not entitled to manage the affairs. This must be left to the directors. (The directors act because they have been appointed directors, not because they are shareholders.)
Taxation	Firms are not liable to pay tax on their profits. The liability to pay tax on their shares of profit rests with the partners individually.	Companies are liable to pay tax on their profits. The tax payable is treated as an appropriation of profit.
Distribution of profit	Partners share profits and losses	Profits are distributed as dividends. Undistributed profits may be retained in the company.

23.5 Profit and Loss Accounts of limited companies

The Companies Act 1985 prescribes various forms for companies' Profit and Loss Accounts. It includes the Trading and Appropriation Accounts in the general term Profit and Loss Account.

The Act recognises that companies do not wish to disclose too much confidential detail about their operations as it might provide an unfair advantage to competitors.

The following is a typical example of a company Profit and Loss Account that students at this level may encounter, and is prepared in a form prescribed by the Companies Act. Students should follow this form as far as possible.

Exhibit Co. Ltd
Profit and Loss Account for the year ended 31 December 2004

	$000	$000
Turnover		1500
Cost of sales[1]		(900)
Gross profit		600
Distribution costs[2]	(234)	
Administrative expenses[3]	(196)	(430)
Operating profit or (loss)		170
Interest receivable[4]		12
		182
Interest payable[5]		(20)
Profit before taxation		162
Taxation[6]		(40)
Profit after taxation		122
Transfer to General Reserve[7]		(60)
		62
Preference dividend paid[8]	16	
Ordinary dividend paid	30	(46)
Retained profit for the year[9]		16

1 Cost of sales: the detail does not have to be shown here but show it as a working.

2 Distribution costs include expenses such as salespersons' salaries, warehousing costs, carriage outwards, depreciation of warehouse and delivery vans etc. Only the total of these needs to be shown, in which case show the detail as workings.

3 Administrative expenses include administrative salaries and wages, property expenses not already included in cost of sales or selling and distribution, and depreciation not dealt with above. Financial items such as discounts allowed, bad debts and doubtful debt provisions are sometimes treated as selling expenses, but otherwise are treated as administration expenses. Only the total of these expenses need be shown, in which case show the detail as workings.

4 Interest receivable will include interest on investments, including debenture interest received from other companies. (Debentures are loans made to companies and will be explained in §23.14.)

5 Interest payable includes interest payable on loans made to the company by other companies or by individuals. (See §23.14.)

6 Taxation is based on the profit for the year.

7 A transfer to a General Reserve may be made when it is considered desirable to plough some profit back into the business.

8 The payment of dividends is explained in §23.8.

9 The Companies Act does not provide for retained profit brought forward from the previous year to be credited in the Profit and Loss Account.

23.6 Balance Sheets of limited companies

The Companies Act 1985 requires companies to prepare their Balance Sheets in a prescribed form.

The example which follows is the form in which students should prepare company Balance Sheets for examination purposes. It follows the pattern required by the Act but shows the fixed assets in more detail than the Act requires.

Exhibit Co. Ltd
Balance Sheet as at 31 December 2004

	$000 Cost	$000 Depn	$000 NBV
Fixed assets			
Intangible			
Goodwill[1]	100	80	20
Tangible			
Freehold land and buildings	800	300	500
Plant and machinery	360	200	160
Office machinery and furniture	145	105	40
	1305	605	700[2]
Fixed asset investments[3]	200	–	200
Total fixed assets	1605	685	920
Current assets			
Stocks			
Debtors			96
Trade debtors			121
Other debtors			43
Prepayments and accrued income			37
			297
Investments[4]			120
Cash at bank and in hand			105
			522
Creditors: amounts falling due within one year[5]			
(Bank loans and overdrafts)[6]			
Trade creditors		94	
Other creditors including taxation[7]		40	
Accruals and deferred income[8]		46	180
Net current assets			342
Total assets less current liabilities			1262
Creditors: amounts falling due after more than one year[9]			
10% debentures 2006/2008			200
			1062
Capital and reserves[10]			
Ordinary shares of $1 each			800
8% Preference shares of $1 each			50
Share Premium account			100
General Reserve			70
Retained profit[11]			42
			1062

1 Goodwill may be shown in the Balance Sheet only if it was included in the purchase price of another business which has been acquired by the company. Goodwill will be considered in more detail later. Other intangible assets may include the costs of developing the company's products, or acquiring patents and trademarks.

2 The Companies Act only requires the total net book value of the tangible fixed assets ($700 000) to be shown on the Balance Sheet. It will allow the full details of cost and depreciation to be shown as a note to the Balance Sheet.

3 Fixed asset investments include shares etc. held in other companies (possibly companies which supply Exhibit Co. Ltd with goods, or companies which distribute or sell Exhibit Co. Ltd's goods) in order to have some influence on those companies. Such shares will be long-term investments.

4 Current asset investments are short-term investments purchased with cash that is surplus to present requirements. The investments will earn interest; idle cash is a waste of a valuable resource.

5 'Creditors: amounts falling due within one year' is how the Act describes current liabilities.

6 There are no bank loans or overdrafts in this example so the item would not be shown. It is simply included here to show where it should appear if needed.

7 Tax due on the current year's profit will not have been paid by the date of the Balance Sheet.

8 This item includes dividends payable to the shareholders. As will be seen later, the final dividend for the year will be accrued in the Balance Sheet.

9 Amounts falling due after more than one year are long-term liabilities.

10 Share capital and reserves are described below.

11 The retained profit is $26 000 more than the profit for the year shown in the Profit and Loss Account. The difference is retained profit brought forward from 2003 and added to this year's undistributed profit.

23.7 Share capital

Issued capital is the total of the shares which have been issued to the shareholders. It is usually less than, but may never be more than, the authorised capital. A company does not 'sell' its shares; it 'issues' them.

Called-up capital is money required to be paid by shareholders immediately. A newly formed company may not require all the money due from shareholders immediately. If it has to have a factory built and then equip it with machinery, the money could lie idle in the company's bank account until those items have to be paid for. It may require the shareholders to pay only part of the amount due on their shares until further sums are required, when it will call on the shareholders to make further payments.

Uncalled capital is any amount of the share capital not yet called up by the company.

Paid-up capital is the money received from shareholders on the called-up capital. Some shareholders may be late in paying their calls, or may fail to pay them at all.

Calls in advance is money received from shareholders who have paid calls before they are due.

Calls in arrear is money due from shareholders who are late in paying their calls.

Forfeited shares are shares which shareholders have forfeited because they have failed to pay their calls. The shares may be re-issued to other shareholders.

23.8 Classes of shares

Shares may be **preference shares** or **ordinary shares**.

Preference shares

Preference shares are so-called because they entitle holders of them to certain rights which ordinary shareholders do not enjoy. These shareholders are entitled to receive dividends at a fixed rate out of profits before the ordinary shareholders become entitled to dividends. The rate of the dividend is expressed as a percentage of the nominal value (see §23.9) in the description of the shares. The preference shareholders in Exhibit Co. Ltd (above) are entitled to a dividend of 8%, or $0.08 for each share of $1 they hold. When a company is **wound up** (ceases to exist), preference shareholders are entitled to have their capital repaid before any repayment is made to the ordinary shareholders. If there are insufficient funds after the preference shareholders have been repaid, the ordinary shareholders will lose some, if not all, of their money.

Non-cumulative preference shares This class of preference share is not entitled to have any arrears of dividend carried forward to future years if the profit of any year is insufficient to pay the dividend in full.

Cumulative preference shares This class of preference share is entitled to have arrears of dividend carried forward to future years when sufficient profits may become available to pay the arrears.

The following example shows the effect of fluctuating profits on non-cumulative preference shares and ordinary shareholders, and also shows the difference between cumulative and non-cumulative preference shares.

Example

Upandown Ltd was formed with a share capital of 10 000 8% non-cumulative preference shares of $1 each and 20 000 ordinary shares of $1 each.

The profits available for dividend were as follows: 1998 $1200; 1999 $900; 2000 $600; 2001 $1000; 2002 $700; 2003 $1300.

The dividends paid to the preference shareholders and the balances of profit available to pay dividends to the ordinary shareholders were as follows.

Year	1998	1999	2000	2001	2002	2003
	$	$	$	$	$	$
Profit	1200	900	600	1000	700	1300
Preference dividend paid	800	800	600	800	700	800
Profit left for ordinary shareholders	400	100	nil	200	nil	500
Maximum ordinary dividend payable	2%	0.5%	0%	1%	0%	2.5%

If the preference shares in Upandown Ltd had been cumulative preference shares, the position would have been as follows.

Year	1998	1999	2000	2001	2002	2003
	$	$	$	$	$	$
Profit	1200	900	600	1000	700	1300
Preference dividend for year	800	800	600	800	700	800
Arrears of dividend brought forward				200		100
Profit left for ordinary shareholders	400	100	nil	nil	nil	400
Maximum ordinary dividend payable	2%	0.5%	0%	0%	0%	2%

Exercise 1

Seesaw Ltd's share capital consists of 60 000 10% preference shares of $1 and 100 000 ordinary shares of $1. Profits for six years were as follows: 1998 $10 000;

1999 $5000; 2000 $7000; 2001 $4000; 2002 $7000; 2003 $12 000.

Required

Prepare tables showing the dividends payable to the preference shareholders and ordinary shareholders if the preference shares are (a) non-cumulative (b) cumulative.

Ordinary shares

The ordinary share capital is known as the **equity** of a company. The profit that remains after any dividend has been paid on preference shares belongs to the ordinary shareholders, and the ordinary dividend will be paid out of that. All the reserves (including retained profit) also belong to the ordinary shareholders. When a company is wound up, after all creditors (including the debenture holders) and the preference shareholders have been paid, the assets remaining belong to the ordinary shareholders, and the proceeds from the sale of the assets will be paid to them. The shareholders may receive more than their original investment in the company, but may receive less than they paid for their shares. It all depends upon the circumstances in which the company is wound up.

23.9 Shares issued at a premium

Shares have a **nominal (or par) value**. For example, shares of $1 have a nominal value of $1, and shares of $0.50 have a nominal value of $0.50. The directors of a company may issue shares at a price exceeding their nominal value if they believe that the issue will attract a lot of subscribers, or the shares are already being bought and sold on the Stock Exchange at a price higher than the nominal value. When shares are issued at a price above their nominal value they are said to be **issued at a premium**. If shares with a nominal value of $1 are issued at, say, $1.25 the premium on each share is $0.25. The premium on each share must be credited to a special account called Share Premium account. Only the nominal value of $1 may be credited to the Share Capital account. The balances on the Share Capital account and the Share Premium account are shown separately in the Balance Sheet.

Example

The directors of The Very Good Company Ltd issued 60 000 Ordinary Shares of $1 at $1.30 per share. All the shares were subscribed for and issued.

Required

Prepare journal entries to record the issue of the shares.

Answer

	$	$
Bank	78 000	
Ordinary Share Capital		60 000
Share Premium account		18 000
Issue of 60 000 ordinary shares of $1 at $1.30 per share.		

(The accounting entries for the issue of shares are actually more complex than those shown in this journal entry. The CIE syllabus does not require candidates to know the full accounting entries, and the journal entry given here is sufficient for the syllabus. The full accounting procedure produces exactly the same result in the end, in any case.)

Exercise 2

The directors of Premium Shares Ltd offered 100 000 10% preference shares of $1 at $1.20 per share. All the shares were subscribed and paid for.

Required

Prepare journal entries to record the issue of the preference shares.

23.10 Reserves

There are two classes of reserves: **revenue reserves** and **capital reserves**. The differences between them are important.

Revenue reserves

Revenue reserves are created by transferring profit from the appropriation section of the Profit and Loss Account to Reserve accounts (debit Profit and Loss Account and credit Reserve account). Revenue reserves may be created for specific purposes (replacement of fixed assets, or planned expansion of the business) or generally to strengthen the financial position of the company. The creation of general reserves reduces the amount of profit available to pay dividends. If the reserves are later considered by the directors to be excessive or no longer required, they may be credited back to the Profit and Loss Account and become available again for the payment of dividends.

Retained profit shown in a Balance Sheet is one of the revenue reserves.

Capital Reserves

Capital reserves are *not normally* created by transferring profit from the Profit and Loss Account. They represent gains that arise from particular circumstances and usually represent gains which have not yet been realised. Capital reserves are part of the capital structure of a company; they may never be credited back to the Profit and Loss Account and can never be used to pay cash dividends to shareholders.

The most common capital reserves, and ones with which you should become familiar, are given below.

Share Premium account This has already been explained in §23.9.

The Companies Act 1985 permits the Share Premium account to be used for certain specific purposes only:

- to pay up unissued shares to existing ordinary shareholders as fully paid-up bonus shares (these are dealt with in chapter 25)
- to write off preliminary expenses (i.e. expenses incurred in the formation of the company)
- to write off expenses incurred in the issue of shares or debentures of the company (this includes any commission payable on the issues)
- to provide any commission payable on the redemption of shares and debentures
- to provide for any premium payable on the redemption of debentures.

(These topics are covered later, and it will be seen that there are certain important restrictions on the use of the Share Premium account to provide for the premium payable on the redemption of shares.)

Capital Redemption Reserve This reserve is created by transferring profit from the Profit and Loss Account. It will be explained more fully in another chapter, but suffice it to say at this point that this reserve must be created when a company redeems any of its shares otherwise than out of the proceeds of a new issue of shares.

The Capital Redemption Reserve may be used to pay up unissued shares to existing ordinary shareholders as fully paid-up bonus shares.

Revaluation Reserves A company may revalue its fixed assets and any gain on the revaluation must be credited to a Revaluation Reserve; it is an unrealised profit and may not be credited to the Profit and Loss Account.

The Revaluation Reserve may be used to pay up unissued shares to members of the company as bonus shares.

Example

An extract from Premises Ltd's Balance Sheet is as follows.

	$
Freehold buildings: cost	60 000
Provision for depreciation	18 000
Net book value	42 000

The buildings have been professionally revalued at $100 000 and the directors have decided to revalue the buildings in the books. The entries in the books are shown by the following journal entry.

Journal	$	$
Freehold buildings at cost	40 000	
Provision for depreciation of freehold buildings	18 000	
Freehold Buildings Revaluation Reserve		58 000

Note. The buildings are being increased from a net book value $42 000 to $100 000, an increase of $58 000. The amount already provided for depreciation must be transferred to the Revaluation Reserve. The Freehold Premises at Cost account will now become Freehold Premises at Valuation account with a debit balance of $100 000.

Exercise 3

Freehold premises are shown in the Balance Sheet of a company as follows: Cost $60000, Net Book Value $42 000. It has been decided to revalue the premises in the books of the company at $80 000.

Required

Prepare the journal entry for the revaluation of the premises in the company's books.

23.11 Calculation of the Balance Sheet value of shares

The value of shares depends upon many factors. Shares are no different from other commodities, the prices of which depend upon supply and demand. The past performance and, more importantly, the future prospects of the company, economic, political and sociological factors at home and abroad may all influence the demand, and the price which has to be paid, for shares on the Stock Exchange. This aspect of share prices is outside the scope of this book.

The Balance Sheet value of shares, however, may be of some importance. It is based on the fact that all the reserves of a company belong to the ordinary shareholders.

Example

The following is the summarised Balance Sheet of Appoggiatura Ltd.

	$000
Total assets less current liabilities	1400
Long-term liabilities: 10% debentures 2006	(300)
	1100
Share capital and reserves	
1 000 000 ordinary shares of $0.50	500
200 000 6% preference shares of $1	200
Share Premium account	180
Capital Redemption Reserve	100
General Reserve	100
Retained profit	20
	1100

Required
Calculate the Balance Sheet value of *one* ordinary share.

Answer
The total of the ordinary share capital and reserves = $900 000.
The value of one ordinary share is

$$\frac{\$900\,000}{1\,000\,000} = \$0.90.$$

Note. The preference share capital is excluded from the total of ordinary share capital and reserves.

Exercise 4

The following is an extract from the Balance Sheet of Gracenote Ltd.

	$
Share capital and reserves	
200 000 ordinary shares of $1	200 000
150 000 8% preference shares of $1	150 000
Share Premium account	50 000
General Reserve	100 000
Profit and Loss Account	(40 000)
	460 000

Required
Calculate the Balance Sheet value of 100 ordinary shares.

23.12 Liabilities, provisions and reserves

The differences between liabilities, provisions and reserves, including how they are created, are important and are summarised here.

Liabilities are amounts owing by a company to trade or other creditors when the amounts can be determined with substantial accuracy. They are created in the books by carrying down credit balances on personal or expense accounts. (See chapter 10.)

Provisions are created to provide for liabilities that are known to exist but of which the amounts cannot be determined with substantial accuracy, for example doubtful debt provisions. Provisions are also made for the depreciation of fixed assets and unrealised profit on stocks of manufactured goods.

Provisions are created by debiting the amounts to the Profit and Loss Account and crediting them to Provision accounts.

Reserves are any other amounts that are set aside and not included in the definition of provisions above. They may be created by debiting the appropriation section of a company's Profit and Loss Account and crediting reserve accounts. They may also be created by revaluing fixed assets.

23.13 Distributable profits and dividends

Distributable profit

The distributable profits of a company consist of

- its accumulated realised profits which have not already been distributed or used for any other purpose *less*
- its accumulated realised losses which have not previously been written off.

For our purposes, distributable profits are the profits for the year after interest and taxation, plus any retained profit brought forward from previous years.

Dividends

Dividends are the means by which shareholders share in the profits of a company. Directors may not pay dividends to shareholders except out of distributable profits as defined above.

Interim dividends may be paid to shareholders during a company's financial year provided the directors are satisfied that profits for the purpose have been earned and the cash resources of the company are sufficient to pay the dividend.

A **final dividend** is paid after the end of the financial year. However, the directors may only recommend the amount of dividend to be paid. Before it can be paid, the shareholders must approve payment by passing a resolution at the company's annual general meeting.

Interim dividends paid and proposed final dividends must be debited in the company's Profit and Loss Account for the year to which they relate. Final dividends must also be shown as current liabilities in the Balance Sheet as they will not have been paid at the year-end.

Dividends are declared either as so many cents per share or as a percentage of the nominal value of the shares.

Example

A company has issued 100 000 ordinary shares of $1 per share.
(a) The directors have recommended a dividend of $0.07 per share. The company will pay a total dividend of $100\ 000 \times \$0.07 = \$7000$.
(b) The directors have recommended a dividend of 5%. The company will pay a total dividend of 5% of $100\ 000 = \$5000$ (or $0.05 per share).

Dividend policy Before paying or recommending dividends, directors of a company must consider the following important matters:

- whether sufficient distributable profits are available
- whether the company's funds will be sufficient to pay the dividend; a cash forecast is needed
- whether there is any need to transfer profits into revenue reserves to strengthen the business
- whether there is a proper balance between dividend growth and capital growth; unless dividends and share values increase, shareholders' wealth is diminished by inflation in the economy (undistributed profit increases the company's reserves and the Balance Sheet value of the ordinary shares)
- a generous dividend policy may increase the value of shares on the Stock Exchange, and a 'mean' policy will have the opposite effect.

23.14 Debentures

A **debenture** is a document given by a company to someone who has lent it money. It states the amount of loan, the annual amount of interest payable, and the dates on which interest is to be paid. It also includes the date on which the loan is to be repaid by the company. Usually, repayment is spread over a period and the dates of commencement and end of the period are included in the description of the debenture. For example, the debentures in Exhibit Co. Ltd's Balance Sheet in §23.6 are entitled to interest of 10% per annum and are due for repayment between 2006 and 2008.

Debentures are usually secured on all or some of the company's assets. If the company gets into financial difficulties, the assets on which the debentures are secured will be sold and the proceeds used to repay the loans to the debenture holders. This gives the debenture holders an advantage over other creditors of the company.

The difference between shares and debentures

Shares	Debentures
Shareholders are members of the company.	Debenture holders are not members of the company.
Share capital is shown in the Balance Sheet under *share capital and reserves*.	Debentures are shown in the Balance Sheet as *long-term liabilities* unless they are due for redemption within one year, when they must be shown as *current liabilities*.
Shareholders are the last people to be repaid when a company is wound up.	Debenture holders are entitled to be repaid before shareholders when a company is wound up.
Dividends may only be paid if distributable profits are available.	Interest on debentures must be paid even if the company has not made a profit.
Dividends are an appropriation of profit.	Debenture interest is an expense which is debited as such in the Profit and Loss Account.

Example

The trial balance of Dillydally Ltd at 30 April 2004 is as follows.

	$	$
Turnover		756 000
Purchases	446 000	
Stock at 1.5.03	32 000	
Sales staff salaries and commission	83 000	
Administration salaries	57 000	
Carriage outwards	24 000	
General expenses	45 000	
Interest on debentures	5 000	
Goodwill at cost	100 000	
Freehold premises at cost	240 000	
Provision for depreciation of freehold premises		71 000
Delivery vans at cost	75 000	
Provision for depreciation of delivery vans		30 000
Office machinery at cost	35 000	
Provision for depreciation of office machinery		10 000
Trade debtors	60 000	
Trade creditors		42 000
Balance at bank	66 000	
100 000 ordinary shares of $1		100 000
80 000 6% preference shares of $1		80 000
10% debentures 2008/2010		100 000
Share Premium account		30 000
General Reserve		40 000
Retained profit brought forward at 1 May 2003		13 900
Interim dividends paid: preference	2 400	
ordinary	2 500	
	1 272 900	1 272 900

Further information

1. Stock at 30.4.04: $54 000.
2. Depreciation for the year ended 30 April 2004 is to be provided as follows.

   Freehold warehouse $4000

   Freehold offices $12 000

   Delivery vehicles: 20% on cost

   Office machinery: 20% on cost
3. Debenture interest is payable half-yearly on 1 May and 1 November.
4. Provision is to be made for taxation on the year's profits in the sum of $25 000.
5. A transfer of $20 000 is to be made to General Reserve.
6. The directors have recommended a final dividend on the ordinary shares of $0.05 per share.

Required

(a) Prepare Dillydally Ltd's Profit and Loss Account for the year ended 30 April 2004 in as much detail as possible.

(b) Prepare the Balance Sheet as at 30 April 2004 in as much detail as possible.

(c) Prepare Dillydally Ltd's Profit and Loss Account for the year ended 30 April 2004 showing the minimum amount of detail required by the Companies Act 1985.

(d) Prepare the Balance Sheet as at 30 April 2004 showing the minimum amount of detail required by the Companies Act 1985.

Answer

(a)

Dillydally Ltd
Profit and Loss Account for the year ended
30 April 2004

		$	$	$
Turnover				756 000
Cost of sales:	Stock at 1 May 2003		32 000	
	Purchases		446 000	
			478 000	
	Stock at 30 April 2004		54 000	424 000
Gross profit				332 000
Selling and distribution				
	Sales staff salaries and commissions	83 000		
	Carriage out	24 000		
	Depreciation: warehouse	4 000		
	delivery vehicles	15 000	126 000	
Administration				
	Administrative salaries	57 000		
	General expenses	45 000		
	Depreciation: office premises	12 000		
	office machinery	7 000	121 000	247 000
Operating profit				85 000
Debenture interest				10 000
Profit before taxation				75 000
Taxation				25 000
Profit after taxation				50 000
Transfer to General Reserve			20 000	
Dividends paid and proposed				
	Preference: paid	2 400		
	proposed	2 400	4 800	
	Ordinary: paid	2 500		
	proposed	5 000	7 500	32 300
Retained profit for the year				17 700

(b)

Balance Sheet at 30 April 2004

Fixed assets		Cost	Depn	NBV
		$	$	$
Intangible:	Goodwill	100 000	-	100 000
Tangible:	Freehold premises	240 000	87 000	153 000
	Delivery vehicles	75 000	45 000	30 000
	Office machinery	35 000	17 000	18 000
		350 000	149 000	201 000
Total fixed assets				301 000
Current assets				
Stock			54 000	
Trade debtors			60 000	
Balance at bank			66 000	
			180 000	
Creditors: amounts falling due within one year				
Trade creditors		42 000		
Debenture interest		5 000		
Taxation		25 000		
Dividends: preference		2 400		
ordinary		5 000	79 400	
Net current assets				100 600
Total assets less current liabilities				401 600
Creditors: amounts falling due after more than one year				
10% debentures 2008/2010				100 000
				301 600
Share capital and reserves				
100 000 ordinary shares of $1				100 000
80 000 6% preference shares of $1				80 000
Share Premium account				30 000
General Reserve				60 000
Retained profit *(13 900 + 17 700)*				31 600
				301 600

(c)

Dillydally Ltd
Profit and Loss Account for the year ended 30 April 2004

	$	$	$
Turnover			756 000
Cost of sales			424 000
Gross profit			332 000
Selling and distribution		126 000	
Administration		121 000	247 000
Operating profit			85 000
Debenture interest			10 000
Profit before taxation			75 000
Taxation			25 000
Profit after taxation			50 000
Transfer to General Reserve		20 000	
Dividends paid and proposed			
Preference: paid	2 400		
proposed	2 400	4 800	
Ordinary: paid	2 500		
proposed	5 000	7 500	32 300
Retained profit for the year			17 700

(d)

Balance Sheet at 30 April 2004

Fixed assets	Cost	Depn	NBV
	$	$	$
Intangible: Goodwill	100 000	–	100 000
Tangible:			201 000
Total fixed assets			301 000
Current assets			
Stock		54 000	
Trade debtors		60 000	
Balance at bank		66 000	
		180 000	
Creditors: amounts falling due within one year			
Trade creditors	42 000		
Debenture interest	5 000		
Taxation	25 000		
Dividends: preference	2 400		
ordinary	5 000	79 400	
Net current assets			100 600
Total assets less current liabilities			401 600
Creditors: amounts falling due after more than one year			
10% debentures 2008/2010			100 000
			301 600
Share capital and reserves			
100 000 ordinary shares of $1			100 000
80 000 6% preference shares of $1			80 000
Share Premium account			30 000
General Reserve			60 000
Retained profit (13 900 + 17 700)			31 600
			301 600

Note. The Companies Act allows the items in current assets and current liabilities to be combined if their individual amounts are not material to assessing the state of affairs of the company. The detail is required to be shown in notes to the accounts. Students are advised to show these items in detail in answers to questions. In any case, students should not adopt the less detailed form of accounts for their answers unless specifically required to do so by the question.

Exercise 5

Molly Coddle Ltd's trial balance at 30 April 2004 was as follows.

	$	$
Turnover		300 000
Stock at 1 May 2003	20 000	
Purchases	113 000	
Sales office salaries	57 000	
Selling expenses	39 000	
General office wages	32 000	
Other general expenses	35 000	
Warehouse machinery at cost	70 000	
Provision for depreciation of warehouse machinery		30 000
Office machinery at cost	42 000	
Provision for depreciation of office machinery		20 000
Trade debtors	38 000	
Balance at bank	28 000	
Trade creditors		11 000
10% debentures 2006/2008		5 000
50 000 ordinary shares of $1		50 000
10 000 6% preference shares of $1		10 000
Share Premium account		15 000
General Reserve		25 000
Retained profit		8 000
	474 000	474 000

Further information

1. Stock at 30 April 2004 was valued at $31 000.
2. Depreciation for the year is to be provided as follows.
    Warehouse machinery $8000;
    office machinery $10 000
3. $10 000 is to be transferred to the General Reserve.
4. Provision is to be made for the payment of dividends as follows.
    Preference dividend $600; ordinary shares $3750

Required

(a) Prepare Molly Coddle Ltd's Profit and Loss Account for the year ended 30 April 2004.
(b) Prepare the Balance Sheet at 30 April 2004.

Exercise 6

The trial balance of Shillyshally Ltd at 30 June 2004 is as follows.

	$	$
Freehold premises at cost	1 000 000	
Provision for depreciation of freehold premises		60 000
Delivery vehicles at cost	80 000	
Provision for depreciation of delivery vehicles		28 000
Office machinery at cost	70 000	
Provision for depreciation of office machinery		21 000
Trade debtors	82 000	
Trade creditors		33 000
Balance at bank	67 000	
12% debentures 2006/2008		100 000
800 000 ordinary shares of $1		800 000
100 000 8% preference shares of $1		100 000
General Reserve		50 000
Profit and Loss Account at 30 June 2003		7 000
Turnover		1 000 000
Stock at 30 June 2003	46 000	
Purchases	630 000	
Sales staff salaries	79 000	
Administration wages	36 000	
Delivery vehicle expenses	38 000	
Advertising	34 000	
Office expenses	24 000	
Debenture interest paid	6 000	
Interim dividends paid: preference	4 000	
ordinary	3 000	
	2 199 000	2 199 000

Further information

1. Stock at 30 June 2004 was valued at $38 000.
2. Account is to be taken of the following at 30 June 2004.
    Accrued expenses: delivery vehicle expenses $2000
    office expenses $3000
    Prepaid expense: advertising $6000
3. Freehold premises were revalued to $1 200 000 at 30 June 2004.
4. Depreciation is to be provided as follows for the year ended 30 June 2004.
    Delivery vehicles: 25% on the reducing balance
    Office machinery: 10% on cost
5. Debenture interest is payable half-yearly on 1 July and 1 January.

6. Taxation is to be provided for in the sum of $16 000.

7. $50 000 is to be transferred to the General Reserve.

8. The directors have recommended a final dividend of 3% on the ordinary shares.

Required

(a) Prepare Shillyshally Ltd's Profit and Loss Account for the year ended 30 June 2004.

(b) Prepare the Balance Sheet at 30 June 2004.

23.15 Examination hints

- Learn the differences between ordinary shares and preference shares.
- Learn the differences between liabilities, provisions and reserves (§23.12).
- Learn the differences between capital reserves and revenue reserves (§23.10).
- Learn the differences between debentures and shares (§23.14).
- Remember that only the nominal amount of the share capital is credited to the Share Capital account. Any premium on the issue of shares must be credited to the Share Premium account.
- Learn the restrictions on the uses of the Share Premium, Revaluation Reserve and the Capital Redemption Reserve (§23.10).
- Learn how to record the revaluation of fixed assets and how to calculate the amount of the Revaluation Reserve.
- Remember that all the reserves of a company belong to the ordinary shareholders.
- Always show proposed dividends as current liabilities in the Balance Sheet.
- Learn the differences between partnerships and limited companies.
- Prepare company Profit and Loss Accounts and Balance Sheets in the forms required by the Companies Act as far as possible.

23.16 Multiple-choice questions

1 A company has an authorised share capital of 100 000 ordinary shares of $0.05. It has issued 70 000 shares. The directors recommend a dividend of 6%.

What will be the amount of the dividend?

A $2100   **B** $3000   **C** $4200   **D** $6000

2 A company with an authorised share capital of $200 000 has issued 100 000 ordinary shares of $1. It has also issued $100 000 6% debentures. Operating profit is $20 000. A transfer of $10 000 is to be made to the General Reserve.

What is the maximum dividend that can be paid on the ordinary shares?

A 2%   **B** 4%   **C** 5%   **D** 7%

3 On 6 April 2004 a company paid a final dividend of $7000 in respect of its financial year ended 31 December 2003. On 1 October it paid an interim dividend of $5000 in respect of the year ending 31 December 2004. The Balance Sheet at 31 December 2004 included a current liability of $10 000 for dividend payable.

How much has been debited for dividends in the Profit and Loss Account for the year ended 31 December 2004?

A $12 000   **B** $15 000   **C** $17 000

D $22 000

4 The following is a company's summarised Balance Sheet.

	$000
Share capital and reserves	
1 200 000 ordinary shares of $0.50	600
100 000 7% preference shares of $1	100
Share premium	200
General Reserve	80
Retained profit	20
	1000

What is the Balance Sheet value of each ordinary share?

A $0.75   **B** $1.50   **C** $0.83   **D** $1.67

5 The following are extracts from a company's Balance Sheet.

Fixed asset:	Freehold premises at cost $400 000	
	Provision for depreciation of freehold premises $160 000	
Share capital and reserves		
		$
Ordinary shares of $1		500 000
8% preference shares of $1		100 000
Share premium		80 000
Retained profit		40 000
		720 000

It has been decided to revalue the freehold premises to $500 000.

What will be the Balance Sheet value of the ordinary shares after the revaluation?

A $1.44

B $1.64

C $1.76

D $1.96

6 Ali holds 500 ordinary shares of $0.50 in Riski Ltd. He has paid in full the amount of $0.35 called up on each share. The company is unable to pay its creditors.

What is the maximum amount that Ali can now be required to pay on his shares?

A $75

B $250

C $325

D $500

7 Which of the following will not be shown as *share capital and reserves* in a company's Balance Sheet?

A debentures

B retained profit

C revaluation reserve

D share premium

8 Which is the safest form of investment in a limited company?

A long-term debentures

B ordinary shares

C preference shares

D short-term debentures

9 A shareholder sold 1000 ordinary shares of $1 for $1500. What effect will this have on the share capital of the company?

A It will decrease by $1000.

B It will decrease by $1500.

C It will increase by $1500.

D It will remain unchanged.

10 A company has an authorised share capital of $1 000 000. The company has issued 800 000 ordinary shares of $1 at $1.20 per share. It pays $48 000 as dividend on the ordinary shares. What was the rate of the dividend?

A 4%

B 4.8%

C 5%

D 6%

23.17 Additional exercises

1 The following is the summarised Balance Sheet of Bracket & Racket Ltd, a limited company wholly owned by its two shareholders, Bracket and Racket.

Balance Sheet as at 31 March 2002			
	$000	$000	$000
Fixed assets at net book value			
Buildings			250
Fixtures and fittings			100
			350
Current assets			
Stock	1540		
Debtors	820		
Cash	3	2363	
Current liabilities			
Creditors for supplies	1210		
Accruals	192		
Bank	203	1605	758
			1108
Share capital: Ordinary shares			25
Retained profits			910
Loan accounts: Bracket		104	
Racket		69	173
			1108

The company accountant resigned at the beginning of April 2002 and proper records were not kept for the six-month period 1 April to 30 September 2002.

The following information is available for that six-month period.

	$000
Payments by cheque for purchases	1996
Payments by cheque for expenses	823
Interest charged on overdraft	20
Cash and cheques banked	2784

Included in the amount banked was $53 000 for the sale of an unused building, book value $70 000.
Prior to banking the takings,
(i) $205 000 was used to pay wages for the six months;
(ii) Bracket and Racket each reduced their loans to the firm by $45 000.

Depreciation on all fixed assets which remain in the company's books at the end of an accounting period is calculated at 25% per annum on the net book value.

At 30 September 2002 the following figures were available.

	$000
Creditors for supplies	510
Accruals	103
Debtors	420
Stock	704
Cash	8
Bank overdraft	195
Unpresented cheques	63

Doubtful debts are estimated at 5% at 30 September 2002 and a provision for doubtful debts at that date is to be created.

Required

(a) A Trading and Profit and Loss Account for Bracket and Racket Ltd for the six months ended 30 September 2002.
(b) A Balance Sheet for Bracket and Racket Ltd at 30 September 2002.

(UCLES, 2003, AS/A Level Accounting, Syllabus 9706/02 May/June)

2 Pecnut Ltd's trial balance at 31 March 2004 was as follows.

	$000	$000
Issued share capital: ordinary shares of $1 each		600
General Reserve		120
10% debentures 2007–2010		360
Freehold buildings at cost	1500	
Provision for depreciation of freehold buildings		180
Motor vehicles at cost	246	
Provision for depreciation of motor vehicles		162
Trade debtors	96	
Bank balance		51
Stock at 1 April 2003	85	
Trade creditors		60
Retained profit at 31 March 2003		69
Sales		2683
Purchases	1152	
Selling and distribution	540	
Administration	648	
Debenture interest	18	
	4285	4285

Further information

1. Stock at 31 March 2004: $105 000.
2. The freehold buildings are to be revalued to $2 000 000 at 31 March 2004.
3. The motor vehicles are to be depreciated at the rate of 25% using the reducing balance method.
4. $10 000 is to be transferred to General Reserve.
5. The directors have recommended a dividend of $0.25 per share.

Required

(a) Prepare Pecnut Ltd's Profit and Loss Account for the year ended 31 March 2004.
(b) Prepare the Balance Sheet as at 31 March 2004.
(c) Companies should prepare their annual accounts on the basis that they are going concerns. Explain what this means and how their annual accounts will be affected if they are not going concerns.

24 Cash flow statements

In this chapter you will learn:
- what a cash flow statement is and why it is an important addition to the annual financial statements of a business
- how and why companies are required to include a cash flow statement in their annual accounts
- how to prepare a cash flow statement
- how to prepare a Balance Sheet with the aid of a cash flow statement
- how to prepare cash flow statements for sole traders and partnerships.

24.1 What is a cash flow statement?

A cash flow statement is one that lists the cash flows of a business over a period of time, usually the same period as that covered by the Profit and Loss Account.

A cash flow is any increase or decrease in cash in a business. **Cash** includes cash in hand and deposits repayable on demand, less overdrafts that are repayable on demand. For our purpose, **deposits** and **overdrafts** will generally be balances at, and overdrafts with, banks. The words **on demand** mean either immediately (e.g. current accounts) or within 24 hours of giving notice of repayment.

24.2 Why cash flow statements are important

While it is necessary to know how much profit or loss a business has made, the business does not pay its creditors out of the balance on its Profit and Loss Account. Creditors are paid out of the money a business has at the bank. No business has ever been forced by its creditors to close down because it has made a loss. But a business can be forced to close down because it has insufficient money in the bank to pay its bills when they fall due. The amount by which the ready money in a business exceeds its immediate liabilities is its **liquidity**. There is a big difference between profit and liquidity. A business may make a big profit but have less money in the bank than at the start of the year.

Over a period of time a business needs to generate **cash inflows** that at least match its **cash outflows**. Outflows include:

- payment of creditors (as already mentioned) and the running costs of carrying on business (e.g. wages etc.)
- renewal of, and additions to, fixed assets
- interest on loans and debentures
- payment of tax on profits (companies)
- costs involved in the growth of the business (expansion and development)
- dividends payable to shareholders, or drawings of sole traders and partners.

24.3 Cash flow statements and companies

Companies are required by an **Accounting Standard (FRS 1)** to include a cash flow statement with their annual Profit and Loss Account and Balance Sheet. It is important for shareholders, people intending to invest in the company, and others, to know how efficient the directors have been as stewards of the company's cash and to be able to make comparisons with other companies. The cash flow statement enables judgements to be made about the liquidity, solvency and financial **adaptability** of the business. Adaptability is the ability of a business to change with changing circumstances or to seize new opportunities.

Accounting Standard FRS 1 requires companies to list their cash flows under the following headings:

- **operating activities** (cash effects of transactions relating to operating or trading, normally shown in the Profit and Loss Account; a separate statement is required to reconcile the operating profit shown in the Profit and Loss Account to the resulting cash flow)

- **dividends from joint ventures and associates** (we shall ignore this one as it is outside the CIE syllabus)
- **returns on investments and servicing finance** (interest received and paid, dividends received, and dividends paid on preference shares)
- **taxation** (tax actually paid, not the tax debited in the current Profit and Loss Account)
- **capital expenditure and financial investment** (payments made for the acquisition of fixed assets and receipts from the disposals of fixed assets; this does not include payments and receipts falling under the heading of 'acquisitions and disposals' below)
- **acquisitions and disposals** (cash flows arising from the acquisition or disposal of trades or businesses)
- **equity dividends paid** (ordinary dividends paid in the period, i.e. a final dividend for a previous period and interim dividends paid for the current period, but *not* a proposed dividend for the current period)
- **management of liquid resources** (payments into, and withdrawals from, short-term deposits; payments made to acquire any other investments held as liquid resources; and receipts for the disposal or redemption of such investments)
- **financing** (cash received from the issue of shares and debentures; cash paid when shares are redeemed or debentures repaid).

It is important that those who receive a company's financial statements should be able to relate the cash flow statement to the Profit and Loss Account and Balance Sheet. FRS 1 therefore requires companies to produce two additional statements as follows:

(i) a reconciliation of the operating profit shown in the Profit and Loss Account to the cash flow from operating activities shown in the cash flow statement
(ii) a reconciliation of the movement of cash in the period and the movement of net debt/net funds.

The above may seem a lot to understand and remember at this stage, but examples and practice with the exercises that follow should take a lot of the pain and suffering away from this topic!

24.4 How to prepare a cash flow statement from Balance Sheets

Cash flow statements are prepared by comparing the amounts for items in the latest Balance Sheet with the amounts for the same items in the previous year's Balance Sheet. Some additional calculations for fixed asset details will be required. The following example, with explanatory notes, demonstrates the procedure.

Example

Hannibal Ltd's Balance Sheets at 30 June 2003 and 2004, and an extract from its Profit and Loss Account for the year ended 30 June 2004, were as shown on page 166.

Further information

1. During the year ended 30 June 2004 the following transactions took place.
   (i) Plant and machinery which had cost $105 000, and on which depreciation of $85 000 had been provided, was sold for $24 000.
   (ii) Motor vehicles which had cost $60 000, and which had had a net book value of $15 000 at the date of sale, were sold for $28 000.
   (iii) A bonus issue of shares was made on the basis of one bonus share for every two ordinary shares already held. This was done by using part of the balance on the Share Premium account.
   (iv) Following the bonus issue in (iii), the company issued a further 300 000 ordinary shares at $1.50 per share.
   (v) $50 000 of 10% debentures 2006/2007 were issued on 1 July 2003.

2. There had been no additions to freehold property in the year to 30 June 2004.

Required

Prepare a cash flow statement for the year ended 30 June 2004.

Balance Sheets

	as at 30 June 2003			as at 30 June 2004		
	$000	$000	$000	$000	$000	$000
Fixed assets	Cost	Depn	NBV	Cost or valuation	Depn	NBV
Freehold property	900	300	600	1000	–	1000
Plant and machinery	700	300	400	800	400	400
Motor vehicles	450	180	270	500	200	300
	2050	780	1270	2300	600	1700
Current assets						
Stock		200			300	
Trade debtors		260			215	
Short-term investments		500			800	
Bank		98			200	
		1058			1515	
Creditors: amounts due within one year						
Trade creditors	220			55		
Taxation	90			86		
Proposed dividends:	116	426		108	249	
Net current assets			632			1266
			1902			2966
Creditors: amounts falling due after more than one year						
10% debentures 2006/2007			150			200
			1752			2766
Capital and reserves						
Ordinary shares of $1			600			1200
8% preference shares of $1			500			500
Share premium			350			200
Freehold Property Revaluation Reserve			–			400
General Reserve			200			300
Retained profit			102			166
			1752			2766

Profit and Loss Account (extract) for the year ended 30 June 2004

	$000	$000	$000
Profit before taxation			400
Taxation			80
Profit after taxation			320
Transfer to General Reserve		100	
Dividends paid and proposed:			
Preference	40		
Ordinary	116	156	256
Retained profit for the year			64

Answer

Step 1 Prepare workings: the following information will be required but will probably not be given in a question.

- Fixed assets: cash paid for fixed assets or received from the sale of fixed assets; amounts provided for depreciation in the Profit and Loss Account; profits and losses on the disposal of fixed assets.
- Dividends, interest and taxation paid.

This information is best discovered by preparing rough 'T' accounts as workings and calculating the missing information as balancing figures.

Plant and machinery (P & M)				Provn for depn P & M				Disposal of P & M			
Bal b/f	700	Disposal	105	Disposal	85	Bal b/f	300	Cost	105	Depn.	85
Additions (bal. fig.)	205	Bal c/f	800	Bal c/f	400	P & L (bal. fig)	185	Profit	4	Cash	24
	905		905		485		485		109		109

Motor vehicles (MV)				Provn for depn. MV				Disposal of MV			
Bal b/f	450	Disposal	60	Disposal	45	Bal b/f	180	Cost	60	Depn	45
Additions (bal. fig.)	110	Bal c/f	500	Bal c/f	200	P & L (bal. fig.)	65	Profit	13	Cash	28
	560		560		245		245		73		73

The creation of the Freehold Property Revaluation Reserve shows that the increase in the freehold property was entirely due to revaluation, and no cash flow was involved.

Taxation				Dividends			
Paid (bal. fig.)	84	Bal b/f	90	Paid (bal fig.)	164*	Bal b/f	116
Bal c/f	86	P & L	80	Bal c/f	108	P & L	156
	170		170		272		272

*Preference dividend = 8% of $500 000: $40 000
 ordinary dividend = $124 000

Step 2 Calculate the cash flow from operating activities by preparing a reconciliation. Start with the operating profit and adjust for

- non-cash items in the Profit and Loss Account, that is, those which have not involved any movement of cash, such as depreciation and profits and losses on the disposals of fixed assets
- increases and decreases in stock debtors and creditors.

The extract from Hannibal Ltd's Profit and Loss Account does not give the operating profit, but we can add the debenture interest back to the profit before taxation to arrive at the operating profit. (If necessary, refer back to §23.5.)

	$400 000
Profit before taxation	$400 000
Add debenture interest (10% of $200 000)	$20 000
Operating profit	$420 000

Step 4 Prepare a reconciliation of net cash flow to movement in net debt/net funds. (Net debt is defined in FRS 1 as borrowings (debentures) less cash and liquid resources (short-term investments). The cash and liquid resources in Hannibal Ltd exceed the borrowings, so the reconciliation will be to the movement in net funds.)

Reconciliation of operating profit to net cash flow from operating activities

	$000	$000
Operating profit		420
Add depreciation of fixed assets:		
Plant and machinery	185	
Motor vehicles	65	250
Deduct profit on sale of fixed assets:		
Plant and machinery	4	
Motor vehicles	13	(17)
Deduct increase in stocks *(This required cash expenditure)*		(100)
Add decrease in trade debtors *(This increased cash)*		45
Deduct decrease in trade creditors *(This reduced the cash)*		(165)
Net cash inflow		433

Reconciliation of net cash flow to movement in net funds

	$000	$000
Increase in funds in the period	102	
Add increase in short-term investments	300	
Less increase in debentures issued	(50)	352
Net funds at 1 July 2003 (98 + 500 − 150)		448
Net funds at 30 June 2004 (200 + 800 − 200)		800

Step 3 Prepare the cash flow statement.

Hannibal Ltd
Cash flow statement for the year ended 30 June 2004

	$000	$000
Net cash flow from operating activities		433
Servicing of finance		
Interest paid on debentures	(20)	
Preference share dividends paid	(40)	(60)
Taxation		(84)
Capital expenditure		
Payment to acquire fixed assets *(205 + 110)*	(315)	
Proceeds for disposal of fixed assets *(24 + 28)*	52	(263)
		26
Equity dividends paid		(124)
		(98)
Management of liquid resources		
Purchase of short-term investments		(300)
		(398)
Financing		
Issue of 10% debentures 2006/2007	50	
Issue of 300 000 ordinary shares of $1	450	500
Increase in cash		102

Exercise 1

Contraflo Ltd's Balance Sheets at 31 December 2003 and 2004, and an extract from its Profit and Loss Account for the year ended 31 December 2004, were as follows.

Balance Sheets

	as at 31 December 2003			as at 31 December 2004		
	$000	$000	$000	$000	$000	$000
Fixed assets	Cost	Depn	NBV	Cost	Depn	NBV
Freehold property	400	–	400	364	–	364
Plant and machinery	80	35	45	150	39	111
Motor vehicles	120	90	30	160	95	65
	600	125	475	674	134	540
Current assets						
Stock		100			85	
Trade debtors		40			52	
Bank		55			36	
		195			173	
Creditors: amounts due within one year						
Trade creditors	30			38		
Taxation	39			43		
Proposed dividends:	30	99		35	116	
Net current assets			96			57
			571			597
Creditors: amounts falling due after more than one year						
10% debentures 2006/2008			100			70
			471			527
Capital and reserves						
Ordinary shares of $1			200			250
8% preference shares of $1			50			50
Share Premium			20			25
General Reserve			100			100
Retained profit			101			102
			471			527

Profit and Loss Account (extract) for the year ended 1 December 2004

	$000	$000
Operating profit		94
Debenture interest		(8)
Profit before taxation		86
Taxation		(40)
Profit after taxation		46
Dividends paid and proposed:		
Preference	6	
Ordinary	39	(45)
Retained profit for the year		1

Further information

During the year ended 31 December 2004 the following transactions took place.

1. Freehold buildings which had cost $36 000 were sold for $50 000. The premises had not been depreciated.

2. Plant and machinery which had cost $20 000, and on which depreciation of $16 000 had been provided, was sold for $1000. New plant and machinery had been purchased.

3. Motor vehicles which had cost $30 000, and which had a net book value of $5000 at the date of sale, were sold for $4000. New motor vehicles had been purchased.

4. 50 000 ordinary shares of $1 each were issued at a premium of £0.10 per share on 1 July 2004.

5. $30 000 of 10% debentures 2006/2008 were redeemed at par.

Required

Prepare a cash flow statement for the year ended 31 December 2004.

24.5 How to prepare a Balance Sheet from a cash flow statement

Examination questions sometimes require Balance Sheets to be prepared from a cash flow statement and the technique for doing this is shown in the next example.

Example 1

Hengist Ltd's Balance Sheet at 31 October 2003 was as follows.

Tangible fixed assets

	At cost	Depn	Net Book Value
	$000	$000	$000
Freehold premises	900	240	660
Plant and machinery	750	220	530
			1190

Current assets

Stock		95	
Debtors		77	
Cash at bank		40	
		212	

Creditors: amounts due within one year

Trade creditors	44		
Dividends (ordinary)	26	70	142
			1332

Creditors: amounts due after more than one year

10% debenture stock 2007/2009			200
			1132

Share capital and reserves

Ordinary shares of $1			750
10% Preference shares of $1			80
Share premium			110
General Reserve			100
Profit and Loss Account			92
			1132

An extract from Hengist Ltd's Profit and Loss Account for the year ended 31 October 2004 and the cash flow statement for that year are as follows.

Extract from the Profit and Loss Account for the year ended 31 October 2004

	$000	$000
Operating profit		214
Debenture interest		(25)
Profit for the financial year		189
Transfer to General Reserve	60	
Preference dividend paid	8	
Ordinary dividends: interim	30	
proposed	60	158
Retained profit for the year		31

Note to budgeted Profit and Loss Account:

Statement of total recognised gains and losses

	$000
Profit for the financial year	189
Unrealised surplus on revaluation of freehold premises	340
Total gains and losses recognised since last annual report	529

Cash flow statement for the year ended 31 October 2004

	$000	$000
Net cash inflow from operating activities		241
Servicing of finance and returns on investments		
Interest paid	(25)	
Preference dividend paid	(8)	(33)
Capital expenditure and financial investment		
Payments for plant and machinery	(130)	
Proceeds from sale of plant and machinery	50	(80)
		128
Equity dividends paid		(56)
		72
Management of liquid resources		
Purchase of short-term investments		(300)
		(228)
Financing		
Issue of 150 000 ordinary shares of $1	200	
Redemption of debentures	(50)	150
Decrease in cash		(78)

Reconciliation of operating profit to cash inflow from operating activities

	$000
Operating profit	214
Depreciation of plant and machinery	50
Profit on disposal of plant and machinery (see note below)	(14)
Decrease in stock	15
Increase in debtors	(18)
Decrease in creditors	(6)
Net cash inflow from operating activities	241

Note. The plant and machinery had cost $96 000.

Required

Prepare Hengist Ltd's Balance Sheet as at 31 October 2004 in as much detail as possible.

Answer

Hengist Ltd
Balance Sheet at 31 October 2004

Tangible fixed assets

	At cost or valuation	Depn.	Net Book Value
	$000	$000	$000
Freehold premises	1000	–	1000
Plant and machinery	784	210	574[1]
	1784	210	1574

Current assets		
Stock (95 – 15)		80
Debtors (77 + 18)		95
Short-term investments		300
		475

Creditors: amounts due within one year			
Bank overdraft (40 – 78)	38		
Trade creditors (44 – 6)	38		
Dividends (ordinary)[2]	60	136	339
			1913

Creditors: amounts due after more than one year	
10% debenture stock 2007/2009	150
	1763

Share capital and reserves	
Ordinary shares of $1 (750 + 150)	900
10% Preference shares of $1	80
Share premium (110 + 50)	160
Revaluation Reserve (1000 – 660)	340
General Reserve (100 + 60)	160
Profit and Loss Account (92 + 31)	123
	1763

1

Plant and machinery at cost				Depn plant and machinery				Disposal			
B/f	750	Disposal	96	Disposal	60	b/f	220	Cost	96	Depn (bal. fig.)	60
Cash	130	c/d (bal. fig.)	784	c/d (bal. fig.)	210	P & L	50	Profit	14	Cash	50
	880		880		270		270		110		110

2

Dividends			
Paid (26 + 30)	56	b/f	26
c/f	60	P & L	90
	116		116

Exercise 2

Horsa Ltd's Balance Sheet at 31 July 2003 was as follows.

Tangible fixed assets

	At cost	Depn	Net Book Value
	$000	$000	$000
Freehold premises	300	130	170
Plant and machinery	125	75	50
			220

Current assets

Stock		36
Debtors		79
Cash at bank		42
		157

Creditors: amounts due within one year

Trade creditors	43		
Dividends (ordinary)	18	61	96
			316

Creditors: amounts due after more than one year

10% debenture stock 2003/2006	50
	266

Share capital and reserves

Ordinary shares of $1	100
10% Preference shares of $1	50
Share Premium	20
General Reserve	40
Profit and Loss Account	56
	266

An extract from Horsa Ltd's Profit and Loss Account for the year ended 31 July 2004 and the cash flow statement for that year are as follows.

Extract from the Profit and Loss Account for the year ended 31 July 2004

	$000	$000
Operating profit		69
Debenture interest		(5)
Profit for the financial year		64
Transfer to General Reserve	20	
Preference dividend paid	4	
Ordinary dividends: interim	25	49
Retained profit for the year		15

Cash flow statement for the year ended 31 July 2004

	$000	$000
Net cash inflow from operating activities		131
Servicing of finance and returns on investments		
Interest paid	(5)	
Preference dividend paid	(4)	(9)
Capital expenditure and financial investment		
Payments for plant and machinery	(48)	
Proceeds from sale of plant and machinery	5	(43)
		79
Equity dividends paid		(23)
		56
Financing		
Issue of 20 000 ordinary shares of $1	40	
Redemption of debentures on 31 July 2004 at par	(20)	20
Increase in cash		76

Reconciliation of operating profit to cash inflow from operating activities

	$000
Operating profit	69
Depreciation: freehold premises	12
plant and machinery	60
Loss on disposal of plant and machinery (cost $30 000)	7
Increase in stock	(4)
Increase in debtors	(19)
Increase in creditors	6
Net cash inflow from operating activities	131

Required

Prepare Horsa Ltd's Balance Sheet at 31 July 2004 in as much detail as possible.

Example 2

Box Ltd's Balance Sheet at 31 May 2004 is as follows.

	Cost or valuation	Depn	Net Book Value
	$000	$000	$000
Fixed assets			
Intangible: Goodwill	–	–	–
Tangible: Freehold premises	800	–	800
Plant and machinery	400	180	220
Motor vehicles	120	90	30
	1320	270	1050
Current assets: Stock		196	
Debtors		81	
		277	
Creditors: amounts falling due within one year			
Bank overdraft	18		
Trade creditors	53		
Ordinary dividend	20	91	186
			1236
Creditors: amounts falling due after more than one year			
10% debentures 2002/2005			80
			1156
Share capital and reserves			
Ordinary shares of $1			500
Share Premium			180
Revaluation Reserve			340
General Reserve			120
Retained profit			16
			1156

Extract from Profit and Loss Account for the year ended 31 May 2004

	$000	$000
Operating profit		65
Interest on debentures		12
		53
Transfer to General Reserve	20	
Ordinary dividends	30	50
Retained profit for the year		3

Cash flow statement for the year ended 31 May 2004

	$000	$000
Cash inflow from operating activities (see below)		108
Servicing finance		
Debenture interest paid	(12)	
Preference share dividend paid	(4)	(16)
Capital expenditure		
Payments to acquire tangible fixed assets		
Plant and machinery	(180)	
Motor vehicles	(60)	
Receipts from sale of tangible fixed assets (see below)	50	(190)
		(98)
Equity dividends paid		(30)
		(128)
Financing		
Issue 100 000 ordinary shares of $1 each	200	
Redemption of preference shares at par	(100)	
Redemption of debentures at par	(50)	50
Decrease in cash		(78)

Reconciliation of operating profit with net cash inflow from operating activities

	$000
Operating profit	65
Goodwill written off	50
Depreciation: plant and machinery	40
motor vehicles	36
Loss on sale of motor vehicle (see 1 below)	6
Profit on sale of plant and machinery (see 2 below)	(10)
Increase in stock	(36)
Increase in debtors	(25)
Decrease in creditors	(18)
Net cash inflow from operations	108

Further information relevant to the year ended 31 May 2004:

1. Motor vehicles which had cost $40 000 were sold for $5000.

2. Plant and machinery which had cost $100 000 was sold for $45 000.

3. The freehold premises were purchased in 1990 for $600 000.

4. $50 000 debentures had been redeemed at par on 31 May 2004.

5. The company redeemed its 6% preference shares on 1 June 2003.

Required

Prepare Box Ltd's Balance Sheet as at 31 May **2003**.

Answer

In this example it is necessary to work *backwards* from the Balance Sheet at 31 May 2004 to arrive at the position of Box Ltd at 31 May 2003. Note the adjustments.

Box Ltd
Balance Sheet as at 31 May 2003

	$000	$000	$000
	Cost	Depn.	NBV
Fixed assets			
Intangible: Goodwill (+ 50 w/o)			50
Tangible: Freehold premises[1]	600	140	460
Plant and machinery[2]	320	205	115
Motor vehicles[3]	100	83	17
	1020	428	592
Total fixed assets			642
Current assets			
Stock (196 – 36)		160	
Debtors (81 – 25)		56	
Bank (78 – 18)		60	
		276	
Creditors: amounts falling due within one year			
Trade creditors (53 + 18)	71		
Preference dividend	4		
Ordinary dividend[4]	20	95	181
			823
Creditors: amounts falling due after more than one year			
10% debentures 2002/5 (80 + 50)			130
			693
Share capital and reserves			
Ordinary shares of $1 (500 – 100)			400
6% Preference shares of $1			100
Share Premium account (180 – 100)			80
(Revaluation Reserve)[5]			–
General Reserve (120 – 20)			100
Retained profit (16 – 3)			13
			693

1 Freehold premises at cost (given) $600 000.

The Revaluation Reserve has been made up as follows:

Increase in freehold premises at cost $200 000

Depreciation at 31 May 2003 $140 000

2 Plant and machinery at cost

	$000
At 31 May 2004	400
Less additions in 2004	(180)
Add disposal in 2004	100
At 31 May 2003	320

Depreciation of P & M

	$000
At 31 May 2004	180
Provided in 2004	(40)
On disposals	65
At 31 May 2003	205

Disposal of P & M

	$000
Cost	100
Proceeds	(45)
Profit on disposal	10
Depreciation to sale	65

3 Motor vehicles at cost

	$000
At May 2004	120
Less additions in 2004	(60)
Add disposal in 2004	40
At 31 May 2003	100

Depreciation of MVs

	$000
At May 2004	90
Provided in 2004	(36)
On disposal	29
At 31 May 2003	83

Disposals of MVs

	$000
Cost	40
Proceeds	(5)
Loss on sale	(6)
Depreciation to sale	29

4 Ordinary dividends

	$000
Accrued at 31 May 2004	20
Paid in 2004	30
Debited in P & L A/c	(30)
Accrued at 31 May 2003	20

5 Include the Revaluation Reserve in the Balance Sheet at 31 May 2003 although it did not exist at that date. Examiners require a positive response if a mark is to be rewarded for correct recognition of the situation. Omission of the item from the answer could suggest that the candidate had overlooked it or had not understood how to deal with it.

Exercise 3

Cox Ltd's Balance Sheet at 30 September 2004 is as follows.

	Cost or valuation	Depn	Net Book Value
	$000	$000	$000
Fixed assets			
Intangible: Goodwill	180	80	100
Tangible: Freehold premises	1000	–	1000
Plant and machinery	742	526	216
Motor vehicles	220	116	104
	1962	642	1320
Total fixed assets			1420
Current assets: Stock		154	
Debtors		106	
Bank		83	
		343	
Creditors: amounts falling due within one year			
Trade creditors		79	
Ordinary dividend		35	114	229
			1649
Creditors: amounts falling due after more than one year			
10% debentures 2004/2008			250
			1399
Share capital and reserves			
Ordinary shares of $1			600
Share Premium account			100
Revaluation Reserve			400
General Reserve			240
Retained profit			59
			1399

Extract from Profit and Loss Account for the year ended 30 September 2004

	$000	$000
Operating profit		164
Interest on debentures		30
		134
Transfer to General Reserve	40	
Ordinary dividends	60	100
Retained profit for the year		34

Cash flow statement for the year ended 30 September 2004

	$000	$000
Cash inflow from operating activities (see below)		492
Servicing finance		
Debenture interest paid	(30)	
Preference share dividend paid	(4)	(34)
Capital expenditure		
Payments to acquire tangible fixed assets		
Plant and machinery	(300)	
Motor vehicles	(84)	
Receipts from sale of tangible fixed assets (see below)	31	(353)
		105
Equity dividends paid		(60)
		45
Financing		
Issue 100 000 ordinary shares of $1 each	150	
Redemption of preference shares at par	(80)	
Redemption of debentures at par	(50)	20
Increase in cash		65

Reconciliation of operating profit with net cash inflow from operating activities

	$000
Operating profit	164
Goodwill written off	80
Depreciation: plant and machinery	120
motor vehicles	70
Loss on sale of plant and machinery (see 1 below)	9
Profit on sale of motor vehicle (see 2 below)	(8)
Decrease in stock	71
Increase in debtors	(32)
Increase in creditors	18
Net cash inflow from operations	492

Further information relevant to the year ended 30 September 2004:

1. Plant and machinery which had cost $180 000 was sold for $20 000.
2. Motor vehicles which had cost $72 000 were sold for $11 000.
3. The freehold premises were purchased in 1992 for $700 000.
4. On 30 September 2004 the company redeemed $50 000 debentures and its 5% preference shares, all at par.

Required

Prepare Cox Ltd's Balance Sheet as at 30 September **2003**.

24.6 Cash flow statements for unincorporated businesses

Although sole traders and partnerships do not have to prepare cash flow statements, they may well find the statements useful. Unlike the statements that must be prepared for companies, they may be prepared in any format, and the 'operating profit' is the profit for the year.

24.7 Examination hints

- Memorise the format in which cash flow statements should be prepared for companies, and the items which should be included under each heading.
- Tick each item in the question as you give effect to it, and show your workings.
- All non-cash items in the Profit and Loss Account must be adjusted in the reconciliation of operating profit to net cash flow from operating activities.
- Make sure you understand the effect of changes in stock, debtors and creditors on cash flow.
- Be prepared to draft a cash flow statement for a sole trader or a partnership.
- Get as much practice as you can at preparing cash flow statements.
- Good examination technique starts to earn marks as quickly as possible. Prepare the cash flow statement in outline, leaving plenty of space between the headings for details to be inserted. Start by filling in the easy items such as payments made to purchase fixed assets, proceeds of disposal, issues and redemptions of shares and debentures, movements in stock, debtors and creditors, etc. Then proceed to the items requiring more detailed calculations.
- If the cash flow in your answer in the examination does not equal the change in the cash balance in the question, do not spend time trying to trace the error(s) if this time is better spent tackling the next question. If you have studied the topic thoroughly before the examination, you will probably have done enough to earn useful marks anyway.

24.8 Multiple-choice questions

1 The following information is extracted from the accounts of a company.

	Year ended 31 December 2003	Year ended 31 December 2004
	$000	$000
Retained profit at 31 December	50	70
Dividends paid and proposed	40	45
Transferred to General fund	100	100
Taxation	35	38
Interest payable on debentures	30	36

What was the operating profit for the year ended 31 December 2003?

A $194 000 **B** $239 000 **C** $244 000

D $289 000

2 The following information is extracted from the accounts of a company.

	Year ended	
	30 June 2003	30 June 2004
	$000	$000
Operating profit	100	100
Loss on disposal of fixed assets	16	29
Closing stock	35	41
Debtors	47	49
Creditors	16	20

How much was the cash inflow from operating activities in the year ended 30 June 2004?

A $67 000 **B** $75 000 **C** $125 000

D $133 000

3 A company acquired an asset worth $5000. In full settlement of the price, the company issued 5000 ordinary shares of $1 as fully paid-up shares to the vendor.

Under which heading in the cash flow statement will this transaction be shown?

A Acquisitions

B Capital expenditure

C Financing

D Not shown under any heading.

4 A company purchased a motor vehicle for $25 000. Settlement was made by a payment of $22 000 and the part exchange of one of the company's own vehicles for $3000. The vehicle given in part exchange had a written down value of $7000, but had a re-sale value of $2000.

Which amount should be shown in the cash flow statement for the acquisition of the vehicle?

A $22 000   **B** $24 000   **C** $25 000
D $29 000

24.9 Additional exercises

1 You have received the following financial statements of Pie Ltd for the year ended 30 April 2003, but you do not have the company's Balance Sheet for the previous year.

Balance Sheet as at 30 April 2003

	Cost or valuation $000	Depn $000	Net Book Value $000
Fixed assets			
Intangible: Goodwill	–	–	–
Tangible: Freehold premises	600	–	600
Plant and machinery	520	280	240
Motor vehicles	135	85	50
	1255	365	890
Current assets: Stock		212	
Debtors		96	
		308	
Creditors: amounts falling due within one year			
Bank		36	
Trade creditors		63	
Ordinary dividend		20	119	189
			1079
Creditors: amounts falling due after more than one year			
10% debentures 2002/2005			80
			999
Share capital and reserves			
Ordinary shares of $1			300
Share Premium account			105
Revaluation Reserve			360
General Reserve			100
Retained profit			134
			999

Extract from Profit and Loss Account for the year ended 30 April 2003

	$000	$000
Operating profit		119
Interest on debentures		10
		109
Transfer to General Reserve	20	
Ordinary dividends: paid	10	
proposed	20	50
		59

Cash flow statement for the year ended 30 April 2003

	$000	$000
Cash inflow from operating activities (see below)		226
Servicing finance		
Debenture interest paid	(10)	
Preference share dividend paid	(3)	(13)
Capital expenditure		
Payments to acquire tangible fixed assets		
Plant and machinery	(250)	
Motor vehicles	(62)	
Receipts from sale of tangible fixed assets (see below)	41	(271)
		(58)
Equity dividends paid		(25)
		(83)
Financing		
Issuing of ordinary share capital	100	
Redemption of preference shares	(115)	
Redemption of debentures	(40)	(55)
Decrease in cash		(138)

Reconciliation of operating profit with net cash inflow from operating activities

	$000
Operating profit	119
Goodwill written off	30
Depreciation: plant and machinery	150
motor vehicles	50
Loss on sale of motor vehicle (see 1 below)	4
Profit on sale of plant and machinery (see 2 below)	(15)
Increase in stock	(40)
Increase in debtors	(28)
Decrease in creditors	(44)
Net cash inflow from operations	226

Further information relevant to the year ended 30 April 2003:

1. Motor vehicles which had cost $35 000 were sold for $6000.

2. Plant and machinery which had cost $90 000 was sold for $35 000.

3. The freehold premises were purchased on 1 May 1993 for $400 000. They had been depreciated annually at a rate of 4% on cost.

4. $40 000 debentures had been redeemed at par on 31 October 2002.

5. The company redeemed its 6% preference shares at a premium of $0.15 on 1 May 2002. The shares had been issued at $1.20. The redemption was financed by an issue of 50 000 ordinary shares at $2.00 each.

Required
Prepare Pie Ltd's Balance Sheet as at 30 April **2002**.

2 *Students should read chapter 25 before attempting this question.*

The following is Prophile plc's Balance Sheet at 31 October 2002.

Tangible fixed assets			
	At cost	Depn	Net Book Value
	$000	$000	$000
Freehold premises	850	90	760
Plant and machinery	1197	469	728
			1488
Current assets			
Stock		191	
Debtors		82	
Cash at bank		25	
		298	
Creditors: amounts due within one year			
Trade creditors	73		
Dividends (ordinary)	40	113	185
			1673
Creditors: amounts due after more than one year			
10% debenture stock 2002/2005			300
			1373
Share capital and reserves			
Ordinary shares of $1			850
8% Preference shares of $1			100
Share premium			150
General Reserve			100
Profit and Loss Account			173
			1373

The company's accountant has prepared a budgeted Profit and Loss Account and a budgeted cash flow statement for the year ending 31 October 2003.

Extract from the budgeted Profit and Loss Account for the year ending 31 October 2003

	$000	$000
Operating profit		243
Debenture interest		(20)
Profit for the financial year		223
Transfer to General Reserve	60	
Preference dividend paid	8	
Ordinary dividends: interim	30	
proposed	50	148
Retained profit for the year		75

Note to budgeted Profit and Loss Account:
Statement of total recognised gains and losses

	$000
Profit for the financial year	223
Unrealised surplus on revaluation of freehold premises	240
Total gains recognised since last annual report	463

Budgeted cash flow statement for the year ending 31 October 2003

	$000	$000
Net cash inflow from operating activities		458
Servicing of finance and returns on investments		
Interest paid	(20)	
Preference dividend paid	(8)	
Net cash outflow from servicing finance and returns on investments		(28)
Capital expenditure and financial investment		
Payments for plant and machinery	(293)	
Proceeds from sale of plant and machinery	41	(252)
		178
Equity dividends paid		(70)
		108
Issue of 150 000 ordinary shares of $1	210	
Redemption of debentures	(100)	
Redemption of 100 000 8% preference shares of $1		
(the shares were originally issued at $1.10 per share)	(120)	(10)
Increase in cash		98

Reconciliation of operating profit to cash inflow from operating activities

	$000
Operating profit	243
Depreciation of plant and machinery	200
Profit on disposal of plant and machinery (see note below)	(20)
Decrease in stock	76
Increase in debtors	(15)
Decrease in creditors	(26)
Net cash inflow from operating activities	458

Note. The plant and machinery had cost $110 000.

Required

Prepare Prophile plc's budgeted Balance Sheet as at 31 October 2003 in as much detail as possible. Show all workings.

(UCLES, 2002, AS/A Level Accounting, Syllabus 9706/4, October/November)

25 Limited companies: more about share capital and debentures; capital reductions and reconstructions

> *In this chapter you will learn:*
> - the effect on the Balance Sheet of an issue of shares
> - more about bonus shares and rights issues
> - how to account for the redemption of shares
> - the effect on the Balance Sheet of the redemption of shares, capital reductions and reconstructions
> - the differences between shares and debentures
> - what convertible loan stock is
> - how to account for the redemption of debentures.

25.1 The Companies Act 1985 and share capital

The Companies Act 1985 contains the following provisions regarding the share capital of companies.

- A company's Memorandum of Association must state the amount of its authorised share capital and the division of the share capital into shares of a fixed amount. The company may not issue shares in excess of its authorised capital without amending its articles in accordance with the procedures laid down in the Act.
- Public limited companies must have an authorised minimum capital of £50 000 (stated thus in the Companies Act). At least one quarter of the nominal amount and the whole of any premium must have been paid up on the shares. The shares may be traded on the Stock Exchange.
- Private limited companies may have an authorised capital of less than £50 000. The shares may not be offered to the public generally. A private company may re-register as a public company if it fulfils the necessary requirements.
- A company may
  - increase its share capital by the issue of new shares
  - consolidate its shares into shares of a larger amount than its existing shares (e.g. if it has a share capital of 10 000 ordinary shares of $1, it can convert them into (say) 2000 shares of $5 or 1000 shares of $10)
  - divide its shares into shares of a lower denomination (e.g. convert its ordinary share capital of 10 000 ordinary shares of $1 into 20 000 shares of $0.50 or 40 000 shares of $0.25, etc.)
  - convert its paid-up shares into stock (Stock may be described as 'bundles of shares'. The advantage of stock is that it may be bought and sold in fractional amounts, e.g. $35.50 or $41.80. If the shares had not been converted into stock they could only be bought in multiples of $1.)
  - re-convert stock back into shares of any nominal value, e.g. shares of $1 may be converted into stock then, later, re-converted back into shares of, say, $0.25, $0.50, $5, $10 or any other amount
  - issue bonus shares
  - reduce its capital by redeeming or purchasing its shares provided it complies with strict conditions laid down under the Companies Act.

25.2 Share issues

Students will recall that a company **issues** its shares to people who wish to invest in it. (It is incorrect to say that it *sells* its shares.) The detailed procedure and accounting entries for the issue of shares are not required by the CIE syllabus.

Share premium A company may issue its shares at a premium if it believes that there will be a good demand for them. This could be the case if the company has already issued shares which are being traded on the Stock Exchange at a price above their nominal value.

When shares are issued at a premium, only the amount received for the nominal value of the shares issued may be credited to the Share Capital account. The amount received for the premium must be credited to a Share Premium account. This topic has already been covered in §23.9, and students may wish to revise that section.

25.3 Bonus shares

The Companies Act gives companies the power to use their reserves to issue shares to the ordinary shareholders as fully paid-up shares. These shares are known as **bonus shares** because the shareholders do not have to pay for them; they own all the reserves, anyway, and are not being given anything they do not already own!

The main reason why companies issue bonus shares is because the issued share capital does not adequately represent the long-term capital of the company. Consider the following summarised Balance Sheet.

	$000
Fixed assets	1000
Net current assets	500
	1500
Share capital and reserves	
Ordinary shares of $1	700
Share premium	200
General reserve	400
Retained profit	200
	1500

The directors could, theoretically, distribute the revenue reserves of $600 000 as a cash dividend to the shareholders. The problem with this suggestion is that the fixed assets are long-term assets which should be financed by long-term capital, but they exceed the share capital of the company by $300 000. In order to make the long-term capital of the company adequately support the long-term assets, the directors may transfer $300 000 of the reserves to the Share Capital account, making the balance on that account $1 000 000, equal to the fixed assets. The directors could use any of the reserves for the purpose, but will no doubt prefer to use the Share Premium account, $200 000, and $100 000 of the General Reserve. This would leave the revenue reserves almost intact and these may be used for other purposes including the payment of cash dividends. The reserves have been left in the most flexible form (see §23.10).

Revised Balance Sheet after the capitalisation of the Share Premium account

	$000
Fixed assets	1000
Net current assets	500
	1500
Ordinary shares of $1	1000
General reserve	300
Retained profit	200
	1500

The balance on the Share Capital account has increased by $300 000, but the shareholders have share certificates for 700 000 shares. They must be issued with certificates for another 300 000 bonus shares on the basis of three shares for every seven shares they already hold.

Another reason for capitalising reserves is concerned with the payment of dividends to the ordinary shareholders. If the directors were to recommend paying the whole of the retained profit of $200 000 as a dividend on a share capital of $700 000, the shareholders would receive a dividend of more than 28%. This could cause problems with

(a) the workforce, who may have had little or no increase in their wages
(b) the company's customers, who think that the company should reduce its prices rather than pay excessive dividends to the shareholders.

In fact, the dividend does not represent 28% of the amount the shareholders have invested in the company; their investment includes the share capital and all the reserves and amounts to $1 500 000. The true return to the shareholders is therefore 13% on the amount invested. If the bonus shares were issued, a dividend payment of $200 000 would look a little more reasonable (20% on the issued capital).

Exercise 1

The following is the summarised Balance Sheet of Otago (Bonus Offers) Ltd.

	$000
Fixed assets	1400
Net current assets	350
	1750
Ordinary shares of $1	800
Share premium	200
Revaluation reserve	600
General reserve	100
Retained profit	50
	1750

The directors have decided to make a bonus issue of three new shares for every four already held. They wish to leave the reserves in the most flexible form.

Required

Redraft Otago (Bonus Offers) Ltd's Balance Sheet to show how it will appear following the bonus issue.

25.4 Rights issues

When a company needs to raise more capital, it may do so by issuing more shares. An invitation to the general public to subscribe for shares is an expensive process because the company must issue a prospectus which gives the past history of the company, its present situation and much other information in great detail. Preparation of a prospectus is very time consuming, requiring perhaps hundreds of labour hours. In addition, the company must employ lawyers, accountants and auditors to advise and check on the preparation of the prospectus.

If a company restricts the invitation to subscribe for shares to existing shareholders, the requirements are less stringent and less costly. In any case, if the company is a private company, it is not permitted to invite the general public to subscribe for shares; it must restrict the invitation to its existing shareholders. Such an issue of shares is known as a **rights issue** because the right to apply for the shares is restricted to existing shareholders.

A rights issue entitles existing shareholders to apply for a specified number of shares, depending on how many they already hold. For example, they may apply for one share (or any other number of shares) for every share they already hold. The offer price will be below the price at which shares are currently changing hands on the Stock Exchange, or their current valuation in the case of private companies.

Shareholders who do not wish to exercise their rights may sell the rights to some other person who might be willing to buy them, if the cost of the rights plus the share offer price is less than the price at which the shares are already being traded. For example, a rights issue may be offered at $1.20 per share. The current price at which shares are changing hands may be $1.60. If the rights can be bought for less than $0.40, the person buying the rights will be able to acquire the new shares at a price below that at which they are being traded.

The accounting entries for a rights issue are no different from those for an ordinary issue of shares. In any case, students are not required to know the bookkeeping entries for share issues, but it is important to note the differences between rights issues and bonus issues.

Rights and bonus issues compared	
Rights issue	**Bonus issue**
Subscribers pay for shares.	Shareholders do not pay for shares.
The company's net assets are increased by the cash received.	The net assets of the company are unchanged.
Shareholders do not have to exercise their right to subscribe for the new shares.	All the ordinary shareholders will receive their bonus shares
Shareholders may sell their rights if they do not wish to exercise them.	Shareholders may sell their bonus shares if they do not wish to keep them.

25.5 How to record issues of bonus shares and rights issues

Example

Handout Ltd's Balance Sheet at 1 April 2004 is summarised as follows.

	$000
Net fixed and current assets	1600
Share capital and reserves	
Ordinary shares of $1	1000
Share premium	400
Retained profit	200
	1600

On 1 April 2004, the directors made a bonus issue of shares on the basis of one new share for every two already held, leaving the reserves in the most flexible form.

Required

(a) Redraft Handout Ltd's Balance Sheet at 1 April 2004 after the issue of the bonus shares.

Answer

(a)

	$000
Net fixed and current assets	1600
Share capital and reserves	
Ordinary shares of $1	1500
Retained profit	100
	1600

Following the bonus issue, Handout Ltd made a rights issue on 7 April 2004 of 150 000 ordinary shares of $1 at a price of $1.50. All the shares were subscribed for by the shareholders.

Required

(b) Redraft Handout Ltd's Balance Sheet at 7 April 2004 after the completion of the rights issue.

Answer

(b)

	$000
Net fixed and current assets	1825
Share capital and reserves	
Ordinary shares of $1	1650
Share premium	75
Retained profit	100
	1825

Exercise 2

The summarised Balance Sheet of Bonarite Ltd at 30 June 2004 was as follows.

	$000
Net fixed and current assets	2000
Share capital and reserves	
Ordinary shares of $1	1000
Share premium	500
Revaluation reserve	300
General reserve	120
Retained profit	80
	2000

On 1 July 2004, before any other transactions had taken place, the company made a bonus issue of shares on the basis of four new shares for every five already held. The directors wished to leave the reserves in the most flexible form.

Required

(a) Show how Bonarite Ltd's Balance Sheet will appear at 1 July 2004 immediately after the issue of the bonus shares.

Following the issue of the bonus shares, the company made a rights issue of one new share for every three shares already held. The shares were offered at $1.25 per share and all the shares were taken up.

Required

(b) Show how Bonarite Ltd's Balance Sheet will appear immediately after the rights issue has been completed.

25.6 Redemption and purchase of own shares by a company

The Companies Act 1985 permits a company to issue **redeemable shares** provided it has issued other shares which are not redeemable. Redeemable shares may later be bought back (redeemed) by the company. The Act also permits companies to purchase their own shares although they were not issued as redeemable shares. The treatment of such shares, whether redeemed or purchased by the company, is the same and no distinction between redemption and purchase will be made in what follows. The shares are cancelled on redemption or purchase so that the issued capital is reduced but the authorised capital is not affected.

The Companies Act is concerned with the protection of creditors, who may suffer if the capital of companies is depleted. The Act requires companies to replace redeemed capital by:

(a) either using the proceeds of a new issue of shares

(b) or ensuring that revenue reserves (which could be distributed as cash dividends to shareholders) are converted into a capital reserve, known as a Capital Redemption Reserve, making them unavailable for cash distributions

(c) or a combination of both of the above.

Example 1

Split Coggs Ltd's summarised Balance Sheet at 30 June 2004 is as follows.

	$000
Fixed assets	1000
Net current assets	700
	1700
Ordinary shares of $1	1000
8% redeemable preference shares	300
General reserve	250
Retained profit	150
	1700

The company has decided to redeem the 8% redeemable preference shares out of the proceeds of a new issue of 200 000 ordinary shares at a price of $1.50. After the redemption of the preference shares, the Balance Sheet will be as follows.

	$000
Fixed assets	1000
Net current assets	700
	1700
Ordinary shares of $1	1200
Share premium	100
General reserve	250
Retained profit	150
	1700

The preference share capital has been replaced by ordinary shares and the Share Premium account. The interests of the creditors have been protected. The $300 000 received from the issue of ordinary shares has been paid to the preference shareholders, and the net current assets have remained unchanged.

Example 2

Details as in example 1. The company decided that the preference shares in Split Coggs Ltd should be redeemed, but that no new ordinary shares should be issued.

	$000
Fixed assets	1000
Net current assets	400
	1400
Ordinary shares of $1	1000
Capital Redemption Reserve	300
Retained profit	100
	1400

The interests of the creditors have been protected by the transfer of revenue reserves to a Capital Redemption Reserve which cannot be used to pay cash dividends to the shareholders. Net assets have been reduced by the cash paid to the preference shareholders.

Exercise 3

Choppers Ltd's summarised Balance Sheet is as follows.

	$000
Fixed assets	1300
Net current assets	550
	1850
Ordinary shares of $1	1000
8% preference shares of $1	300
Share premium	200
General reserve	200
Retained profit	150
	1850

The company has decided to redeem the preference shares out of the proceeds of a new issue of 150 000 ordinary shares of $1 at a price of $2.00.

Required

(a) Prepare Choppers Ltd's Balance Sheet immediately after the redemption of the preference shares.

The company has decided to redeem the preference shares without the issue of any new shares.

Required

(b) Prepare Choppers Ltd's Balance Sheet immediately after the redemption of the preference shares.

Premium paid on the redemption of shares

Companies may pay a premium on shares when they redeem them. As an example, a company may redeem $1 preference shares at $1.20; shareholders will receive $1.20 for every preference share they hold, the $0.20 being the premium. The accounting treatment of the premium requires great care.

In some circumstances, the premium paid on redemption may be debited to the Share Premium account (see §23.10). However, the creditors must be protected against any improper reduction of a company's capital. The Companies Act places the following restrictions on the right of a company to debit the premium to Share Premium account:

- the shares being redeemed must have been issued at a premium
- the shares are being redeemed out of the proceeds of a fresh issue of shares made for the purpose
- the amount of the premium debited to Share Premium account must be the lesser of:
  - the amount of premiums received on the new issue of shares
  - the balance on the Share Premium account (including the premiums received on the new issue of shares); this is to prevent a debit balance on the Share Premium account.

If the premium being paid on the redemption of shares exceeds the amount permitted to be debited to the Share Premium account (as explained above), the difference must be charged to the Profit and Loss Account.

If the shares being redeemed were not issued at a premium, or are not being redeemed out of the proceeds of a new issue made for the purpose, the whole of the premium on redemption must be charged to the Profit and Loss Account.

Example 3

Spin Ltd's summarised Balance Sheet is as follows.

	$000
Fixed assets	1100
Net current assets	600
	1700
Ordinary shares of $1	1000
6% redeemable preference shares	200
Share Premium account	150
Profit and Loss Account	350
	1700

The 6% redeemable preference shares are to be redeemed at a premium of $0.20 per share. No new issue of shares is to be made for the purpose,

Required

Show how Spin Ltd's Balance Sheet will appear immediately after the redemption of the preference shares.

Answer

	$000
Fixed assets	1100
Net current assets (600 – 240)	360
	1460
Ordinary shares of $1	1000
Share Premium account	150
Capital Redemption Reserve	200
Profit and Loss Account (350 – 240)	110
	1460

Example 4

Given the summarised Balance Sheet of Spin Ltd before the redemption of the preference shares as given in example 3 above, in this case the preference shares were redeemed partly out of the proceeds of a new issue of 100 000 ordinary shares of $1 issued at a premium of $0.15. The premium paid on the redemption of the preference shares was $0.20.

Required

Show how the Balance Sheet of Spin Ltd will appear immediately after the redemption of the preference shares.

Answer

	$000
Fixed assets	1100
Net current assets (600 + 115 – 240)	475
	1575
Ordinary shares of $1	1100
Share Premium account (150 + 15 – 15)[1]	150
Capital Redemption Reserve[2]	100
Profit and Loss Account [350 – (100 + 25)][3]	225
	1575

1 The Share Premium account has been increased by the amount of the premium received on the issue of the ordinary shares ($15 000), but the company has been allowed to apply this amount towards the premium payable on the redemption of the preference shares. The company cannot debit the whole of the premium paid on redemption ($40 000) to the Share Premium account as this exceeds $15 000.

2 The balance of the preference share capital not covered by the new issue of the ordinary shares must be covered by a transfer of $100 000 from the Profit and Loss Account to a Capital Redemption Reserve.

3 The amount of the premium paid on the redemption of the preference shares ($40 000) less the amount of the premium charged to Share Premium account ($15 000) is $25 000 and must be debited to the Profit and Loss Account.

Exercise 4

The summarised Balance Sheet of Twist Ltd is as follows.

	$000
Fixed assets	2000
Net current assets	800
	2800
Ordinary shares of $1	2000
10% preference shares of $1	250
Share Premium account	200
Profit and Loss Account	350
	2800

The preference shares had been issued at a premium of $0.20 per share.

The preference shares are to be redeemed at $1.20 per share. No new issue of shares is to be made for the purpose of the redemption.

Required

(a) Show how the Balance Sheet of Twist Ltd will appear after the redemption of the preference shares.

The preference shares are to be redeemed after a new issue of 200 000 ordinary shares of $1 has been made at $1.10 per share.

Required

(b) Show how the Balance Sheet of Twist Ltd will appear after completion of the new issue of ordinary shares and the redemption of the preference shares.

The preference shares are to be redeemed after a new issue of 250 000 ordinary shares of $1 has been made at $1.25.

Required

(c) Show how the Balance Sheet of Twist Ltd will appear after the new issue of ordinary shares and the redemption of the preference shares.

25.7 The redemption or purchase of own shares by a private company

The Companies Act recognises that the rules which apply to public companies may be too strict for private companies for the following reasons.

- As shares in private companies cannot be traded on the Stock Exchange, such companies are restricted in their ability to raise capital. Potential investors may hesitate to buy shares in private companies unless they can be certain that they can dispose of their shares in an emergency.
- Many private companies are 'family' concerns. If one of the shareholders dies, his or her family may need the money invested in the shares urgently, especially if death duties or taxes have to be paid out of the deceased's estate.

If a private company's distributable reserves are insufficient to create the Capital Redemption Reserve, the Act allows the company to use its capital reserves to make up the shortfall. If the company's total reserves (i.e. revenue and capital reserves) are insufficient to create the full amount of the Capital Redemption Reserve, the Act allows the Capital Redemption Reserve to be less than the nominal amount of the shares being redeemed.

25.8 Redemption of debentures

A debenture is a loan to a company and redemption of debentures by a company is simply the repayment of a loan. The rules applying to the redemption of shares do not apply to the redemption of debentures but the following should be noted:

- any premium payable to the debenture holders on redemption may be charged to Share Premium account if there is one
- it is not necessary to create a Redemption Reserve for debentures; if the directors consider it wise to create a reserve, it will be made by a transfer from the Profit and Loss Account, but should probably not be called a *Capital* Redemption Reserve.

25.9 Convertible loan stock

Convertible loan stock is similar to debentures, but it gives the holder of the stock the option to convert the stock into shares in the company on a pre-determined date at a pre-determined price. If, when the time arrives, the pre-determined price is less than the market price of the shares, it could be advantageous to exercise the option. If the pre-determined price is higher than the market price, the option will not be exercised.

25.10 Capital reduction and reconstruction

The Companies Act 1985 permits companies to reduce their share capital provided the interests of creditors are preserved. Losses on the Profit and Loss Account lead to a reduction of capital and, if the situation appears to be permanent, it will be necessary to recognise the fact by undertaking a scheme of capital reduction. A Capital Reduction account is opened in the books for this purpose.

Example

D. Pleet Ltd's summarised Balance Sheet at 31 September 2004 is as follows.

	$000
Goodwill	100
Fixed assets	
Land and buildings	600
Plant and machinery	250
Motor vehicles	50
Net current assets	350
	1350
1 600 000 ordinary shares of $1	1600
Profit and Loss Account (debit balance)	(250)
	1350

Further information

1. Goodwill is now considered to be valueless.
2. The fixed assets are considered to be overvalued and have been valued more realistically as follows.

	$000
Land and buildings	420
Plant and machinery	150
Motor vehicles	30

3. Stock has been overvalued by $125 000. A major debtor owing $25 000 has become bankrupt.

The company has not paid any dividends for some years but the directors believe that the company can become profitable again and start paying dividends once more. They propose to carry out a scheme of capital reduction with the agreement of the shareholders.

The scheme of capital reduction:

The Balance Sheet value of the shares is $0.84375 [$(1 600 000 − 250 000) ÷ 1 600 000]. After taking the overvaluation of the assets into account, the value of the shares is $0.50.

		$000
Nominal value of share capital		1600
Less:	Debit balance on Profit and Loss Account	(250)
	Reductions in value of: Goodwill	(100)
	land and buildings	(180)
	plant and machinery	(100)
	motor vehicles	(20)
	stock	(125)
	debtors	(25)
Real value of share capital		800

($800 000 ÷ 1 600 000 = $0.50)

Examination candidates may be required to prepare journal entries for a capital reconstruction but will not be required to prepare the Capital Reduction or other ledger accounts.

Journal entries

	$000	$000
Capital Reduction account	800	
Profit and Loss Account		250
Goodwill		100
Land and buildings		180
Plant and machinery		100
Motor vehicles		20
Stock		125
Bad debt written off		25

Reduction in asset values and writing off Goodwill.

	$000	$000
Ordinary Share Capital account	800	
Capital Reduction account		800

Reduction of share capital.

The balance on the Share Capital account has now been reduced from $1 600 000 to $800 000, but the shareholders still hold share certificates for 1 600 000 shares of $1. The directors may correct this situation in various ways, but the two most likely are:

- to give the shareholders certificates for one ordinary share of $0.50 for every share of $1 they already hold
- to give the shareholders a certificate for one share of $1 for every two shares they already hold.

Follow any advice given in the question. The student is advised to show the working for the reconstruction as follows.

	$000		$000
Goodwill	100	– 100	–
Fixed assets			
Land and buildings	600	– 180	420
Plant and machinery	250	– 100	150
Motor vehicles	50	– 20	30
Net current assets	350	– (125 + 25)	200
	1350		800
1 600 000 ordinary shares of $1	1600	– 800	800
Profit and Loss Account (debit balance)	(250)	+ 250	–
	1350		

The Balance Sheet can now be copied out as the answer.

D. Pleet Ltd
Balance Sheet immediately after the capital reduction

	$000
Fixed assets	
Land and buildings	420
Plant and machinery	150
Motor vehicles	30
Net current assets	200
	800
1 600 000 ordinary shares of $0.50*	800

* Alternatively, 800 000 ordinary shares of $1

Exercise 5

The summarised Balance Sheet of Downsize Ltd is as follows.

	$000
Fixed assets	
Freehold property	400
Fixtures and fittings	100
Office furniture	80
	580
Net current assets	230
	810
1 000 000 ordinary shares of $1	1000
Profit and Loss Account	(190)
	810

The directors propose to write off the debit balance on the Profit and Loss Account and to write the assets down to more realistic values as follows.

	$000
Freehold property	340
Fixtures and fittings	80
Office furniture	70

Stock has been overvalued by $15 000 and a debtor for $5000 has become bankrupt. The shareholders have agreed to a scheme of capital reduction on condition that they receive one new share for every share they already hold.

Required
Re-draft the Balance Sheet of Downsize Ltd as it will appear immediately after the completion of the capital reduction.

25.11 Examination hints

- Memorise the differences between bonus shares and a rights issue.
- Read questions carefully to see whether they are about bonus shares, a rights issue or both.
- Make bonus issues out of capital reserves rather than out of revenue reserves to leave the reserves in the most flexible form.
- In a question based on the redemption of shares a company should be assumed to be a public company unless the question clearly states that it is a private company.
- A Capital Redemption Reserve must be created when shares are not wholly redeemed out of the proceeds of a new issue.
- Make sure you know when the premium on the redemption of shares may be charged to the Share Premium account and the limitations placed on this.
- Make sure you know how capital reductions work, and show the number of the shares issued and their nominal value following the reduction.
- Remember that companies may consolidate their shares into shares of a higher amount or divide them into shares of lower amount.

25.12 Multiple-choice questions

1 A company redeems 60 000 $1 redeemable preference shares at a premium of $0.25 per share. The shares were originally issued at par. No new issue of shares was made to finance the redemption.

What effect does the redemption have on the Profit and Loss Account and the Capital Redemption Reserve?

	Profit and Loss Account	Capital Redemption Reserve
A	decrease by $60 000	increase by $60 000
B	decrease by $60 000	increase by $75 000
C	decrease by $75 000	increase by $60 000
D	decrease by $75 000	increase by $75 000

2 A company issues bonus shares. How does this affect the cash flow statement?

A It will increase the management of liquid resources.

B It will increase financing.

C It will increase cash flow from operating activities.

D It will not appear in the cash flow statement.

3 A company has issued 300 000 ordinary shares of $0.50 each. It makes a bonus issue of two shares for every three already held. It follows that with a rights issue of one share for every two already held at $0.75 per share. The rights issue was fully taken up.

What was the increase in the Share Capital account as a result of the bonus and rights issues?

A $150 000

B $175 000

C $225 000

D $275 000

4 A company redeems its debentures at a premium. How may the company treat the premium on the redemption?

A debit Bank account

B debit Capital Redemption Reserve

C debit Share Capital account

D debit Share Premium account

5 A company, which has already issued ordinary shares of $1 each, issues 200 000 bonus shares and follows this with a rights issue of 100 000 ordinary shares at $1.50 per share.

What is the increase in the share capital and reserves of the company after these transactions?

A $100 000

B $150 000

C $300 000

D $350 000

25.13 Additional exercises

1. The summarised Balance Sheet of Omicron Ltd at 31 December 2002 was as follows.

	$000
Fixed assets	1900
Net current assets	1500
	3400
10% debentures 2003/2004	400
	3000
Share capital and reserves	
Ordinary shares of $1	1000
8% preference shares of $1	800
Share Premium account	180
Profit and Loss Account	1020
	3000

On 1 January 2003 before any other transactions had taken place the following had occurred:

1. redemption of all the debentures at a premium of 5%

2. redemption of all the preference shares at $1.25 per share.

The shares had originally been issued at $1.10 per share.

Required

A revised Balance Sheet at 1 January 2003 as it appeared after the redemption of the debentures and the preference shares.

(UCLES, 2003, AS/A Level Accounting, Syllabus 9706/04, May/June)

2 Istaimy plc's summarised Balance Sheet at 30 April 2001 was as follows.

	$000
Fixed assets	1300
Net current assets	740
	2040
Ordinary shares of $1	1200
10% preference shares of $1	300
Share Premium account	200
Profit and Loss Account	340
	2040

On 1 May 2001, before any further transactions had taken place, it was decided to redeem all the preference shares at a premium of $0.30. The shares had originally been issued at $1.20 per share. In order to provide funds for the redemption, the company issued a further 100 000 ordinary shares at a premium of $0.25.

Required

Prepare Istaimy plc's Balance Sheet as it will appear immediately after the issue of the additional ordinary shares and the redemption of the preference share capital

(UCLES, 2002, AS/A Level Accounting, Syllabus 9706/4, October/November)

3 The following is the Balance Sheet of Joloss plc at 30 April 2002.

	$000	$000
Intangible fixed asset – Goodwill		50
Tangible fixed assets		650
		700
Current assets		
Stock	32	
Debtors	80	
Bank	6	
	118	
Creditors: amounts falling due within one year	42	76
		776
Share capital and reserves		
Ordinary shares of $1		1000
Profit and Loss Account		(224)
		776

Over the past few years Joloss plc has traded at a loss and no dividends have been paid to the shareholders during that time.

The directors are of the opinion that Goodwill is now valueless. The tangible fixed assets are overvalued by $150 000. Some stock which cost $10 000 now has no value. Included in debtors is an amount of $16 000 from a customer who has now become insolvent.

The directors are confident that, as a result of improved efficiency and the introduction of new products, the company can look forward to annual net profits of $50 000. They have proposed to the shareholders a scheme of capital reduction whereby each shareholder will receive one ordinary share with a nominal value of $0.55 for every $1 share presently held. This will enable the debit balance on the Profit and Loss Account to be eliminated and adjustments to be made to the company's assets to take account of the matters mentioned above.

The directors' policy in future will be to pay dividends which will be covered twice by earnings.

The shareholders have agreed to the directors' proposals and the capital reduction was effected on 1 May 2002.

Required

(i) Prepare the Balance Sheet as it will appear immediately after the capital reduction.
(ii) Explain the reasons why the shareholders agreed to the reduction in the nominal value of their shares.

(UCLES, 2002, AS/A Level Accounting, Syllabus 9706/4, May/June)

26 Business purchase

In this chapter you will learn:
- the difference between the purchase of a business and the purchase of the assets of a business
- Goodwill arising on the purchase of a business
- how to prepare a journal entry to record the purchase of a business in the books of the purchasing company
- the preparation of a Balance Sheet following the purchase of a business
- how to calculate the return on an investment in a new business.

26.1 What is the difference between the purchase of a business and the purchase of the assets of a business?

It is important to distinguish between a company buying the assets of another business, and the purchase by the company of that other business. Some students get confused between the two different kinds of purchase. A company may buy the assets of another business which may then cease to trade. The customers of that other business must find another supplier. That is very different from a company buying another business; the company takes over the assets and liabilities of that business together with its customers and carries on the trade of the business taken over. The distinction is important because the purchase only of assets does not involve any payment for Goodwill; the purchase of a business usually does involve payment for Goodwill.

A company often issues shares to the owner of a business as payment. The shares may be issued at a premium.

Sometimes a sole trader or a partnership may decide to convert their business into a limited company. This is done by forming a new company which purchases the partnership business.

Example

Aiisha has traded for some years as a sole trader. On 1 October 2004 she decided to form a limited liability company to take over her business. She will hold ordinary shares of $1 in the company as her capital.

Aiisha's summarised Balance Sheet at 1 October 2004 was as follows.

	$
Fixed assets	20 000
Net current assets	14 000
	34 000
Capital account	34 000

The summarised Balance Sheet of the new company will appear as follows.

Aiisha Ltd	
	$
Fixed assets	20 000
Net current assets	14 000
	34 000
Share capital	
Ordinary shares of $1	34 000

26.2 Goodwill

When a company purchases a business, it will usually buy the assets less the liabilities at an agreed valuation. In addition, it usually pays for the advantage of acquiring an established trade. The company does not have to build up a new business from nothing; the business has been built up by the previous owner who will normally expect to be rewarded for his efforts.

Goodwill is the amount paid for the acquisition of a business in excess of the fair value of its separable net assets. The term 'separable net assets' is used to describe the piecemeal sale of the assets of a business and the settlement of its liabilities out of the proceeds.

It is important to distinguish between **purchased Goodwill** and **inherent Goodwill**. Purchased Goodwill has been paid for. Inherent Goodwill has not been paid for and will arise, for instance, if a trader decides that he wants to show the Goodwill of his business in his Balance Sheet; he debits a Goodwill account in his books and credits his Capital account with any amount that he wishes to show as Goodwill. An Accounting Standard (FRS 10) states that *only purchased Goodwill* should be shown in company Balance Sheets and should be shown as an 'intangible' fixed asset. FRS 10 also has some other important things to say about Goodwill, which will be considered in chapter 27.

If the amount paid for a business is less than the fair value of its separable net assets, the difference is called **negative Goodwill** (not Badwill!) and must be shown as a negative amount among the intangible fixed assets in the Balance Sheet. (Before December 1997, when FRS 10 was published, negative Goodwill had to be shown as a Reserve in the Balance Sheet.)

26.3 How to make journal entries in the books of a company to record the purchase of a business

Before any entries for the purchase of a business are made in a company's ledger accounts, the transaction must be recorded in the journal. The entries should include the Bank and Cash accounts if these are taken over. However, the bank and cash balances of the business being acquired are not usually taken over unless a sole trader or a partnership converts their business into a limited company.

Example

Bortit Ltd purchased the business of A. Sellit, a sole trader, on 1 October 2004. Sellit's Balance Sheet at that date was:

	$	$
Fixed assets		
Land and buildings		60 000
Plant and machinery		35 000
Motor vehicles		21 000
		116 000
Current assets		
Stock	7 000	
Debtors	4 000	
Bank	5 000	
	16 000	
Less Current liabilities		
Creditors	2 000	14 000
		130 000
Capital		130 000

The assets were taken over at the following values:

Land and buildings	80 000
Plant and machinery	28 000
Motor vehicles	16 000
Stock	5 000
Debtors	3 000
Creditors	2 000

Bortit Ltd did not take over Sellit's Bank account.

Bortit Ltd paid A. Sellit $150 000, made up as follows: cash $20 000 and 100 000 ordinary shares of $1 each.

Required

Prepare the journal entries in Bortit Ltd's books to record the purchase of A. Sellit's business.

Answer

	Dr	Cr
	$	$
Land and buildings	80 000	
Plant and machinery	28 000	
Motor vehicles	16 000	
Stock	5 000	
Debtors	3 000	
Goodwill	20 000[1]	
Creditors		2 000
Cash		20 000
Ordinary share capital		100 000
Share Premium account	____	30 000[2]
	152 000	152 000

The purchase of the business of A. Sellit on 1 October 2004 for the sum of £150 000 payable as follows: cash $20 000 and by the issue of 100 000 ordinary shares of $1 at $1.30 per share.

1 Goodwill = purchase consideration ($150 000) less value of net assets acquired ($130 000).

2 The shares were valued at $(150 000 – 20 000) = $130 000. $30 000 is the share premium.

Bortit Ltd's Balance Sheet at 1 October 2004 before it acquired the business of A. Sellit was as follows.

	$	$
Tangible fixed assets		
Land and buildings		200 000
Plant and machinery		75 000
Motor vehicles		40 000
		315 000
Current assets		
Stock	21 000	
Debtors	16 000	
Bank	32 000	
	69 000	
Current liabilities		
Creditors	7 000	62 000
		377 000
Capital and reserves		
Ordinary share capital		300 000
Retained profit		77 000
		377 000

Required

Prepare Bortit Ltd's Balance Sheet immediately after the purchase of the business of A. Sellit.

Answer

Add the journal entries to Bortit Ltd's assets, liabilities, share capital and reserves.

(Workings are shown in brackets.)

Bortit Ltd Balance Sheet at 1 October 2004 after the acquisition of A. Sellit's business

		$	$
Intangible fixed asset			
Goodwill			20 000
Tangible fixed assets			
Land and buildings	(200 000 + 80 000)		280 000
Plant and machinery	(75 000 + 28 000)		103 000
Motor vehicles	(40 000 + 16 000)		56 000
			439 000
Total fixed assets			459 000
Current assets			
Stock	(21 000 + 5000)	26 000	
Debtors	(16 000 + 3000)	19 000	
Bank	(32 000 – 20 000)	12 000	
		57 000	
Current liabilities			
Creditors	(7000 + 2000)	9 000	48 000
			507 000
Capital and reserves			
Ordinary share capital (300 000 + 100 000)			400 000
Share premium			30 000
Retained profit			77 000
			507 000

Exercise 1

Hamil Ltd purchased the business of Abdul, a sole trader, on 30 June 2004. The Balance Sheets of both businesses at that date were as follows.

	Abdul		Hamil Ltd	
	$	$	$	$
Fixed assets				
Freehold property		40 000		100 000
Plant and machinery		15 000		60 000
Office equipment		–		14 000
Office furniture		7 000		–
		62 000		174 000
Current assets				
Stock	4 000		10 000	
Debtors	6 000		7 000	
Bank	1 000		25 000	
	11 000		42 000	
Current liabilities				
Creditors	3 000	8 000	6 000	36 000
		70 000		210 000
Capital account		70 000		
Share capital and reserves				
Ordinary shares of $1				150 000
Share Premium account				20 000
Retained profit				40 000
				210 000

It was agreed that Abdul's assets should be valued as follows.

	$
Freehold property	70 000
Plant and machinery	12 000
Office furniture	4 000
Stock	2 500
Debtors	5 500

Hamil Ltd did not acquire Abdul's bank account.

The consideration for the sale was $120 000 and was satisfied by the payment to Abdul of $20 000 in cash and the issue to him of 80 000 ordinary shares in Hamil Ltd.

Required

(a) Prepare the journal entries in Hamil Ltd's books to record the purchase of Abdul's business.

(b) Prepare Hamil Ltd's Balance Sheet immediately after the acquisition of Abdul's business.

26.4 Purchase of a partnership business

The purchase of a partnership business by a company follows a similar procedure to that for the purchase of a sole trader's business. When one of the partners has made a loan to the firm and the company takes the loan over, it is usual for the company to issue a debenture to the partner concerned. If the rate of interest on the debenture is different from the rate previously received by the partner on the loan, the amount of the debenture will usually ensure that the partner continues to receive the same amount of interest each year as previously. To calculate the amount of the debenture, find the capital sum which, at the new rate, will produce the same amount of interest. Multiply the amount of the loan by the rate paid by the partnership and divide by the rate of interest on the debenture, as shown in the following example.

(i) Partner's loan to partnership: $100 000 at 8% interest per annum. Annual interest = $8000.
A 10% debenture producing annual interest of $8000 will be $100 000 \times \frac{8}{10} = $80 000$.

(ii) If in (i) the rate of interest on the debenture is 5% the amount of debenture is: $100 000 \times \frac{8}{5} = $160 000$.
(Interest on $160 000 at 5% per annum = $8000.)

Exercise 2

Carol has lent $60 000 at 5% interest per annum to the firm in which she is a partner. A company has offered to buy the partnership business. Part of the purchase price consists of a debenture to be issued to Carol to ensure that she continues to receive the same amount of interest annually as she had been receiving from the partnership.

Required

(a) Calculate the amount of the debenture to be issued to Carol if the debenture carries interest at 8% per annum.

(b) Calculate the amount of the debenture if it carries interest at 4% per annum.

Exercise 3

Spaid and Shuvell are partners in a business and their Balance Sheet at 31 December 2004 is as follows.

	$	$
Fixed assets		
Land and buildings		50 000
Fixtures and fittings		18 000
Office machinery		12 000
		80 000
Current assets		
Stock	17 000	
Debtors	8 000	
Bank	4 000	
	29 000	
Current liabilities		
Creditors	12 000	17 000
		97 000
Long-term liability		
Loan from Spaid at 10% per annum		12 000
		85 000
Capitals		
Spaid		50 000
Shuvell		35 000
		85 000

The partners have accepted an offer from Digger Ltd to purchase the business for $118 000. The company will take over all the assets and liabilities of the partnership except the bank account. The partnership assets are to be valued as follows.

	$
Land and buildings	60 000
Fixtures and fittings	14 000
Office machinery	10 000
Stock	15 000
Debtors	6 000

Digger Ltd will settle the purchase price as follows:

- a payment of cash, $28 000
- an 8% debenture issued to Spaid to ensure that he continues to receive the same amount of interest annually as he has received from the partnership
- the balance to be settled by an issue of ordinary shares of $1 in Digger Ltd at $1.25 per share.

Digger Ltd's Balance Sheet at 31 December 2004 is as follows.

	$	$
Fixed assets		
Land and buildings		90 000
Fixtures and fittings		30 000
Office machinery		15 000
		135 000
Current assets		
Stock	20 000	
Debtors	5 000	
Bank	60 000	
	85 000	
Current liabilities		
Creditors	16 000	69 000
		204 000
Share capital and reserves		
Ordinary shares of $1		200 000
Retained profit		4 000
		204 000

Required

Prepare Digger Ltd's Balance Sheet immediately after the company has acquired the partnership business.

26.5 Return on investment

It is important that a company purchasing another business succeeds in making the new business as profitable as its existing business. Profitability is measured by expressing profit as a percentage of capital invested. If a company has purchased a business for $100 000 and the business has made a profit of $12 000 in the first year, the profitability is 12%. This is the **return on capital invested**. If it is equal to, or more than, the return on capital the company was earning on its existing business, the investment may be considered to have been worthwhile. If it is less, overall profitability of the business will be **diluted** (or decreased). However, it is better to measure the profitability over a number of years to get a reliable picture.

The new business may have been merged with the existing business so closely that separate results for the new business are not available. In such a case, the incremental (that is, the additional) profit is measured against the additional capital invested in the business.

Example

X Ltd had a capital of $300 000. Its average annual profit was $54 000. Its return on capital was

$$\frac{\$54\,000}{\$300\,000} \times 100 = 18\%.$$

X Ltd purchased another business on 1 January 2004 for $100 000 which was settled by the issue to the vendor of shares in X Ltd. X Ltd's profit for the year ended 31 December 2004 was $84 000. The profitability of X Ltd has increased by 3% to 21%

$$\left(\frac{\$84\,000}{\$400\,000} \times 100\right).$$

A more reliable picture is obtained if the additional profit of $30 000 is calculated as a percentage of the price paid for the new business:

$$\frac{\$30\,000}{\$100\,000} \times 100 = 30\%.$$

X Ltd has benefited from the purchase of the new business.

26.6 Examination hints

- Goodwill is the difference between the values of the net assets acquired and the purchase price.
- Show Goodwill as an intangible fixed asset, even if it is negative Goodwill.
- When a debenture is issued to a partner, and the partner is to receive the same amount of annual interest as he/she received before the sale of the firm; check that you have calculated the amount of the debenture correctly.
- If you are required to prepare journal entries in a company's books to record the purchase of a business, do *not* show the entries in the books of the business being taken over.
- Make sure you prepare the journal entries in good form.
- Show all workings when preparing the company's Balance Sheet after the new business has been acquired.

26.7 Multiple-choice questions

1 The following is information about the assets and liabilities of a business.

	Book value	Market value
	$	$
Tangible fixed assets	90 000	101 000
Current assets	32 000	29 000
	122 000	
Current liabilities	(14 000)	14 000
	108 000	

Goodwill is valued at $50 000.

What should be paid for the net assets of the business?

A $116 000

B $119 000

C $166 000

D $169 000

2 A company paid $1.8 million to acquire the business of a sole trader. The sole trader's assets and liabilities were valued as follows.

	$
Fixed assets	700 000
Current assets	300 000
Current liabilities	50 000
Long-term loan	100 000

How much was paid for Goodwill?

A $650 000

B $750 000

C $850 000

D $950 000

3 The Balance Sheet of a sole trader is as follows.

	$
Fixed assets	
Intangible: Goodwill	30 000
Tangible	100 000
Net current assets	50 000
	180 000

A company purchased the business, paying for the tangible fixed assets and the net current assets at the valuations shown above.

The company settled the purchase price by issuing 200 000 ordinary shares of $1 at $1.50 per share.

How much did the company pay for Goodwill?

A $30 000

B $50 000

C $120 000

D $150 000

26.8 Additional exercises

1 The following is the Balance Sheet of the Erchetai partnership at 30 April 2002.

	$	$
Goodwill		50 000
Tangible fixed assets		928 000
		978 000
Current assets		
Stock	40 000	
Debtors	76 000	
Bank	80 000	
	196 000	
Current liabilities: Creditors	29 000	167 000
		1 145 000
Long-term liability		
Loan (carrying interest at 8% per annum)		100 000
		1 045 000
Partners' capitals		1 045 000

On 30 April 2002, Istaimy plc acquired the business of the Erchetai partnership. The following matters were taken into consideration in fixing the terms of the acquisition.

1. No depreciation had been provided on freehold buildings. It was agreed that a provision of $128 000 should have been made.

2. On 1 April 2002 Erchetai had purchased a machine. The cost was $60 000. $20 000 was paid immediately. The balance is payable by four equal instalments on 1 May, 1 June, 1 July and 1 August, together with interest at the rate of 12% per annum. Only the initial payment of $20 000 had been recorded in the partnership's books. It was Erchetai's policy to depreciate machinery at the rate of 15% per annum on cost, and to provide for a full year's depreciation in the year of purchase.

3. A debtor owing $5000 at 30 April 2002 has since become bankrupt. Erchetai has been advised that a dividend of 20 per cent will be paid.

4. Stock has been valued at cost. Investigation shows that if stock had been valued at net realisable value it would have been valued at $28 000. If separate valuation at the lower of cost and net realisable value had been applied to each item of stock it would have been valued at $30 000.

The purchase consideration was satisfied as follows:

- The long-term loan was satisfied by the issue of $80 of 10% debenture stock 2008/10 for every $100 of the loan.

- The partners were issued, for every $50.00 of capital, with:

  3 × 8 percent preference shares at $1.20 per share, and 3 ordinary shares of $10.00 each at $12.50.

Required

Prepare the journal entry to record the purchase of the partnership business in the books of Istaimy plc. Your answer should include cash transactions.

(UCLES, 2002, AS/A Level Accounting, Syllabus 9706/4, October/November)

2 On 1 April 2004 Joel Ltd acquired the partnership business of Kay and Ola. The partnership Balance Sheet at 31 March 2004 was as follows.

	$000	$000
Fixed assets		
Land and buildings		150
Plant and machinery		280
		430
Current assets		
Stock	150	
Debtors	141	
Bank	69	
	360	
Current liabilities		
Creditors	130	230
		660
Long-term liability		
Loan from Kay at $12\frac{1}{2}$% per annum		100
		560
Financed by capital accounts: Kay		300
Ola		260
		560

Further information

1. The assets (including the bank account) and current liabilities were taken over at the following valuations.

	$000
Land and buildings	220
Plant and machinery	170
Stock	128
Debtors	105
Creditors	138

2. Kay received sufficient 10% Convertible Loan Stock to ensure that she continued to receive the same amount of interest annually as she had received as a partner. The terms of this issue give Kay the option to have the debenture stock converted to ordinary shares in Joel Ltd on 1 June 2006 at $1.25 per share.

3. The balance of the purchase price was settled by the allocation of 300 000 shares in Joel Ltd to Kay and Ola at $1.50 per share.

Joel Ltd's Balance Sheet at 31 March 2004 was as follows.

	$000	$000	$000
Fixed assets			
Land and buildings			1425
Plant and machinery			803
			2228
Current assets			
Stock		381	
Debtors		519	
Bank		420	
		1320	
Creditors: amounts falling due within one year			
Trade creditors	500		
8% debentures 2004/2005	450	950	
			370
			2598
Share capital and reserves			
Ordinary shares of $1			1350
Profit and Loss Account			1248
			2598

Immediately following the acquisition of the partnership, Joel Ltd redeemed its 8% debentures 2004/2005 at a premium of 4%. In order to preserve the capital structure of the company, a reserve equal to the amount of the debentures redeemed was created.

Required

(a) Prepare Joel Ltd's Balance Sheet as it appeared immediately after it had acquired the partnership of Kay and Ola and redeemed the 8% debentures. (Show all workings.)

(b) Calculate the profit required on Joel Ltd's investment in the partnership business to produce a return of 25% on the investment.

On 1 June 2006 the market price of Joel Ltd's shares was $1.37.

Required

(c) (i) State, with reason, whether Kay should convert her 10% convertible loan stock into ordinary shares in Joel Ltd.

(ii) State the effect that the conversion of Kay's 10% convertible loan stock into shares would have on Joel Ltd's Balance Sheet.

27 Published company accounts

In this chapter you will learn:
- the financial statements and reports that must be published and sent to shareholders
- reporting standards relating to Profit and Loss Accounts
- reporting standards relating to Balance Sheets
- the contents of directors' reports
- the importance of auditors' reports.

27.1 Introduction to published company accounts

Shareholders are not permitted to manage their company unless they are also directors of the company. The directors act as stewards of the shareholders' investments in the company; they are in a position of trust. The Companies Act 1985 ensures that the directors account to the shareholders regularly for their stewardship of the company. The documents which are required to be prepared and published annually are:

- Profit and Loss Account
- Balance Sheet
- cash flow statement
- directors' report
- auditors' report.

These documents must be sent to shareholders in advance of every annual general meeting. They must also be sent to debenture holders. The directors must file an annual return, which includes the annual accounts, with the Registrar of Companies, and the returns may be inspected by any member of the public. Apart from shareholders and debenture holders, other persons who may be interested in a company's accounts are:

- trade and other creditors
- providers of long-term finance such as banks and finance houses
- trade unions, representing the company's workforce
- financial analysts employed by the financial press
- fund managers managing clients' investments
- the Stock Exchanges.

27.2 The Companies Act 1985

The Companies Act requires the Profit and Loss Account to give a **true and fair view** of the profit or loss of the company for the financial year, and the Balance Sheet to give a *true and fair view* of the state of affairs of the company as at the end of the financial year. The word *true* may be explained in simple terms as meaning that, if financial statements indicate that a transaction has taken place, then it has actually taken place. If a Balance Sheet records the existence of an asset, then the company has that asset. The word *fair* implies that transactions, or assets, are shown in accordance with accepted accounting rules of cost or valuation.

Window dressing describes attempts by directors of a company to make a Balance Sheet show the financial position of company to be better than it really is. For example, the directors may cause cheques to be drawn and entered in the books of account on the last day of the financial year but not send the cheques to the creditors until the next financial year. This would have the effect of artificially reducing a company's liabilities in the Balance Sheet, but it would not give a true and fair view because the creditors had not, in fact, been paid. An attempt to inflate the retained profit figure in the Balance Sheet by including unrealised profits in the Profit and Loss Account would not give a true and fair view. The Companies Act 1985 states that only profits which have been realised at the Balance Sheet date shall be included in the Profit and Loss Account.

The accounting principle of **substance over form** (see §9.12) is one accounting principle intended to give a true and fair view.

Schedule IV of the Companies Act 1985 sets out rules for the presentation of company accounts. If accounts prepared in accordance with those rules do not provide sufficient information to meet the requirement to present a true and fair view,

- any necessary information must be provided in the Balance Sheet or Profit and Loss Account, or in notes to the accounts
- if necessary, because of special circumstances, the directors shall depart from the normal rules in order to present a true and fair view and state why they have departed from the normal rules.

27.3 Generally accepted accounting principles (GAAP)

Accounting standards have been published as Statements of Standard Accounting Practice (SSAPs) but, since 1991, as Financial Reporting Standards (FRSs), by the recognised professional accounting bodies in the United Kingdom. The purpose of the standards is to ensure compliance with the true and fair view concept, and they are officially recognised in the Companies Act 1985. All companies are required to comply with the standards, or to publish reasons for departing from them

Company auditors are required to ensure that company accounts are prepared in accordance with the standards and to report any significant departure from the standards to the shareholders. The standards help to increase uniformity in the presentation of company accounts and to reduce the subjective element in the disclosure of information.

Students are not required to know the historical background to the origin of the accounting standards. It is very important, however, for students to learn the requirements of the standards referred to in this chapter. (Not all accounting standards are relevant to the CIE syllabus. Most will not be mentioned here, and those that are mentioned will be dealt with only in so far as they are appropriate at this level.)

27.4 FRS 18 Accounting policies

FRS 18 has replaced a former standard (SSAP 2) and requires two policies (or principles) to be applied in the presentation of accounts:

- **going concern** (see §9.11)
  Companies must prepare their financial statements on a going concern basis unless they are being wound up or have ceased trading, or the directors have no realistic alternative but to wind the company up or to cease trading.
- **accruals** (see §9.9)
  Companies must compile their financial statements (except cash flow statements) on an accruals basis. Cash flow statements must, of course, be on a 'cash' basis.

Two more policies are mentioned as desirable:

- **consistency** (see §9.7)
- **prudence** (see §9.10).

Directors must decide how appropriate the policies mentioned above are to their particular companies at the time the financial statements are prepared and published. The policies should be selected with four objectives in mind:

- **relevance**
  Information should have the ability to influence the economic decisions of the users of the statements, and be provided in time to influence those decisions.
- **reliability**
  Information is reliable if it faithfully represents the facts and is free from bias and material error. It must be complete 'within the bounds of materiality' and prudently prepared.
- **comparability**
  It should be possible to compare information with similar information about the company in a previous period (trend analysis – see chapter 28) and with similar information about other companies (inter-firm comparison – see chapter 28)
- **understandability**
  Information should be able to be understood by users who have a reasonable knowledge of business and accounting, and who are willing to study the information reasonably diligently.

27.5 SSAP 25 Segmental reporting

Companies that carry on different classes of business, or carry on their business in several geographical areas, are required to prepare their accounts in a form that provides information about each individual class (or segment) of the business or geographical area. **Segmental reporting**, as it is called, provides users of financial statements with information that might not otherwise be available to them. They are then better able to assess a company's past and possible future performance.

In their financial statements, companies should define their separate classes of business and the geographical areas in which they operate. They should give, for each segment:

- turnover
- profit before taxation
- net assets employed.

Other information, such as costs common to all the activities, does not need to be shown separately.

Example

Multido Ltd operates in three distinct industries: aerospace, civil engineering and automotive.

The segmental report for the year ended 31 March 2004 is as follows.

	Aerospace $m.	Civil engineering $m.	Automotive $m.	Total $m.
Turnover	80	120	65	265
Profit before taxation				
Segmental profit	16	23	16	55
Common costs				(30)
				25
Net interest				(3)
Profit before taxation				22

27.6 FRS 3 Reporting financial performance

FRS 3 is another standard designed to help users of Profit and Loss Accounts to make better assessments of a company's past and future performance. It requires

- details of turnover to be shown separately for continuing, new and discontinued businesses owned by the company
- separate operating profits for continuing, new and discontinued businesses
- the following to be shown separately in the Profit and Loss Account
  - profits or losses on sale or cessation of an operation*
  - costs of fundamental reorganisation or restructuring*
  - profits or losses on the disposal of fixed assets*
  - exceptional items
  - extraordinary items
- a statement of total recognised gains and losses
- a reconciliation of movements in shareholders' funds.

Exceptional items are shown with an asterisk (*) above. They are defined in the FRS as material items which derive from events or transactions that fall within the ordinary activities of the company and which, because of the amounts involved, need to be disclosed if the financial statements are to give a true and fair view.

Exceptional items should be shown under their natural heading in the format of the Profit and Loss Account as prescribed by the Companies Act 1985. They should be identified with the continuing new or discontinued operations as appropriate.

Extraordinary items, since the introduction of FRS 3, are now so rare that identifying them causes some difficulty. Students are not likely to be questioned on such items.

Statement of total recognised gains and losses Only realised gains and losses are recognised in the Profit and Loss Account; but the net worth of a company is determined by unrealised gains and losses as well as those that have been realised. An example of an unrealised gain or loss occurs when, for example, an asset is revalued, or shares are issued at a premium.

Example
(Based on assumed figures)

Lladnar Ltd
Profit and Loss Account for the year ended 30 September 2004

	$000	$000
Turnover: Continuing operations	5000	
Acquisitions	460	
	5460	
Discontinued operations	134	5594
Cost of sales		3845
Gross profit		1749
Net operating expenses		957
Operating profit/(loss)		
Continuing operations	968	
Acquisitions	80	
	1048	
Discontinued operations	(256)	792
Profit on disposal of properties in continued operations		86
Loss on disposal of discontinued operations		(100)
Profit on ordinary activities before interest		778
Interest payable		(25)
Profit on ordinary activities before taxation		753
Taxation on profit on ordinary activities		(32)
Profit on ordinary activities after taxation		721
Dividends		(70)
Retained profit for the year		651

Statement of total recognised gains and losses	$000
Profit on ordinary activities after taxation	721
Unrealised surplus on revaluation of property	100
Unrealised loss on trade investment	(70)
Net gain in year ended 30 September 2004	751

Reconciliation of movements in shareholders' funds	$000
Profit for the year after taxation	721
Less dividends	(70)
	651
Other recognised gains less losses in the year	30
New share capital*	125
Net addition to shareholders' funds in the year	806
Shareholders' funds at 30 September 2003	2300
Shareholders' funds at 30 September 2004	3106

*Issue during the year of 100 000 ordinary shares of $1 at $1.25 per share.

The Companies Act 1985 requires companies to provide information regarding movements in reserves during the year. The following note should be given in Lladnar Ltd's accounts.

Reserves	Share Premium account	Revaluation Reserve	Profit and Loss Account	Total
	$000	$000	$000	$000
At 30 September 2003	150	–	410	560
Premium on issue of shares				
(nominal value $100 000)	25			25
Surplus on revaluation of				
property		100		100
Retained profit for the year			651	651
	175	100	1061	1336

27.7 Earnings per share (EPS)

The earnings of a company are the profits for the year that are attributable to the ordinary shareholders. The profits in question are after deduction of interest, taxation and preference dividends.

Example

The following is an extract from the Profit and Loss Account of a company for the year ended 31 May 2004.

	$000
Operating profit	400
Interest payable	(36)
Profit before taxation	364
Taxation	(59)
Profit after taxation	305
Transfer to General Reserve	(60)
Preference dividend	(75)
Ordinary dividend	(100)
Retained profit for the year	70

The earnings are $(305\,000 - 75\,000) = \$230\,000$.

Earnings per share (EPS) is the amount, in cents, attributable to each ordinary share.

If the company's issued share capital includes 1 000 000 ordinary shares, the earnings per share are

$$\frac{\$230\,000}{1\,000\,000} = \$0.23 \text{ per share}$$

Earnings per share should be shown as a note to the Profit and Loss Account and always expressed in cents per share.

27.8 FRS 4 Capital instruments

The term 'instrument' describes any document that includes the terms of a contract. The definition of a **capital instrument** is wide ranging and includes share certificates, debentures, loans, convertible loan stocks and other items which need not concern the student using this book.

The Companies Act 1985 requires the following information regarding a company's share capital and debentures to be given by way of a note to the accounts:

- the authorised share capital
- the number and total value of shares of each class allotted
- the earliest and latest dates on which the company has power to redeem redeemable shares
- the premium, if any, payable on the redemption of shares
- the reason for any issue of shares during the year, details of the shares and the cash received
- the reason for any issue of debentures during the year, details of the debentures issued and the cash received.

The purpose of FRS 4 is to ensure that companies provide a 'clear, logical and consistent' treatment of capital instruments in their financial statements. The instruments must be entered under different categories as appropriate.

Liabilities

Debentures and other loans must differentiate between convertible and non-convertible debt. Different types of debts must be distinguished:

- those which are repayable in one year or less, or on demand
- those which are repayable between one and two years
- those which are repayable between two and five years
- those which are repayable in five years or more.

FRS 4 requires that the total finance cost of the debt (i.e. interest payable on the debt) must be spread evenly over the period of the debt.

Shareholders' funds (i.e. share capital and reserves) must differentiate between equity interests (i.e. ordinary shares and reserves) and non-equity interests (preference shares). All dividends must be shown as appropriations of profit.

27.9 FRS 5 Reporting the substance of transactions

The object of FRS 5 is to ensure that the **substance** of an entity's transactions is reported in its financial statements, which should show the **commercial** effect of the transactions on the company's assets, liabilities, gains or losses. The doctrine of **substance over form** is demonstrated in the treatment of assets acquired on hire purchase (see § 9.12).

27.10 FRS 10 Goodwill and intangible assets

Apart from Goodwill, other intangible assets include patents and trade marks, development costs, brand names, etc. The CIE syllabus only specifies Goodwill as examinable, so this text will be confined to that.

Purchased Goodwill is defined by FRS 10 as the difference between the cost of an acquired business and the aggregate of the fair values of the identifiable assets and liabilities of that business.

Negative Goodwill arises when the aggregate of the fair values of the identifiable assets and liabilities of the purchased business exceeds the price paid for the business. Negative Goodwill may arise when the owner of a business urgently requires cash and sells the business for less than its net assets are worth in order to gain a quick sale.

Inherent (or non-purchased) Goodwill (see §26.2) cannot be valued on any objective basis and possibly may not even exist. FRS 10 requires that inherent Goodwill should not be recognised in company accounts.

Purchased Goodwill should be shown as an intangible asset in the Balance Sheet. Negative Goodwill should be shown under the Goodwill heading and deducted from positive Goodwill (if any).

Amortisation of Goodwill Goodwill should be written off to the Profit and Loss Account by the straight-line method over the period of its useful economic life. FRS 10 states that the estimated useful life should not exceed 20 years. This period may only be exceeded if it can be demonstrably proved that the purchased business has a useful economic life exceeding 20 years, perhaps by reference to its continuing potential to generate income.

Goodwill should be reviewed at the end of the first full financial year following acquisition, and in other periods if there are changes in circumstances which indicate that the book value may not be recoverable. Any amount of the book value that is not recoverable should be written off to the Profit and Loss Account immediately.

Revaluation of Goodwill The book value of Goodwill may not be increased unless it can be shown that amortisation provided in the past has been excessive. This situation could arise, for example, if A Ltd purchased a business with shops that offered a dry-cleaning service for clothes. Soon after the acquisition, B Ltd started up in opposition to A Ltd. The Goodwill acquired by A Ltd might have been amortised heavily as a result of the competition. In time, B Ltd ceased business. It could be shown that, in the light of events, the exceptional amortisation of Goodwill had been excessive and an increase in the book value is now justified. However, Goodwill should not be revalued more highly than the price originally paid for it.

Disclosures by way of note to the Balance Sheet FRS 10 requires the following to be disclosed by way of a note to the Balance Sheet:

* the basis on which Goodwill has been valued
* the basis on which Goodwill has been amortised
* the basis on which any revaluation has taken place
* details of negative Goodwill
* details of exceptional depreciation ('impairment') of Goodwill.

27.11 FRS 11 Impairment of assets and Goodwill

The object of FRS 11 is to ensure that:

* fixed assets and Goodwill are recorded in the financial statements at no more than their recoverable amount
* any resulting impairment loss is measured and recognised on a consistent basis
* sufficient information is disclosed in the financial statements to enable users to understand the impact of the impairment on the financial position and performance of the reporting entity.

Impairment loss has been described under **exceptional depreciation** in §11.6.

27.12 FRS 15 Tangible fixed assets

FRS 15 seeks to ensure that:

* tangible fixed assets are valued on a consistent basis when first recorded in the books
* revaluation of tangible fixed assets is carried out and recorded on a consistent basis and regularly reviewed
* sufficient information is disclosed in the accounts to enable users of the accounts to understand the company's accounting policies regarding the amount at which tangible fixed assets are stated in the accounts, revalued and depreciated.

Tangible fixed assets should be recorded initially in the books at cost. 'Cost' is restricted to those costs which are incurred in bringing an asset into working condition for its intended use. Cost will include:

* delivery charges to bring the asset to its intended location
* expenses of preparing the site for its installation
* installation costs, including a proper proportion of the wages of the user's own workforce involved in the installation
* professional fees (e.g. surveyors, lawyers, etc.)
* interest on money borrowed specifically to finance the acquisition of the asset.

A policy of revaluing fixed assets should be applied to individual classes of fixed assets and consistently to all assets in each of the selected classes. The amount at which an asset is carried forward in a Balance Sheet should be its current value at the Balance Sheet date. The current value should be reviewed regularly, though not necessarily annually.

Revaluation of property should be based upon the valuation of the property by a qualified valuer.

Disclosure of information in the accounts

Certain information must be disclosed by way of notes to the Balance Sheet to enable users of the accounts to understand the company's accounting policies regarding fixed assets.

Published Balance Sheets do not have to show detailed information for the tangible fixed assets. Balance Sheets usually show only the total net book value of the fixed assets. The Companies Act 1985 requires a note to be added to the accounts to show:

- the separate classes of fixed assets and their amounts at the beginning of the financial year
- acquisitions of fixed assets during the year
- disposals of fixed assets during the year
- any revaluation of fixed assets during the year
- the amounts of depreciation provisions and movements on the depreciation provision accounts to correspond with the information provided (above) for the fixed assets
- the total of the net book values of the fixed assets at the end of the financial year to agree with the amount shown in the Balance Sheet.

The following is an example of such a note.

Fixed assets at cost	Premises	Plant and machinery	Motor vehicles	Total
	$000	$000	$000	$000
At cost at 31 December 2003	800	400	230	1430
Revaluation	200	–	–	200
Purchases	–	246	170	416
Disposals	–	(80)	(96)	(176)
At cost at 31 December 2004	1000	566	304	1870
Depreciation				
Balance at 31 December 2003	400	256	164	820
Revaluation	(400)			(400)
Provided in the year	–	115	70	185
Disposals		(70)	(80)	(150)
At 31 December 2004	–	301	154	455
Net book value				
at 31 December 2004	1000	265	150	1415

Note. A revaluation reserve of $600 000 will have been created in the year ended 31 December 2004 for the revaluation of the premises.

Depreciation

FRS 15 requires a note to be appended to the accounts to show:

- the depreciation methods used
- the useful economic lives of the assets or the depreciation rates used
- the total depreciation charged for the period
- the financial effect, where material, of any change during the financial year of the estimated useful economic lives of the assets or of their residual values
- if there has been a change in the depreciation method used, the effect of the change, if material.

27.13 SSAP 9 Stocks and long-term contracts

The valuation of stock has been dealt with in chapter 20. Long-term contracts are not in the CIE syllabus.

27.14 FRS 12 Provisions, contingent liabilities and contingent assets

Provisions are created to provide for liabilities that are known to exist but of which the amounts cannot be determined with substantial accuracy.

A **contingent liability** is a liability, the existence of which, at the date of a Balance Sheet, depends upon the occurrence or non-occurrence of a future event. For example, at the date of its Balance Sheet, a company may be involved in a legal action of which the outcome is uncertain. It is possible that the company may be liable to pay substantial compensation if it loses the case, but this and the amount of the compensation, will not be known until later.

A **contingent asset** is a possible asset, the existence of which, at the date of the Balance Sheet, depends upon the occurrence or non-occurrence of a future event. It may be thought of as the opposite of a contingent liability. The purpose of FRS 12 is to ensure that contingencies are recognised in a company's financial statements and are quantified on appropriate bases. Companies must disclose sufficient information in notes to the financial statements to enable users to understand the nature, timing and amounts of the contingencies.

27.15 Accounting for post Balance Sheet events

Post Balance Sheet events are those events, both favourable and unfavourable, which occur between the Balance Sheet date and the date on which the financial statements are approved by the board of directors.

Adjusting events are events which provide additional evidence of conditions existing at the Balance Sheet date. Such events, if material, require amounts included in the financial statements to be adjusted; they may indicate that the going concern concept is not appropriate to the financial statements.
Examples:

The purchase price or proceeds of sale of assets purchased or sold before the year-end are not known until after the Balance Sheet date.

The valuation of property after the Balance Sheet date provides evidence that the property had already suffered a material loss in value at the Balance Sheet date.

The receipt of proceeds from the sale of stock after the Balance Sheet date provides evidence that the stock should have been valued at net realisable value rather than at cost.

A debtor at the Balance Sheet date subsequently becomes bankrupt.

Non-adjusting events are post Balance Sheet events which concern conditions that did not exist at the Balance Sheet date. Material non-adjusting events may affect the ability of the user of financial statements to understand the financial position of the company properly. These events should be disclosed by way of a note to the financial statements stating:

- the nature of the event
- an estimate (if possible) of the financial effect.

Examples: Issues of shares and debentures
Capital reductions and reconstructions
Losses of fixed assets or stocks as a result of fire, flood, theft or other catastrophe

27.16 FRS 1 Cash flow statements

Companies are required to include a cash flow statement in their published accounts. This topic has been covered in chapter 24.

27.17 Directors' report

The Companies Act 1985 requires directors to prepare a report for each financial year. The purpose of the report is to supplement the information given by the financial statements, which, by themselves, cannot convey all the information that users of the accounts need to know to form an assessment of the past and future performance of the business.

The Companies Act states that the directors' report shall contain the following information.

1. A review of the business during the year and its position at the end of the year.

   [The Profit and Loss Account and Balance Sheet only provide information which can be expressed in monetary terms (concept of money measurement). They cannot describe the conditions under which the company has traded, for example.]

2. The principal activities carried on by the company during the year and significant changes in those activities.

   [The accounting statements prepared for FRS 3 cannot explain the activities carried on by the company or give complete information about new and discontinued activities.]

3. Particulars of important events that have occurred after the end of the financial year and which affect the company.

   [Post Balance Sheet events take place after the end of a company's financial year and may affect items in the Balance Sheet or Profit and Loss Account (adjusting events).

   Non-adjusting events occur after the date of the Balance Sheet but do not require the Profit and Loss Account or Balance Sheet items to be changed.]

4. Recommended dividends.

   [These must be approved by the members of the company at the annual general meeting.]

5. Names of the directors of the company, their remuneration, pension details and their interests in shares or debentures of the company.

   [Shareholders are entitled to know who have been stewards of their interests during the year and the extent of each director's commitment to the company as a shareholder or debenture holder.]

6. Donations to political parties or charities during the year.

   [Shareholders may not wish their money to be used for political purposes, or may wish that some of the profits be used for charitable purposes.]

7. Arrangements for promoting the health, safety and welfare at work of the employees.

   [Shareholders are entitled to be re-assured that the company is abiding by current legislation concerning health and safety and that it is concerned with the welfare of its employees (good labour relations).]

8. Information about research and development being carried on by the company.

   [Shareholders are able to see the extent of the company's involvement in the development of its product, which may be a guide to the future prospects of the company.]

9. An indication of the future developments in the company's business.

   [An indication of likely future growth and/or diversification) or disposing of non-core activities.]

10. Significant changes in fixed assets during the financial year.

    [Shareholders are informed of any material differences between the Balance Sheet values of fixed assets and their current market values.]

11. Policy regarding the payment of creditors.

    [This requirement arose from the practice of many large companies of improving their cash flows by delaying payments to creditors, whose cash flows suffered in consequence. Many suppliers of large companies are small businesses who are largely reliant upon prompt payments. There is an ethical dimension to the requirement to disclose this information.]

12. Details regarding employment of disabled persons.

    [Companies must not discriminate against disabled persons. They should provide information concerning the provision of facilities for disabled employees.]

27.18 Auditors' report

Directors are stewards of the company in which shareholders have invested their capital. The shareholders are unable to inspect the company's books but they are, along with the debenture holders, entitled to receive copies of the annual accounts. It is important that shareholders and debenture holders can be sure that the directors can be trusted to conduct the company's business well and that the financial statements and directors' report are reliable.

The shareholders appoint auditors to report at each annual general meeting whether

- proper books of account have been kept
- the annual financial statements are in agreement with the books of account
- in the auditors' opinion, the Balance Sheet gives a true and fair view of the position of the company at the end of the financial year and the Profit and Loss Account gives a true and fair view of the profit or loss for the period covered by the account.
- the accounts have been prepared in accordance with the Companies Acts and all current, relevant accounting standards.

If auditors are of the opinion that the continuance of a company is dependent on a bank loan or overdraft, they have a duty to mention that fact in their report as it is relevant to the going concern concept.

The auditors' responsibility extends to reporting on the directors' report and stating whether the statements in it are consistent with the financial statements. They must also report whether, in their opinion, the report contains misleading statements.

Auditors must be qualified accountants and independent of the company's directors and their associates. They report to the shareholders and not to the directors; as a result, auditors enjoy protection from wrongful dismissal from office by the directors.

27.19 Examination hints

- Make sure you are familiar with the requirements of the Companies Act 1985 and the accounting standards regarding published company accounts. They link very strongly with what you have already learnt and with the understanding and interpretation of accounts, which will be covered in the next chapter.
- Multiple-choice questions are often based on a knowledge this topic.
- Practise answering discursive type questions based on published accounts. Answers should be clear, concise and relevant.

27.20 Multiple-choice questions

1 FRS 18 (Accounting policies) lists four accounting principles. Which of the following is stated by the standard to be a desirable principle?

   A accruals

   B consistency

   C going concern

   D historical cost

2 SSAP 25 (Segmental reporting) requires companies to give separate figures for certain items for each segment. For which of the following are separate figures *not* required?

   A cost of sales

   B net assets employed

   C profit before taxation

   D turnover

3 On which amount are earnings per share calculated?

   A profit after interest, tax and preference dividend

   B profit after interest, tax, preference dividend and transfer to general reserve

   C profit before interest, tax and preference dividend

   D profit before interest, tax, preference dividend and transfer to general reserve

4 Which of the following is required by FRS 4 (Capital instruments) to be disclosed by way of a note to the accounts?

  A exceptional items

  B the basis on which depreciation has been calculated

  C the number of shares held by directors

  D the reason for any issue of shares during the year.

5 What should be disclosed by way of a note to the Balance Sheet regarding depreciation of fixed assets?

  A date of acquisition

  B estimated proceeds of disposal

  C estimated net residual value

  D useful economic lives of the assets

6 Which of the following, occurring after the Balance Sheet date, is an adjusting event?

  A a capital reconstruction

  B a debtor at the Balance Sheet date subsequently becoming bankrupt

  C an issue of shares

  D loss of stock in a fire

27.21 Additional exercises

1 Explain what is meant by an adjusting event. Describe the action that needs to be taken when one occurs and explain why the action is necessary.

2 What is segmental reporting and what does it entail? Why is it helpful to the users of financial statements?

Part III
Financial reporting and interpretation

28 Interpretation and analysis

In this chapter you will learn:
- **the limitations of financial statements**
- **how to analyse and interpret financial statements**
- **how to calculate ratios**
- **how to use ratios**
- **how to explain (and how not to explain) ratios.**

28.1 The limitations of financial statements for shareholders and other interested parties

The purpose of financial statements such as Profit and Loss Accounts and Balance Sheets is to present information in a meaningful way. That is why items in financial statements are placed in groups of similar items: fixed assets, current assets, current liabilities etc. It also explains why you should compile financial statements with every item in its correct place.

Accounting standards are intended to ensure that items included in financial statements and described in similar terms are calculated, as far as possible, on the same bases. The Companies Act and the accounting standards require companies to add numerous notes to their financial statements to throw more light on the items in the accounts.

To be useful, information must be clear, complete, reliable and timely. In spite of the efforts of the Companies Act and the numerous accounting standards to ensure some sort of uniformity in the preparation of financial statements, the published accounts of limited companies have a number of limitations as communicators of information.

- They are not clear to people who have an inadequate knowledge of accounting and finance.
- The information they give is not complete. Legislation and accounting standards recognise that companies are entitled to keep certain information confidential because publication would give competitors an unfair advantage.

- The reliability of financial statements is only relative because companies are permitted to exercise a fair degree of subjectivity in selecting their accounting policies. Depreciation, provisions for doubtful debts, stock valuation and treatment of Goodwill are examples of areas where there is no uniformity.
- Companies are allowed to depart from accounting standards if such departure is justified by the nature of their business and will improve the quality of the information provided by the accounting statements.
- By their very nature, published accounts are of historic interest. They may not be published for many months after the end of the financial year they cover. In the meantime, many circumstances may have changed: the economy may have improved or worsened; the political scene may have altered; new technologies may have been developed; fashions may have changed. A company's performance may have improved or worsened between the date of the Balance Sheet and its publication.

The directors' report may help to overcome some of the limitations of the financial statements, but not completely.

Only people with some knowledge of accounting are able to make much sense of the mass of figures in a company's financial statements. Even accountants need to interpret the figures before they are able to understand their significance. As a useful tool for interpreting accounts, accountants calculate ratios that relate certain items in the accounts to other items where there should be some sort of sensible relationship.

28.2 A pyramid of ratios

The ratios that accountants use may be represented as a pyramid, which classifies the ratios into useful types and shows how they relate to one another.

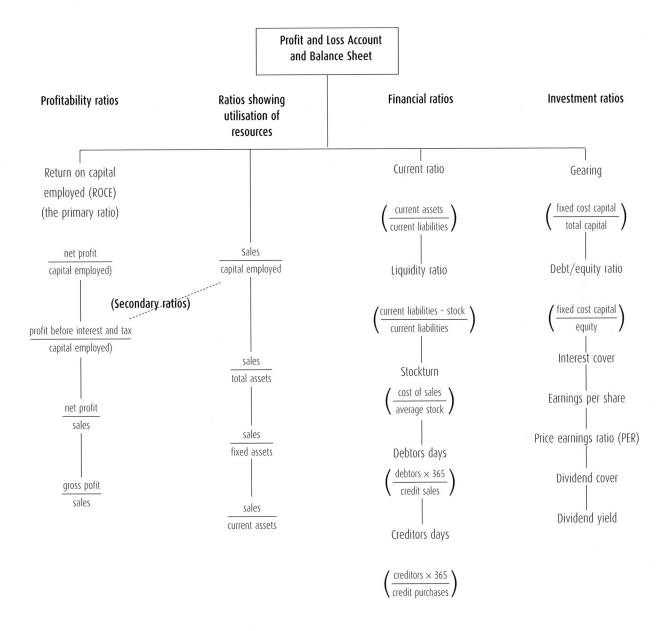

28.3 How to calculate and analyse ratios

All the ratios shown in the pyramid are explained in §§28.4–28.7 and illustrated with the aid of the following financial statements of Lladnar Ltd.

Lladnar Ltd
Profit and Loss Accounts for the years ended 31 December

	2003			2004	
	$000	$000		$000	$000
Turnover		1200			1600
Cost of sales					
Stock at 1.1.03	42		(1.1.04)	54	
Purchases	800			1166	
	842			1220	
Stock at 31.12. 03	54	788	(31.12.04)	100	1120
Gross profit		412			480
Salaries and wages	102			121	
Rent	66			66	
Electricity	30			32	
Sundry expenses	5			8	
Depreciation	27			37	
Debenture interest	10	240		15	279
Net profit		172			201
General reserve	40			60	
Preference dividend	8			10	
Ordinary dividend	60	108		64	134
Retained profit		64			67

Balance Sheets at 31 December

	2003			2004		
	$000	$000	$000	$000	$000	$000
Fixed assets			670			900
Current assets						
Stock		54			100	
Debtors		115			200	
Bank		100			29	
		269			329	
Current liabilities						
Creditors	101			190		
Dividends	40	141	128	44	234	95
			798			995
Long-term liability						
10% Debentures 2007/2008			100			150
			698			845
Share capital and reserves						
Ordinary shares of $1			400			400
10% Preference shares of $1			80			100
General Reserve			100			160
Retained profit			118			185
			698			845

Most ratios are appropriate for both incorporated and unincorporated businesses. Lladnar Ltd's Profit and Loss Account has been prepared in a form which, down to net profit, could apply to any business.

The ratios explained and analysed in §§28.4–28.7 are calculated to three decimal places but rounded to two decimal places. This is the usual requirement in examinations, but the particular requirement of any question must be observed.

28.4 Profitability ratios

The primary ratio: return on capital employed (ROCE)

The test of a good investment is its profitability, that is, the reward it yields on the amount invested in it. (Profit and profitability should not be confused. Profit is expressed as an amount of money: $172 000 for 2003 and $201 000 for 2004 in Lladnar Ltd's case; profitability is a ratio that relates profit to the amount invested.) The **first (or primary) ratio** for investors in a business is the **return on capital employed**. It relates net profit before interest and tax to the capital employed in the business. The formula is:

$$\frac{\text{profit before interest and tax}}{\text{capital employed}} \times 100$$

(remember it easily as $\dfrac{\text{PROBIT}}{\text{capital employed}} \times 100$)

(PROBIT = profit before interest and tax)

Lladnar Ltd's return on capital employed is:

2003	2004
$\frac{182}{798} \times 100 = 22.81\%$	$\frac{216}{995} \times 100 = 21.71\%$

Note. Debentures and other long-term loans are included in capital employed.

Comment In 2003, $22.81 of every $100 of turnover was left on the bottom line as net profit. (The net profit is known as the 'bottom line'. Items in accounts may be described as 'above the line' or 'below the line'.) In 2004, the return had decreased by 1.1% to 21.71%. The decrease, although only small, contrasts with the preferred result, which would be an improvement in profitability. Whether or not a rate of return is satisfactory depends upon the return that may be expected on suitable alternative investments.

Profit before interest and tax

Profit before interest and tax is calculated as a percentage of sales. For Lladnar Ltd this is:

2003	2004
$\frac{182}{1200} \times 100 = 15.17\%$	$\frac{216}{1600} \times 100 = 13.5\%$

Comment Profit before interest and tax has fallen by 1.67%. When the gross profit percentage is calculated, that ratio will be seen to have fallen even more (by 4.33%). It is not surprising, therefore, to find that the profit before interest and tax has fallen although it should not fall by the same amount as most overheads are more or less fixed and do not vary with turnover.

Net profit percentage

Net profit can be related to sales by the following formula: $\frac{\text{net profit}}{\text{sales}} \times 100$. For Lladnar Ltd this is:

2003	2004
$\frac{172}{1200} \times 100 = 14.33\%$	$\frac{201}{1600} \times 100 = 12.56\%$

Comment The net profit percentage has fallen by 1.77% from 14.33% in 2003 to 12.56% in 2004, even though turnover has risen by $33\frac{1}{3}\%$ from $1 200 000 to $1 600 000. The causes for the change in the net profit percentage may be analysed by examining gross profit percentage and the overheads as a percentage of sales.

Gross profit percentage

The formula for gross profit percentage is $\frac{\text{gross profit}}{\text{sales}} \times 100$. For Lladnar Ltd this is:

2003	2004
$\frac{412}{1200} \times 100 = 34.33\%$	$\frac{480}{1600} \times 100 = 30.00\%$

Comment Gross profit percentage has decreased by 4.33% from 34.33% to 30.00%. In theory, the gross profit percentage should match the margin the business expects to make on all its sales. In practice, it is not as simple as that because most businesses sell more than one kind of good and a different mark up may be added to each kind. The gross profit percentage is affected by changes in the mix of the different products making up the turnover.

The reduction in the gross profit percentage may be explained by a number of factors:

- a rise in the price of goods purchased may not have been passed on to customers
- it may have been necessary to purchase the goods from a different supplier at a higher price
- the margin on sales may have been cut
  - to increase the volume of sales
  - to fight competition from other businesses
  - as an introductory offer for a new product
  - as a result of seasonal sales
  - to dispose of out-of-date or damaged stocks
  - to increase cash flow when the business is short of cash
- the cost of sales may have been increased by the theft of stock.

Overheads

Overheads expressed as percentage of sales are given as follows for Lladnar Ltd:

2003	2004
$\frac{240}{1200} \times 100 = 20\%$	$\frac{279}{1600} \times 100 = 17.44\%$

The overhead percentage is calculated more quickly by finding the difference between the gross and net profit percentages.

Comment Although sales have increased in 2004 by $33\frac{1}{3}\%$, the ratio of overheads to sales has decreased from 20% to 17.44%. Sometimes overheads may increase as a percentage of sales, but the increase should not match the increase in gross profit percentage. The reason is that most overheads, such as rent, do not vary as a result of an increase in sales. Other overheads may vary, but not in proportion to sales. Salespeople's remuneration, for example, may consist of a fixed salary plus a bonus based on sales.

It is possible to analyse overheads further by expressing the individual items as percentages of sales but this is usually of very limited value because of the absence of any direct link between the individual overheads and sales.

28.5 Ratios showing the utilisation of resources

The profitability of a business depends on how efficiently it uses its resources, and the next group of ratios is designed to test this aspect of the business.

Sales as a percentage of capital employed

Capital invested in a business must be utilised efficiently if it is to produce a good ROCE. Capital of $100 producing sales of $300 is being used more efficiently than the same capital producing sales of only $200. Sales are expressed as a percentage of capital employed. For Lladnar Ltd, this is:

2003	2004
$\frac{1200}{798} \times 100 = 150.38\%$	$\frac{1600}{995} \times 100 = 160.80\%$

Comment In 2003, sales were only $1\frac{1}{2}$ times the amount of capital employed. This is very low, but further comment would be unhelpful without knowing the kind of business being carried on by Lladnar Ltd. A low percentage may be normal for some businesses. The percentage for 2004 has only improved slightly.

The ratios of profit before tax and interest percentage, and sales as a percentage of capital employed, are known as **secondary ratios** because they help to explain the primary ratio (ROCE). If the two ratios are multiplied together, they give the primary ratio:

$$\frac{\text{net profit}}{\text{sales}} \times \frac{\text{sales}}{\text{capital employed}} = \frac{\text{net profit}}{\text{capital employed}}$$

(Sales in the denominator of the first fraction cancel out sales in the numerator of the second fraction to give the third fraction.) For Lladnar Ltd:

2003	2004
$15.17\% \times 150.38\% = 22.81\%$	$13.5\% \times 160.80\% = 21.71\%$

Some textbooks state that the net profit percentage is one of the secondary ratios, but this is only true if no interest is involved.

The ratio of sales to capital employed may be further refined by relating sales to total assets, then to fixed assets and current assets.

Utilisation of total assets

The number of times sales cover the capital invested in the assets of a business is calculated as follows.

$$\frac{\text{sales}}{\text{total assets}} = X \text{ times}$$

Lladnar Ltd's utilisation of total assets is as follows.

2003	2004
$\frac{1200}{670 + 269} = 1.28 \text{ times}$	$\frac{1600}{900 + 329} = 1.30 \text{ times}$

Comment These ratios are on the low side but further comment is limited by lack of information about the nature of the business.

Notice that this 'ratio' is expressed as a 'number of times' the total assets are 'turned over'.

Fixed asset turnover

A business purchases fixed assets with the intention that they will earn revenue. Fixed asset turnover is calculated as $\frac{\text{sales}}{\text{total of fixed assets}}$. The ratios for Lladnar Ltd are:

2003	2004
$\frac{1200}{670} = 1.79 \text{ times}$	$\frac{1600}{900} = 1.78 \text{ times}$

Comment There has not been a significant change in the ratio in 2004. Assets that are not owned for a full year will not earn a full year's revenue and, unless information is given about the dates the assets were purchased, further comment is impossible.

Current asset turnover

Current assets include stock, debtors and cash. The relationship of these to sales is of interest because stock and debtor levels may well be determined by the level of sales. Current asset turnover is calculated as $\frac{\text{sales}}{\text{total of current assets}}$. The ratios for Lladnar Ltd are:

2003	2004
$\frac{1200}{269} = 4.46 \text{ times}$	$\frac{1600}{329} = 4.86 \text{ times}$

Comment There would appear to be very little change but other ratios, stockturn and debtors' days (see below), will show if the situation is as satisfactory as it appears.

Net current assets (or working capital) to sales

This is another ratio that may be used to measure performance. It is calculated as

$$\frac{turnover}{net\ current\ assets}.$$ For Lladnar Ltd:

2003	2004
$\frac{1200}{128} = 9.38$ times	$\frac{1600}{95} = 16.84$ times

Comment The increase from 9.38 times to 16.84 times may appear to be a good result, but comment should be reserved until creditors' days (see below) have been calculated.

28.6 Financial ratios

Current ratio

Current assets are the fund out of which a business should pay its current liabilities; it should never have to sell fixed assets to pay its creditors. It follows that there should be a margin of safety between the current assets and the current liabilities. The current ratio expresses the margin in the form of a true ratio:

current assets : current liabilities

Lladnar Ltd's current ratios are:

2003	2004
269 : 141 = 1.91 : 1	329 : 234 = 1.41 : 1

The right-hand figure in the ratio should always be expressed as unity (i.e. 1); divide the current liabilities into the current assets.

Comment The ratios show that, although the current assets comfortably exceed the current liabilities, the safety margin has been reduced by 0.5 in 2004. Textbooks often state that the current ratio should be between 1.5 : 1 and 2 : 1 to take account of slow-moving stocks and slow-paying debtors, but much depends upon the kind of business. While a low ratio could signal danger, a high ratio may indicate that a business has resources that are not being used efficiently. High levels of stock, debtors and cash mean that capital is lying idle in the business instead of being used profitably.

The current ratio is sometimes described as an indication of liquidity but that is incorrect. The liquidity of a business depends upon the liquidity of its current assets. A **liquid asset** is one that is in the form of cash (cash and bank balances) or in a form that may become cash in the short term (debtors). Stock is not a liquid asset – no buyer has yet

been found for it! The current ratio calculation includes stock, so is not a measure of liquidity. Liquidity is measured by the **liquidity ratio** (or acid test or quick ratio).

Liquidity ratio (acid test or quick ratio)

The liquidity ratio excludes stock from the calculation and shows the proportion of liquid assets (debtors and cash) that is available to pay the current liabilities. The ratio is calculated as

current assets – stock : current liabilities

The liquidity ratios of Lladnar Ltd are:

2003	2004
(269 – 54) : 141 = 215 : 141 = 1.52 : 1	(329 – 100) : 234 = 229 : 234 = 0.98 : 1

Comment The liquidity ratio has fallen by 0.54 in 2004 and the cash plus debtors are now less than the current liabilities. Textbooks often state that the liquidity ratio should not fall below 1 : 1, or perhaps 0.9 : 1. This is generally a good guide, but supermarkets' sales are on a cash basis while they enjoy a period of credit before they have to pay for their supplies. In the meantime, they have a constant inflow of cash from sales. Their liquidity ratio may not exceed 0.4 : 1. Without knowing more about Lladnar Ltd's business, further comment may not be helpful. However, it would not appear to be a supermarket.

Debtors, stock and creditors may be examined in a little more detail.

Debtors' ratio (debtors' days)

A business should have set a limit on the amount of time it allows its debtors to pay. Many debtors take longer than the time allowed and the debtors' ratio calculates the average time debtors are taking to pay. The formula is

$$\frac{debtors \times 365}{credit\ sales}$$

The debtors' days for Lladnar Ltd are:

2003	2004
$\frac{115 \times 365}{1200} = 34.98$ or 35 days	$\frac{200 \times 365}{1600} = 45.63$ or 46 days

As there is no information about any of Lladnar Ltd's sales being on a cash basis, it has been assumed that all sales were on credit. It is sensible to round all fractions of days up to the next day.

Comment The debtors are taking 11 more days in 2004 to pay their bills. It is usual in many businesses to allow debtors 30 days, or 1 month, to pay. The company seems to be losing control over its debtors' payments and to have a deteriorating cash flow. Debtors' payments may be affected by a deterioration in the national economy or in the business sector. A business may try to attract new customers by offering more favourable payment terms. When debtors are slow to pay there is an increased risk of incurring bad debts.

Stockturn

Stockturn is the rate at which the stock is turned over, or the time that elapses before stock is sold. This ratio is important for the following reasons.

- The more quickly stock is sold, the sooner the profit on it is realised and the more times the profit is earned in the financial year.
- A slow stock turnover may indicate that excessive stocks are held and the risk of obsolete or spoiled stocks increases. Large quantities of slow-moving stocks mean that capital is locked up in the business and is not earning revenue.

However, different trades have their own expected rates of stock turnover. Food shops will expect to have a fast stock turnover if their food is not to deteriorate before it is sold. On the other hand, shops selling furniture, refrigerators, radios and television sets, etc. will have slower stock turnovers, while manufacturers of large items of plant and shipbuilders will have very long stockturns. Generally, fast-moving stocks have lower profit margins than slow-moving stocks. (Compare the profit margin to be expected on the sale of food with that expected on the sale of motor cars.)

The formula for calculating stockturn is

$$\frac{\text{cost of sales}}{\text{average stock}} \quad \text{where average stock} = (\text{opening stock} + \text{closing stock}) \div 2$$

It is important to take average stock because closing stock may not be representative of the normal stock level. If opening stock is not given, use closing stock for the calculation.

It is usual to express stockturn as the number of times a year the stock is turned over, but it is also acceptable to express it as the average number of days stock remains in the business before it is sold.

The stockturns for Lladnar Ltd are:

2003	2004
$\dfrac{788}{(42 + 54) \div 2} = 16.4$ times a year	$\dfrac{1120}{(54 + 100) \div 2} = 14.55$ times a year
or $\dfrac{365}{16.4} = 23$ days	$\dfrac{365}{14.55} = 26$ days

Comment The rate of stockturn has slowed a little in 2004. Without more knowledge about the company's business further comment would only be speculation.

The cash at bank

It is not necessary to make up a formula for a cash ratio; it is sufficient to refer to the balances and, in the case of Lladnar Ltd, to draw attention to the fact that the bank balance has fallen from $98 000 to $29 000. When a balance at bank is converted into an overdraft, it may be appropriate to recognise the fact with a suitable comment.

Creditors' ratio (creditors' days)

Creditors' days are calculated using the formula

$$\frac{\text{creditors} \times 365}{\text{purchases on credit}}$$

Assuming that all Lladnar Ltd's purchases were made on credit, the creditors' days are:

2003	2004
$\dfrac{101 \times 365}{800} = 47$ days	$\dfrac{190 \times 365}{1166} = 60$ days

Comment The company is taking 13 days longer to pay its creditors and this is beneficial to its cash flow. However, it may be dangerous if it is greatly exceeding the period of credit allowed by suppliers as they may withdraw their credit facilities and require Lladnar Ltd to pay cash with orders in future.

Overtrading

Overtrading may occur when a business increases its turnover rapidly with the result that its stocks, debtors and creditors also increase, but to a level that threatens its liquidity. The business may become insolvent and unable to pay its creditors as they fall due. The result may be that the business is forced to close.

Lladnar Ltd has increased turnover by $33\frac{1}{3}\%$ in 2004. Stock has increased by $56 000 (over 100%). Debtors' days have increased from 35 to 46 days (31%) suggesting poor credit control by the company. Stockturn has increased, but only slightly. Lladnar Ltd may be overtrading.

The cash operating cycle

The cash operating cycle measures the time it takes for cash to circulate around the working capital system. It calculates the interval that occurs between the time a business has to pay its creditors and the time it receives cash from its customers. It is calculated using the following formula:

stockturn in days + debtors' days - creditors' days

The cash operating cycle for Lladnar Ltd is found as follows.

	2003 days	2004 days
Stockturn	23	26
Debtors' days	35	46
	58	72
Creditors' days	47	60
Cash operating cycle	11	12

In both years the company received its money from sales, on average, 11/12 days after it had paid its suppliers. During this time, the company was financing its customers out of its own money!

28.7 Investment (stock exchange) ratios

Investment ratios are of particular interest to people who have invested, or are intending to invest, in a company. These people include shareholders and lenders such as debenture holders and banks.

Gearing

Gearing is fixed-cost capital expressed as a percentage of total capital. Fixed-cost capital is the money that finances a company in return for a fixed return and includes debentures and preference share capital. Total capital includes the equity interests (ordinary share capital and reserves) plus the fixed-cost capital.

The formula is

$$\frac{\text{debentures + preference share capital}}{\text{ordinary share capital and reserves + debentures + preference shares}} \times 100$$

Lladnar Ltd's gearing is:

2003
$$\frac{\$100\,000 + \$80\,000}{\$618\,000 + \$100\,000 + \$80\,000} \times 100 = 22.56\%$$

2004
$$\frac{\$150\,000 + 100\,000}{\$745\,000 + £150\,000 + \$100\,000} \times 100 = 25.13\%$$

A company is described as highly geared if the gearing is more than 50%. If it is less than 50%, it is low geared. 50% is neutral gearing. Lladnar Ltd is low geared.

Comment The key word in understanding the importance of gearing is risk. Lenders of money to a company may be concerned if it is highly geared; this may indicate that a large slice of profit is applied in the payment of interest. Risk arises if profits fall and fail to cover the interest payments. Banks approached by a highly geared company will question why, when the company is already heavily dependent upon loans, the shareholders are unwilling to invest more of their own money in their company. Perhaps they lack confidence in the company's future.

The risk to ordinary shareholders is increased in a highly geared company as the following example shows.

	Low geared company	Highly geared company
Gearing	20%	80%
	$	$
Ordinary share capital	800 000	200 000
10% debentures	200 000	800 000
	1 000 000	1 000 000
Year 1		
Profit before interest	100 000	100 000
Debenture interest	20 000	80 000
Profit left for ordinary shareholders	80 000	20 000

Profit as a percentage of ordinary share capital:

$\frac{80\,000}{800\,000}$	10%	$\frac{20\,000}{200\,000}$	10%

Year 2		
Profit before interest	150 000	150 000
Debenture interest	20 000	80 000
Profit left for ordinary shareholders	130 000	70 000

Profit as a percentage of ordinary share capital

$\frac{130\,000}{800\,000}$	16.25%	$\frac{70\,000}{200\,000}$	35%

Year 3		
Profit before interest	50 000	50 000
Debenture interest	20 000	80 000
Profit left for ordinary shareholders	30 000	(30 000)

Profit as a percentage of ordinary share capital

$\frac{30\,000}{800\,000}$	3.75%	$\frac{(30\,000)}{200\,000}$	-15%

The above example shows that if profit varies by ± $50 000 (50%) in the low geared company, the profit left for the ordinary shareholders varies by ± 6.25%. In the highly geared company, the variation is ± 25%. The swings in the fortunes of ordinary shareholders are greater (more risky) in a highly geared company than in a low geared company.

Debt/equity ratio

The formula for the debt/equity ratio is

$$\frac{\text{debentures + preference share capital}}{\text{ordinary share capital + reserves}}$$

Lladnar Ltd's debt/equity ratio is

2003
$$\frac{\$100\ 000 + \$80\ 000}{\$618\ 000} \times 100 = 29.13\%$$
2004
$$\frac{\$150\ 000 + \$100\ 000}{\$745\ 000} \times 100 = 33.56\%$$

Comment This ratio is often taught as an alternative method of calculating the gearing ratio, but it is arguable whether expressing fixed-cost capital as a percentage of equity is as useful as expressing it as a percentage of total capital employed. In contrast to the debt/equity ratio, the gearing ratio is consistent with the formula for return on capital employed.

If the debt/equity ratio is less than 100%, the company is low geared; if it exceeds 100% the company is highly geared; 100% is neutral gearing.

Interest cover

Debenture holders and other lenders to a company need to be sure that the profit before interest adequately covers the interest payments. Interest must be paid even if a company makes a loss, but it is reassuring if the profit before interest covers the interest payments several times; a good cover provides a safety margin against a fall in profits in the future. Shareholders are also concerned to see a good interest cover as their dividends can only be paid if profit is left after charging the interest in the Profit and Loss Account.

The formula for calculating interest cover is

$$\frac{\text{profit before interest}}{\text{interest payable}}$$

The interest cover for Llandar Ltd is:

2003	2004
$\frac{182^*}{10} = 18.2$ times	$\frac{216^*}{15} = 14.4$ times
* 172 + 10	* 201 + 15

Comment Lladnar Ltd's interest cover has decreased by 3.8 times in 2004, but is still very satisfactory.

Earnings per share

Earnings are the profit left for the ordinary shareholders after interest, tax and preference dividends have been provided for in the Profit and Loss Account. Ordinary dividends are paid out of earnings, and any earnings not distributed increase the reserves and the Balance Sheet value of the shares. Earnings per share are expressed in cents ($0.00) per share, and are calculated using the formula:

$$\frac{\text{earnings}}{\text{the number of ordinary shares issued}}$$

Lladnar Ltd's earnings per share are:

2003	2004
$\frac{\$16\ 400\ 000^*}{400\ 000} = \$0.41$ per share	$\frac{\$19\ 100\ 000^*}{400\ 000} = \$0.4775$ per share

* Net profit less the preference dividend × 100

Comment Earnings per share have increased by $0.0675 in 2004 and have allowed an increased dividend to be paid and a small increase in the retained profit for the year (added to the reserves).

Price earnings ratio (PER)

The price earnings ratio calculates the number of times the price being paid for the shares on the market exceeds the earnings per share; it is calculated using the formula:

$$\frac{\text{market price per share}}{\text{earnings per share}}$$

The market price of Lladnar Ltd's ordinary shares at 31 December 2003 was $1.80, and at 31 December 2004 it was $2.10. The price earnings ratios are:

2003	2004
$\frac{\$1.80}{\$0.41} = 4.39$	$\frac{\$2.10}{\$0.4775} = 4.40$

Comment The price earnings ratio has remained steady over both years. Shareholders have been prepared to pay 4.4 times the earnings per share. This is a measure of confidence in the ability of Lladnar Ltd to maintain its earnings in future. A PER of 4.4 is not particularly good for a long-term investment in a company. PER is an important ratio for investors as it gives a quick and easily understandable indicator of the market's assessment of a company's prospects.

Dividend cover

The formula for dividend cover is

$$\frac{\text{profit after tax and preference dividend}}{\text{dividend on ordinary shares}}$$

Dividend cover is the number of times the profit out of which dividends may be paid covers the dividend. If the cover is too low, a decline in profits may lead to the dividend being restricted or not paid at all. On the other hand, if the cover is high, shareholders may decide that the directors are adopting a mean dividend policy.

Dividend cover for Lladnar Ltd is:

2003	2004
$\dfrac{\$164\,000}{\$60\,000} = 2.73$ times	$\dfrac{\$191\,000}{\$64\,000} = 2.98$ times

Comment A dividend cover of 2 to 3 times may be considered normal and safe.

Dividend yield

Companies usually declare dividends as a certain number of cents per share, representing a certain percentage return based on the nominal value of the share. For example, a dividend of $0.03 per share of $0.50 is a dividend of 6% on the share. Shareholders who have paid the market price for their shares need to know the return based on the price they have paid. This is the dividend yield and is calculated using the following formula:

$$\text{dividend yield} = \text{declared rate of dividend} \times \frac{\text{nominal value of share}}{\text{market price of share}}$$

Lladnar Ltd's declared rates of dividend are:

2003	2004
$\dfrac{\$60\,000}{\$400\,000} \times 100 = 15\%$	$\dfrac{\$64\,000}{\$400\,000} \times 100 = 16\%$

The dividend yields are:

2003	2004
$15\% \times \dfrac{\$1}{\$1.80} = 8.33\%$	$16\% \times \dfrac{\$1}{\$2.10} = 7.62\%$

Comment The small decrease in the dividend yield in 2004 is the result of the share price increasing fractionally more than the increase in the dividend. There may be a connection between the increase in the market price and the small increases in the earnings per share and the dividend cover.

Earnings yield

The earnings yield is calculated in a similar manner to the dividend yield. Lladnar Ltd's earnings as a percentage of ordinary share capital are:

2003	2004
$\dfrac{\$164\,000}{\$400\,000} \times 100 = 41$	$\dfrac{\$191\,000}{\$400\,000} \times 100 = 47.75\%$

The earnings yield is calculated using the formula

$$\text{earnings yield} = \text{earnings}\% \times \frac{\text{nominal value of share}}{\text{market price of share}}$$

For Lladnar Ltd, the earnings yields are:

2003	2004
$41\% \times \dfrac{\$1}{\$1.80} = 22.78\%$	$47.75\% \times \dfrac{\$1}{\$2.10} = 22.74\%$

Comment The change in the earnings yield in 2004 is not significant.

28.8 Trend analysis and inter-firm comparison

Individual ratios are usually of very limited value. The ratios of a business for past years are necessary if trends in progress or deterioration of performance are to be seen. The examples of Lladnar Ltd have given the results for 2003 and 2004 and some limited trends have been observed. Given the results for, say, four, five or six years, more reliable trends may be discerned.

Trends may signal to investors whether they should stay with their investment, or sell it and re-invest in a more promising venture.

Inter-firm comparison (IFC) is possible when information about the performance of other similar businesses is available. Trade associations collect information from their members and publish the statistics as averages for the trade or industry. It is thus possible to compare the results of one company with the averages for businesses of the same type. Comparisons, however, must be made with care. It is not realistic to compare the statistics of a small trader with results achieved by large companies. Comparison should always be on a like-for-like basis as far as possible.

Inter-firm comparison can inform shareholders whether they have invested their money in the most profitable and stable institutions.

28.9 The limitations of ratios

- To be useful and reliable, ratios must be reasonably accurate. They should be based on information in accounts and notes to the accounts. Some useful information may not be disclosed in the accounts and some account headings may not indicate the contents clearly.
- Information must be timely to be of use. It may not be available until some long time after the end of a company's financial year.
- Ratios do not explain results but may indicate areas of concern; further investigation is usually necessary to discover causes of the concern.
- Ratios usually do not recognise seasonal factors in business:
  - profit margins will be lower than normal during periods of seasonal sales
  - stock and debtors are unlikely to remain at constant levels throughout the year.
  - Companies, even in the same trade, will have different policies for such matters as providing for depreciation, doubtful debts, profit recognition, transferring profits to reserves, dividend policy, etc.

Such limitations should be borne in mind when making comparisons between businesses.

Exercise 1

(Based on the accounts of a sole trader)
Najim wants to analyse the results of his trading for the year ended 31 December 2005 and has prepared his Trading and Profit and Loss Account and Balance Sheet. He compares these with the final accounts for the previous year. The Trading and Profit and Loss Accounts and Balance Sheets for the two years are as follows.

Trading and Profit and Loss Accounts				
	for the year ended 31.12.04		for the year ended 31.12.05	
	$	$	$	$
Sales		172 308		187 500
Less cost of sales				
Opening stock	12 000		16 000	
Purchases	116 000		125 500	
	128 000		141 500	
Closing stock	16 000	112 000	14 000	127 500
Gross profit		60 308		60 000
Less expenses		38 769		32 678
Net profit		21 539		27 322

Balance Sheets at				
	31.12.04		31.12.05	
	$	$	$	$
Fixed assets (net book values)		78 322		93 750
Current assets				
Stock	16 000		14 000	
Trade debtors	9 914		12 511	
Bank	4 851		7 185	
	30 765		33 696	
Current liabilities				
Trade creditors	13 984	16 781	17 192	16 504
		95 103		110 254
Opening capital		81 176		95 103
Add profit		21 539		27 322
		102 715		122 425
Deduct drawings		7 612		12 171
		95 103		110 254

Further information

1. 60% of Najim's sales are on credit.
2. Najim purchases all his stock of goods on credit.
3. The only current assets are stock, trade debtors and a bank balance.

Required

(a) Calculate the following ratios to *two* decimal places for each of the years ended 31 December 2004 and 2005.
  (i) gross profit percentage
  (ii) net profit percentage
  (iii) fixed asset turnover
  (iv) stockturn
  (v) debtors' days
  (vi) creditors' days
  (vii) current ratio
  (viii) liquid (acid test) ratio

(b) Compare the performance of Najim's business in 2005 with its performance in 2004, using the ratios calculated in (a), and comment on the comparison.

Exercise 2

(Based on the accounts of limited companies)
A financial consultant has been asked by his client for advice on the relative performance of two companies, Dunedin Ltd and Wellington Ltd. Extracts from the Profit and Loss Accounts for the year ended 31 December 2004 and the Balance Sheets at that date of the two companies are as follows.

Profit and Loss Accounts for the year ended 31 December 2004

	Dunedin Ltd	Wellington Ltd
	$000	$000
Operating profit	300	420
Debenture interest	(60)	(120)
	240	300
Transfer to General Reserve	(100)	(50)
Preference dividend	(6)	(60)
Ordinary dividend	(90)	(150)
Retained profit	44	40

Balance Sheet extracts at 31 December 2004

Dunedin Ltd		Wellington Ltd	
	$000		$000
Long-term liabilities		Long-term liabilities	
10% debentures 2007/8	600	12% debentures 2006/7	1 000
Ordinary shares of $1	200	Ordinary shares of $2	1 500
6% preference shares of $1	100	8% preference shares of $1	750
General reserve	120	General reserve	200
Retained profit	80	Retained profit	350
	500		2 800

The market values of the ordinary shares at 31 December 2004 were as follows.

Dunedin Ltd $2.70   Wellington Ltd $3.60

Required

(a) Calculate the following ratios to *two* decimal places for each company.
   (i) gearing
   (ii) interest cover
   (iii) earnings per share (EPS)
   (iv) dividend per share
   (v) dividend cover
   (vi) price earnings ratio (PER)
   (vii) dividend yield
(b) Compare and comment on the performance of the two companies in 2004 using the ratios calculated in (a).

28.10 How to prepare a Profit and Loss Account and Balance Sheet from given ratios

A Profit and Loss Account and Balance Sheet may be prepared from a list of accounting ratios provided at least one item is given as a numerical term. The method begins with the given numerical term and progresses by steps from that.

Example

Pulchra's stock at 31 December 2004 was $35 000, which was $5000 less than her stock at 1 January 2004. Further information about her business for the year ended 31 December 2004 is as follows.

Stockturn   7 times

Gross profit/sales   44%

Net profit/sales $17\frac{1}{2}$%

Distribution cost to administration expenses   1:3

Debtors' days   32 (70% of sales are on credit)

Creditors' days   65 (all purchases were made on credit)

Fixed asset turnover $2\frac{1}{2}$ times

Current ratio   1.8:1

Interest cover   12.2 times

The current assets consist of stock, trade debtors and bank balance only.

Pulchra has received a long-term loan on which she pays interest at 10% per annum.

Pulchra has drawn $1000 from the business each week.

Required

Prepare Pulchra's Trading and Profit and Loss Account for the year ended 31 December 2004 and her Balance Sheet at that date in as much detail as possible. Make all calculations to the nearest $.

Answer

The stock at 31 December 2004 is the starting point. Proceed as follows, in the order given by the numbered steps.

Pulchra
Trading and Profit and Loss Account for the year ended 31 December 2004

		$	$
Step 6	Sales (100/56* × 262 500)		468 750
	Cost of sales		
Step 2	Stock at 1.1.04 (35 000 + 5000)	40 000	
Step 5	Purchases (balancing figure)	257 500	
Step 4	(262 500 + 35 000)	297 500	
Step 1	Stock at 31.12.04 (given)	35 000	
Step 3	(cost of sales $\frac{40\ 000 + 35\ 000}{2} = \times\ 7$)		262 500
Step 7	Gross profit (468 750 − 262 500)		206 250
Step 10	Distribution costs (124 219 × $\frac{1}{4}$)		31 055
Step 11	Administration expenses (124 219 × $\frac{3}{4}$)		93 164
Step 9	(balancing figure)		124 219
Step 8	Net profit (17$\frac{1}{2}$% of 468 750)		82 031
Step 12	Interest on long-term loan at 10% (82 031 ÷ 12.2)		6 724
Step 13			75 307

*Gross profit/sales = 44%, therefore cost of sales = 56% of sales.

Balance Sheet at 31 December 2004

		$	$
Step 14	Fixed assets (468 750 ÷ 2$\frac{1}{2}$)		187 500
	Current assets		
Step 15	Stock	35 000	
Step 16	Trade debtors (468 750 × $\frac{7}{10}$ × $\frac{32}{365}$)	28 767	
Step 20	Bank (balancing figure)	18 774	
Step 19	(45 856 × 1.8)	82 541	
Step 17	Trade creditors (257 500 × $\frac{65}{365}$)	45 856	
Step 18	(balancing figure)		36 685
Step 21			224 185
Step 22	Less long-term loan at 10% (6724 × 10)		67 240
Step 23			156 945
Step 28	Capital at 1.1.04 (balancing figure)		133 638
Step 24	Profit for the year		75 307
Step 25			208 945
Step 26	Drawings (1000 × 52)		52 000
Step 27			156 945

Note. The steps show the order in which the items should be tackled but the step numbers do not form part of the answer and should not be shown in answers to questions. It is important in examinations to gain as many marks as possible as quickly as possible. It is a good idea to start with an outline for the Trading and Profit and Loss Account and Balance Sheet (leaving spaces to insert additional items if necessary), and to fill in the items as soon as the figures are known. For example, stock in the Balance Sheet can be inserted immediately it has been entered in the Trading Account. Similarly, net profit can be inserted in the Balance Sheet as soon as it has been calculated in the Profit and Loss Account.

Exercise 3

Patience has mislaid her final accounts for the year ended 31 December 2004 but has found the report, which her accountant has prepared, based on those accounts. She has decided to reconstruct the accounts from the information contained in the report.

The accountant's report contained the following data.

At 31 December 2004

Stock $54 000. (This was 20% more than the stock at 1 January 2004.)

For the year ended 31 December 2004

Stockturn	10 times
Gross profit margin	35%
Net profit margin	22%
Fixed asset turnover	4 times
Debtors' days	34 (based on 365 days in the year)
Creditors' days	42 (based on 365 days in the year)
Current ratio	2.5 : 1

The current assets consist of stock, trade debtors and bank balance.

All sales and purchases were made on credit.

Patience drew $140 000 from the business during the year.

Required

(a) Prepare, in as much detail as possible, Patience's Trading and Profit and Loss Account for the year ended 31 December 2004 and the Balance Sheet at that date. Make all calculations to the nearest $.

Virtue carries on a similar business to that of Patience and has the following data for the year ended 31 December 2004.

Stockturn	12 times
Gross profit margin	40%
Net profit margin	20%
Fixed asset turnover	5 times
Debtors' days	31
Creditors' days	36

Required

(b) Compare Virtue's performance with that of Patience and indicate the ratios that show which business is the more efficient.

You should write your answer in sentence form and include supporting figures.

28.11 Examination hints

- Learn the headings under which ratios are shown in the pyramid of ratios and which ratios are included under each heading.
- Remember how each ratio is calculated (the model).
- Take care to calculate ratios on the correct figures and check your arithmetic.
- Express every ratio in the correct terms, for example as a percentage, a number of times or days, a true ratio, etc. Marks will not be awarded in an examination if the correct terms are omitted.
- Make sure you understand what each ratio is intended to explain.
- Your comments on ratios should be based on the information you are given and justified by the ratios you have calculated. Do not assume facts you are not given.
- Avoid making definite statements that cannot be supported by the information given. You may *suggest* reasons for the comments you make.
- Your comments should be concise and relevant; avoid repetition of the same point. Long rambling answers that stray from the point do not impress the examiner.

28.12 Multiple-choice questions

1 Information about a business is given in the following table.

	year 1	year 2
	$	$
Turnover	200 000	250 000
Cost of sales	125 000	140 000
	75 000	110 000
Operating expenses	32 000	64 000
Profit before interest and taxation	43 000	46 000
Fixed assets	140 000	120 000
Net current assets	60 000	80 000
Long-term loans	(80 000)	(40 000)

Which of the following is true in year 2?

	Gross profit margin	Return on capital employed
A	decreased	decreased
B	increased	decreased
C	decreased	increased
D	increased	increased

2 Extracts from the Profit and Loss Accounts for two years for a business are given in this table:

	Year 1	Year 2
	$	$
Sales	100 000	200 000
Gross profit	30 000	70 000

What might explain the change in the gross profit margin in year 2?

A an increase in sales

B an increase in the sales price

C a reduction in stock

D suppliers offering higher cash discounts

3 What is the effect on the current ratio and quick ratio of a business if it uses cash to buy stock?

	Current ratio	Quick ratio
A	decrease	decrease
B	decrease	increase
C	no change	decrease
D	no change	increase

4 The quick ratio (acid test) of a business has fallen. What is the reason for the fall?

A a decrease in creditors

B a decrease in stock

C an increase in cash

D an increase in the bank overdraft

5 The closing stock of a business was $30 000 and the cost of goods sold was $600 000. Stock turnover is based on the average value of the opening and closing stocks.

If the stock turnover was 15 times, what was the opening stock?

A $10 000

B $40 000

C $50 000

D $80 000

6 The following information is extracted from the final accounts of a business.

	$
Opening stock	6 000
Purchases (all on credit)	220 000
Closing stock	28 000
Creditors at end of year	21 096

What is the period taken to pay the creditors?

A 31 days   **B** 32days   **C** 34 days   **D** 35 days

7 The following is an extract from the Profit and Loss Account of a company.

	$
Operating profit	360 000
Debenture interest	24 000
Profit after interest	336 000
Preference dividend	(16 000)
Ordinary dividend	(200 000)
Retained profit	120 000

The company's share capital is as follows.

> Authorised: $1 000 000
>
> Issued: 200 000 8% preference shares of $1
>
>   800 000 ordinary shares of $1

What is the company's earnings per share?

A $0.32   **B** $0.40   **C** $0.42   **D** $0.45

8 A company has an authorised share capital of 750 000 ordinary shares of $1 of which it has issued 500 000 shares. The following is an extract from its Profit and Loss Account.

	$
Operating profit	400 000
Debenture interest	(60 000)
	340 000
Transfer to general reserve	(100 000)
Ordinary dividend	(200 000)
Retained profit	40 000

The current market price of the shares is $3.60. What is the price earnings ratio?

A 5.29   **B** 7.5   **C** 8   **D** 11.25

28.13 Additional exercises

1 On 1 October 2001 Manny Kyoor and his wife formed a limited company, Kyoor Ltd, to run a beautician's business, and each paid in $37 500 as share capital. The bank loaned the company a further $80 000 at 9% interest per annum.

At 30 September 2002 the business's final accounts were drawn up as follows.

Trading and Profit and Loss Account for the year ended 30 September 2002

Sales and fees		$350 000
Less Cost of sales		
Stock bought on 1 October 2001	$31 500	
Purchases	$280 000	
	$311 500	
Stock at 30 September 2002	$66 500	$245 000
Gross Profit		$105 000
Less Expenses		
Rent and Rates	$3 950	
Advertising	$1 750	
Wages	$29 000	
Heat and Light	$5 250	
Interest due	$7 200	
Depreciation	$12 000	$59 150
Net Profit		$45 850

Balance Sheet as at 30 September 2002

Fixed Assets	Cost	Depreciation	NBV
Premises	$124 000		$124 000
Fixtures and fittings	$48 000	$12 000	$36 000
	$172 000	$12 000	$160 000
Current assets			
Stock	$66 500		
Debtors	$21 500	$88 000	
Amounts to be settled within one year			
Creditors	$21 000		
Interest due	$7 200		
Bank	$18 950	$47 150	$40 850
			$200 850
Amounts to be settled after more than one year			
Long-term loan			$80 000
			$120 850
Share Capital and Reserves			
75 000 ordinary shares of $1			$75 000
Retained profit			$45 850
			$120 850

Industry average ratios and other relevant data concerning businesses similar to Kyoor Ltd were as follows.

(i)	Gross Profit percentage	30.00%
(ii)	Net Profit percentage	18.07%
(iii)	Current ratio	2.21 : 1
(iv)	Liquid (Quick) ratio	1.02 : 1
(v)	Stock Turnover ratio	8 times
(vi)	Fixed Assets to Sales	50.18%
(vii)	Return on Total Assets	25.37%
(viii)	Return on Net Assets	34.93%
(ix)	Debtors' Payment period	25 days
(x)	Creditors' Payment period	30 days

(a) Calculate each of the above ratios, to 2 decimal places, for Kyoor Ltd.

(b) Comment on the business's performance in the light of the data for the industry.

Note. It is not sufficient to say that a ratio is 'higher' or 'lower' than the industry average – it must be made clear whether you think it is *better* or *worse* than the industry average and you must give reasons for your comments.

(UCLES, 2002, AS/A Level Accounting, Syllabus 9706/2 (October/November)

2 The following information summarises the latest set of final accounts of Worky Tout & Co., a partnership.

At 30 April 2001

Stock $45 000. (This was 50% more than the stock at 30 April 2000.)

For the year ended 30 April 2001

Stockturn 12 times

Gross profit margin 40%

Net profit margin 18%

Fixed asset turnover 3 times

Average time taken by debtors to pay: 36 days (based on a year of 365 days).

Average time taken to pay creditors: 40 days (based on a year of 365 days).

The current ratio is 3 : 1.

The only current assets of the firm consist of stock, debtors and balance at bank.

Partners' drawings for the year $125 000.

All sales and purchases were on a credit basis.

(a) Prepare, in as much detail as possible, the Trading and Profit and Loss Account of Worky Tout & Co. for the year ended 30 April 2001 and a Balance Sheet as at that date. (All calculations should be made to the nearest $000.)

The following information is available for Zenapod, a similar business, for the year ended 30 April 2001.

Stockturn 10 times

Gross profit margin 45%

Net profit margin 20%

Fixed asset turnover $3\frac{1}{2}$ times

| Time taken by debtors to pay | 30 days (based on a year of 365 days) |
| Time taken to pay creditors | 28 days (based on a year of 365 days) |

(b) Compare the performance of Worky Tout & Co. with that of Zenapod. Indicate the ratios which show that one business is more efficient than the other. Your answer should be in sentence form with supporting figures.

(UCLES, 2001, AS/A Level Accounting, Syllabus 8427/2, May/June)

3 An extract from Oitar plc's Profit and Loss Account for the year ended 30 April 2002 was as follows.

	$000	$000
Operating profit		1000
Debenture interest ($12\frac{1}{2}$%)		250
		750
Ordinary dividend paid and proposed	350	
Preference dividend paid and proposed	120	
Transfer to General Reserve	200	670
Retained profit for the year		80

Oitar plc's issued share capital and reserves at 30 April 2002 consisted of:

	$000
Ordinary shares of $10	4000
8% preference shares of $5	1500
Capital and revenue reserves	900

The market price of the ordinary shares at 30 April 2002 was $30.

Required

(a) Calculate the following ratios for Oitar plc.
  (i) interest cover
  (ii) dividend cover
  (iii) earnings per share
  (iv) price earnings ratio
  (v) dividend yield
  (vi) gearing

(b) Explain why each of the ratios in (a) is important for investors in ordinary shares in the company.

Oitar plc's accounting ratios at 30 April 2001 were as follows.

interest cover	5.5 times
dividend cover	2.5 times
price earnings ratio	22
gearing (calculated as a percentage of long term debentures and preference share capital to total long-term capital)	36%

Required

(c) Compare the ratios for 2001 with the same ratios in 2002 as calculated in (a), and comment on the changes that you find.

(d) State, with reasons, any further information you might require and what other documents you might wish to see to enable you to assess the likely future performance of Oitar plc.

(UCLES, 2002, AS/A Level Accounting, Syllabus 9706/4, May/June)

29 Company financing

In this chapter you will learn:
- the sources of company financing
- principles that are important for the financing of companies
- the bases and limitations of modern financial reporting
- the critical appraisal of accounting reports
- what window dressing is
- the nature of company forecasts.

29.1 Sources of company finance

Every company must have share capital, and the maximum amount of share capital it may issue must be stated in its Memorandum of Association, which it files with the Registrar of Companies when it is formed. There are provisions to enable the authorised capital to be increased at a later date if need be. A company may issue redeemable shares, but only if it has already issued shares which are not redeemable. This ensures that some part of a company's financing must be provided by the members of the company as an insurance for the creditors if the company gets into financial difficulties.

Besides share capital, other sources of finance are

- loans – debentures, bank loans, other loans
- bank overdrafts
- hire purchase and leasing of assets
- trade and other creditors.

Some forms of finance are more suitable than others; it depends upon the purpose for which the finance is required. It will be useful to recall the main features of each source.

29.2 Share capital

Ordinary shares, together with a company's reserves, are known as the **equity** of the company. Ordinary shareholders can be paid dividends only if there are profits available after all other claims by debenture holders and preference shareholders have been met. When a company is wound up, the ordinary shareholders are entitled to the funds that remain after all creditors (including debenture holders and other lenders) and

preference shareholders have been repaid. Thus ordinary shareholders may receive back more than they originally paid for their shares, or they may receive nothing at all. The Companies Act allows companies to convert their fully paid-up shares into stock. Stock may be thought of as 'bundles of shares' which may be bought and sold in fractional amounts. For example, shares with a nominal value of, say, \$1 may only be traded in multiples of \$1 (nominal value). It is not possible to buy, say, $100\frac{1}{2}$ shares. Stock, however, may traded in any amounts and it is possible to trade in, say, \$945.86 of stock. Companies may re-convert stock back into fully paid-up shares of any nominal value.

Preference shares entitle the holders to a fixed rate of dividend each year provided the company has made sufficient profit. **Participating preference shares** entitle the holders to have any arrears of dividend made good in later years when profits are sufficient. Preference shares are participating unless they are specifically described as non-participating. Preference dividends are payable before any dividends are payable to the ordinary shareholders, and holders of the preference shares are entitled to have their capital returned in priority to the ordinary shareholders when the company is wound up, subject to funds being available.

Rights issues are shares offered to existing shareholders of a company at a price below the current market price. Shares may never be issued at a discount, that is, at a price below their nominal value. A rights issue ensures that existing shareholders do not lose control of the company, as could be the case if the shares were offered to the general public. A private company may only increase its capital by a rights issue because it is prevented from offering shares to the public.

Bonus issues are not a new source of funding as they do not create any additional cash for the company. Bonus shares are created by transferring the balances from a company's reserves to the Ordinary Share Capital account and issuing certificates for the new shares to the ordinary shareholders in proportion to their existing shareholdings

29.3 Other sources of finance

Debentures

Debentures are loans to a company. Debenture holders are entitled to a fixed rate of interest on their loan regardless of whether or not the company has made a profit. If a company lacks the cash to pay debenture interest when it is due, and the loan is secured on the assets of the company, the debenture holders are entitled to have the assets sold to pay the interest and to repay the loan immediately. Debentures are usually repayable on a date or within a period of time specified at the time they are issued. They are a long-term, but not a permanent, form of finance.

Convertible loan stock

Convertible loan stock entitles the holders to a fixed rate of interest payable on defined dates, and the right to convert the stock into shares at a pre-determined price on a set date. Because of the option to convert, convertible loan stock usually carries a lower rate of interest than ordinary debentures and is usually not secured on the assets of the business.

If, when the time to convert arrives, the market price of the shares is higher than the pre-determined price, it will be advantageous to convert the stock into shares. The holder of the stock exchanges the right to a fixed income payable on settled dates for the uncertainty of receiving dividends which may be more or less than the interest on the stock. The company, on the other hand, is relieved of having to pay loan interest regardless of the profitability of the company, and need only pay dividends if profits are available. Conversion of the stock decreases the company's gearing.

Bank loans

Bank loans are available to a company provided it can satisfy the bank that the funds are required for a sound purpose such as capital investment or expansion, and that the company will be able to pay the interest on the due dates, and repay the loan in due course. The loan may be for a short term such as three months or for a longer term of a number of years depending on the purpose for which it is required. A bank will usually be unwilling to lend to a company that has got into difficulties through bad management. Loans will usually be secured on the assets

of the company. The rate of interest charged may be fixed or variable. The interest is charged on the full amount of the loan whether it is used or not.

Bank overdrafts

Bank overdrafts are temporary facilities that allow companies to become overdrawn on their bank accounts. Interest is calculated on the overnight amount of the overdraft so that interest is only paid by a company on the amount of the facility it uses day by day. Banks may cancel overdraft facilities at any time without notice, exposing the borrower to the risk of financial embarrassment.

Hire purchase

Hire purchase enables a purchaser to have the beneficial use of an asset while the ownership of the asset remains with the hire purchase company. At the end of the hire purchase agreement the purchaser may become the owner of the asset on payment of a (usually) nominal sum. Under the principle of substance over form, the purchaser shows the asset as a fixed asset in the Balance Sheet at its normal cash price and shows the outstanding liability to the hire purchase company as a creditor.

Leasing

Leasing allows a company leasing an asset (the lessee) to use the asset while the ownership of the asset remains with the company from which it is leased (the lessor). The asset will never become the property of the lessee and the rental is shown in the lessee's Profit and Loss Account as an expense.

A company may raise money by selling some of its fixed assets to a leasing company and leasing them back, so retaining their use. This is known as 'sale and lease back'. It receives a capital sum for the sale and charges the leasing rental in its Profit and Loss Account.

Factoring

Some companies sell their book debts to a factoring company either with or without **recourse**. The factoring company makes a charge for collecting the debts and this is deducted from the book value of the debts sold. If the debts were sold *with recourse*, the factoring company will require the company that sold the debts to make good any loss resulting from bad debts. If the debts were sold *without recourse*, the factoring company will increase the charge for collecting the debts to allow for the risk of bad debts.

The advantage of factoring is that a company receives the money owing by debtors early and is relieved of the expense of credit control and debt recovery.

Creditors

Some of a company's finance is provided by its trade and expense creditors. This is a short-term form of finance. However, a company that abuses this source of finance risks losing the goodwill of its suppliers and sacrificing advantageous credit terms. The creditors may insist that future dealings are on a cash basis, or may even withdraw supplies or services altogether.

29.4 Important principles that should decide how companies are financed

The main principles that should decide how a company is financed are briefly explained below.

Long-term capital

Long-term requirements should be financed by long-term sources. Financing the acquisition of fixed assets, for example by short-term loans, runs the very great risk that the loans will have to be repaid before the assets in question have generated sufficient funds for the repayment. The fixed assets of a company should be adequately covered by share capital and reserves, and possibly by long-dated debentures.

An acquisition of a fixed asset may be financed by a bank loan for an agreed term to allow the asset to generate the funds for repayment by the time the term has expired. Alternatively the funds may be raised by an issue of debentures which will be repayable when the asset has started to earn revenue. This enables the shareholders to enjoy all the benefits accruing from the asset without having to share them with the provider of the capital used to purchase the asset.

Working capital

A positive current ratio (greater than 1 : 1) shows that the current assets are not wholly financed by the current liabilities (short-term creditors). The possibility that stock turnover may be low (slow-moving stock), and that debtors may take a long time to pay means that some of the current liabilities should be funded by long-term finance.

Share and debenture issues compared

- Issues of shares to the public are costly because of the need to meet the requirements of the Companies Act. Rights issues are less costly because they are limited to existing shareholders. A rights issue will fail if existing shareholders are not able to subscribe the additional funds required. Issues of debentures are less costly than issues of shares.

- An issue of ordinary shares to the public may result in a loss of control by existing shareholders. The shareholders' control will not be affected if the issue is one of preference shares or debentures, neither of which carry the right to vote in company meetings.
- Share dividends may be paid only if profits are available for the purpose. Debenture interest must be paid regardless of whether a company makes a profit or a loss.
- Issues of preference shares and debentures increase gearing. High gearing is associated with increased risk to the ordinary shareholders. However, very low or a 'nil' gearing is not necessarily good. When interest rates generally are low, the cost of servicing debenture interest may be less than the rate of dividend the company is paying on its shares. A company will fail its shareholders if it does not take advantage of raising some of its capital cheaply.
- While shareholders may like to have a substantial amount of long-term capital raised by borrowing at cheap rates, banks and other providers of finance may be unwilling to provide further funds to companies in which the shareholders seem unwilling to risk more of their own money.

29.5 The critical appraisal of accounting reports

The basis of modern financial reporting and its limitations

The annual accounting reports of limited companies consist of Profit and Loss Accounts, Balance Sheets, Cash Flow Statements and directors' reports. These reports are prepared within an accounting framework made up of the requirements of the Companies Act and the various published accounting standards. These requirements are intended to ensure a degree of uniformity that will enable the users of the reports to interpret them in a generally accepted context. The framework has been considered in chapter 27.

Limitations of interpreting financial reports may be summarised as follows.

- While the accounting framework is intended to ensure that financial reports provide the information necessary for an understanding of a company's performance, the rules do not require confidential information which might provide an unfair advantage to competitors to be disclosed. The undisclosed information might, however, contain important clues to the better understanding of the company's performance.
- Companies are required to supplement Profit and Loss Accounts and Balance Sheets with additional notes to explain how the items in those financial statements are made up. However, companies differ in their

classification of many items of income and expenditure, and the notes may not be in sufficient detail to identify the differences. This may cast doubt on the usefulness of some accounting ratios calculated from the financial statements.

- Where accounting standards do not fit a particular business, the directors may adapt them, or even ignore them, provided they have good reason for doing so.
- Companies have different policies for the treatment of expenditure on fixed assets; some will capitalise all such expenditure while others will treat the expenditure as revenue expenditure if it is not material compared with the size of the amounts shown in its Balance Sheet.
- A company may own its extensive properties or it may operate solely from rented accommodation. The one will pay no rent, while the other may be burdened with very high rental payments.
- There are limits to the extent to which companies of considerably different sizes can be compared. For example, it would hardly be helpful to compare the performance of a company with an issued capital of $50 000 with the performance of a company with an issued capital of $5 million. There may also be difficulty in making a sensible comparison between a company with nil gearing and one that is very highly geared.
- Companies in the same line of business are often not comparable. For example, some may simply retail their goods while others manufacture and retail them. Some companies may act as manufacturers and wholesalers only.
- Financial reports may be too historical to be useful by the time they are published. Public companies are allowed seven months before the directors must present the accounts to the members at an annual general meeting.
- The interpretation of financial reports may be subject to external factors such as developments in the industry, general political and economic conditions at home and overseas, changes in fashion, market demand and so on.
- The financial accounts and reports of companies in countries where there is high inflation can be seriously misleading if the accounts have been based on historical costs.

Window dressing

Company directors naturally desire annual financial reports to present the company performance in as favourable a light as possible. This may lead to 'window dressing' which may take various forms, including:

- reducing creditors in the Balance Sheet by drawing cheques at the end of the financial period to pay the creditors but not posting the cheques until the start of the next financial year, or even cancelling them on the first day of the next financial year
- reducing the debtors in the Balance Sheet by pressing them to pay before the end of the financial period.

Other methods of window dressing, such as changing the bases of calculating depreciation of fixed assets and the provision for doubtful debts, of stock valuation, etc. are not permissible and contravene accounting standards. They may even amount to fraud.

Income smoothing techniques

Income should be recognised as soon as it is realised and not before. A company carrying out work under a contract which spans two or more financial periods is required to spread the anticipated profit on the contract over the financial periods concerned. The amount of profit to be credited in each year is calculated on a formula which apportions the profit according to the amount deemed to have been earned in each period less a prudent provision for any future unanticipated losses. (A more detailed explanation of contract accounts is outside the scope of this text as students are not required to have a knowledge of the topic.)

When the directors of a company anticipate that a good trading year will be followed by a poor one, they may decide to delay invoicing some customers in the good year until the following one for the sake of appearances. This contravenes the concept of realisation and, if the financial statements are subject to audit, should not be allowed to happen without being reported.

Similarly, if customers are allowed to pay by instalments for work done or services rendered, and some of the instalments are payable in a subsequent financial period, any attempt to smooth income by partly deferring it until the instalments are received would be a contravention of the realisation principle.

29.6 The nature of company forecasts

Directors' reports and future developments

Directors' reports are required to include an indication of likely future developments in the business of the company. These statements are usually quite brief and lack sufficient detail to enable shareholders and others to form an accurate assessment of the future funding requirements of the business.

Company budgets

Every company, except some very small private companies, prepares budgets. Budgets are based on forecasts and express in money terms the plans and policies the directors intend to implement to achieve a company's long-term objectives. The budgets usually cover periods of five, ten or, for large companies, even more years ahead. Separate budgets are prepared for each of the company's activities: sales, production, purchasing, stock holding, etc. Cash budgets are prepared from these budgets to show if and when the company is likely to need additional cash. Master budgets, which take the form of forecast Profit and Loss Accounts and Balance Sheets, will indicate when additional long-term finance is required.

The budgets are for internal use within the company and are not published, but they are an essential management tool if the directors are to avoid the embarrassment, and possibly the catastrophe, of suddenly finding that the company has insufficient funds to continue in business. Banks and others approached to provide additional capital will require to see the budgets before deciding whether or not to lend to the business. Budgeting is covered in chapter 34.

Exercise 1

Explain the difference between stocks and shares.

Exercise 2

Explain the difference between debentures and convertible loan stock.

29.7 Examination hints

- Learn the main short-, medium- and long-term sources of company financing and their advantages and disadvantages.
- Remember that long-term requirements for funds should be financed by long-term sources.
- Learn the limitations of financial reports and their effect upon interpretation.
- Be prepared to describe window dressing and income smoothing techniques.
- Note the importance of forecasting and budgeting as regards business financing.

29.8 Multiple-choice questions

1 Information extracted from the Balance Sheets of company P and company Q is as follows.

	P	Q
	$000	$000
Ordinary share capital	500	600
12% debentures	400	200

Which of the following would experience the greatest degree of risk in times of declining profits?

A debenture holders in company P

B debenture holders in company Q

C ordinary shareholders in company P

D ordinary shareholders in company Q

2 Which of the following is a method of 'window dressing' financial statements?

A omitting an asset acquired on hire purchase

B overstating Goodwill

C transferring a large amount to General Reserve

D writing off debts before they become bad

3 Which of the following may be used to smooth earnings per share from one year to another?

A asset revaluation reserve

B capital redemption reserve

C General Reserve

D preference share dividend

4 A company proposes to purchase an expensive machine which will pay for itself in five years. General interest rates are low and the company wishes to avoid a change in the control. From which source of finance should it obtain the necessary funds?

A a rights issue

B an issue of convertible loan stock

C an issue of debentures

D an issue of redeemable preference shares

29.9 Additional exercises

1 Explain why the fixed assets of a company should be funded by long-term finance.

2 Explain why long-term finance should exceed the amount of a company's long-term assets.

3 State *five* limitations that may be relevant to the appraisal of company financial reports.

4 Explain what is meant by 'window dressing' and why directors may wish to use it.

5 What means are available to enable directors to foresee future needs for additional funds?

Part IV
Elements of managerial accounting

30 Costing principles and systems: total (or absorption) costing

In this chapter you will learn:
- the nature and purpose of cost accounting
- how to analyse costs into direct and indirect costs
- how to record materials and labour
- how to allocate and apportion overheads
- how to calculate overhead absorption rates (OARs)
- the causes of over-/under-absorption of overheads.

30.1 The purpose and nature of total (absorption) costing

Cost accounting is one of the management tools included in a number of systems of accounting known as **management accounting**. Management accounting provides management with information which is not obtainable from the financial accounts of a business. Consider the following example.

Makeit & Co. Manufacturing Account for the year ended 30 June 2004		
	$000	$000
Direct materials Stock at 1 July 2003	10	
Purchases	140	
Carriage inwards	24	
	174	
Less Stock at 30 June 2004	18	156
Direct labour		222
Direct expenses		46
Prime cost		424
Indirect materials	45	
Indirect labour	72	
Rent of factory	100	
Heating, lighting and power	45	
Depreciation: factory	20	
machinery	36	318
		742
Work in progress 1 July 2003	38	
Work in progress 30 June 2004	(20)	18
Factory cost of finished goods		760

This manufacturing account has been prepared as part of the company's financial accounting system. It provides us with information about prime cost, overheads and the cost of producing goods. If only one type of good has been produced, the unit cost can easily be found by dividing the factory cost by the number of units produced. The selling price for the good is fixed by adding the required amount of profit per unit. So far, so good, but it does not go far enough to help management make important decisions.

Assuming that Makeit & Co. manufactures only one type of product and that the output for the year was 1000 units of that product, each unit has cost $760. If the managers want to find the cost of producing 1001 units, the answer will not be $760\,000 \times \frac{1001}{1000} = \$760\,760$, that is $\$(760\,000 + 760)$. The additional unit will not result in additional costs of $760 because not all costs (rent and depreciation, for example) will be affected by the addition of one unit of output; they are fixed costs, which do not vary with the number of units produced. The effect on costs of increasing numbers of units produced is covered in chapter 33 on marginal costing.

The problem is even more complicated if Makeit & Co. manufactures more than one type of product, and each type requires different types and quantities of materials, different numbers of labour hours and different processes. Management must know how much it costs to make a single unit of each product if they are to fix selling prices. This problem is considered now.

30.2 Direct and indirect costs

In chapter 19 we saw that a distinction is made in manufacturing accounts between direct costs and indirect costs.

Direct costs include direct materials (those materials from which goods are made, and carriage inwards paid on the materials), direct labour (the wages of workers who actually make goods) and direct expenses (royalties, licence fees, etc.).

Indirect costs are indirect materials (purchased for the factory, e.g. cleaning materials, lubricating oil for the machinery), indirect wages (the wages of all factory workers who do not actually make the goods (factory managers, supervisors, stores staff, cleaners, etc.) and other overheads (rent, heating and lighting, depreciation, etc.)

30.3 The behaviour of costs

Direct expenses are deemed to vary in proportion to the number of units produced. If 1 kg of material is required for one unit of production, 2 kg will be required for two units produced, 10 kg for ten units, and so on. It will be true for royalties and other direct expenses; if a royalty of $0.05 has to be paid for every unit produced, the royalties payable will always be equal to the number of units produced × $0.05. At one time, it might have been common for direct workers to be paid according to the amount they produced so that direct wages would be

proportionate to output. Now, direct workers are usually paid a fixed or basic wage regardless of their output. This wage may or may not be supplemented by a productivity bonus. In practice, therefore, wages paid to direct labour will not be in relation to output, but we still tend to treat them in a theoretical way as being proportionate to production.

Indirect expenses may be **fixed** or **variable**. They are fixed if they are not linked directly to the level of activity. Rent is an example; it is fixed by a lease agreement. Straight-line depreciation is another fixed expense. However, it is important to remember that even fixed expenses are only fixed within certain parameters (or limits). For example, it may be possible to increase the number of units produced only if additional machines are purchased, and that will increase the total depreciation charge. If production is increased still further and more machines have to be purchased, it may be necessary to lease more factory space and the rent will increase. Fixed costs then become 'stepped costs' and may be represented by a chart as follows.

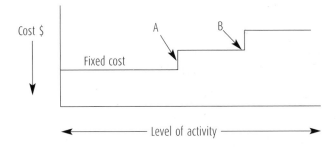

At A it has been necessary to buy an additional machine in order to increase production, and the depreciation of machinery charge has increased. At B, a further machine has been bought, and it has been necessary to rent additional factory space so that both the depreciation charge and the rent have increased.

30.4 Recording materials, labour and overheads

Cost accounting requires materials purchased and wages paid to be classified as direct or indirect. If expenditure has been incurred for particular departments within the business, it must be analysed by departments. Invoices for goods and services must be coded by the purchasing department to show the type of expenditure that has been incurred. The purchase journal must have additional columns so that the expenditure can be analysed according to the codes shown on the invoices. Analysed purchase journals have already been encountered in departmental accounts in chapter 18.

Wages are analysed into different departments and then classified into direct and indirect wages on payroll summaries.

If the systems of analysis outlined above have been carried out, all expenses can be posted in the ledger to appropriate accounts to enable the allocation and appropriation of expenses to cost centres as described below.

30.5 How to apportion overheads to cost centres

Cost centres

A **cost centre** is any location in a business to which costs may be attributed. A cost centre is usually a department or process, but may be an item of equipment (a machine) or even a person (e.g. a marketing manager). **Production cost centres** are directly involved in producing goods, for example moulding or shaping raw material, assembling components, painting, etc. **Service cost centres** are not involved in the production of goods, but provide services for the production cost centres, for example stores, building and plant maintenance, canteen, etc.

Allocation and apportionment of costs to production cost centres

Direct expenses and some overhead expenses can be identified with specific cost centres and are **allocated** to them.

Overheads which may be identified with, and allocated to, specific cost centres include:

- wood, metal, plastic, chemicals, components, etc. (production departments)
- paint (paint shop)
- packing materials (packing department)
- lubricating oil (the machine shop)
- maintenance of handling equipment (the stores or warehouse)
- food (the canteen).

Other overheads are incurred for the business generally and are **apportioned** to cost centres on suitable bases.

Overhead	Basis of apportionment
Heating and lighting (when not separately metered to the cost centres)	In proportion to the respective floor areas of the departments
Rent	
Insurance of buildings	
Power (if metered separately to cost centres)	Actual consumption (this is allocation rather than apportionment)
Insurance of plant, machinery and other assets	On cost or replacement values of assets in each department
Depreciation of fixed assets	On the cost or book value of assets in each department

Example 1

Oar Manufacturers & Co. has four production cost centres: moulding, machining, painting and packing. The following information is available.

Cost centres	Moulding	Machining	Painting	Packaging
Floor area (metres^2)	1000	700	500	300
Plant and machinery at cost ($000)	50	40	20	10

Details of expenditure for the year ended 31 December 2004 are as follows.

	$
Direct materials: Moulding	50 000
Machining	7 000
Painting	9 000
Packaging	6 000
Direct labour Moulding	96 000
Machining	80 000
Painting	40 000
Packaging	18 000
Indirect labour Moulding	11 000
Machining	9 000
Painting	4 000
Packaging	1 000
Factory rent	45 000
Repairs and maintenance of factory	5 000
Factory depreciation	6 000
Insurance of factory	2 500
Heating and lighting	5 500
Depreciation of plant and machinery	12 000
Maintenance of plant and machinery	18 000
Insurance of plant	3 000

The overhead apportionment will be as follows.

Expense	Basis	Total $	Moulding $	Machining $	Painting $	Packaging $
Indirect labour	allocation	25 000	11 000	9 000	4 000	1 000
Factory: rent	floor area	45 000	18 000	12 600	9 000	5 400
repairs and maintenance	floor area	5 000	2 000	1 400	1 000	600
depreciation	floor area	6 000	2 400	1 680	1 200	720
insurance	floor area	2 500	1 000	700	500	300
heating and lighting	floor area	5 500	2 200	1 540	1 100	660
Plant and machinery:						
depreciation	cost	12 000	5 000	4 000	2 000	1 000
maintenance	cost	18 000	7 500	6 000	3 000	1 500
insurance	cost	3 000	1 250	1 000	500	250
Total overhead		122 000	50 350	37 920	22 300	11 430

The total cost per cost centre includes direct expenditure:

Expense	Basis	Total $	Moulding $	Machining $	Painting $	Packaging $
Direct costs: materials	actual	72 000	50 000	7 000	9 000	6 000
labour	actual	234 000	96 000	80 000	40 000	18 000
Total direct cost		306 000	146 000	87 000	49 000	24 000
Apportionment of overhead		122 000	50 350	37 920	22 300	11 430
Total cost per cost centre		428 000	196 350	124 920	71 300	35 430

Exercise 1

Teepops Ltd manufactures a single product which passes through four stages of production: machining, painting, assembly and packing. The following expenditure has been incurred by the company in the year ended 31 March 2005.

		$000
Direct materials:	Machining	80
	Painting	20
	Assembly	5
	Packing	12
Direct labour:	Machining	136
	Painting	74
	Assembly	68
	Packing	45
Indirect labour:	Machining	51
	Painting	32
	Assembly	28
	Packing	14
Factory expenses:	Rent	90
	Heating and lighting	70
	Maintenance	30
	Insurance	20
Plant and machinery:	Depreciation	80
	Repairs	32
	Insurance	16

Further information

1. The floor areas of the departments are:

	metres^2
Machining	500
Painting	200
Assembly	200
Packing	100

2. Plant and machinery at cost is:

	$000
Machining	90
Painting	40
Assembly	10
Packing	20

Required

(a) Calculate the total overhead cost for each department.
(b) Calculate the total cost of production for each department.

Apportionment of service cost centre overheads to production cost centres

The total cost of goods produced includes all overhead expenditure, including the overheads of service departments; these must be apportioned to the production departments on suitable bases. The bases usually adopted are:

Service cost centre	Apportioned on
Stores	number or value of stores requisitions raised by production cost centre
Canteen	number of persons in each production cost centre
Building maintenance	area occupied by each production cost centre*
Plant and machinery maintenance	number or value of machines in each cost centre*

*However, records of actual maintenance costs may be kept and the costs allocated accordingly.

There are a number of ways of apportioning service cost centre overheads to production cost centres and they all usually produce very similar results. The simplest, and quickest, way is the elimination method.

Example 2

(Apportionment of service cost centre overheads by elimination)
Eliminator Ltd has three production and two service departments for which the following information is available.

	Foundry	Finishing	Assembly	Stores	Canteen
No. of stores requisitions	200	100	50	–	70
No. of staff	40	15	20	7	10
Overheads ($000)	110	60	50	35	30

The overheads are first tabulated under the cost centres. The overhead of one service department is then apportioned over the other cost centres and that service department is eliminated from future apportionments. If there are more than two service cost centres, there will be more steps until the last service cost centre is apportioned over the production cost centres.

	Foundry $000	Finishing $000	Assembly $000	Stores $000	Canteen $000
Overheads ($000)	110.00	60.00	50.00	35.00	30.00
First apportionment*	16.67	8.33	4.17	(35.00)	5.83
Second apportionment†	19.11	7.17	9.55	–	(35.83)
	145.78	75.50	63.72	–	–

* Based on 420 requisitions. † Based on 75 staff.

Exercise 2

Luvlibix Foods has three production departments: mixing, bakery and packaging. It also has two service departments: stores and canteen. The following information is provided.

	Mixing	Bakery	Packaging	Stores	Canteen
Overheads ($000)	165	124	87	80	90
No. of staff	60	80	40	15	18
No. of stores requisitions	300	80	20	–	40

Required

Apportion the service department overheads to the production departments on appropriate bases.

30.6 How to calculate overhead absorption rates

Once overheads have been apportioned to cost centres, the next step is to calculate overhead absorption rates (OARs). The OARs are then used to calculate the amount of overhead to be attributed to each cost unit in each cost centre.

Cost units are units of production, for example:

a computer (computer manufacturer)

a garment   (dress maker)

a thousand electric lamps (manufacturer of electric lamps)

a barrel of oil (oil well)

passenger-mile (bus or train company)

tonne-mile (freight transport)

a kilowatt-hour (electricity generation)

Overhead absorption rates are calculated for future periods because the cost of production must be known in advance to enable selling prices to be fixed. Calculations are based on planned volumes of output and budgeted overhead expenditure.

The amount of overhead absorbed by a cost unit is usually calculated by reference to the time taken to produce it. There are other methods but they are generally considered to be less satisfactory for reasons that will be discussed later. The two methods about to be described assume that a unit of production absorbs overheads (rent, heat and lighting, for example) proportionately to the time spent on processing it in the cost centres. This time is measured either in direct labour hours or machine hours.

Direct labour overhead absorption rate

A process is labour intensive when it requires the use of labour rather than machines, and the labour cost is greater than the cost of using machinery. The time is measured in direct labour hours.

Example 1

Manhour Ltd makes two products, P and Q. The output for September is budgeted as follows.

Product P	10 000 units
Product Q	8 000 units

Each unit of P requires $1\frac{1}{2}$ direct labour hours to make, and each unit of Q requires $\frac{3}{4}$ direct labour hour.

The total number of direct labour hours required to produce 10 000 units of P and 8000 units of Q is

$$(10\ 000 \times 1\tfrac{1}{2}) + (8000 \times \tfrac{3}{4}) = 21\ 000$$

If Manhour Ltd's overheads for September are $131 250, the overhead absorption rate is

$$\frac{\text{total budgeted overhead expenditure}}{\text{total budgeted no. of direct labour hours}} = \frac{\$131\ 250}{21\ 000} = \$6.25 \text{ per direct labour hour}$$

The amount of overhead absorbed by each unit of P is $6.25 \times 1\frac{1}{2}$ = $9.375 and the amount absorbed by Q is $\frac{3}{4}$ × $6.325 = $4.6875. The total overhead is therefore fully absorbed as follows.

	$
Product P: 10 000 × $9.375	93 750
Product Q: 8000 × $4.6875	37 500
Total overhead absorbed	131 250

Exercise 3

Trimble Ltd manufactures two products, Dimbles and Gimbles.

The number of direct labour hours required for each unit is: Dimbles 1.3; Gimbles 0.7.

In July the company plans to produce 5000 Dimbles and 7000 Gimbles.

Trimble Ltd's estimated overhead expenditure for July is $129 276.

Required

(a) Calculate the direct labour overhead absorption rate:
   (i) per unit of Dimble (ii) per unit of Gimble.

(b) Show how the overhead for July is absorbed by the planned production for the month.

Machine hour overhead absorption rate

A cost centre is capital intensive when the operations carried out in the centre are mechanised and the machinery running cost is greater than the direct labour cost. Overhead should then be absorbed on a machine hour rate (machine hour OAR).

Example

Jigsaw Ltd has six machines which are used 9 hours each day in a five-day working week. The number of machine hours in a six-month period is $6 \times 9 \times 5 \times 26$ or 7020 machine hours.

If Jigsaw Ltd's overheads for the six months are $114 075, the machine hour absorption rate is $\frac{\$114\,075}{7020}$ or $16.25 per machine hour.

Exercise 4

Makeit-by-Robot Ltd uses 10 machines to produce its goods. The machines are used 7 hours a day for 6 days per week. In a period of 13 weeks it is planned to produce 1200 units, and the overheads are estimated to amount to $141 960.

Required

(a) Calculate the machine hour overhead absorption rate.

(b) Calculate the amount of overhead absorbed by each unit of production.

Example 2

Jenx Ltd manufactures two products, L and P, each of which requires processing in the company's three production departments, I, II and III.

The following information is available from the company's budget for the next six months.

Products		L	P
No. of units to be produced		4000	5000
Cost of direct materials per unit		$17	$16
Direct wages per unit		$10	$8
Machine hours per unit	Dept I	3	2
	Dept II	1	1
	Dept III	2	3
Direct labour hours per unit	Dept I	1	2
	Dept II	2	3
	Dept III	3	4

Production departments	I	II	III
Budgeted overheads	$95 920	$86 250	$96 000
Budgeted machine hours	22 000	9 000	23 000
Budgeted labour hours	14 000	23 000	32 000

Required

(a) Calculate an appropriate overhead absorption rate for each department.

(b) Calculate the overhead absorption for each unit of L and P, in each of the departments, and in total.

(c) Prepare a statement to show how the overhead of each department is absorbed by production.

(d) Calculate the total cost of each unit of L and P.

Answer

Department I is capital intensive and Departments II and III are labour intensive.

(a)

OARs Dept I Machine hour $\frac{\$95\,920}{22\,000} = \$4.36$

Dept II Direct labour hours $\frac{\$86\,250}{23\,000} = \$3.75$

Dept III Direct labour hours $\frac{\$96\,000}{32\,000} = \$3.00$

(b)

OAR per unit	Dept	I		II		III		Total
Product L	($4.36 × 3)	$13.08	($3.75 × 2)	$7.50	($3 × 3)	$9.00		$29.58
Product P	($4.36 × 2)	$8.72	($3.75 × 3)	$11.25	($3 × 4)	$12.00		$31.97

(c)

Total overhead recovery	Dept.	I		II		III	Total
		$		$		$	$
Product L	(4000 × $13.08)	52 320	(4000 × $7.50)	30 000	(4000 × $9) 36 000	118 320
Product P	(5000 × $8.72)	43 600	(5000 × $11.25)	56 250	(5000 × $12) 60 000	159 850
		95 920		86 250	96 000	278 170

(d)

Total cost per unit	Product L	Product P
	$	$
Direct material	17.00	16.00
Direct labour	10.00	8.00
Overhead	29.58	31.97
Total cost	56.58	55.97

Exercise 5

Egbert Ltd manufactures two products which it markets under the brand names 'Sovrin' and 'Ginny'. The following information is available for a six-month period.

No. of units	Sovrin 6000	Ginny 3000	
Production cost centres:	Moulding	Machinery	Paint shop
Direct materials per unit: Sovrin	$80	$10	$12
Ginny	$65	$5	$15
Direct labour per unit: Sovrin	$120	$40	$30
Ginny	$96	$40	$15
Machine hours per unit:			
Sovrin	$2\frac{1}{2}$	2	1
Ginny	2	2	$\frac{1}{2}$
Direct labour hours per unit:			
Sovrin	4	1	1
Ginny	$3\frac{1}{2}$	$1\frac{1}{4}$	1
Budgeted overhead expenditure	$301 875	$115 200	$47 250
Budgeted machine hours	21 000	18 000	7 500
Budgeted direct labour hours	34 500	9 750	9 000

Required

(a) Calculate an appropriate overhead absorption rate for each department.
(b) Calculate the overhead absorption for each unit of Sovrin and Ginny, in each of the departments, and in total.
(c) Prepare a statement to show how the overhead of each department is absorbed by production.
(d) Calculate the total cost of each unit of Sovrin and Ginny.

30.7 Other bases for calculating OARs

The following bases for calculating overhead absorption rates are generally unsatisfactory, for the reasons stated, and are seldom used.

Direct material cost Overhead absorption is not related to the cost of material. A product which is made of expensive material would be charged with a greater share of overheads than one which is made of cheap material but which requires the same time to make.

Direct labour cost The labour cost incurred in making a product depends partly on the rate paid to the workers engaged on making it. A product made by highly skilled workers would be charged with a greater share of overheads than one which is made by unskilled workers but which takes the same time to make.

Prime cost This method combines the disadvantages of the direct material cost and the direct labour cost.

Cost unit This method is restricted to the production of one type of good which is made by a common process.

30.8 Under-/over-absorption of overheads

As explained above, overhead absorption rates are calculated on planned levels of production and budgeted overhead expenditure. It is most likely that the actual volume of goods produced and the actual overhead expenditure will turn out to differ from the forecasts. The result will be that overhead expenditure will be either under-absorbed or over-absorbed.

Under-absorption occurs when actual expenditure is more than budget and/or production is less than the planned level.

Over-absorption occurs when actual expenditure is less than budget and/or actual production is more than the planned level.

Example

A company calculated its overhead absorption rates for the six months to 30 June and the next six months to 31 December as follows.

	6 months to 30 June	6 months to 31 December
Budgeted overhead expenditure	$200 000	$240 000
Planned production in units	80 000	100 000
Actual results were: expenditure	$215 000	$230 000
goods produced	76 000	106 000
OAR	$\frac{$200\,000}{80\,000} = 2.50	$\frac{$240\,000}{100\,000} = 2.40
Overhead recovered	76 000 × $2.50 $190 000	106 000 × $2.40 $254 400
(Under-)/Over-absorption	$(215 000 – 190 000) ($25 000)	(230 000 – 254 400) $24 400

Exercise 6

Upandown Ltd has provided the following information about its overhead expenditure for four quarterly periods ended 31 December.

	3 months to 31 March	3 months to 30 June	3 months to 30 September	3 months to 31 December
Budgeted overhead	$124 000	$128 000	$130 000	$131 000
Planned productions (units)	1 000	1 000	1 000	1 000
Actual overhead	$128 000	$125 000	$129 500	$132 800
Actual output (units)	900	1 050	1 100	980

Required

Calculate the under-absorption or over-absorption of overhead in each of the four quarterly periods. State clearly in each case whether the overhead was under- or over-absorbed.

30.9 Examination hints

- Learn the definitions of **cost centre** and **cost unit** and be prepared to explain their functions.
- Be prepared to apportion overheads to cost centres and to re-apportion service cost centre overheads to production cost centres.
- Practise calculating overhead absorption rates.
- Be prepared to state when direct labour OARs and machine hour OARs should be used and to explain why other methods of calculating OARs are normally unsuitable.
- Learn how to calculate under-absorption and over-absorption of overheads.
- Check all calculations carefully; arithmetical mistakes cost marks.
- Make sure you understand the causes of under-absorption and over-absorption. This is a weak spot for many candidates in examinations.

30.10 Multiple-choice questions

1 A company provides the following information:

Actual direct labour hours worked	13 000
Actual overhead expenditure	$520 000
Budgeted direct labour hours	14 000
Budgeted overhead expenditure	$532 000

What is the overhead absorption rate based on direct labour hours?

A $37.14
B $38
C $40
D $40.42

2 Which of the following could cause an under-absorption of overhead expenditure?

1. absorption rate calculated on actual production and actual number of units produced
2. units produced exceeding the budgeted production
3. units produced being less than the planned production
4. overhead expenditure exceeding budget

A 1 and 2
B 1 and 3
C 2 and 4
D 3 and 4

3 The following information is provided by a company.

Actual direct labour hours	12 400
Actual overhead expenditure	$198 400
Budgeted direct labour hours	11 000
Budgeted overhead expenditure	$170 500

Which of the following correctly describes the overhead absorbed?

	Under-absorbed	Over-absorbed
A	$6 200	
B		$6 200
C	$21 700	
D		$21 700

30.11 Additional exercises

1 (a) Explain the following terms:

(i) Cost Centre

(ii) Cost Unit

(b) Julie and Cleary Ltd manufactures toy soldiers. The company has three production departments – Moulding, Sanding and Painting – and two service departments – Canteen and Maintenance. Estimated indirect overheads for the year ended 30 April 2002 are as follows:

Overhead	Cost or Calculation	Basis of Apportionment or Allocation
Administration	$104 000	Number of employees
Electricity	$70 000	Kilowatt hours used
Depreciation	10%	Cost of Fixed Asset
Indirect wages	$360 000	Allocated
Rent	$80 500	Floor area (square metres)

Relevant information on the five departments is as follows:

	Moulding	Sanding	Painting	Canteen	Maintenance
No. of employees	40	50	40	38	40
Power (kW hours)	1400	1600	150	160	190
Cost of Fixed Asset	$162 000	$175 000	$40 000	$43 000	$80 000
Floor area (sq m)	625	475	500	300	400
Indirect wages	$6 000	$11 250	$6 375	$18 750	$36 190
Direct Labour hours	8 000	7 800	7 500		
Direct Machine hours	7 750	5 625	1 250		

Canteen costs are shared among all the other departments on the basis of number of employees. Maintenance costs are shared among the three production departments on the basis of floor area.

(i) Prepare an overhead analysis sheet for the year ending 30 April 2002 detailing the total overheads for Moulding, Sanding and Painting.

(ii) Moulding and Sanding department overhead rates are calculated on a Direct Machine hour basis. Painting department overhead rate is calculated on a Direct Labour hour basis. Calculate the Overhead absorption rate for each of the three production departments for the year ending 30 April 2002. Calculations should be shown to two decimal places.

(UCLES, 2001, A/AS Level Accounting, Syllabus 8706/2, May/June)

2 Auckland (Manufacturers) Ltd has two manufacturing departments: (i) Machining and (ii) Assembly. It also has two service departments: (i) Maintenance and (ii) Power house. The information in the table below is available for the coming year.

Required

(a) Analyse the above indirect costs between the four departments showing the bases of apportionment you have used.

(b) Re-apportion the costs of the service departments over the two production departments using appropriate bases.

(c) Calculate an overhead absorption rate for the machining department based on machine hours and an overhead absorption rate for the assembly department based on direct labour hours.

3 (a) Define the term 'overhead expenses'.

(b) Explain the meaning of the following terms as they relate to overhead expenditure:

(i) allocation

(ii) apportionment.

(c) Explain the meaning of the terms:

(i) overhead absorption

(ii) overhead under-absorption

(iii) overhead over-absorption.

(d) State reasons why a company might recover more in overheads than the amount spent on overheads in the period.

(e) Explain why estimated figures are used to calculate overhead absorption rates.

	Machining	Assembly	Maintenance	Power house	Total
	$000	$000	$000	$000	$000
Indirect materials	298	482	132	152	1064
Indirect labour	706	918	282	672	2578
Rent and local taxes					1426
Supervision					660
Plant depreciation					1650
					7378

Further information is available as follows.

	Machining	Assembly	Maintenance	Power house
No. of employees	40	80	20	10
Area (metres²)	3 000	5000	1000	200
Plant valuation ($000s)	13 000	5000	2400	1600
Direct labour hours	3 200	4800		
Machine hours	11 080	2320		
Maintenance hours	1 800	600		
Units of power used	4 200	1200	600	

31 Unit, job and batch costing

31.1 Continuous and specific order operations

Costing systems may be applied to every type of business including:

- public or privately owned organisations
- manufacturers of goods such as motor cars, breakfast cereals, etc.
- providers of services, for example hospitals, hotels, restaurants, lawyers, accountants, etc.

Each type of business must choose a costing system that suits its particular operation; no one system will serve every type of business.

The operations of a business may be classified as either **continuous** or **specific order**.

Continuous operations are typically those in which a single type of good is produced and the cost units are identical. Production may involve a sequence of continuous or repetitive operations. Examples are:

- manufacture of computers
- production of mineral water
- oil refining
- production of medicines
- passenger and freight transport.

Continuous operations will almost certainly involve a product passing through a number of processes. Process costing will be covered in chapter 32.

Specific order operations are those which are performed in response to special orders received from customers and may be classified according to whether the operations consist of individual jobs, or the production of batches of identical units for a customer.

31.2 Continuous costing

For a business with continuous operations, continuous costing is used to find the cost of a single unit of production or service (**unit costing**). A single unit may be a single item; but a manufacturer of large volumes of a single product may find it more convenient to regard a number of items as a single unit. For example, for a company producing hundreds of thousands of packets of breakfast cereal, the unit may be, say, 1000 packets. Other examples of cost units are a pallet of bricks in brick making (a pallet is a wooden platform on which a given number of bricks is stacked after manufacture), and barrels for the output of oil wells.

Example

The following information is given for a business producing a single type of product for a period of one year.

Number of units produced:	30 000
Expenditure: Direct labour	$108 000
Direct materials	$54 000
Indirect	$66 000

The cost per unit is

$$\frac{\$(108\ 000 + 54\ 000 + 66\ 000)}{30\ 000} = \$7.60$$

Exercise 1

Luvlibrek manufactures breakfast cereal. Its cost unit is 1000 packets of the cereal. The following information is given.

Number of packets of cereal produced	425 000
Expenditure: Direct materials	$398 000
Direct labour	$996 000
Overheads	$1 687 250

Required

Calculate the cost of one unit of breakfast cereal.

31.3 Specific order costing

Job costing

For a company with specific order operations, that is, those which are performed in response to special orders received from customers, **job costing** can be carried out. Each order becomes a cost unit and can be costed as a separate job. Examples of jobs are:

- re-painting a house
- repairing a television set
- servicing a motor car.

Example 1

Jobbings Ltd is asked to quote a price to install central heating in a house. The quotation is based on estimated costs as follows.

	Estimated costs
	$
Materials*	3 000
Labour*	1 700
Overhead (200% of labour)	3 400
Total cost	8 100
Add profit (25% of cost)	2 025
Amount of quotation	10 125

* All the materials and labour are direct costs of the job.

If the quotation is accepted, the costs will be recorded on a job card as they are incurred by Jobbings Ltd.

Job No. 107 Installation of central heating at xxxxxx	Estimated	Actual
	$	$
Materials*	3 000	2 740
Labour*	1 700	1 920
Overhead (200% of labour)	3 400	3 840
Total cost	8 100	8 500
Add profit (25% of cost)	2 025	1 625
Amount of quotation	10 125	10 125

* All the materials and labour are direct costs of the job.

When the job has been completed, the actual costs have been entered on the job card, which shows that actual cost exceeded the estimated cost by $400 and the profit made is only $1625 instead of $2025. The job card will provide useful information the next time Jobbings Ltd quotes for a similar job.

Exercise 2

Geoffrey Pannell is a professional researcher. He has been commissioned to conduct research into allegations that mobile phones are bad for public health. Geoffrey estimates that the project will require 200 hours of his time, which he charges at $100 per hour. He will also require the services of Susan, his research assistant, for 100 hours at $60 per hour. Overheads are recovered at the rate of $40 per labour hour.

Required

Prepare a statement to show the amount Geoffrey will charge for carrying out this research.

Batch costing

Batch costing is very similar to job costing and is applied when an order from a customer involves the production of a number of identical items. All the costs incurred are charged to the batch and the cost per unit is found by dividing the cost of the batch by the number of units in the batch.

Example 2

Evocation Ltd sells reproductions of antique furniture. It places an order with Fakerfabs Ltd for 500 dining chairs at an agree price of $30 000 for the batch.

Fakerfabs Ltd has four production departments for which the following information is given.

Machining:	OAR $35 per machine hour
Finishing:	OAR $20 per direct labour hour
French polishing:	OAR $10 per direct labour hour
Assembly:	OAR $15 per direct labour hour

The costs incurred in the production of 500 dining chairs were:

Direct materials	$5000	
Direct labour:	Machining	125 hours at $10 per hour
	Finishing	180 hours at $9 per hour
	French polishing	220 hours at $12 per hour
	Assembly	100 hours at $8 per hour

160 machine hours were booked against the batch of chairs in the machining department.

Fakerfabs Ltd recovers its administration expenses at 15% on the total cost of production.

The batch cost, cost per chair and profit per chair are calculated as follows.

Costs for batch of 500 chairs		
	$	$
Direct materials		5 000
Direct labour: Machining (125 × $10)	1250	
Finishing (180 × $9)	1620	
French polishing (220 × $12)	2640	
Assembly (100 × $8)	800	6 310
Prime cost		11 310
Production overhead recovered		
Machining (160 × £35)	5600	
Finishing (180 × $20)	3600	
French polishing (220 × $10)	2200	
Assembly (100 × $15)	1500	12 900
Cost of production		24 210
Add administration costs recovered ($24 210 × 15%)		3 632
Total cost of batch of 500 chairs		27 842
Profit		2 158
		30 000

$$\text{Cost per chair} = \frac{\$27\ 842}{500} = \$55.684$$

$$\text{Profit per chair} = \frac{\$30\ 000}{500} - \$55.684 = \$4.316$$

Exercise 3

Wipup Ltd has received an order for 1000 packs of paper towels. Each pack contains six rolls of towels. The following information is given.

	$
Raw materials per roll of towels	0.08
Labour hourly rate	6.00
Cost of setting up machinery	30.00
Overhead absorption rate per labour/hour	9.35

100 packs of towels are manufactured per hour.

Required
(a) Calculate the cost of manufacturing the batch of 1000 packs of paper towels.
(b) Calculate the cost of one roll of paper towels.

31.4 Examination hints

- Make sure you understand the difference between continuous operations and specific order operations.
- Learn the characteristics of job costing and be prepared to give examples.
- Be prepared to explain the difference between job costing and batch costing.
- Make sure you can calculate continuous costs, job costs and batch costs. Set all calculations out in a neat and orderly form.

31.5 Multiple-choice questions

1 Which of the following operations would involve a system of continuous costing?

A construction of houses
B generating electricity
C hiring out boats in a fun park
D publishing newspapers

2 Retep Ltd hired a drilling machine for use on job 160. The machine was not used on any other job. Which of the following statements is true?

A Rent of the machine will be charged as a direct expense to job 160.
B Rent of the machine will be charged as an indirect expense to job 160.
C Rent and depreciation of the machine will be charged as a direct expense to job 160.
D Rent and depreciation of the machine will be charged as an indirect expense to job 160.

31.6 Additional exercises

1 Borlix Ltd makes a number of products, one of which is Super Borlix, which passes through three production departments, A, B and C. The following details are relevant to the production of Super Borlix.

Monthly production		4000 units
Direct material per unit		$8
Direct labour per unit	Dept A	$1\frac{1}{2}$ hours
	Dept B	1 hour
	Dept C	$\frac{1}{2}$ hour

Other information is as follows.

Direct labour rate (all depts.)		$8.75
Departmental overhead	Dept A	$36 000
	Dept B	$26 000
	Dept C	$24 000
Total direct labour hours	Dept A	24 000
	Dept B	20 000
	Dept C	8 000

Departmental overhead absorption is based on direct labour hours.

Required
Calculate the cost of one month's production of Super Borlix.

2 Curepipe Successful Promotions Ltd has two departments: (i) Printing and (ii) Marketing and Promotion. The following information is available for the next six months.

	Printing	Marketing and Promotion
Direct wage rate per hour	$8	$12
Budgeted overheads	$127 400	$267 540
Budgeted labour hours	3640	6370

Departmental overhead is recovered on the basis of the number of direct labour hours.

The company has been asked to promote a new product under the brand name 'Port Louis Chox'.

The cost of the job is based on the following estimates.

	Printing	Marketing and Promotion
Materials	$1300	$1600
Direct labour	120 hours	300 hours

Curepipe Successful Promotions Ltd charges to clients are based on cost plus 40%.

Required
Calculate the amount which Curepipe Successful Promotions Ltd will charge its client for the promotion of Port Louis Chox. Your answer should be prepared in the form of a fully itemised financial statement.

3 The Kelang Gum Boots Company has received a contract to manufacture 2000 pairs of children's boots. The boots pass through three departments: Moulding, Lining and Finishing. The following information is given.

	Moulding	Lining	Finishing
Direct material per pair of boots	$2	$3	–
Direct labour rate per hour	$7	$6	$6
Budgeted overhead expenditure	$21 840	$11 375	$4368
Budgeted machine hours	7280	–	–
Budgeted direct labour hours	–	4550	1820
Direct labour hours per pair of boots	0.25	0.5	0.25
Machine hours per pair of boots	0.5	–	–

Overhead absorption is calculated as follows.

Moulding: machine hours
Lining and finishing: direct labour hours

Required
(a) Calculate the total cost of producing the batch of 2000 pairs of children's boots.
(b) Calculate the cost of each pair of boots.

32 Process costing

32.1 Process costing explained

Continuous production usually involves a product passing through a series of processes. Each process is a cost centre to which costs are allocated. The raw material of each process consists of the cost of the production transferred from the previous process. Further costs will be added in each process in the form of added material, labour and overheads. The following diagram illustrates the procedure.

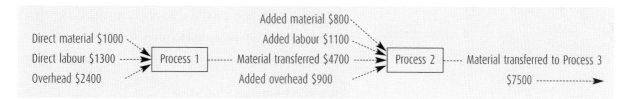

An account is prepared for each process to show the cost of the output from the process.

Example

1000 units of a product passed through three processes for which the following information is available.

	Process 1	Process 2	Process 3
	$	$	$
Direct material	15 000	8 000	2 000
Direct labour	23 000	11 000	5 000
Overhead	19 000	16 000	12 000

All of the units of the product were completed. The process accounts are as follows.

Process 1

	$		$
Direct material	15 000	Completed units transferred to Process 2	57 000
Direct labour	23 000		
Overhead	19 000		
	57 000		57 000

Process 2

	$		$
Material transferred from Process 1	57 000	Completed units transferred to Process 3	92 000
Added material	8 000		
Direct labour	11 000		
Overhead	16 000		
	92 000		92 000

Process 3

	$		$
Material transferred from Process 2	92 000	Completed units transferred to finished goods	111 000
Added material	2 000		
Direct labour	5 000		
Overhead	12 000		
	111 000		111 000

Exercise 1

The Sitrah Processing Company, which passes its product through three refining processes, provides the following information for one month.

	Process I	Process II	Process III
	$000	$000	$000
Direct material	10 000	4000	7000
Direct labour	400	350	275
Overhead	900	864	423

All the material which was input to process I completed processes II and III.

Required

Prepare the cost accounts for processes I, II and III.

32.2 Work in progress

It is usual that at any particular time some units of production will not have been completely processed; these are **work in progress** and must be valued for accounting purposes. The incomplete units are expressed as **equivalent units** of production and valued according to the cost that has been incurred in processing them so far.

Example

The budgeted cost of processing 1000 units of product X is made up as follows.

	$
Material transferred from a previous process (1000 units)	15 000
Added material	4 500
Direct labour in this process	20 000
Overhead (recovery based on 200% of direct labour)	40 000

Only 900 units have been completely processed. The other 100 are complete as to 80% material and 50% labour.

The cost of the 900 completed units is

90% of $(15\,000 + 4500 + 20\,000 + 40\,000) = \$71\,550$.

The cost of 100 incomplete units is:

		$
Material transferred $\frac{100}{1000} \times \$15\,000$		1500
Added material $\frac{100}{1000} \times \$4500 \times 80\%$		360
Direct labour $\frac{100}{1000} \times \$20\,000 \times 50\%$		1000
Overhead	$200\% \times \$1000$	2000
		4860

The incomplete units are carried down on the Process account as work in progress.

The Process account

	$		$
Material transferred from previous process	15 000	Transferred to next process	
Added material (90% of $4500 + $360)	4 410	(or finished goods)	71 550
Direct labour (90% of $20 000 + $1000)	19 000	Work in progress c/d	4 860
Overhead (90% of $40 000 + $2000)	38 000		
	76 410		76 410
Opening work in progress b/d	4 860		

32.3 Joint products

A single process may yield two or more products known as **joint products**. They are not distinguishable when material enters the process, but at some stage in the process they become separately identifiable.

Examples of joint products are:

- oil refining, which results in the production of petrol, diesel oil, lubricating oil and paraffin
- cattle farming, which results in milk, cream, butter, meat and hides
- clay pits, which result in ceramics, bricks, roofing tiles and chemically resistant materials.

Joint products become recognisable at the point of separation. Up to that point they have shared all the processing costs. After separation each product will be charged with the further costs incurred in putting it into a saleable condition. The following diagram illustrates the emergence of joint products in a process:

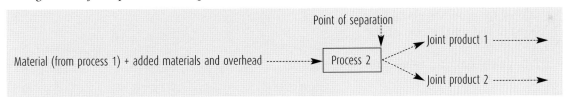

The joint costs up to the point of separation may be apportioned between the products on the basis of respective quantities, provided the products are measured in the similar terms, for example in kilograms, litres, etc.

Example

A process incurs the following costs.

	$
Common material input to process	30 000
Additional material	7 000
Direct labour	42 000
Overhead	51 000
Total cost of process	130 000

The process yielded two products: A 17 000 kilograms, B 9000 kilograms.

After separation, A incurred further processing costs of $3400, and B incurred further processing costs of $13 500.

The cost of 17 000 kg of A up to the point of separation is $130 000 \times \frac{17\,000}{26\,000} = \$85\,000$

The cost of 1 complete kilogram of A is
$\frac{85\,000 + 3400}{17\,000} = \$5.20$

The cost of 9000 kg of B up to the point of separation is $130\,000 \times \frac{9000}{26\,000} = \$45\,000$

The cost of 1 complete kilogram of B is
$\frac{45\,000 + 13500}{9000} = \$6.50$

Exercise 2

The Trinbago Refining Company produces two substances know as Animo and Lactino. In one week, 3400 litres of Animo and 5100 litres of Lactino were produced. The input to the process was as follows.

	$
Material: Animacto	21 000
Direct labour	11 000
Overheads	23 000

After separation, further processing costs to completion were: Animo $4624; Lactino $13 362.

Required

Calculate the cost of each complete litre of (a) Animo and (b) Lactino.

32.4 By-products and waste

A **by-product** is similar to a joint product except that its sales value is low compared with the sales value of the main product. The cocoa and chocolate industry provides a good example of a by-product: the shells of cocoa beans constitute about 8–10% of the weight of the beans and have to be removed. They are of no use in the chocolate industry but are used as fertiliser, mulch and fuel. Other examples of by-products are remnants of material in garment manufacture, and wood off-cuts and sawdust in the timber industry.

Any income from the sale of by-products should be credited to the Process account to reduce the cost of the main or joint products.

Waste describes material which has no value and therefore has no effect upon the Process accounts; nor will it be included in stock.

Example

Slag produced by an iron foundry is sold as hard core for $2000 to a firm of civil engineers. It is recorded in the foundry's Process accounts as follows.

	$
Material input to process	50 000
Direct wages	76 000
Overhead	94 000
	220 000
Less sale of slag	2 000*
Cost attributed to main product	218 000

* The proceeds from the sale of the slag were less than 1% of the process cost.

32.5 Normal losses in processing

Losses of material are unavoidable in many processes and the quantity of the product produced is less than the quantity of the material input to the process. If the loss is within the range expected for the process it is recognised as a **normal loss**. The unspoiled production will bear the cost of the loss.

Example

In a certain process, 1000 kg of material costing $4000 was used. The direct wages paid were $16 000 and overhead expenditure amounted to $24 160. The output from the process was 920 kg. The normal loss expected for the process is 10%. The output per kg will be valued at $(4000 + 16 000 + 24 160) \div 920 = \$48$.

In this example, there has in fact been an abnormal gain because the actual loss was less than the expected 10%. However, students are not expected to know the treatment of abnormal gains and losses.

Exercise 3

Okara Quality Carpets Ltd makes a product which involves two processes. Process 1 results in the production of a low-priced by-product which the company sells. 2000 units of the product were made in process 1 and transferred to process 2. Work in progress at the end of process 2 consisted of 800 units complete as to 75% material and 50% labour. Further production details are as follows.

Data per unit	Process 1	Process 2
Material	4 kg	2.5 kg
Cost of material	$12 per kg	$3.25 per kg
Labour hours per unit	3	5
Labour hourly rate	$14	$11
Production overhead absorption	$36 per labour hour	$27 per labour hour
Sale proceeds of by-product	$1630	–

Required

Prepare Process accounts 1 and 2 to show the cost of producing 2000 units. Show detailed workings for the valuation of finished units and work in progress in process 2.

32.6 Examination hints

- Remember that the total cost of production in one process is the cost of material input to the next process.
- Make sure you can express partly completed work in terms of equivalent units.

- Learn how to apportion cost between joint products.
- Remember that the proceeds from the sale of by-products are credited in the Process accounts.
- Allow for waste when valuing completed production.

32.7 Multiple-choice questions

1 Which of the following industries would use process costing?

   A building construction

   B chemical

   C hotel

   D road haulage

2 The following information is given about a process in which normal waste of 10% is incurred.

	$
Direct material	57 000
Direct labour	88 000
Overhead	79 000
Sale of by-product	3 000

What is the prime cost of production?

   A $127 000   **B** $142 000   **C** $145 000

   D $148 000

32.8 Additional exercises

1 The Taranaki Milk Products Company manufactures products which pass through three processes. The costing records for processes 1 and 2 give the following information.

	Process 1	Process 2
Materials per unit	2 litres	1 litre
Cost of materials per kg/litre	$1.25	$1.5
Materials used in process at cost	$60 000	
Additional materials used in process		to be calculated
Direct labour per unit	30 minutes	15 minutes
Labour cost per hour	$12	$12
Variable overhead per unit	$5 per direct labour hour	$4 per direct labour hour
Fixed overhead absorption rate	$9 per direct labour hour	$6 per direct labour hour

Further information

Process 1. There were no opening or closing stocks of work in progress. All production from this process was passed to process 2.

Process 2. There was no opening stock of work in progress. There was a closing stock of work in progress consisting of 2000 units which were complete as to 80% materials and 60% labour.

Required

(a) Prepare the accounts for processes 1 and 2.

(b) Calculate the cost of:
   (i) one completed unit of production in process 1
   (ii) one completed unit of production in process 2
   (iii) one unit of work in progress in process 2.

10 000 units from process 2 were used in process 3 as a result of which two joint products X and Y were produced. The costs of this process were as follows: materials $9050; labour $18 500; variable overheads $5400; fixed overheads $10 800.

   10% of production in process 3 was spoiled. X represented 75% of the good production, and Y the remainder. There were no opening or closing stocks of work in progress.

Required

(c) Calculate the quantities of (i) X and (ii) Y produced in process 3.

(d) Calculate the cost of each unit of output of process 3.

(e) Calculate the values of the finished stocks of (i) X and (ii) Y.

(f) (i) Explain what is meant by a by-product.
   (ii) State how by-products are accounted for in process cost accounting.

2 The Harare Metal Alloy Company manufactures two products which involve three processes. They pass through processes 1 and 2 as a single product and separate into product X and product Y in process 3.

   The following information has been extracted from the cost records.

	Process 1	Process 2
Materials per unit	7 kg	4.5 kg
Cost of material per litre	$1.50	$2
Cost of materials used in process 1	$42 000	–
Cost of materials used in process 2	–	to be calculated
Direct labour hours per unit	4	3.5
Hourly labour cost	$8	$6
Variable overhead per unit	$16 per direct labour hour	$15 per direct labour hour
Fixed overhead absorption rate	$30 per direct labour hour	$29 per direct labour hour
Sale of by-product	$1 000	–
Opening stock of work in progress	nil	nil
Closing stock of work in progress	nil	1000 units

The closing stock of work in progress in process 2 is complete as to 100% materials and 75% labour.

Required

(a) Prepare the ledger account for process 1.

(b) Prepare the ledger account for process 2.

The completed units in process 2 are transferred to process 3 where they separate into joint products, X and Y. 70% of the finished units are X and 30% are Y. The costs in process 3 are as follows.

Added materials: 3.5 kg per unit at $3 per kg

Direct labour: 2 hours per unit at $7 per hour

Variable overheads: $18 per direct labour hour

Fixed overhead absorption rate: $27 per direct labour rate.

10% of the production in process 3 was spoiled.

Required

(c) Prepare the ledger account for process 3.

33 Marginal costing

33.1 Marginal cost

In chapter 30 we have seen how total costing can be used to determine price and profit but, beyond that, its uses are limited. For many management decisions it is necessary to know the **marginal cost** of a unit of production. Marginal cost can be described as the cost of making one extra unit of an item. It is based on the principle that an additional unit of production will only entail an increase in the variable costs and that the fixed costs will not be affected. **Marginal cost of production** is the total of the variable costs of manufacture.

Example 1

The cost of producing 1000 units of a good are shown in the table on this page (with the unit cost shown in the second column).

The marginal cost of production for 1000 units is $150 000 (or $150 for a single unit). The difference between the total cost of production (i.e. including fixed overheads) and the selling price gives the profit of $40 000 (or $40 per unit – not shown). Fixed overheads + profit = $90 000, or $90 per unit. This is called the **contribution** because it is the contribution that each unit of production makes towards covering the overheads and providing a profit. The contribution per unit is calculated as follows: selling price per unit less the total of the variable costs per unit or SP – VC (per unit).

	Cost for 1000 units $	Cost per unit $
Variable costs		
Direct material	30 000	30
Direct labour	100 000	100
Direct expenses	5 000	5
Prime cost	135 000	135
Variable overheads	15 000	15
Marginal cost of production	150 000	150
Fixed overheads	50 000	
Total cost of production	200 000	
Profit (20% of total cost)	40 000	
Contribution		90
Selling price	240 000	240

The cost of making 1001 units will be $(240 000 + 150) = $240 150, not $240 240 as it might seem if we only had a total cost statement.

The ratio of the contribution to the selling price is known as the **C/S ratio**. In this example the C/S ratio is $\frac{90}{240} \times 100 = 37.5\%$. This is a very useful ratio that can be used to calculate the answers to many problems. The use of the C/S ratio can avoid the need to spend valuable time calculating marginal cost.

Example 2

The following is a summarised statement of producing 2000 units of product X.

	$
Marginal cost	81 900
Contribution	44 100
Sales	126 000

Fixed costs amount to $26 000

Profit = contribution – fixed costs: $(44 100 – 26 000) = $18 100

What will the profit or loss be if production is
(i)   increased to 2400 units
(ii) reduced to 1800 units
(iii) reduced to 1100 units?

Answer

(i) The contribution from 1 unit is $44 100 ÷ 2000 = $22.05.
   Therefore the contribution from 2400 units is 2400 × $22.05 = $52 920.

   Profit = contribution – fixed costs = $(52 920 – 26 000) = $26 920

(ii) The contribution from 1800 units will be 1800 × $22.05 = $39 690.

   Profit = $(39 690 – 26 000) = $13 690

(iii) The contribution from 1100 units will be 1100 × $22.05 = $24 255.

   Loss = $(26 000 – 24 255) = $1745

Exercise 1

The following is the marginal cost statement for the production of 3000 units of product Q.

	$
Marginal cost	178 750
Contribution	146 250
Sales	325 000

Fixed costs amount to $82 000.

Required

Calculate the profit or loss from the sale of (i) 3000 units (ii) 4000 units (iii) 1200 units of product Q.

33.2 The break-even point

The point at which a business or a product makes neither a profit nor a loss is the **break-even point**. Managers need to know the break-even point of a product when making decisions about pricing, production levels and other matters.

Break-even occurs when contribution equals fixed costs. It is found by dividing the total fixed costs by the contribution per unit. The calculation gives the number of units that have to be produced and sold before the fixed costs are covered.

Example

The following information relates to the production of a chemical.

	$
Marginal cost per litre	26
Selling price per litre	50
Total of fixed costs	72 000

The contribution per litre is $(50 – 26) = $24.

Break-even point $= \frac{\$72\,000}{\$24} = 3000$ litres.

The sales revenue at which the product will break even is 3000 × $50 = $150 000. This may also be found as follows:

$$\frac{\text{total fixed costs}}{\text{contribution per \$ of selling price}} = \frac{\$72\,000}{0.48} = \$150\,000$$

(contribution per $ of selling price = $24 ÷ 50 = $0.48).

When the calculation of break-even point results in a fraction of a unit of production, the answer should be rounded up to the next complete unit, for example:
Contribution per unit of product $23; total fixed costs $32 000.

Break-even $= \frac{\$32\,000}{\$23} = 1391.304$, shown as 1392 units.

33.3 Break-even charts

A **break-even chart** is a diagrammatic representation of the profit or loss to be expected from the sale of a product at various levels of activity. The chart is prepared by plotting the revenue from the sale of various volumes of a product against the total cost of production. The break-even point occurs where the sales curve bisects the total cost curve and there is neither profit nor loss.

Example

The marginal cost of product X is $10 per litre. It is sold for $22.50 per litre. Fixed costs are $50 000.

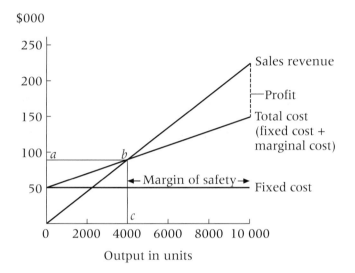

Break-even chart for product X

The line *ab* shows the revenue at break-even point ($90 000). The line *bc* shows the output in units at break-even point (4000). At 10 000 units, the sales revenue is $225 000 and total cost is $150 000. The distance between those two lines shows the profit of $75 000.

The area between the sales revenue line and the total cost line *before* the break-even point represents the loss that will be made if the output falls below 4000 units. The area *beyond* the break-even point represents profit.

The difference between the break-even point and 10 000 units is the **margin of safety**, or the amount by which output can fall short of 10 000 units before the business risks making a loss on product X. It may be expressed as a number of units, 6000, or as a percentage, $\frac{6000}{10\,000} \times 100 = 60\%$.

The break-even charts of two products, A and B, will now be compared. Both products have similar total costs and revenues, but product A has high fixed costs while product B has low fixed costs.

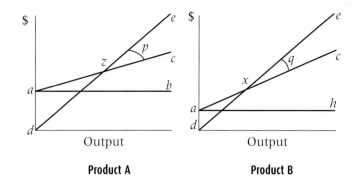

In each case, line *ab* represents fixed costs, line *ac* represents total cost, and line *de* represents sales revenue. The break-even point *x* for product A occurs further to the right of the chart (i.e. later) than that for product B. This shows that high fixed costs tend to result in high break-even points. Product B with a low fixed cost has a lower break-even point even though the marginal cost is greater.

The angle *p* at which the revenue line *de* intersects the total cost line *ac* for product A is greater than the angle *q* for product B. The size of the angle of intersection is an indication of the **sensitivity** of a product to variations in the level of activity. It can be seen that, as output increases for the two products, the profitability of product A increases at a faster rate than the profitability of product B. On the other hand, if output decreases for both products, the profitability of A decreases at a faster rate than for B. Product A is more sensitive to changes in output than product B. When the proportion of fixed cost to total cost is high, the risk to profitability is also high. Profit and break-even points are said to be sensitive to changes in prices and cost. This aspect will be considered later in §33.9.

Note. The CIE syllabus requires candidates to be able to prepare break-even charts from given information.

Exercise 2

Production of 5000 units of Product Q is planned. The following information is given.

	$
Variable cost per unit	65
Selling price per unit	95
Total of fixed costs	75 000

Required

(a) Calculate:
  (i) the break-even point of product Q in terms of units and revenue
  (ii) the margin of safety.
(b) Draw a break-even chart for product Q.

Profit/volume charts

Break-even charts may also be drawn to show only the profit or loss at each level of output. The cost and revenue lines are omitted. The break-even chart for product X given in the example above could be drawn as a profit/volume chart:

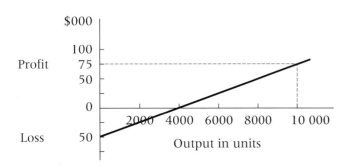

Profit/volume chart for product X

At zero output, the loss equals the total of the fixed costs, £50 000. At 10 000 units, the profit is equal to $75 000. A straight line joining the two points intersects the output line at the break-even point.

33.4 The limitations of break-even charts

Break-even charts are useful visual aids for the study of the effect of changes in output, costs and revenues on the break-even point, especially for managers with little accounting knowledge. The charts, however, have their limitations.

- Some costs are not easily classified as fixed or variable.
- Many fixed costs are fixed only within certain limits and may increase with the level of activity; they are 'stepped' costs (see §30.3).
- If sales revenue and costs are represented by straight lines they may be misleading. Maximum sales revenue may only be achieved if customers are given attractive discounts, while variable costs may be affected by quantity discounts when output is increased. These

factors would be more accurately represented on charts by curves than straight lines.

The charts may mislead people whose accounting knowledge is limited, but trained accountants will know when to make allowances for the charts' limitations.

33.5 Marginal costing and pricing

The price at which a good may be sold is usually decided by a number of factors:

- the need to make a profit
- market demand
- a requirement to increase market share for a product
- maximum utilisation of resources
- competition from other firms
- economic conditions
- political factors (price regulation etc.).

Marginal costing can help management to decide on pricing policy but first it is necessary to understand that some expenses, such as selling expenses, may be variable. An example is salespeople's commission based on the number of units sold. When variable selling expenses are included in marginal cost, the result is the **marginal cost of sales**:

	$000
Direct materials	100
Direct wages	80
Direct expenses	30
Marginal cost of production	210
Variable selling expenses	15
Marginal cost of sales	225
Other fixed expenses	175
Total cost	400

It is important to use the correct marginal cost when using marginal costing for decision making.

Example

(Increasing market share)
The Larabee Gamebusters Company produces and sells a computer game that sells at $30 per game.

Each year 6000 of the games are sold. The marketing director suggests that, if the price is reduced to $28, sales will increase to 8000 games. The sales manager thinks that sales will increase to 11 000 games if the price is reduced to $25.

The following information is available for 6000 computer games.

	$
Direct materials	48 000
Direct labour	66 000
Variable selling expenses (commission)	12 000
Fixed expenses	48 000

Required

Calculate the profit or loss from the sale of (i) 6000 (ii) 8000 (iii) 11 000 units and recommend which option should be adopted.

Answer

Every unit sold incurs a variable selling expense (commission) and the marginal cost of sales is used.

Per unit:	$	$	$
Selling price	30	28	25
Direct material	8		
Direct labour	11		
Variable selling expense	2		
Marginal cost of sales	21	21	21
Contribution	9	7	4
	6000 units	8000 units	11 000 units
	$	$	$
Total contribution	54 000	56 000	44 000
Fixed expenses	48 000	48 000	48 000
Profit/(loss)	6 000	8 000	(4 000)

The Larabee Gamebusters Company should reduce the price of the game to $28.

Exercise 3

Veerich Ardson Ltd makes and sells mobile phones. The following information is given.

Per phone:	$
Selling price	50
Direct materials	18
Direct labour	20
Variable selling expenses	3

Fixed overheads amount to $70 000.

Required

Calculate the profit or loss from the sale of (i) 10 000 phones at $50 each (ii) 15 000 phones at $48 each, (iii) 20 000 phones at $42 each.

33.6 Acceptance of orders below normal selling price

There are occasions when orders may be accepted below the normal selling price. These may be considered when there is spare manufacturing capacity and in the following circumstances:

- when the order will result in further contribution to cover fixed expenses and add to profit
- to maintain production and avoid laying off a skilled workforce during a period of poor trading
- to promote a new product
- to dispose of slow-moving or redundant stock.

The selling price must exceed the marginal cost of production.

Example

K2 Altimeters Ltd makes altimeters that it sells at $80 each. It has received orders for:
(i) 1000 altimeters for which the buyer is prepared to pay $60 per altimeter
(ii) 2000 altimeters at $48 each.
The following information is available.

	$
Direct material per altimeter	21
Direct labour per altimeter	32

Fixed expenses will not be affected by the additional production.

Required

State whether K2 Altimeters Ltd should accept either of the orders.

Answer

Order for 1000 altimeters at $60 each:

Contribution per altimeter $(60 – 53) = $7
Additional contribution from order: $7000

K2 Altimeters Ltd should accept the order.
Order for 2000 altimeters at $48 each:

Contribution per altimeter $(48 – 53) = $(5)

K2 Altimeters Ltd would make a loss of $10 000 on the order and should not accept it.

Exercise 4

El Dugar Peach Ltd sells canned fruit for which the following information is given.

	$
Per 1000 cans of fruit:	
Direct materials	5500
Direct labour	8750

The company has received orders for:
(i) 5000 cans of fruit at $16 000 per 1000 cans
(ii) 3000 cans of fruit at $14 100 per 1000 cans.
The additional production will not require any additional fixed expenses.

Required

State which of the two orders, if any, El Dugar Peach Ltd should accept.

33.7 Make or buy decisions

We have already seen in §19.2 that a Manufacturing Account may suggest that it would be more profitable for a business to buy goods from another supplier than make the goods itself. This involves a **'make or buy' decision**. It may be relevant for goods that are already being produced, or to the introduction of a new product.

The decision will be based primarily on whether the cost of buying the goods from another supplier is more or less than the marginal cost of production. Notice that the marginal cost of sales is not relevant to this type of decision as any variable selling costs will have to be incurred whether the goods are manufactured or purchased.

Example

Uggle Boxes Ltd makes and sells uggle boxes for which the following information is available.

Per box	$
Selling price	25
Direct material	9
Direct labour	6
Variable selling expenses	7

Uggle Boxes Ltd's fixed overheads amount to $60 500.

The variable selling expenses are ignored as they will have to be incurred anyway. The marginal cost of production is $(9 + 6) = $15. The contribution per unit is $(25 − 22) = $3. The current break-even point is $\frac{\$60\,500}{\$3}$ = 20 167 boxes.

Uggle boxes may be bought from Ockle Cockle Boxes Ltd for $13 per box, and from Jiggle Boxes Ltd for $16 per box.

Purchase of the boxes from Jiggle Boxes Ltd will increase the marginal cost to $23 and reduce the contribution to $2. Profit will be reduced and the break-even point will increase to $\frac{\$60\,500}{\$2}$ or 30 250 boxes. This option should not be considered.

If the boxes are bought from Ockle Cockle Boxes Ltd, the marginal cost will be $20 and the contribution will increase to $5. Profit will be increased and the break-even

point will reduce to $\frac{\$60\,500}{\$5}$ or 12 100 boxes. This appears to be a good option.

Note. There are other matters which Uggle Boxes Ltd should consider before finally deciding to buy the boxes from another supplier:

- How certain is it that Ockle Cockle Boxes Ltd will not increase the price above $13? If the price is increased to more than $15 it may not be easy for Uggle Boxes Ltd to recommence manufacturing the boxes if it has rid itself of its workers and other resources.
- Will Ockle Cockle Boxes Ltd supply boxes of the proper quality?
- Will Ockle Cockle Boxes Ltd deliver the boxes promptly? Uggle Boxes Ltd cannot afford to keep its customers waiting because it is out of stock.
- Has Uggle Boxes Ltd an alternative use for the resources which will become free when it ceases to make the boxes? Unless it can utilise the resources profitably to make another product it will either have to shed the resources (labour, machines, etc.) or increase its unproductive costs.
- Can Uggle Boxes Ltd afford to lose the services of a skilled and loyal workforce which it may be difficult to replace at a later date when the need arises?

As we shall see again in chapter 36 on capital investment appraisal, managers often need to take non-financial factors into account before deciding which course of action to take.

Exercise 5

Canterbury Planes Ltd supplies the following information for the production of 15 000 tools.

	$
Direct materials	45 000
Direct labour	37 500
Other direct expenses	15 000
Variable selling expenses	30 000

Fixed expenses total $74 000. The tools sell for $16 each.

Canterbury Planes Ltd has received the following quotations for the supply of the tools:

North Island Tool Co.	$6000 per 1000 tools
South Island Tool Co.	$6800 per 1000 tools

Required

(a) Calculate the effect on profit and the break-even point of the quotations of
  (i) North Island Tool Co.
  (ii) South Island Tool Co.
  if either was awarded the contract to supply the tools to Canterbury Planes Ltd.

(b) State whether Canterbury Planes Ltd should continue to produce the tools or whether it should buy them, and if so, from whom. Support your answer with figures.

33.8 Making the most profitable use of limited resources

Anything which limits the quantity of goods that a business may produce is known as a **limiting factor**. Limiting factors include:

- shortage of materials
- shortage of labour
- shortage of demand for a particular product.

When faced with limited resources, a company making several different products should use the limited resources in a way that produces the most profit. The products must be ranked according to the amount of contribution they make from each unit of the scarce resource. Production will then be planned to ensure that the scarce resource is concentrated on the highest-ranking products.

Example 1

(Shortage of material)
Hillbilly Ltd makes three products: Hillies, Billies and Millies. All three products are made from a material called Dilly. Planned production is as follows: Hillies 2000 units; Billies 3000 units; Millies 4000 units. The following information is given for the products.

	Hillies	Billies	Millies
Selling price per unit	$54	$50	$105
Direct material per unit	2 kg	4 kg	5 kg
Direct labour hours per unit	3	2	6

Direct material costs $6 per kg; direct labour is paid at $10 per hour.

Fixed expenses amount to $72 000.

Hillbilly Ltd has discovered that the material Dilly is in short supply and only 30 000 kg can be obtained.

Required
Prepare a production plan that will make the most profit from the available material.

Answer
Calculation of contributions per kg of Dilly:

	Hillies	Billies	Millies
	$	$	$
Direct material per unit	12	24	30
Direct labour per unit	30	20	60
Marginal cost per unit	42	44	90
Selling price per unit	54	50	105
Contribution per unit	12	6	15
Contribution per kg of material	6	1.5	3
Ranking	1	3	2

Revised plan of production:

	Units	Direct material kg	Contribution $
Hillies	2000	4 000	24 000
Millies	4000	20 000	60 000
Billies	1500	6 000	9 000
		30 000	93 000
Deduct fixed expenses			72 000
Profit			21 000

Example 2

(Shortage of direct labour hours)
The data for the manufacture of Hillies, Billies and Millies is as given for example 1 but the number of direct labour hours available is limited to 33 000. There is no shortage of material.

Required
Prepare a production plan that will make the most profit from the available labour hours.

Answer
Calculation of contributions per direct labour hour:

	Hillies	Billies	Millies
	$	$	$
Contribution per unit (as above)	12	6	15
Contribution per direct labour hour	4	3	2.5
Ranking	1	2	3

Revised plan of production:

	Units	Direct labour hours	Contribution
			$
Hillies	2000	6 000	24 000
Billies	3000	6 000	18 000
Millies	3500	21 000	52 500
		33 000	94 500
Deduct fixed expenses			72 000
Profit			22 500

Exercise 6

Castries Ltd makes three products: Gimie, Gros and Petit. The budgeted production for three months is as follows.

	Gimie	Gros	Petit
No. of units	1000	2000	800
Selling price per unit	$14	$25	$20
Direct material per unit (litres)	2.5	3.25	4
Direct labour per unit (hours)	0.5	1.4	0.6

Direct material costs $2 per litre. Direct labour is paid at $10 per hour.

Fixed expenses are $10 000.

Castries Ltd has been informed that only 10 575 litres of material are available.

Required

Prepare a revised production budget that will produce the most profit from the available materials.

Exercise 7

Castries Ltd has been informed that supplies of material are not limited, but only 3395 direct labour hours are available. All the other information is as in exercise 6.

Required

Prepare a revised production budget that will produce the most profit from the available direct labour hours.

33.9 Sensitivity analysis

In §33.3 the sensitivity of profit and break-even points to changes in costs and revenue was mentioned. This topic will now be covered in more detail as errors in estimates of revenue and costs will affect profit. By definition, estimates are rarely likely to be accurate and allowances should be made in budgets for possible differences between estimates and actual costs and revenue. The point will be illustrated by taking the example of a high-risk situation.

Example

The following information relates to the budget for a certain product.

No. of units produced and sold: 10 000	
	$
Sales revenue	180 000
Variable costs	50 000
Fixed costs	100 000
Profit	30 000

(Break-even occurs at $\frac{\$100\,000}{\$13} = 7692$ units)

If fixed costs rise by 10% and the increase is not passed on to customers, profit will be reduced by $10 000 to $20 000. Break-even will be increased to $\frac{\$110\,000}{\$13} = 8462$ units.

If fixed costs do not increase but variable costs rise by 10%, and the increase is not passed on to customers, the profit will be reduced by $5000 to $25 000, and the break-even point will be increased to $\frac{\$100\,000}{\$12.5} = 8000$ units.

If costs do not increase but sales revenue is only 90% of expectation, profit will be reduced by $18 000 to $12 000, and break-even will be increased to $\frac{\$100\,000}{\$11.2} = 8929$ units.

If fixed costs increase by 10% and are not passed on to customers, and sales revenue is only 90% of expectation, profit will be reduced by $(10 000 + 18 000) to $2000, and break-even will be increased to $\frac{\$110\,000}{\$11.2} = 9822$ units.

If all costs increase by 10% and are not passed on to customers, and sales revenue is only 90% of expectation, a loss of $3000 ($30 000 − $15 000 − $18 000) will be incurred, and break-even will be increased beyond the budgeted production at $\frac{\$110\,000}{\$10.7} = 10\,281$ units.

Exercise 8

The following budget has been prepared for the production and sales of 20 000 units of a product.

	$
Fixed costs	80 000
Variable costs	60 000
Total costs	140 000
Sales	175 000
Profit	35 000

Break-even occurs at $\frac{\$80\,000}{\$5.75} = 13\,914$ units.

Required

Calculate the profit and the break-even point if
(i) fixed costs increase by 15% and are not passed on to customers

(ii) variable costs increase by 15% and are not passed on to customers (there is no increase in fixed costs)

(iii) fixed and variable costs increase by 15% and the increases are passed on to the customers.

Exercise 9

Cohort Ltd makes three products: Legion, Centurion and Praefect. All three products are made from the same material. The production budget for June 2004 is as follows.

	Legion	Centurion	Praefect
Budgeted production (units)	1000	2000	4000
Materials per unit (kg)	2	4	5
Direct labour per unit (hours)	3	5	6
Selling price per unit	$80	$130	$150

Material cost: $10 per kg   Labour rate of pay: $12 per hour

Total fixed expenses for June 2004: $115 000

Required

(a) Calculate the budgeted profit for June 2004. Show your workings.

After the budget for June 2004 was prepared, Cohort Ltd learned that there was a shortage of the material and that it would not be able to obtain more than 28 000 kg in June.

Required

(b) Prepare a revised production budget which will ensure that Cohort Ltd obtains the maximum profit from the available material.

(c) Prepare a calculation to explain the difference between the original budgeted profit you have calculated in (a) and the revised profit you have calculated in (b).

Exercise 10

The Cockpit Country Industrial Co. Ltd has a maximum production capacity of 20 000 units. Each unit sells for $25.

The following are the costs for a single unit of production.

Direct materials	4 kilograms at $4.10 per kilogram
Direct labour	$12 per hour. 3 units are produced in one hour.
Variable expenses	$1.80 per unit for the first 16 000 units
	$1.70 per unit for all units in excess of 16 000 units
Fixed expenses	$1.50 per unit at full production

Required

(a) Using marginal costing, calculate the net profit if:
  (i)   15 000 units are produced and sold
  (ii) 18 000 units are produced and sold.

(b) Calculate the number of units required to break even.

(c) Calculate the profit at full production capacity if all production is sold at the reduced price of $24.

(d) State the possible advantages and disadvantages of reducing the normal selling price.

(e) State *five* assumptions which are made in the preparation of break-even charts, and state *one* limitation of each assumption.

33.10 Examination hints

- Make sure you are able to distinguish between variable and fixed costs.
- Learn the definition of 'marginal cost'.
- The C/S ratio is most important and is certain to be required in marginal cost questions. Make sure you know how to calculate the ratio and when to use it.
- Learn how to calculate the break-even point and the margin of safety. Break-even point is calculated by dividing the total fixed costs by the contribution per unit. If you are given the fixed cost per unit, multiply it by the number of units to find the total fixed costs.
- Practise drawing break-even charts. Choose as large a scale as possible for the chart to achieve a good degree of accuracy. Give every chart a proper heading and label the x and y axes clearly. Indicate the break-even point and other features. Take a ruler, pencil and rubber to the exam.
- Make sure you know how to use limited resources most profitably. Products should be ranked according to the contribution per unit of the limited resource.

33.11 Multiple-choice questions

1 Information about a product is given.

	per unit
	$
Selling price	110
Direct materials	50
Direct labour	40

Fixed costs total $50 000 and planned production is 2000 units. Which action is necessary to break even?

Decrease cost of:

A direct labour by 20%

B direct labour by 25%

C direct material by 10%

D direct material by 20%

2 The annual results of a company with three departments are as follows.

Department	X	Y	Z
	$	$	$
Sales	210 000	100 000	140 000
Less: variable costs	100 000	80 000	90 000
head office fixed costs	75 000	35 000	50 000
Net profit (loss)	35 000	(15 000)	0

Head office fixed costs have been apportioned on the basis of the respective sales of the departments and will not be reduced if any department is closed. Which action should the company take, based on these results?

A close department Y

B close departments Y and Z

C close department Z

D keep all the departments open

3 A company makes three products, X, Y and Z, all of which require the use of the same material. Information about the products is as follows.

	Product X	Product Y	Product Z
	$	$	$
Per unit:			
Selling price	260	200	240
Direct material	96	80	90
Direct labour	50	40	50
Variable overhead	40	30	36
Fixed overhead	54	36	36
Profit	12	14	27

The material is in short supply. Which order of priority should the company give to the products to maximise profit?

	Order of priority		
	1	2	3
A	Y	X	Z
B	Y	Z	X
C	X	Y	Z
D	X	Z	Y

4 The following information relates to product Q.

	$
Sales revenue at break even point	72 000
Unit sales price	24
Fixed costs	18 000

What is the marginal cost of each unit of product Q?

A $4.00 **B** $6.00 **C** $10.00 **D** $18.00

33.12 Additional exercises

1 Barkis & Co. Ltd manufacture specialised containers for use under water. The business uses two machines. These machines have different levels of efficiency. The following information applies to production and costs.

Machine	X	Y
Hourly rate of production	160	250
Material cost per unit	$5.00	$4.60
Hourly labour rate	$10	$10
Number of operatives	4	5
Fixed costs per order	$200	$500
Variable costs per order	$2.40	$2.60

Orders have been received from different customers for (a) 800 and (b) 1000 containers. Which machine should be used for each order, in order to minimise cost? Orders may not be split between machines, but the same machine may be used for more than one order.

(a) Order 123/P for 800 containers

(b) Order 382/Q for 1000 containers

(c) Calculate the contribution to be made for order 123/P to make a profit of 25% on total cost, using each machine.

(d) Barkis & Co. Ltd require more funds to purchase an additional machine to complete further orders.

Three methods of doing so have been discussed:

(i) a rights issue;

(ii) an issue of shares to the public;

(iii) an issue of debentures.

Give *one* advantage and *one* disadvantage of each method.

(UCLES, 2002, AS/A Level Accounting, Syllabus 9706/2, May/June)

2 Angelicus and Co. manufactures three different qualities of lock, Domestic, Commercial and Industrial. The company's results for the year ended 31 March 2003 were as follows.

	Domestic	Commercial	Industrial	Total
Sales (units)	120 000	45 000	56 250	221 250
	$000	$000	$000	$000
Sales (total value)	240	180	450	870
Total costs				
Direct material	108	66	84	258
Direct labour	60	30	150	240
Variable overheads	24	54	120	198
Fixed overheads	54	33	42	129
	246	183	396	825
Profit (loss)	(6)	(3)	54	45

Fixed overheads are absorbed on the basis of 50% of direct materials.

Required

(a) For the year ended 31 March 2003 calculate, for each type of lock,
   (i) the contribution per unit;
   (ii) the contribution as a percentage of sales.
   Give answers to a maximum of *three* decimal places.
   Show *all* workings

(b) Calculate the break-even point for each type of lock in both units and dollars.

(c) Advise whether Angelicus should cease production of Domestic and Commercial locks. Give your reasons.

(UCLES, 2003, AS/A Level Accounting, Syllabus 9706/2, May/June)

34 Budgeting

In this chapter you will learn:
- how budgets differ from forecasts
- how budgets help management to plan and control
- factors to be considered in the preparation of budgets
- how to prepare sales, production, purchasing, expense and cash budgets
- how to prepare master budgets
- what flexible budgets are.

34.1 The difference between a forecast and a budget

A business **forecast** is an estimate of the likely position of a business in the future, based on past or present conditions. For example, Cindy's sales over the past five years have been $100 000, $105 000, $110 250, $115 750 and $121 500; the sales have been increasing at the rate of about 5% each year. Based on this information, and assuming that trading conditions will continue unchanged, the forecast sales for the next year might be about $127 600.

A **budget** is a statement of *planned* future results which are expected to follow from actions taken by management to change the present circumstances. Cindy may want sales to grow by 10% each year in future by introducing new products, or by increasing advertising, or by offering improved terms of trading. Her budgeted sales for next year will then be $133 650 ($121 500 × 110%), and $147 000 and $161 700 for the following two years. A budget expresses management's plans for the future of a business in money terms.

34.2 Budgets as tools for planning and control

Planning

Managers are responsible for planning and controlling a business for the benefit of its owners, and budgets are essential tools for planning and controlling. Well-managed businesses have short-term budgets for, say, the year ahead. Small businesses may function well enough with these, but larger businesses need to plan further ahead and may prepare long-term budgets, in addition to the short-term ones, for the next five, ten or even more years ahead. These plans are often known as **rolling budgets** because, as each year passes, it is deleted from the budget and a budget for another year is added. A budget for one year ahead will be detailed, but budgets for the following years may be less precise because of uncertainty about future trading conditions.

The manager of each department or function in a business is responsible for the performance of his or her department or function. Separate operational, or functional, budgets must be prepared for each department or activity detailing the department's revenue (if any) and expenses for a given period. The budgets will be prepared for sales, production, purchasing, personnel, administration, treasury (cash and banking), etc. Opinions differ as to who should prepare these budgets.

Top-down budgets are prepared by top management and handed down to departmental managers, who are responsible for putting them into effect. Such budgets usually have the merit of being well co-ordinated so that they all fit together as a logical and consistent plan for the whole business. However, departmental managers may not feel committed to keeping to these budgets as they have had little or no say in their preparation and may be of the opinion that the budgets are unrealistic.

Bottom-up budgets are prepared by departmental managers and may be unsatisfactory because:

- they may not fit together with all the other departmental budgets to make a logical and consistent overall plan for the business

- managers tend to base their own budgets on easily achievable targets to avoid being criticised for failing to meet them; this will result in departments performing below their maximum level of efficiency and be bad for the business as a whole.

A budget committee, which should include the accountant, should co-ordinate the departmental budgets to ensure that they achieve top management's plans for the business.

The benefits of budgets may be summarised as follows.

1. They are formal statements in quantitative and financial terms of management plans.

2. Their preparation ensures the co-ordination of all the activities of a business.

3. Budgets identify limiting factors (shortages of demand or resources – see §33.8).

4. When managers are involved in the preparation of their budgets, they are committed to meeting them.

5. Budgets are a form of responsibility accounting as they identify the managers who are responsible for implementing the various aspects of the overall plan for the business.

6. Budgets avoid 'management by crisis', which describes situations in which managers have not foreseen problems before they arise and prepared for them in advance. These managers spend their time grappling with problems that should never have arisen had they been foreseen. The managers are sometimes described as 'fire fighters' when they should be 'fire preventers'.

Control

Control involves measuring actual performance, comparing it with the budget and taking corrective action to bring actual performance into line with the budget. It is important that deviations from budget are discovered early before serious situations arise. Annual departmental budgets are broken down into four-weekly or monthly, or even weekly, periods, and departmental management accounts are prepared for those periods. These management accounts compare actual performance with budget and must be prepared promptly after the end of each period if they are to be useful. If actual revenue and expenditure are better than budget, the differences (or variances) are described as **favourable** because they increase profit. On the other hand, if 'actual' is worse than budget, the variance is described as **adverse**.

Departmental management accounts usually contain many items of revenue and expenditure with a mixture of favourable and adverse variances. Managers should concentrate their attention on items with adverse variances and, to help managers focus their attention on these, management accounts may report only the items with adverse variances. This is known as **management by exception** or **exception reporting**.

Flexible budgets Experience shows that sales and costs rarely conform to the patterns anticipated by management when they prepare a 'fixed' budget, that is, one that does not allow for different levels of activity and changing conditions. Fixed budgets may lose their usefulness as management tools as a result. Invariably, the number of units produced and sold is more or less than the number in a fixed budget. To overcome this, budgets may be 'flexed' to reflect various levels of activity and costs. Flexing budgets makes use of marginal costing and is an important process when standard costing techniques (chapter 35) are employed. Flexing budgets is described in chapter 35.

34.3 Limiting (or principal budget) factors

Limiting factors, sometimes called **principal budget factors**, are circumstances which restrict the activities of a business. Examples are:

- limited demand for a product
- shortage of materials, which limits production
- shortage of labour, which also limits production.

Limiting factors must be identified in order to decide the order in which the departmental budgets are prepared. If the limiting factor is one of demand for the product, a sales budget will be prepared first. The other budgets will then be prepared to fit in with the sales budget. If the limiting factor is the availability of materials or labour, the production budget will be prepared first and the sales budget will then be based on the production budget.

34.4 How to prepare a sales budget

Sales budgets are based on the budgeted volume of sales. The volume is then multiplied by the selling price per unit of production to produce the sales revenue. For the sake of simplicity, the examples which follow assume that only one type of product is being sold.

Example

Xsel Ltd's sales for the six months from January to June 2005 are budgeted in units as follows:
January 1000; February 800; March 1100; April 1300; May 1500; June 1400.
The current price per unit is $15 but the company plans to increase the price by 5% on 1 May.

The sales budget will be prepared as follows.

	2005						Total
	January	February	March	April	May	June	
Units	1000	800	1100	1300	1500	1400	7100
Price	$15	$15	$15	$15	$15.75	$15.75	
Sales	$15 000	$12 000	$16 500	$19 500	$23 625	$22 050	$108 675

Exercise 1

Flannel and Flounder Ltd's sales budget in units for six months ending 30 June 2005 is as follows:
January 1000; February 1200; March 1300; April 1500; May 1700; June 1800.
The price per unit will be $20 for the three months to 31 March but will be increased to $22 from 1 April.

Required

Prepare Flannel and Flounder Ltd's sales budget for the new product for the six months ending 30 June 2005. (Keep your answer; it will be needed later.)

34.5 How to prepare a production budget

Manufacturing companies require production budgets to show the volume of production required monthly to meet the demand for sales. It is important to check that production is allocated to the correct months.

Example

Xsel Ltd (see the example in §34.4) manufactures its goods one month before they are sold. Monthly production is 105% of the following month's sales to provide goods for stock and for free samples to be given away to promote sales. Budgeted sales for July 2005 are for 1800 units.

Required

Prepare Xsel Ltd's monthly production budget for the period from December 2004 to December 2005.

Exercise 2

Flannel and Flounder Ltd (see exercise 1, §34.4) manufacture their goods one month before the goods are sold. Monthly production is 110% of the following month's sales. Budgeted sales for July 2005 are 2000 units.

Required

Prepare Flannel and Flounder Ltd's production budget. (Keep your answer; it will be needed later.)

34.6 How to prepare a purchases budget

A purchases budget may be prepared for either

1. raw materials purchased by a manufacturer, or

2. goods purchased by a trader.

A manufacturing company's purchases budget is prepared from the production budget while a trader's purchases budget is prepared from the sales budget. The purchases budget is calculated as follows:

> Units produced per production budget × quantity of material per unit produced × price per unit of material

Take care to ensure that the purchases are made in the correct month.

Answer

	2004	2005					
	December	January	February	March	April	May	June
Production for sales(units)	1000	800	1100	1300	1500	1400	1800
Add 5% for stock and samples	50	40	55	65	75	70	90
Monthly production	1050	840	1155	1365	1575	1470	1890

Example

Xsel Ltd (see the example in §34.5) purchases its raw materials one month before production. Each unit of production requires 3 kg of material, which costs $2 per kg.

Required

Prepare the purchases budget for the materials to be used in the production of goods for the period from December 2004 to June 2005.

Answer

	2004		2005				
	November	December	January	February	March	April	May
No. of units	1050	840	1155	1365	1575	1470	1890
Material required (kg)	3150	2520	3465	4095	4725	4410	5670
Purchases ($2 per litre)	6300	5040	6930	8190	9450	8820	11 340

Exercise 3

Flannel and Flounder Ltd (see exercise 2, §34.5) use 2.5 litres of material in each unit of their product. The price of the material is currently $4.10 per litre, but the company has learned that the price will be increased to $4.25 in March 2005. The raw materials are purchased one month before production; 2100 units are budgeted to be produced in August 2005.

Required

Prepare Flannel and Flounder Ltd's purchases budget based on its production budget for the seven months from December 2004 to June 2005. (Make all calculations to the nearest $.)

34.7 How to prepare an expenditure budget

An expenditure budget includes payments for purchased materials (from the purchases budget) plus all other expenditure in the period covered by the budget. Take care to ensure that:

- purchased materials are paid for in the correct month
- all other expenses are included in the budget in accordance with the given information.

Example

Xsel Ltd pays for its raw materials two months after the month of purchase (see §34.6). Its other expenses are as follows.

1. Monthly wages of $4000 are paid in the month in which they are due.

2. The staff are paid a commission of 5% on all monthly sales exceeding $15 000. The commission is paid in the month following that in which it is earned (see §34.4).

3. General expenses are paid in the month in which they are incurred and are to be budgeted as follows: January $6600; February $7100; March $6900; April $7000; May $7300; June $7500.

4. Xsel Ltd pays interest of 8% on a loan of $20 000 in four annual instalments on 31 March, 30 June, 30 September and 31 December.

5. A final dividend of $2000 for the year ended 31 December 2004 is payable in March 2005.

Required

Prepare an expenditure budget for Xsel Ltd for the six months ending 30 June 2005. All amounts should be shown to the nearest $.

Answer

	2005					
	January	February	March	April	May	June
	$	$	$	$	$	$
Purchases	6 300	5 040	6 930	8 190	9 450	8 820
Wages	4 000	4 000	4 000	4 000	4 000	4 000
Commission	–	–	–	75	225	431
General expenses	6 600	7 100	6 900	7 000	7 300	7 500
Loan interest	–	–	400	–	–	400
Dividend	–	–	2 000	–	–	–
Total expenditure	16 900	16 140	20 230	19 265	20 975	21 151

Exercise 4

Flannel and Flounder Ltd's overheads and other expenses for six months to 30 June 2005 are budgeted as follows.

1. Purchases are paid for in the following month.

2. Wages of $4000 per month are paid in the same month as they are earned.

3. Staff are paid a bonus equal to 4% of the amount by which monthly sales exceed $20 000. The bonus is paid in the month following that in which it is earned.

4. Electricity bills are expected to be received in January 2005, for $2400, and in April for $1800. The bills will be paid in the month following their receipt.

5. Other expenses are expected to amount to $6000 per month. From April 2005 they are expected to increase by 10%. They are paid in the month they are incurred.

6. Flannel and Flounder Ltd have a loan of $20 000 on which interest at 10% is payable in four quarterly instalments on 31 March, 30 June, 30 September and 31 December.

7. The company will purchase a machine in May 2005 for $15 000.

8. A final dividend of $4000 for the year ended 31 December 2004 will be paid in April 2005.

Required

Prepare Flannel and Flounder Ltd's expenditure budget for the six months ending 30 June 2005. Save your answer; it will be needed later.

34.8 How to prepare a cash budget

Cash budgets are prepared from the sales and expenses budgets. Special care must be taken with respect to the following.

- Sales revenue must be allocated to the correct months. Receipts from credit customers who are allowed cash discounts must be shown at the amounts after deduction of the discounts. The discounts should not be shown separately as an expense.

- Payments to suppliers (purchases) must be shown in the correct months; read the question carefully.

Example

Xsel Ltd's sales in November 2004 were $18 000, and in December 2004 were $17 600.

Of total sales, 40% are on a cash basis; 50% are to credit customers who pay within one month and receive a cash discount of 2%. The remaining 10% of customers pay within two months.

$10 000 was received from the sale of a fixed asset in March 2005. The balance at bank on 31 December 2004 was $12 400.

Required

Prepare Xsel Ltd's cash budget for the six months ending 30 June 2005. All amounts should be shown to the nearest $.

Answer

(a)

	January $	February $	March $	April $	May $	June $
			2005			
Receipts						
Cash sales[1]	6 000	4 800	6 600	7 800	9 450	8 820
Debtors – 1 month[2]	8 624	7 350	5 880	8 085	9 555	11 576
Debtors – 2 months[3]	1 800	1 760	1 500	1 200	1 650	1 950
Sales of fixed asset	–	–	10 000	–	–	–
	16 424	13 910	23 980	17 085	20 655	22 346
Expenditure	January $	February $	March $	April $	May $	June $
Purchases	6 300	5 040	6 930	8 190	9 450	8 820
Wages	4 000	4 000	4 000	4 000	4 000	4 000
Commission	–	–	–	75	225	431
General expenses	6 600	7 100	6 900	7 000	7 300	7 500
Loan interest	–	–	400	–	–	400
Dividend	–	–	2 000	–	–	–
	16 900	16 140	20 230	19 265	20 975	21 151
Net receipts/(payments)	(476)	(2 230)	3 750	(2 180)	(320)	1195
Balance brought forward	12 400	11 924	9 694	13 444	11 264	10 944
Balance carried forward	11 924	9 694	13 444	11 264	10 944	12 139

1 Cash sales = 40% of sales for month.

2 Cash received from debtors after one month = sales for previous month × 50% × 98%.

3 Cash received from debtors after two months = 10% of sales for two months previously.

Note. At 30 June 2005:

Debtors for sales:	$
10% of May sales ($23 625)	2 362.50
98% of 50% of June sales ($22 050)	10 804.50
10% of June sales	2 205.00
	15 372.00

Creditors for supplies: May purchases (paid for in July) = $11 340 + June purchases for production in July.

Accrued expenses: staff commission, 4% of $2050 = $82

Stock: If information for July and August had been available the following would be known:

raw materials – purchased in June

finished goods – made in June

Exercise 5

Flannel and Flounder Ltd's sales in November 2004 were $18 000 and in December 2004 were $17 600.

Of total sales revenue, 50% is on a cash basis, 40% is received one month after sale. Cash discount of $2\frac{1}{2}$% is allowed to customers who pay within one month. 10% of sales revenue is received two months after sale.

The company sold plant and equipment for $12 000 in February 2005. The balance at bank on 31 December 2004 was $31 750.

Required

(a) Prepare Flannel and Flounder Ltd's cash budget for the six months ending June 2005. Make all calculations to the nearest $.

(b) State the amount of Flannel and Flounder Ltd's trade debtors and creditors, and expense creditors at 30 June 2005.

34.9 How to prepare a master budget

A **master budget** is a budgeted Profit and Loss Account and Balance Sheet prepared from sales, purchases, expense and cash budgets. The purpose of the master budget is to reveal to management the profit or loss to be expected if management's plans for the business are implemented, and the state of the business at the end of the budget period.

It is important to remember that the Profit and Loss Account must be prepared on an accruals basis, and the information in the functional budgets must be adjusted for accruals and prepayments; it is advisable to identify these when preparing the cash budget. Much information additional to that required for the functional budgets mentioned above will usually be given. Details of fixed assets which are to be sold or purchased will often be supplied; this information will usually be included in a **capital budget**.

Example
Meadowlands Ltd's Balance Sheet at 31 December 2004 was as follows.

Fixed assets	Cost	Depreciation	Net
	$	$	$
Equipment	13 000	6 000	7 000
Motor vehicles	11 000	7 000	4 000
	24 000	13 000	11 000
Current assets			
Stock		9 600	
Trade debtors		33 600	
Cash at bank		15 000	
		58 200	
Current liabilities			
Trade creditors		6 200	52 000
			63 000
Share capital and reserves			
Ordinary shares of $1			40 000
Profit and Loss Account			23 000
			63 000

Further information

1. Goods are purchased one month before the month of sale.

2. Budgeted quarterly purchases and sales for the year ending 31 December 2005 are as follows:

	Purchases	Sales
	$	$
January – March	72 000	132 000
April – June	96 000	156 000
July – September	84 000	168 000
October – December	96 000	144 000

3. Meadowlands Ltd receives one month's credit on all purchases and allows one month's credit on all sales.

4. The following expenses will be incurred in the year ending 31 December 2005:

   (i)   rent of $1600 per quarter paid in advance on 1 January, 1 April, 1 July, and 1 October

   (ii) wages of $7200 payable each month

   (iii) an insurance premium of $3000 for 15 months to 31 March 2006 paid on 1 January 2005

   (iv) other expenses of $20 000 paid quarterly.

5. The company will purchase additional equipment costing $15 000 on 1 April 2005.

6. A new motor vehicle will be purchased on 1 April 2005 for $12 000.

7. A motor vehicle which cost $6000 and has a written down value of $3000 at 31 December 2004 will be sold for $2000 on 1 July 2005.

8. The company depreciates equipment at 10% per annum on cost. It depreciates motor vehicles at $12\frac{1}{2}\%$ per annum on cost.

9. The company's stock at 31 December 2005 will be valued at $32 000.

Required

(a) Prepare a cash budget for the year ending 31 December 2005.

(b) Prepare Meadowlands Ltd's budgeted Profit and Loss Account for the year ending 31 December 2005 and a budgeted Balance Sheet as at that date.

Answer

Meadowlands Ltd Cash budget for the year ending 31 December 2005

	Jan/Mar	Apr/Jun	Jul/Sept	Oct/Dec
	$	$	$	$
Receipts				
Sales	121 600[1]	148 000[2]	164 000[2]	152 000[2]
Proceeds from sale of van	–	–	2 000	–
	121 600	148 000	166 000	152 000
Payments				
Purchases	54 200[3]	88 000[4]	88 000[4]	92 000[4]
Rent	1 600	1 600	1 600	1 600
Wages	21 600	21 600	21 600	21 600
Insurance	3 000	–	–	–
Other expenses	20 000	20 000	20 000	20 000
Purchase of equipment	–	15 000	–	–
Purchase of motor vehicle	–	12 000	–	–
	100 400	158 200	131 200	135 200
Net receipts/(payments)	21 200	(10 200)	34 800	16 800
Balance brought forward	15 000	36 200	26 000	60 800
Balance carried forward	36 200	26 000	60 800	77 600

1 Debtors at 31 December 2004 + $\frac{2}{3}$ of sales for January/March.

2 $\frac{1}{3}$ of previous quarter's sales + $\frac{2}{3}$ of current quarter's sales.

3 Creditors at 31 December 2004 + $\frac{2}{3}$ of purchases for January/March

4 $\frac{1}{3}$ of previous quarter's purchases + $\frac{2}{3}$ of current quarter's purchases.

Budgeted Profit and Loss Account for the year ending 31 December 2005

	$	$	$
Sales			600 000
Less Cost of sales:			
Stock at 1.1.05		9 600	
Purchases		348 000	
		357 600	
Stock at 31.12.05		32 000[5]	325 600
Gross profit			274 400
Less expenditure			
Wages		86 400	
Rent		6 400	
Insurance ($\frac{12}{15} \times \$3000$)		2 400	
Other expenses		80 000	
Loss on sale of motor vehicle		1 000	
Depreciation: equipment	2800[6]		
motor vehicles	2125[6]	4 925	181 125
Net profit			93 275

5 Stock purchased in December 2005 for sale in January 2006 ($\frac{1}{3}$ of $96 000).

6 See fixed assets in Balance Sheet.

Budgeted Balance Sheet at 31 December 2005

Fixed assets	Cost	Depreciation	Net
	$	$	$
Equipment	28 000	8 800	19 200
Motor vehicles	17 000	6 125	10 875
	45 000	14 925	30 075
Current assets			
Stock		32 000	
Trade debtors		48 000[7]	
Prepaid insurance		600	
Balance at bank		77 600	
		158 200	
Current liabilities			
Trade creditors		32 000[8]	126 200
			156 275
Share capital and reserves			
Ordinary shares of $1			40 000
Profit and Loss Account (23 000 + 93 275)			116 275
			156 275

7 December sales.

8 December purchases.

Exercise 6

The directors of Greenfields Ltd have prepared functional budgets for the four months ending 30 April 2005. To discover the effect that the budgets will have on the company at the end of the four months, they require the accountant to prepare master budgets. The accountant is provided with the following data.

Greenfields Ltd Balance Sheet at 31 December 2004

Fixed assets	Cost	Depreciation	Net
	$	$	$
Freehold premises	50 000	10 000	40 000
Plant and machinery	37 500	22 500	15 000
	87 500	32 500	55 000
Current assets			
Stock		30 000	
Trade debtors		42 500	
Balance at bank		20 750	
		93 250	
Current liabilities			
Trade creditors		22 500	70 750
			125 750
Long-term liability			
12% debentures 2009/10			25 000
			100 750
Share capital and reserves			
Ordinary shares of $1			65 000
General reserve			30 000
Retained profit			5 750
			100 750

Further information

1. Sales and purchases for the four months from January to April 2005 are budgeted to be:

	Sales	Purchases
	$	$
January	62 500	25 000
February	70 000	20 000
March	75 000	30 000
April	82 500	37 500

2. 40% of sales are to cash customers; one month's credit is allowed on the remainder.

3. The company pays for its purchases in the month following purchase.

4. Selling and distribution expenses amount to 10% of sales and are paid in the month in which they are incurred.

5. Administration expenses amount to $20 000 per month and are paid in the month in which they are incurred.

6. Stock at the 30 April 2005 is estimated to be valued at $22 500.

7. Additional plant and machinery costing $60 000 will be purchased on 1 March 2005.

8. Annual depreciation of fixed assets is based on cost as follows: Freehold premises 3%; plant and machinery 20%. 50% of all depreciation is to be charged to selling and distribution expenses, and the balance to administration expenses.

9. Debenture interest is payable half-yearly on 30 June and 31 December.

10. A dividend of $0.10 per share will be paid on the ordinary shares on 30 April 2005.

11. $25 000 will be transferred to the General Reserve on 30 April 2005.

Required

(a) Prepare a cash budget for each of the four months from January 2005 to 30 April 2005.

(b) Prepare a budgeted Profit and Loss Account for the four months ending 30 April 2005 in as much detail as possible.

(c) Prepare a budgeted Balance Sheet as at 30 April 2005 in as much detail as possible.

34.10 Examination hints

- Practise the preparation of the functional and master budgets. They are not too difficult provided you read questions carefully to ascertain exactly when transactions are to take place. Failure to allocate sales, purchases, receipts and payments to the correct periods is a common cause of the loss of valuable marks.

- Preparation of budgets is often an exercise in arithmetic, so be accurate; but note if the question states the degree of accuracy required (e.g. to nearest $ or nearest $000).

34.11 Multiple-choice questions

1 A bedside table is made from 4 kg of raw material. Production for six months is based on the following data.

Budgeted sales	5000 tables
Budgeted decrease in stock of raw material	1200 kg
Budgeted increase in stock of tables	800 tables

How many kilograms of raw material will be purchased for the six months?

A 18 000 kg

B 18 800 kg

C 22 000 kg

D 23 200 kg

2 Debtors at the year-end are $40 000. It is planned to double turnover in the next year and to reduce the debtors' collection period from 45 days to 30 days.

What will the debtors be at the end of the next year?

A $26 667

B $53 334

C $60 000

D $80 000

3 The sales budget for four months from January to April is as follows.

January $80 000

February $100 000

March $110 000

April $130 000

The cost of the raw material used in the goods is 40% of sales. The material is purchased one month before the goods are made, and manufacture takes place one month before sale. 50% of the material is paid for one month after purchase and the balance is paid for two months after purchase.

How much will be paid for raw materials in March?

A $40 000

B $42 000

C $46 000

D $48 000

4 A company plans to purchase a new machine costing $40 000. It will part exchange one of its existing machines for the new one. The existing machine has a net book value of $4000 and the part exchange will result in a loss on disposal of the machine of $1000. The company will pay the balance due on the new machine by cheque.

How will the transaction be recorded in the cash budget?

A payment for new machine $37 000

B payment for new machine $40 000

C payment for new machine $40 000; cash received for old machine $3000

D payment for new machine $40 000; cash received for old machine $4000

34.12 Additional exercises

1 The sales budget for Roh Ltd for the six months to 30 November 2003 is as follows.

	Units
June	600
July	800
August	1000
September	900
October	980
November	1020

Further information is as follows:

1. All units are sold for $60. Customers are allowed 1 month's credit.
2. Monthly production of the units is equal to the following month's sales plus 10% for stock.
3. Costs per unit are as follows:

Material	3 kilos
Cost of material	$4.00 per kilo
Labour	2 hours
Labour rate of pay	$8.00 per hour
Absorption rates	
Variable overhead	$14.00
Fixed overhead	$3.50

4. Materials are purchased one month before they are needed for production and are paid for two months after purchase.
5. Wages and variable overheads are paid in the current month.
6. Fixed overheads are paid in the following month.
7. The following information is to be taken into account:
   (i) cash book balance at 30 June 2003: $16 000;
   (ii) stock of finished goods at 31 July 2003: $56 420.

Required

(a) The following budgets for the month of August 2003 *only*.
   (i) Production budget (in units only)
   (ii) Purchases budget
   (iii) Sales budget

(b) Calculate the cash book balance at 31 July 2003.

(c) A cash budget for the month of August 2003 *only*.

(d) (i) Explain the advantages and uses of budgets.
   (ii) Explain how principal budget factors affect the preparation of budgets.

(UCLES, 2003, AS/A Level Accounting, Syllabus 9706/04, May/June)

2 Banner Ltd's budget for the four months from January to April includes the following data.

1.

Month	Sales	Materials	Wages	Overheads
	$000	$000	$000	$000
January	615	114.4	30	360
February	636	118.8	33	390
March	690	132.0	36	412
April	684	128.0	39	420

2. One third of sales revenue is received one month after sale and the remainder is received two months after sale. The sales in the previous two months were: November $600 000; December $540 000.

3. One quarter of purchases of materials are paid for in the month of purchase. The remainder are paid for two months later. Purchases in the previous two months were: November $108 000; December $106 000.

4. Two thirds of the wages are paid in the month in which they are earned, and the balance is paid in the following month. The wages for the previous December amounted to $30 000.

5. One half of the overhead expenditure is paid in the month in which it is incurred, and the balance is paid in the following month. The overheads for the previous December were $380 000.

6. Old machinery will be sold for $4000 in April. New machinery will be purchased in March for $90 000 but only one half of the price will be paid in that month. The balance will be paid in August.

7. Banner Ltd has an overdraft $63 000 at the bank at 31 December.

Required

(a) Prepare Banner Ltd's cash budget for each of the four months from January to April. The budget should be prepared in columnar form.

(b) Prepare a statement to show the accruals in part (a) which would appear in a Balance Sheet at 30 April.

35 Standard costing

35.1 What is standard costing?

Standard costing is an accounting system that records the cost of operations at pre-determined standards. If the standards are realistic, the system informs managers of the material, labour and overhead costs that should be incurred if the business is managed efficiently. Standard costs are an essential tool for realistic budgeting. However, the costs actually incurred may differ from the standards for a variety of reasons:

• the quantity of goods produced may be more or less than budget
• the quantity of material used in each unit of production may be more or less than budget
• the cost of material may be more or less than budget because the price paid may have increased or decreased since the budget was prepared, or the material has been obtained from alternative suppliers
• workers may have been more or less efficient than expected in the budget
• the rates of pay for workers may be more or less than those on which the budget was based.

Standards are also set for sales revenue, and causes for differences between actual revenue and the standard may be highlighted.

The link between the profit calculated on standard costs and the profit shown in a traditional Profit and Loss Account is provided by the preparation of a reconciliation statement between the standard profit or loss and the actual profit or loss.

The differences between actual costs and budgeted costs are known as *variances*.

35.2 The advantages of standard costing

• The preparation of budgets is made easier if they are based on standard costs, and the budgets are likely to be more realistic.
• Differences between actual and budgeted results (**variances**) are easier to identify if standard costs are used.
• The activities that are responsible for variances are highlighted.
• Because it highlights activities that give rise to variances, standard costing is an essential part of responsibility accounting (see §34.2).
• Calculated standards facilitate the preparation of estimates for the costs of new products and quotations for orders.
• Although standard costing is usually associated in people's minds with manufacturing industries, it is of equal use in all kinds of businesses, including service industries such as hotels and hospitals.
• Valuation of stock at standard cost is acceptable for the purposes of the Companies Act 1985 and the accounting standards, if the standard costs approximate to actual costs and are reviewed regularly.

35.3 Setting standards

Standards must be realistic if they are to be useful and not misleading. Unrealistic standards result in the loss of the advantages listed above in §35.2. The various types of standards may be described, as follows.

- **Ideal standards** are standards that can only be met under ideal conditions. Since the conditions under which businesses work are very rarely ideal, these standards are unrealistic and are never likely to be attained. As a result, they may actually demotivate managers and cause them to perform less, rather than more, efficiently. Ideal standards should not be used.
- **Current standards** are based on present levels of performance, which may be quite inappropriate for the future. They do not offer management or workers any incentive to perform more efficiently. Current standards should only be used when present conditions are too uncertain to enable more appropriate standards to be set.
- **Attainable standards** recognise that there is normally some wastage of materials and not all the hours worked are productive. Time spent unproductively by workers is called **idle time** and may occur when machinery breaks down or the machinery has to be 'set up' for a production run. The standards should take reasonable account of these factors and give the workers an incentive to use their time and materials efficiently. The standards set should therefore be attainable ones.

Standard hours of production are measures of quantity of work and should not be confused with a period of time. If, under normal, or standard, working conditions, 20 units of output can be produced in one hour, the standard hour is 20 units. This concept of standard hours is useful when budgets are being prepared for departments that produce two or more different products. For example, in one month a department's output may consist of:

	Standard hours
200 Xs which take 1 hour each to make:	200
400 Ys which take 1½ hours each to make	600
327 Zs which take 40 minutes each to make	218
Total standard hours of production	1018

The output of the department can conveniently be expressed as 1018 standard hours for budgeting purposes. Similarly, standard minutes are a quantity of work that can be done in a stated number of standard minutes.

35.4 How to flex budgets

The actual volume of goods produced is seldom the same as the volume on which a budget has been based. Sensible comparisons can only be made if 'like is compared with like', and the budget is based on the actual volume of output. This is done by **flexing** the budget.

The variable expenses in the budget must be adjusted to take account of the actual volume of goods produced.

Example 1

Variable Grommets Ltd produced the following budget for the production and sale of 10 000 grommets for the six months ending June 2005.

Budget for 10 000 grommets Six months ending June 2005	
	$
Variable expenses	
Direct materials	50 000
Direct labour	100 000
Production overheads	40 000
Selling and distribution	8 000
	198 000
Fixed expenses	
Production overheads	78 000
Selling and distribution	43 000
Administration	91 000
Total cost	410 000

The output for the six months ended 30 June was 12 000 grommets. The budget is flexed by multiplying the variable expenses by $\frac{12\,000}{10\,000}$, that is by 1.2.

Flexed Budget for 12 000 grommets Six months ended June 2005	
	$
Variable expenses	
Direct materials	60 000
Direct labour	120 000
Production overheads	48 000
Selling and distribution	9 600
	237 600
Fixed expenses	
Production overheads	78 000
Selling and distribution	43 000
Administration	91 000
Total cost	449 600

The fixed expenses have not changed. The flexed budget is the one that would have been prepared as the original budget if it had been known that the output would be 12 000 grommets.

Exercise 1

Brekkifoods Ltd's budget for the production of 100 000 packets of Barleynuts in the year ending 31 December 2005 was as follows.

	$
Variable expenses	
Direct materials	20 000
Direct labour	15 000
Production expenses	6 000
	41 000
Fixed expenses	
Production expenses	13 000
Administration	29 000
	83 000

The actual output for the year ended 31 December 2005 was 110 000 packets of Barleynuts.

Required

Prepare a flexed budget for the production of 110 000 packets of Barleynuts.

Flexing budgets with semi-variable expenses

Budgets may not show a distinction between fixed and variable expenses. In these cases, the distinction must be found by inspection.

Example 2

Obskure Ltd has prepared flexed budgets for the production of (i) 5000 and (ii) 6000 pairs of sun glasses.

	5000 pairs of glasses	6000 pairs of glasses
	$	$
Direct materials	10 000	12 000
Direct labour	15 000	18 000
Production overheads	16 000	18 000
Selling and distribution	19 000	22 000
Administration	12 000	12 000
	72 000	82 000

8000 pairs of glasses were produced and a flexed budget for that output is required.

Answer

Some expenses vary directly with output: direct materials are $2 per pair of spectacles, and direct labour is $3 per pair. The cost of these items for 8000 pairs of glasses will be: direct materials $16 000; direct labour $24 000.

Production overheads and selling and distribution expenses have not increased proportionately with the increased production. Each of these items contains a fixed element. To find the variable elements of these costs, deduct the costs for 5000 units from the costs for 6000 units to find the variable costs for 1000 units

Production overheads

Production overheads for 1000 units = $(18 000 – 16 000) = $2000, or $2 per unit.

Fixed production costs are now found by deducting the variable cost for 5000 units from the total production cost: $(16 000 – 10 000) = $6000.

Production cost for 8000 pairs of spectacles is $6000 + (8000 × $2) = $22 000.

Selling and distribution

Selling and distribution for 1000 units = $(22 000 – 19 000) = $3000, or $3 per unit.

Fixed selling and distribution cost is found by deducting the variable cost for 5000 units from the total selling and distribution cost: $(19 000 – 15 000) = $4 000.

Selling and distribution cost for 8000 pairs of spectacles is $4000 + (8000 × $3) = $28 000.

The flexed budget for 8000 pairs of spectacles is:

	$
Direct materials	16 000
Direct labour	24 000
Production overheads	22 000
Selling and distribution	28 000
Administration	12 000
	102 000

Exercise 2

Flexers Ltd has prepared the following budgets for the production of time locks.

No. of locks	6000	8000
	$	$
Direct materials	15 000	20 000
Direct labour	36 000	48 000
Production overhead	25 000	31 000
Selling and distribution	24 000	28 000
Administration	80 000	80 000
	180 000	207 000

Required

Prepare a flexed budget for the production of 9000 time locks.

35.5 Variances

A **variance** is the difference between a standard cost and an actual cost or, in the case of revenue, between budgeted revenue and actual revenue. Variances may be calculated for:

- sales
- direct materials
- direct labour
- overheads.

Variances highlight activities that may need management intervention if the budgeted profit is to be achieved or, at least, to limit any adverse effect on profit. The variances may be further analysed into sub-variances to indicate the activities or operations that are performing adversely. An adverse variance decreases profit while a favourable variance increases profit. Every variance must be described as either favourable (F) or adverse (A). Any variance not so described is meaningless and is of no help to management. *No marks will be awarded in an examination for a variance that is not described as (F) or (A), even if it has been calculated correctly.*

35.6 Acrobat Ltd

Acrobat Ltd makes a product which it markets under the name of 'Capers'. The budget for one month is based on the following standards.

No. of Capers produced and sold: 20 000	
Per Caper:	
Selling price per Caper	$32
Direct material (kg)	1.25
Cost of material per kg	$4
Direct labour (minutes)	40
Labour rate per hour	$12
Production overhead:	
fixed	$30 000
variable per unit	$7
Selling and distribution:	
fixed	$16 000
variable per unit	$4
Administration (fixed)	$75 000

The master budget based on the above information is as follows.

	Master budget 20 000 Capers	Flexed budget 23 000 Capers
	$	$
Sales revenue	640 000	736 000
Direct materials	100 000	115 000
Direct labour	160 000	184 000
Production overhead	170 000	191 000
Selling and distribution	96 000	108 000
Administration	75 000	75 000
	601 000	673 000
Profit	39 000	63 000

The actual number of Capers sold was 23 000 and a flexed budget for this number is shown next to the master budget.

Further information about the actual revenue and costs is as follows.

The increased sales resulted from a reduction in the selling price from $32 to $30.50.

The actual cost of the material was $4.15 and each Caper used 1.10 kg of the material

The hourly rate paid to the workers was $10 but each Caper took 45 minutes to make.

Actual variable production overhead was $7.20 per Caper, and the variable selling and distribution overhead was $3.90 per Caper.

The actual outcome for the production and sale of 23 000 Capers was therefore:

	$
Sales revenue	701 500
Direct materials	104 995
Direct labour	172 500
Production overhead	195 600
Selling and distribution	105 700
Administration	75 000
	653 795
Profit	47 705

All the information is now available to enable variances to be calculated.

35.7 How to calculate sales variances

When a business sells more than one type of product, sales variances will occur when the mix of products sold differs from the budgeted mix and gives rise to a mix variance. However, it is only necessary in this text to consider situations involving a single product.

The sales variances for a single product are:

- **volume variance**, which equals the difference between the master budget and the flexed budget

Acrobat Ltd's sales volume variance is $(736 000 - 640 000) = $96 000 (F)

- **price variance**, which is the difference between the flexed budget sales and actual sales

Acrobat Ltd's sales price variance is $(736 000 - 701 500) = $34 500 (A)

Check: Actual sales – budgeted sales = $(701 500 – 640 000) = $61 500 (F)

Sales volume variance - sales price variance = $(96 000 - 34 500) = $61 500 (F).

35.8 How to calculate total cost variances

Cost variances may be summarised as follows.

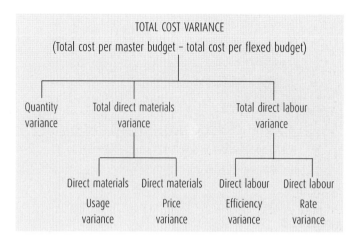

The CIE syllabus does not require the calculation of overhead variances and these will not be covered in this text except as an overhead expenditure variance.

Note. When calculating cost variances, always start with the standard and deduct the 'actual'. A positive remainder will indicate that the variance is favourable, and a negative remainder will indicate that the variance is adverse. Always describe variances as favourable (F) or adverse (A).

Total cost variance This is the difference between the total costs per the master budget and the actual total costs incurred. In the case of Acrobat Ltd the total cost variance is $(601 000 – 653 795) = $52 795 (A).

Quantity variance This is the amount of the total cost variance which is due to the actual level of activity being more or less than budget. It is found by deducting the flexed budget costs from the master budget costs. Acrobat Ltd's quantity variance is $(601 000 – 673 000) = $72 000 (A).

Note. Once the quantity variance has been calculated, the master budget is not used to calculate the remaining variances; we shall calculate the all the variances which follow using the flexed budget.

Total direct materials variance This is the difference between the flexed budget direct materials cost and the actual direct materials cost. Acrobat Ltd's total direct materials variance is $(115 000 – 104 995) = $10 005 (F).

Total direct labour variance This is the difference between the flexed budget labour cost and the actual labour cost. Acrobat Ltd's total labour cost variance is $(184 000 – 172 500) = $11 500 (F).

The quantity, direct materials and direct labour variances can be reconciled to the total cost variance if the overhead expenditure variance is also taken into account:

	$
Quantity variance	72 000 (A)
Direct materials variance	10 005 (F)
Direct labour variance	11 500 (F)
Overhead expenditure variance†	2 300 (A)
Total cost variance	52 795 (A)

†Production overhead $(191 000 – 195 600) = $4600 (A)

Selling and distribution $(108 000 – 105 700) = $2300 (F)

Net variance = $2300 (A)

Exercise 3

Enigma Ltd has prepared a budget based on standard costs. It is shown below together with the actual results.

	Budget	Actual
No. of units	4000	4250
	$	$
Direct material	20 000	23 400
Direct labour	46 000	47 236
Variable overhead	10 000	10 500
Fixed overhead	50 000	50 000
Total costs	126 000	131 136

Required

(a) Prepare a flexed budget for 4250 units
(b) Calculate:
   (i)   total cost variance
   (ii) expenditure variance
   (iii) direct material variance
   (iv) direct labour variance.
(c) Reconcile the actual cost incurred with the budgeted costs, using the variances calculated in (b).

Exercise 4

Underpar Ltd has prepared a budget based on standard costs. It is shown below together with the actual results.

	Budget	Actual
No. of units	7000	6300
	$	$
Direct material	23 800	20 890
Direct labour	47 250	44 065
Variable overhead	3 500	3 250
Fixed overhead	62 000	62 000
Total costs	136 550	130 205

Required

(a) Prepare a flexed budget for 6300 units.
(b) Calculate:
   (i)   total cost variance
   (ii) expenditure variance
   (iii) direct material variance
   (iv) direct labour variance.
(c) Reconcile the actual cost incurred with the budgeted costs, using the variances calculated in (b).

35.9 How to calculate material and labour sub-variances

Total material and labour cost variances reveal the main components of the difference between flexed budget total cost and actual total cost. However, this information is of limited use to management as it falls short of real responsibility accounting. A material variance may be caused by the price paid for material being more or less than standard, or by the quantity of material used for each unit made being more or less than standard. The purchasing manager is responsible for price, and the factory manager is responsible for usage. The total materials variance can be broken down into price and usage variances for which the purchasing and factory managers must give explanations.

Similarly, a total labour variance may be caused by the hourly rate being paid to workers being more or less than standard, or by the time taken in production being more or less than standard. The personnel manager is responsible for fixing rates of pay, and the factory manager is responsible for the time taken in production. A total labour variance is therefore broken down into rate and efficiency variances.

Direct material usage variance The formula is (SM – AM)SP, where SM is the standard quantity of materials (per the flexed budget), AM is the actual quantity of materials used, and SP is the standard price of materials (per the master budget).

Example

The cost of direct material in Acrobat Ltd's (§35.6) flexed budget for 23 000 Capers was $115 000 based on a standard use of 1.25 kg of material per Caper at a cost of $4 per kg. Only 1.10 kg of material were used for each Caper and the cost per kg was $4.15. The usage variance is calculated as follows.

Standard materials (SM) = 23 000 × 1.25	28 750 kg	
Actual materials used (AM) = 23 000 × 1.10 kg	25 300 kg	
Variance (favourable)	3 450 kg (F)	
Usage variance at standard price per kg ($4)	$13 800 (F)	

Direct material price variance The formula is (SP – AP)AM where SP is the standard price and AP is the price actually paid. In the example of Acrobat Ltd the standard price was $4 per kg, and the price actually paid was $4.15 per kg. The price variance is calculated as follows.

	$
Standard price (per kg)	4.00
Actual price	4.15
Variance (adverse)	0.15 (A)
Actual quantity of material	25 300 kg
Price variance (25 300 × $0.15)	$3 795 (A)

Check: Usage variance – price variance = total material variance: $13 800 (F) – $3795 (A) = $10 005 (F) (See p.185.)

Exercise 5

Dandelion Ltd manufactures a health food known as 'Pickup'. The standard material cost of a packet of Pickup is as follows: 3 litres at $5 per litre. In one month Dandelion Ltd produced 12 000 packets of Pickup using 2.8 litres of material per packet at a total cost of $4.80 per litre.

Required

Calculate the direct material usage and price variances for 12 000 packets of Pickup.

Direct labour efficiency variance This variance is calculated using the formula (SH – AH)SR where SH is the standard hours, AH is the actual hours taken and SR is the standard rate of pay.

Acrobat Ltd's standard hours were 40 minutes per Caper, or a total of $\frac{40}{60}$ × 23 000 = 15 333.33 hours

The actual time taken was 45 minutes per Caper, or a total of $\frac{45}{60}$ × 23 000 = 17 250.00 hours

Variance = 1916.67 hours (A)

1916.67 hours × Standard rate at $12 = $23 000 (A)

Direct labour rate variance This is calculated using the formula (SR – AR)AH where AR is the actual hourly rate of pay.

Acrobat Ltd's actual hourly rate of pay was $10 and the rate variance is $(12 – 10)17 250 = $34 500 (F).

Check: Efficiency variance – rate variance = total labour variance: $23 000 (A) – 34 500 (F) = $11 500 (F) (See p.281.)

Exercise 6

Dandelion Ltd has a standard direct labour cost for the production of one packet of Pickup based on 1 labour hour at $10 per hour. The production of 12 000 packets of Pickup required 1.25 hours paid at $8.50 per hour.

Required

Calculate the direct labour efficiency and rate variances for 12 000 packets of Pickup.

35.10 How to comment on variances

Questions may require candidates to comment on variances they have calculated. This is not a difficult task if the following advice is heeded.

- Variances highlight operations that do not match standards. They do not explain the causes of differences but show management where further investigation is required if effective corrective action is to be taken.
- Without the further investigation mentioned above, it is not possible to do more than suggest possible reasons for variances. Some checks to support comments are suggested below.
- A favourable material usage variance may result from:
  1. use of material of a better quality than the standard: check for an adverse material price variance, or for a favourable labour efficiency variance (material easier to work with)
  2. the labour being of a higher skill than the standard skill, e.g. skilled labour used instead of semi-skilled; check for an adverse labour rate variance.
- An adverse material variance may indicate:
  1. the use of substandard material – check for a favourable material price variance or for an adverse labour efficiency variance
  2. the employment of lower skilled labour – check for a favourable labour rate variance.
- A favourable labour rate variance may result from the employment of a lower grade of labour than standard – check for an unfavourable labour efficiency variance or an adverse material usage variance.

- An unfavourable labour rate variance may result from:
  1. employment of a higher skill of labour than standard – check for a favourable efficiency variance
  2. a wage increase (the standard should be revised).
- A favourable sales volume variance may occur because:
  1. selling price has been reduced to increase volume
  2. seasonal sales have increased volume
  3. special discounts have been given to selected customers to increase orders
  4. local competition from other firms has disappeared.
- An adverse sales volume variance may occur because:
  1. selling price has been increased to pass increased costs onto customers
  2. the goods have become unfashionable or obsolete
  3. customers have heard that new, improved products will be available soon and are waiting for those
  4. local competition from other firms may have increased.
- A favourable sales price variance may occur because:
  1. increased costs have been passed onto customers in the selling price
  2. prices have been increased in line with inflation
  3. fewer discounts have been allowed to favoured customers
  4. improved products have allowed prices to be increased.
- An adverse sales price variance may occur because:
  1. local competition has necessitated a price reduction
  2. selling prices have been reduced in seasonal sales
  3. some favoured customers have been given price concessions to increase volume of orders
  4. prices have been reduced generally to increase sales volume.
- All comments should be consistent and not contradict each other. Explain possible links between variances. Be clear and concise.

Exercise 7

Larabee Ltd prepared a budget for the production of 300 units in April 2004 as follows.

	$
Direct materials (4 kg per unit)	7200
Direct labour ($11 per hour)	6600

The production for the month was 400 units and the costs were as follows.

	$
Direct materials ($6.25 per kg)	9 000
Direct labour (2.25 hours per unit)	10 890

Required

(a) Calculate the following variances for April 2004:
  (i) direct material usage
  (ii) direct material price
  (iii) direct labour efficiency
  (iv) direct labour rate.
(b) Comment on the variances in (a) and suggest possible causes.

35.11 Reconciliation of budgeted profit and actual profit

Actual profit should be reconciled to the budgeted profit by summarising the variances.

Example

The actual profit made by Acrobat Ltd is reconciled to the budgeted profit, using the variances that have been calculated above, as follows.

	$	$
Profit per master budget		39 000
Add: favourable variances		
Sales volume		96 000
Materials usage		13 800
Labour rate		34 500
		183 300
Deduct: adverse variances		
Quantity	72 000	
Selling price	34 500	
Material price	3 795	
Labour efficiency	23 000	
Overhead expenditure (p.282)	2 300	135 595
Actual profit (p.281)		47 705

Exercise 8

Cantab Ltd's standard costing records provide the following information for three month's production and sales.

	$
Master budget profit	98 970
Variances	
Quantity	17 009 (A)
Sales volume	6 210 (F)
Sales price	3 730 (A)
Material usage	6 280 (A)
Material price	9 635 (F)
Labour efficiency	10 500 (F)
Labour rate	7 840 (A)
Overhead expenditure	5 760 (A)

Required

Prepare a statement to show the actual profit made by Cantab Ltd in the three months covered by the given information.

35.12 Examination hints

- Learn the formulae for calculating the variances.
- Describe every variance as favourable (F) or adverse (A).
- Every variance must be shown with a $ sign, otherwise it is meaningless and will gain no marks in an exam.
- Use common sense when commenting on variances; remember that variances only indicate operations that require further investigation to reveal the causes.

35.13 Multiple-choice questions

1 A company manufactures a product which requires 2 hours of direct labour per unit. Normal output is 1400 units and the standard labour rate is $6.50 per hour.

In one month the company manufactured 1300 units of the product in 2500 direct labour hours costing $17 550.

What is the direct labour efficiency variance?

A $650 (favourable)   **B** $675 (favourable)

C $1300 (favourable)   **D** $1350 (favourable)

2 A company makes a single product which requires two types of raw material: ionium and zetonium. The standard cost of materials to produce one unit of the product is shown:

Material	kg	Standard cost ($ per kg)
Ionium	30	2
Zetonium	45	3

100 units of the product have been made using 3100 kg of ionium and 4400 kg of zetonium.

What is the total material usage variance?

A $100 (adverse)   **B** $100 (favourable)

C $500 (adverse)   **D** $500 (favourable)

3 A company's standard cost statement shows the following variances: (F favourable; A adverse).

		$
1	Sales total variance	1300 (A)
2	Sales volume variance	1500 (A)
3	Sales price variance	?
4	Materials total variance	950 (A)
5	Materials usage variance	670 (F)
6	Materials price variance	?
7	Labour total variance	660 (F)
8	Labour efficiency variance	415 (F)
9	Labour rate variance	?

What is the effect *in total* of variances 3, 6 and 9 on the profit of the company?

A $1175 (A)   **B** $1175 (F)   **C** $1575 (A)

D $1665 (A)

4 The following information is available about a product.

Standard selling price per unit	$17
Budgeted sales (units)	45 000
Actual sales (units)	48 000
Total sales revenue	$744 000

What is the sales price variance?

A $51 000 (A)   **B** $51 000 (F)   **C** $72 000 (A)

D $72 000 (F)

5 Details of direct material costs are as follows.

Budget	Actual
41 500 kg at $12 per kg	44 000 kg at £13.20 per kg

What is the direct material price variance?

A $49 500 (A)   **B** $49 500 (F)   **C** $52 800 (A)

D $52 800 (F)

6 A company's cost of production is made up of the cost of direct materials and the cost of direct labour. The following variances have been calculated at the end of three month's production:

	$	
Direct materials usage	1600	adverse
Direct materials price	1300	favourable
Direct labour efficiency	820	favourable
Direct labour rate	900	adverse

The actual cost of production was $23 440.
What was the standard cost of production?

A $22 220 **B** $23 020 **C** $23 060
D $24 580

35.14 Additional exercises

1 Kings Ltd makes an electronic device for finding lost keys, which it has patented under the trademark 'Gonkeys'. The product passes through two processes and the budget for the production of 10 000 Gonkeys is as follows.

	Process 1	Process 2
Costs per Gonkey		
Material	2 kg	4 litres
Cost of material per kg/litre	$8	$6
Labour hours per Gonkey	2	4
Labour rate per hour	$10	$12
Production overhead absorption	$20 per labour/hour	$23 per labour/hour

Required
(a) Prepare budgeted accounts for processes 1 and 2 to show the cost of producing 10 000 Gonkeys.

The actual production for process 1 was 10 000 Gonkeys. In process 2, completed production was 9000 Gonkeys, and 1000 Gonkeys were completed as to 50% of material and wages.

Required
(b) Prepare a flexed budget for process 2 based on actual production.

Actual costs per Gonkey were as follows.

	Process 1	Process 2
Material	2.22 kg	3.75 litres
Cost of material per kg/litre	$8.25	$6.2
Labour hours per Gonkey	2.25	4.5
Labour rate per hour	$11.50	$11.50
Production overhead absorption	$20 per labour/hour	$23 per labour/hour

Required
(c) Prepare ledger accounts for processes 1 and 2 based on actual expenditure
(d) Calculate the following variances for process 1
   (i) material price
   (ii) material usage
   and the following variances for process 2
   (iii) labour efficiency
   (iv) labour rate.
(e) State *four* advantages of using a system of standard costs.

2 Pembroke Ltd makes an item of furniture known as a Tripos. The standard cost per Tripos is as follows.

Direct material: 2 kg at $7 per kg
Direct labour: 3 hours at $10 per hour
Production overhead: direct (variable) $14 per direct labour hour
   indirect (fixed) based on overhead absorption rate of $30 per direct labour hour

Further information for the three months ending 30 June 2005:
1. The budgeted amount for direct labour: $120 000.
2. Administration and selling overheads for three months ending 30 June 2005: $32 000.
3. Factory profit is 20% of cost of production.
4. The budgeted selling price per Tripos: $250.
5. No stocks of raw materials, work in progress or finished goods are held.

Required
(a) Prepare a budgeted Manufacturing, Trading and Profit and Loss Account for the three months ending 30 June 2005 to show the budgeted net profit or loss.
(b) Calculate, using the information in (a), the break-even point and margin of safety. The margin of safety should be shown as a percentage.

The actual production of Tripos and the related revenue and costs for the three months ended 30 June 2005 were as follows.

No. of Tripos produced	4180
Materials used	8990 kg
Cost of materials	$61 132
Direct labour hours	14 630
Direct labour cost	$138 985
Fixed overhead expenditure:	
Production	$372 000
Administration and selling	$42 000
Selling price per Tripos	$248

The overhead absorption rate for variable production overhead was not affected. All Tripos produced were sold.

Required

(c) Prepare
   (i) a flexed budget based on the actual number of Tripos produced and sold and
   (ii) a financial statement based on actual results.
(d) Calculate the following variances:
   (i) quantity (the additional profit arising from increased production)
   (ii) sales volume
   (iii) sales price
   (iv) direct materials usage
   (v) direct materials price
   (vi) direct labour efficiency
   (vii) direct labour rate.
(e) Calculate the break-even point based on actual revenue and expenditure. (Show your workings.)
(f) Prepare a financial statement to reconcile the original budgeted profit with the actual profit.

36 Investment appraisal

In this chapter you will learn:
- what investment appraisal is
- how to calculate accounting rate of return (ARR)
- how to calculate payback period
- how to calculate net present value (NPV)
- how to calculate internal rate of return (IRR)
- how to calculate the sensitivity investment to errors in estimates.

36.1 What is investment appraisal?

Investment appraisal is a process of assessing whether it is worthwhile to invest funds in a project. The project may be replacement of an existing asset, acquiring an additional asset, introducing a new product, opening a new branch of a business, etc. Funds invested in a project may include additional working capital as well as expenditure on fixed assets. These projects always involve making choices, including whether or not to proceed with the project, which assets to buy, which new products to introduce, and so on.

Accounting techniques are essential tools when these decisions have to be made. However, projects must sometimes be undertaken even when the accounting techniques appear to advise against them. For example, a business that is causing an environmental nuisance may face being closed down by health and safety inspectors unless it spends a considerable sum of money to abate the nuisance. It is well to remember that investment decisions should only be made after all relevant matters, economic, political, environmental, social, etc. have been considered.

This chapter is concerned principally with the financial techniques of appraisal:

- accounting rate of return (ARR)
- payback period
- net present value (NPV)
- internal rate of return (IRR).

These techniques are designed to assess the quality of projects, benefits arising from them, and degrees of risk involved. Only accounting rate of return is concerned with profitability; the others are based on cash flows. The net present value and internal rate of return take the time value of money into account They are all based on additional benefits and costs which will arise from a project. These are referred to **incremental** profits and cash flows. Existing profit and cash flows are ignored as being irrelevant because they will continue whether the new project is undertaken or not. There are two new terms to learn.

- **Sunk costs** consist of expenditure that has been incurred before a new project has been considered. For example, a company plans to introduce a new product that will require the use of a machine it acquired some years ago and has used in the production of an existing product. The cost of the machine is a sunk cost because it has already been incurred and is not *incremental*. Its cost is a historical fact and cannot have any bearing on future decisions.
- **Opportunity costs** are the values of benefits that will be sacrificed if resources are diverted from their present uses to other applications. For example, if a machine that has been earning annual net revenue of $50 000 is to be used exclusively for another operation, it will cease to earn the $50 000. The lost revenue is an opportunity cost. If the machine will earn net revenue of $70 000 in its new capacity, the incremental net revenue will be $20 000 ($70 000 – $50 000).

36.2 How to calculate the accounting rate of return (ARR)

The **accounting rate of return** expresses average profit as a percentage of the average of the capital investment:

$$\frac{\text{average profit}}{\text{average investment}} \times 100.$$

Average profit is the average of the incremental profit (i.e. the profit arising from the investment) expected to be earned over the life of the project. For example, if the expected profit over a period of five years is: year 1 $26 000; year 2 $30 000; year 3 $33 000; year 4 $34 000; year 5 $35 000, the average profit for the purpose of calculating ARR is:

$(26\,000 + 30\,000 + 33\,000 + 34\,000 + 35\,000) \div 5 = \$31\,600$

Fixed assets will be depreciated over the period in which they will be employed on a project and the average investment is therefore the average book value of the assets during that period. Unfortunately, there are different opinions as to how the average investment should be calculated. Students for the CIE exams need only be aware of the simplest method, which is

$\dfrac{\text{the cost of the assets acquired}}{2}$.

Example

Baggins Ltd requires a new machine that will cost $160 000 and have a useful life of five years. The machine is expected to earn profits in those five years of $15 000, £18 000, $21 000, $21 000 and $20 000. The average profit is $95 000 ÷ 5 = $19 000. The average investment is $160 000 ÷ 2 = $80 000. Average rate of return is

$\dfrac{\$19\,000}{\$80\,000} \times 100 = 23.75\%$

Baggins Ltd is able to compare 23.75% with the rate of return that it expects to earn on capital to decide whether the project will be worthwhile. If it is currently earning a return on capital employed (ROCE) of less than 23.75%, the project should improve its overall profitability; if the present ROCE is more than 23.75%, the project will dilute its profitability.

Notes

- ARR is the only technique being considered that takes depreciation of the investment into account.
- A project may require an increase in working capital because this may result in increased stock and debtors. Any increase in working capital will be assumed to remain constant throughout the life of the project and no calculation is required to find the average increase. For example, if a project involves the purchase of a machine at a cost of $60 000 and an increase in working capital of $40 000, the average investment is

$\left(\dfrac{\$60\,000}{2} + \$40\,000\right) = \$70\,000.$

Advantages of ARR

1. The expected profitability of a project can be compared with the present profitability of the business.

2. ARR is comparatively easy to calculate.

Disadvantages of ARR

1. The average annual profit used to calculate ARR is unlikely to be the profit earned in any year of the life of the project.

2. 'Profit' is a subjective concept. It depends upon a number of variable policies such as provisions for depreciation and doubtful debts, valuation of stock, and other matters.

3. The method does not take account of the timing of cash flows. The initial outlay on the project is at risk until the flow of cash into the business has covered the initial cost.

4. ARR ignores the time value of money. Every $ received now is more useful to a business than a $ received at a later date.

5. No account is taken of the life expectancy of a project.

Exercise 1

Baseball Ltd intends to introduce a new product that is expected to produce the following profits over a period of six years.

	$		$
Year 1	23 000	Year 4	26 000
Year 2	24 000	Year 5	29 000
Year 3	25 000	Year 6	23 000

The project will require the use of a machine that was purchased some years ago at a cost of $16 000 and the use of a second machine that will have to be purchased for $120 000. It is estimated that stock held will increase by $10 000, and debtors will increase by $15 000.

Required

Calculate the accounting rate of return that will be earned from the new product.

36.3 How to calculate payback period

Until the initial expenditure on a project has been covered by net receipts (cash inflow – cash outflow) from the venture, a business is at risk of being worse off than if it had not launched the project. Calculation of the **payback period** indicates the time over which the business is at risk. Short payback periods are preferred.

The payback method is concerned with cash flows, not with profitability; depreciation does not enter into the calculations.

Example

Dumbells Ltd is proposing to market a new product which will involve the purchase of new plant costing $100 000. The net receipts from the new product are expected to be as follows: year 1 $30 000; year 2 $40 000; year 3 $50 000; year 4 $45 000.

The payback period is calculated as follows. In the first two years, net receipts will amount to $70 000. The balance of $30 000 will be received in the third year: $\frac{30\,000}{50\,000} \times 12 = 7.2$ months. The payback period is therefore 2 years 8 months. (It would be unrealistic to be more precise than this.)

Advantages of payback

1. It is relatively simple to calculate.
2. Payback can compare the relative risks of different projects.
3. Cash flow is less subjective than profitability.
4. Payback highlights the timing and size of cash flows.
5. Short payback periods result in increased liquidity and enable businesses to grow more quickly.

Disadvantages of payback

1. The life expectancy of a project is ignored.
2. Projects with the same payback period may have different cash flows. For example:

	Project 1	Project 2
	$	$
Year 0 Initial cost	(80 000)	(80 000)
Year 1 Net cash inflow	15 000	30 000
Year 2	25 000	40 000
Year 3	40 000	10 000

Both projects have a payback period of three years and similar amounts of cash inflows, but project 2 is more attractive as the cash flow is better in the early years.

Note. The initial outlay is shown as made in year 0 because it is assumed, simply as a matter of convenience, that cash flows occur on the last day of the year. The initial outlay should be shown as occurring on the first day of year 1, and the last day of year 0 is the nearest we can get to the first day of year 1.

3. The simple payback method ignores the time value of money, but it is possible to apply discounting techniques to it to overcome this failing.

Exercise 2

Mapleduck Ltd is planning to replace one of its machines. It has two choices of replacements: Duckbill and Kwak, each costing $90 000.

The following information is available for the machines.

	Duckbill		Kwak	
	Cash inflow	Cash outflow	Cash inflow	Cash outflow
	$	$	$	$
Year 0	–	90 000	–	90 000
1	80 000	50 000	60 000	20 000
2	90 000	54 000	68 000	28 000
3	100 000	60 000	72 000	32 000

Required

Calculate the payback periods for Duckbill and Kwak and state, with reasons, which machine Mapleduck Ltd should purchase.

36.4 How to calculate net present value (NPV)

Net present value recognises the time value of money. $1 received now is more useful than $1 received some time in the future because it can be used now. If, for example, $100 is invested now at 10% compound interest it will be worth $100 \times \frac{110}{100}$, or $110, in one year's time, and in two years it will be worth $121. To put it another way, $90.91 invested at 10% compound interest now will be worth $90.91 \times \frac{110}{100}$, or $100, in one year's time, and $100 receivable in one year's time has a present value of $90.91 when discounted at 10%.

The time value of money is important when future cash flows are compared with present cash flows because 'like should be compared with like'. Future cash flows are discounted to present day values so that they can be compared with the initial outlay on a realistic basis.

Future cash flows are the estimated cash receipts less the estimated cash payments attributable to an investment and will usually be known as **net receipts** or **net payments**. If assets purchased for the project are sold at the end of the venture, the proceeds of sale should be included in the net receipts in the last year.

The discounting rate taken for net present values is the cost of capital. For example, if money has to be borrowed at 8% interest per annum to finance the investment in a project, the cost of capital is 8% and the future cash flows will be discounted using the factors for that rate. A table of discounting factors can be found in Appendix 1 (page 295) although the necessary rates are always given in examination questions.

Notes

- It is widely thought that cash flows are discounted to net present value to allow for inflation, but that is not so. The rate used for discounting is the cost of capital, not the rate of inflation.
- The payback period is sometimes calculated using the net present values of the cash flows.

Example

Netpres Ltd is undertaking a project which involves an initial outlay of $100 000. Its net receipts from the project for the next five years are estimated to be as follows.

Year 1	$40 000
Year 2	$42 000
Year 3	$48 000
Year 4	$46 000
Year 5	$38 000

Netpres Ltd's cost of capital is 10%. The discounting factors for the present value of $1 at 10% are: year 1 0.909; year 2 0.826; year 3 0.751; year 4 0.683; year 5 0.621.

Required

Calculate the net present value of the project.

Answer

Year	Net cash inflow/(outflow)	Factor	Net present value
	$		$
0	(100 000)	1.000	(100 000)
1	40 000	0.909	36 360
2	42 000	0.826	34 692
3	48 000	0.751	36 048
4	46 000	0.683	31 418
5	38 000	0.621	23 598
Net present value			62 116

The net present value is positive, showing that the project may be undertaken. A negative NPV would mean that the net receipts in present day terms would not cover the initial outlay and the project should not be undertaken. The higher the net present value, the better the project. If two or more projects are being considered, the one with the higher or highest NPV would be preferred to the other(s).

Exercise 3

Nomen Ltd is considering buying a machine and has three options, machine A, B or C, only one of which it will buy. Each machine costs $135 000 and will have a five-year life with no residual value at the end of that time.

The net receipts for each machine over the five-year period are as follows.

	Machine A	Machine B	Machine C
	$	$	$
Year 1	50 000	38 000	26 000
2	50 000	38 000	26 000
3	38 000	38 000	38 000
4	26 000	38 000	50 000
5	26 000	38 000	50 000

Nomen Ltd's cost of capital is 12%.

The discounting factors at 12% are: year 1 0.893; year 2 0.797; year 3 0.712; year 4 0.636 year 5 0.567.

Required

Calculate the net present value of each option and state which machine Nomen Ltd should choose.

36.5 How to calculate internal rate of return (IRR)

Net present value compares future cash inflows with present cash outflow when the future cash flows are discounted to present day values, but it does not give the **rate of return** on investment based on discounted values. The internal rate of return enables managers to calculate the return on an intended investment and to compare it with the company's present return on capital.

The internal rate of return is the percentage required to discount cash flows to give a nil net present value. The percentage is found by selecting two discounting rates sufficiently wide apart to give positive and negative net present values. The results are then **interpolated** to find the percentage that will give a nil net present value. (**Interpolation** means finding an intermediate value between the two discounting rates.) Interpolation involves using the formula

$$P + \left[(P - N) \times \frac{p}{p + n}\right] = IRR$$

where P is the rate giving a positive net present value
N is the rate giving a negative net present value
p is the positive net present value
n is the negative net present value.

For example, if NPV at 10% is $14 000 and at 18% is $(6000), then

$$IRR = 10\% + \left(8\% \times \frac{14\,000}{14\,000 + 6000}\right) = 10\% + 5.6\% = 15.6\%$$

Therefore, discounted at 15.6%, the investment would have nil net present value.

Example

Netpres Ltd (see §36.4) has a net present value of $62 116 when discounted at 10%. To obtain a negative net present value it may be discounted at 40% as follows.

	$	at 40%	$
Year 0	(100 000)	1.000	(100 000)
1	40 000	0.714	28 560
2	42 000	0.510	21 420
3	48 000	0.364	17 472
4	46 000	0.260	11 960
5	38 000	0.186	7 068
Net present value			(13 520)

$$IRR = 10\% + \left(30\% \times \frac{62\ 116}{62\ 116 + 13\ 520}\right) = 34.6\%$$

Exercise 4

The information is given as for Nomen Ltd in exercise 3 in §36.4, with the addition of the discounting factors for 20%: year 1 0.833; year 2 0.694; year 3 0.579; year 4 0.482; year 5 0.402.

Required

Calculate the internal rate of return for machines A and B.

Notes

- IRR can be calculated from two positive net present values but will be less accurate. The denominator of the fraction in the formula must be amended as follows: $P + [(P - N) \times \frac{p}{p - n})]$. If the discounting factors in a question produce only positive net present values, do *not* try to find another discounting rate; the examiner expects you to use the ones supplied in the question.

- When the receipts are constant for a number of consecutive years, the net present value of those receipts may be calculated quickly if the annual amount is multiplied by the sum of the factors for the years concerned. For example, if net receipts are $25 000 in each of the first five years and the cost of capital is 10%, the NPV for the five years is $25 000 × (0.909 + 0.826 + 0.751 + 0.683 + 0.621) = $25 000 × 3.790 = $94 750

Exercise 5

Baxter Ltd requires a new machine to use in the manufacture of a new product. Two machines are available: Big Gee and Maxi-Shadbolt. Baxter Ltd depreciates machinery using the straight-line method. Baxter Ltd will obtain a bank loan at interest of 10% per annum to buy the machine.

Further information

	Big Gee	Maxi-Shadbolt
Cost of machine	$140 000	$180 000
	$	$
Additional receipts Year 1	98 000	101 000
2	112 000	118 000
3	126 000	126 000
4	126 000	140 000
5	100 000	110 000

Additional costs (including depreciation and bank interest):

	$	$
Year 1	70 000	84 000
2	84 000	98 000
3	91 000	105 000
4	98 000	112 000
5	95 000	100 000
Useful life of machine	5 years	5 years
Estimated proceeds of disposal after 5 years	$20 000	$30 000
Present value of $1	10%	40%
Year 1	0.909	0.714
2	0.826	0.510
3	0.751	0.364
4	0.683	0.260
5	0.621	0.186

Required

(a) Calculate for each machine:
  (i) the accounting rate of return (ARR)
  (ii) the payback period
  (iii) the net present value
  (iv) the internal rate of return (IRR).
(b) State, with reasons, which machine Baxter Ltd should purchase.

36.6 Sensitivity analysis

Appraisal of future capital expenditure is based on estimated future profitability and cash flows. Inaccuracies in the estimates may be very misleading, and acceptable margins of error must be recognised. **Sensitivity analysis** indicates the maximum acceptable margin of error; a greater margin might produce disastrous results especially as very large sums of money are involved.

The percentages of error that could produce unacceptable results must be determined and compared with the likely margins of error as shown by past forecasting experience.

Example

A project needs $100 000 to buy a machine. Net receipts in each of the four years of the project are expected to be $35 000. The cost of capital is 10%.

The net present value = $100 000 − $(35 000 × 3.169) = £10 915. The net present value will be negative if:

- the cost of the machine exceeds £110 915, that is an increase of 11%; or
- the annual net receipts are less than $100 000 ÷ 3.169 = $31 555, that is a decrease of 9.8%.

The company should compare its past degrees of accuracy in estimating capital expenditure and forecasts of revenue with the percentages calculated above.

Exercise 6

A company proposes to replace an existing machine with a new one costing $150 000. It is estimated that the use of the new machine will result in net savings over the next four years of $50 000 per annum. The company will borrow $150 000 at an interest rate of 10% per annum to pay for the machine.

Required

Calculate the degrees of sensitivity as regards the cost of the machine and the annual operational savings.

36.7 Examination hints

- Learn the methods of calculating ARR, payback periods, NPV and IRR.
- Remember that only ARR is calculated on profitability; payback, NPV and IRR are calculated on cash flows. Depreciation must be included for ARR but not for the other methods.
- Understand the importance of profitability and risk in investment, and why the time value of money is important.
- Be prepared to describe, explain or discuss the advantages and disadvantages of the various methods of investment appraisal.
- Take the utmost care to perform all calculations accurately.
- Look out for sunk costs and opportunity costs in problems.

36.8 Multiple-choice questions

1 The net present value of a project has been calculated as follows:

	NPV ($)
at 10%	30 000
at 20%	(8 000)

What is the internal rate of return on the project?

A 10%

B 12.1%

C 17.9%

D 20%

2 Why are cash flows discounted for investment appraisal?

A $1 now is more useful than $1 receivable at a future time.

B It is prudent to state future cash flows at a realistic value.

C Money loses its value because of inflation.

D The risk of not receiving money increases with time.

3 Which method of investment appraisal may be based on either actual cash flows or discounted cash flows?

A accounting rate of return

B internal rate of return

C net present value

D payback

4 A company has $4 million to invest. Its investment opportunities are as follows.

Amount of investment for a period of 5 years	NPV($)
1. $3 mill.	600 000
2. $2.5 mill.	350 000
3. $1.5 mill.	280 000
4. $1 mill.	50 000

In which opportunities should the company invest?

A 1 and 3

B 1 and 4

C 2 and 3

D 2 and 4

36.9 Additional exercises

1 The directors of Joloss plc intend to purchase an additional machine to manufacture one of their new products. Two machines are being considered: Milligan and Bentine. The company depreciates its machinery using the straight-line method.

Joloss plc will borrow the money required to purchase the machine and pay interest of 10% per annum on the loan.

Estimates for the machines are as follows.

		Milligan	Bentine
		$	$
Cost of machine		100 000	130 000
Additional receipts	Year 1	70 000	72 000
	2	80 000	84 000
	3	90 000	90 000
	4	90 000	100 000
Additional costs	Year 1	50 000	60 000
(see note)	2	60 000	70 000
	3	65 000	75 000
	4	70 000	80 000

Note. These costs include the charges for depreciation and interest on the loans.

	Milligan	Bentine
Useful life of the machine	4 years	4 years
Value at end of useful life	nil	nil
Present value of $1	10%	20%
Year 1	0.909	0.833
2	0.826	0.694
3	0.751	0.579
4	0.683	0.482

Required

(i) Calculate the net present value of each machine. (Base your calculations on the cost of capital.)

(ii) State, with your reason, which machine Joloss plc should purchase.

The directors require the machine to produce a return on outlay of not less than 25%.

Required

(iii) Calculate the internal rate of return on the machine you have selected in (ii) to see if it meets the required return on outlay.

(UCLES, 2002, AS/A Level Accounting, Syllabus 9706/4, May/June)

2 Jane Pannell Ltd proposes to purchase a new machine costing $120 000. It will be sold at the end of four years for $20 000. The company depreciates machinery using the straight-line method.

The machine will earn revenue of $80 000 per annum and involve additional expenditure of $46 000 each year. The company's cost of capital is 10%.

The present value of $1 is as follows.

	10%	15%
Year 1	0.909	0.870
2	0.826	0.756
3	0.751	0.658
4	0.683	0.572

Required

Calculate:

(a) the accounting rate of return
(b) the net present value
(c) the internal rate of return.

Appendix 1: Table showing net present value of $1

Present value of $1

Years	5%	6%	7%	8%	9%	10%	11%	12%	13%	14%	15%	16%	17%
1	0.952	0.943	0.935	0.926	0.917	0.909	0.901	0.893	0.885	0.877	0.870	0.862	0.855
2	0 907	0.890	0.873	0.857	0.842	0.826	0.812	0.797	0.783	0.769	0.756	0.743	0.731
3	0.864	0.840	0.816	0.794	0.772	0.751	0.731	0.712	0.693	0.675	0.658	0.641	0.624
4	0.823	0.792	0.763	0.735	0.708	0.683	0.659	0.636	0.613	0.592	0.572	0.552	0.534
5	0.784	0.747	0.713	0.681	0.650	0.621	0.593	0.567	0.543	0.519	0.497	0.476	0.456
6	0.746	0.705	0.666	0.630	0.596	0.564	0.535	0.507	0.480	0.456	0.432	0.410	0.390
7	0.711	0.665	0.623	0.583	0.547	0.513	0.482	0.452	0.425	0.400	0.376	0.354	0.333
8	0.677	0.627	0.582	0.540	0.502	0.467	0.434	0.404	0.376	0.351	0.327	0.305	0.285
9	0.645	0.592	0.544	0.500	0.460	0.424	0.391	0.361	0.333	0.308	0.284	0.263	0.243
10	0.614	0.558	0.508	0.463	0.422	0.386	0.352	0.322	0.295	0.270	0.247	0.227	0.208

Years	18%	19%	20%	21%	22%	23%	24%	25%
1	0.847	0.840	0.833	0.826	0.820	0.813	0.806	0.800
2	0.718	0.706	0.694	0.683	0.672	0.661	0.650	0.640
3	0.609	0.593	0.579	0.564	0.551	0.537	0.524	0.512
4	0.516	0.499	0.482	0.466	0.451	0.437	0.423	0.410
5	0.437	0.419	0.402	0.386	0.370	0.355	0.341	0.328
6	0.370	0.352	0.335	0.319	0.303	0.289	0.275	0.262
7	0.314	0.296	0.279	0.263	0.249	0.235	0.222	0.210
8	0.266	0.249	0.233	0.218	0.204	0.191	0.179	0.168
9	0.225	0.209	0.194	0.180	0.167	0.155	0.144	0.134
10	0.191	0.176	0.162	0.149	0.137	0.126	0.116	0.107

Answers to exercises and multiple-choice questions

Chapter 1

Exercise 1 Martine

Bank

		$			$
May 1	Martine Capital	3000	May 3	Rent Payable	100
May 2	Charline – Loan	1000	May 4	Shop Fittings	400
May 5	Purchases Returns	20	May 4	Purchases	300
May 6	Sales	40	May 7	Wages	60
			May 8	Drawings	100

Martine Capital

		$			$
			May 1	Bank	3000

Charline – Loan

		$			$
			May 2	Bank	1000

Rent Payable

		$		$
May 3	Bank	100		

Shop Fittings

		$		$
May 4	Bank	400		

Purchases

		$		$
May 4	Bank	300		

Purchases Returns

	$			$
		May 5	Bank	20

Sales

	$			$
		May 6	Bank	40

Wages

		$		$
May 7	Bank	60		

Drawings

		$		$
May 8	Bank	100		

Exercise 2 Noel

		Debit account	Credit account
1.	Noel pays his cheque into his business Bank account	Bank	Noel – Capital
2.	Purchases stock and pays by cheque	Purchases	Bank
3.	Sells stock and banks the takings	Bank	Sales
4.	Pays rent by cheque	Rent Payable	Bank
5.	Purchases shop fittings	Shop Fittings	Bank
6.	Cashes cheque for personal expenses	Drawings	Bank
7.	Pays wages	Wages	Bank
8.	Returns stock to supplier and banks refund	Bank	Purchases Returns
9.	Receives rent from tenant	Bank	Rent Receivable
10.	Refunds money to customer by cheque for goods returned	Sales Returns	Bank
11.	Motor vehicle purchased and paid for by cheque	Motor Vehicles	Bank
12.	Pays for petrol for motor vehicle	Motor Expenses*	Bank

*The costs of running motor vehicles (petrol, licence, insurance, repairs etc.) are not debited to the Motor Vehicles account.

1.5 Multiple-choice questions

1 B   **2** B   **3** D   **4** B

Chapter 2

Exercise 1 Geraud

Khor

	$		$
June 10 Purchases Returns	200	June 1 Purchases	2700
30 Bank	2375		
30 Discounts Received	125		

Lim

	$		$
June 30 Bank	2394	June 15 Purchases	2520
June 30 Discounts Received	126		

Lai

	$		$
June 5 Sales	600	June 25 Sales Returns	200
		June 30 Bank	380
		June 30 Discounts Allowed	20

Chin

	$		$
June 20 Sales	1300	June 30 Bank	1235
		June 30 Discounts Allowed	65

Purchases

	$		$
June 1 Khor	2700		
June 15 Lim	2520		

Purchases Returns

	$		$
		June 10 Khor	200

Sales

	$		$
		June 5 Lai	600
		June 20 Chin	1300

Sales Returns

	$		$
June 25 Lai	200		

Bank

	$		$
June 30 Lai	380	June 30 Khor	2375
June 30 Chin	1235	June 30 Lim	2394

Discounts Received

	$		$
		June 30 Khor	125
		June 30 Lim	126

Discounts Allowed

	$		$
June 30 Lai	20		
June 30 Chin	65		

2.5 Multiple-choice questions

1 A   **2** B   **3** A

Chapter 3

Exercise 1 Murgatroyd

Purchases Journal		Sales Journal	
	$		$
March 1 Tikolo	8 000	March 4 Snyman	1080
March 6 Walters	7 200	March 10 Karg	2250
March 13 Burger	5 250	March 17 Kotze	2700
March 18 Tikolo	4 800	March 25 Snyman	1620
	25 250		7650

Purchases Returns Journal		Sales Returns Journal	
	$		$
March 12 Tikolo	400	March 11 Snyman	200
March 22 Burger	1000	March 20 Karg	300
	1400		500

Bank

	Discounts $	Bank $		Discounts $	Bank $
March 31 Snyman	100	2400	March 31 Tikolo	620	11 780
March 31 Karg	78	1872	March 31 Walters	360	6 840
March 31 Kotze	135	2565	March 31 Burger	170	4 080
	313			1150	

Purchases

	$		$
March 31 Purchases journal total	25 250		

Purchases Returns

	$		$
		March 31 Purchases returns journal total	1400

Sales

	$		$
		March 31 Sales journal total	7650

Sales Returns

	$		$
March 31 Sales returns journal total	500		

Discounts Allowed

	$		$
		March 31 Cash book total	313

Discounts Received

	$		$
		March 31 Cash book total	1150

Tikolo

	$		$
March 12 Purchases Returns	400	March 1 Purchases	8000
March 31 Bank	11 780	March 18 Purchases	4800
March 31 Discounts	620		

Walters

	$		$
March 31 Bank	6840	March 6 Purchases	7200
March 31 Discounts	360		

Burger

	$		$
March 22 Purchases Returns	1000	March 13 Purchases	5250
March 31 Bank	4080		
March 31 Discounts	170		

Snyman

	$		$
March 4 Sales	1080	March 11 Sales Returns	200
March 25 Sales	1620	March 31 Bank	2400
		March 31 Discounts	100

Karg

	$		$
March 10 Sales	2250	March 20 Sales Returns	300
		March 31 Bank	1872
		March 31 Discounts	78

Kotze

	$		$
March 17 Sales	2700	March 31 Bank	2565
		March 31 Discounts	135

Exercise 2 Joshua

	Disc $	Cash $	Bank $		Disc $	Cash $	Bank $
March 1 Sales		1100		March 2 Electricity		130	
March 3 Sales		900		March 4 Bank ¢		1700	
March 4 Cash ¢			1700	March 5 Sundry expenses		25	
March 6 Bank ¢		800		March 6 Cash ¢			800
				March 7 Purchases		750	

Table title: Bank and Cash

Exercise 3

	Dr $	Cr $
1. A and Co. Ltd.	120	
A. Cotter		120

Correction of credit note no. 964 received from A and Co. Ltd. in the sum of $120 debited to A. Cotter in error.

2. Purchases	400	
Hussain		400

Correction of invoice no. 104 in the sum of $400 received from Hussain omitted from the purchases journal.

3. Maya	45	
Sales		45

Correction of posting error: invoice no. 6789 in the sum of $150 sent to Maya entered in the sales journal as $105.

4. Machinery	2300	
Purchases		2300

Correction of purchase of machine posted in error to Purchases account.

5. Sales Returns	68	
Hanife		68

Correction of omission of credit note no. 23 for $68 and sent to Hanife, omitted from the sales returns journal.

3.12 Multiple-choice questions
1 C   2 B   3 B   4 C

Chapter 5

Exercise 1 Capital – personal; Sales Returns – revenue; Delivery Vans – fixed asset; Purchases – expense; Rent Payable – expense; Debtors – personal (and current assets); Stock-in-trade – current asset; Discounts Allowed – expense; Drawings – personal; Bank – current asset; Rent Receivable – other income; Creditors – personal; Computer – fixed asset; Wages – expense; Discounts Receivable – other income.

Chapter 6

Exercise 1 Achilles' trial balance at 31 December 2003:

	$	$
Premises	50 000	
Motor Vans	8 000	
Office Furniture	2 000	
Computer	3 000	
Sales		60 000
Sales Returns	700	
Purchases	4 000	
Purchases Returns		500
Motor Vehicle Running Expenses	4 200	
Wages	1 800	
Rent	2 000	
Bank	1 650	
Capital		20 000
Drawings	3 150	
	80 500	80 500

Exercise 2 (a) Complete reversal of entries (b) Error of principle (c) Error of omission (d) Compensating errors (e) Error of commission (f) Error of original entry

6.5 Multiple-choice questions
1 B   2 B   3 C   4 C

Chapter 7

Exercise 1

Corrine
Trading and Profit and Loss Account for the year ended 31 December 2003

	$	$
Sales		200 000
Less Sales returns		6 300
		193 700
Cost of sales		
Purchases	86 500	
Less Purchases returns	5 790	
	80 710	
Less Stock at 31 December 2003	10 000	70 710
Gross profit		122 990
Add Rent received		3 000
Discounts received		3 210
		129 200
Less		
Wages	61 050	
Rent payable	12 000	
Electricity	5 416	
Insurance	2 290	
Motor van expenses	11 400	
Discounts allowed	5 110	
Sundry expenses	3 760	
Loan interest	1 000	102 026
Net profit		27 174

Exercise 2

Khor
Trading Account for the year ended 31 December 2003

	$	$	$
Sales			48 000
Less Sales returns			1 600
			46 400
Less Cost of sales			
Opening stock		4 000	
Purchases	21 000		
Less Purchases returns	900	20 100	
		24 100	
Less Closing stock		7 500	16 600
Gross profit			29 800

Exercise 3

Perkins
Trading and Profit and Loss Account for the year ended 31 March 2004

	$	$	$
Sales			104 000
Less Sales returns			3 700
			100 300
Less Cost of sales			
Opening stock		6 000	
Purchases	59 000		
Less Purchases returns	2 550	56 450	
		62 450	
Less Closing stock		10 000	52 450
Gross profit			47 850
Rent receivable			1 800
Discounts receivable			770
			50 420
Less Overheads			
Wages		13 000	
Rent payable		2 000	
Heating and lighting		2 700	
Repairs to machinery		4 100	
Discounts allowed		1 030	
Loan interest		750	23 580
Net profit			26 840

Exercise 4

Sara Trading and Profit and Loss Account for the year ended 31 March 2004			
	$	$	$
Sales			40 000
Less Cost of sales			
Stock at 1 April 2003		5 000	
Purchases	20 500		
Carriage inwards	1 320	21 820	
		26 820	
Less Stock at 31 March 2004		3 000	23 820
Gross profit			16 180
Less			
Wages		6 000	
Rent		10 000	
Electricity		2 600	
Carriage outwards		1 080	
Sundry expenses		1 250	20 930
Net loss			4 750

7.7 Multiple-choice questions

1 A **2** C **3** C **4** D **5** A

Chapter 8

Exercise 1

Corrine Balance Sheet at 31 December 2003		
	$	$
Fixed assets		
Land and buildings		84 000
Plant and machinery		22 000
Motor vans		19 000
		125 000
Current assets		
Stock	10 000	
Trade debtors	12 425	
Bank	5 065	
	27 490	
Current liabilities		
Trade creditors	4 220	23 270
		148 270
Long-term liability		
Loan		20 000
		128 270
Represented by		
Capital at 1 January 2003		127 000
Add net profit		27 174
		154 174
Deduct Drawings		25 904
		128 270

Exercise 2

Perkins
Balance Sheet at 31 March 2004

	$	$
Fixed assets		
Premises		60 000
Plant and machinery		12 000
		72 000
Current assets		
Stock	10 000	
Trade debtors	1 624	
Bank	5 000	
	16 624	
Current liabilities		
Trade creditors	1 880	14 744
		86 744
Long-term liability		
Loan		15 000
		71 744
Represented by		
Capital at 1 April 2003		55 000
Net profit		26 840
		81 840
Drawings		10 096
		71 744

8.4 Multiple-choice questions

1 D   **2** A   **3** A   **4** C

Chapter 9

9.14 Multiple-choice questions

1 B   **2** A   **3** A   **4** B   **5** B   **6** D

Chapter 10

Exercise 1 Alex

Rent Payable

2003		$	2003		$
Dec 31 Bank		1000	Dec 31 Profit and Loss		800
			Dec 31 Rent prepaid c/d		200
		1000			1000
2004					
Jan 1 Balance b/d		200			

Electricity

2003	$	2003	$
Dec 31 Bank	630	Dec 31 Profit and Loss	810
Dec 31 Amount owing c/d	180		—
	810		810
		2004	
		Jan 1 Balance b/d	180

Stationery

2003	$	2003	$
Dec 31 Bank	420	Dec 31 Profit and Loss	410
Dec 31 Amount owing c/d	130	Dec 31 Stock c/d	140
	550		550
2004		2004	
Jan 31 Balance b/d	140	Jan 31 Balance b/d	130

Rent Receivable

2003	$	2003	$
Dec 31 Profit and Loss	400	Dec 31 Bank	300
	—	Dec 31 Rent owing b/d	100
	400		400
2004			
Jan 1 Balance b/d	100		

Exercise 2

(a)

Devram
Profit and Loss Account for the year ended
31 December 2003

	$	$
Gross profit b/d		30 000
Rent	2300	
Electricity	1168	
Stationery	389	
Motor expenses	885	
Interest on loan	1000	5 742
Net profit		24 258

Note. Unpaid interest on the loan must be accrued although it is not mentioned in the question.

(b)

Balance Sheet at 31 December 2003

	$	$	$
Fixed assets			40 000
Current assets			
Stock in trade	7000		
Stock of stationery	100	7 100	
Trade debtors		1 600	
Prepaid rent		300	
Bank		2 524	
		11 524	
Current liabilities			
Trade creditors	1400		
Expense creditors	986	2 386	9 138
			49 138
Less Long-term loan			10 000
			39 138
Capital at 1 January 2003			20 000
Net profit			24 258
			44 258
Drawings			5 120
			39 138

10.8 Multiple-choice questions

1 D   **2** B   **3** B   **4** A

Chapter 11

Exercise 1 (a)

Provision for Depreciation of Motor Vehicles

			$				$
Year 1	Balance c/d		2 000	Year 1	Profit and Loss		2 000
Year 2	Balance c/d		4 000	Year 2	Balance b/d		2 000
			___		Profit and Loss		2 000
			4 000				4 000
Year 3	Balance c/d		6 000	Year 3	Balance b/d		4 000
			___		Profit and Loss		2 000
			6 000				6 000
Year 4	Balance c/d		8 000	Year 4	Balance b/d		6 000
			___		Profit and Loss		2 000
			8 000				8 000
Year 5	Balance c/d		10 000	Year 5	Balance b/d		8 000
			___		Profit and Loss		2 000
			10 000				10 000
Year 6	Balance c/d		12 000	Year 6	Balance b/d		10 000
			___		Profit and Loss		2 000
			12 000				12 000
Year 7	Balance c/d		14 000	Year 7	Balance b/d		12 000
			___		Profit and Loss		2 000
			14 000				14 000
Year 8				Year 8	Balance b/d		14 000

(b)

Balance Sheet extracts

		Cost	Depreciation	Net book value
		$	$	$
Year 1	Motor vehicles	18 000	2 000	16 000
Year 2	Motor vehicles	18 000	4 000	14 000
Year 3	Motor vehicles	18 000	6 000	12 000
Year 4	Motor vehicles	18 000	8 000	10 000
Year 5	Motor vehicles	18 000	10 000	8 000
Year 6	Motor vehicles	18 000	12 000	6 000
Year 7	Motor vehilces	18 000	14 000	4 000

Exercise 2 (a)

Provision for Depreciation of Machinery

	$		$
Year 1 Balance c/d	12 000	Year 1 Profit and Loss	12 000
Year 2 Balance c/d	20 400	Year 2 Balance b/d	12 000
		Profit and Loss	8 400
	20 400		20 400
Year 3 Balance c/d	26 280	Year 3 Balance b/d	20 400
		Profit and Loss	5 880
	26 280		26 280
Year 4 Balance c/d	30 396	Year 4 Balance b/d	26 280
		Profit and Loss	4 116
	30 396		30 396
Year 5 Balance c/d	33 277	Year 5 Balance b/d	30 396
		Profit and Loss	2 881
	33 277		33 277
Year 6		Year 6 Balance b/d	33 277

(b)

Balance Sheet extracts

	Cost	Depreciation	Net book value
	$	$	$
Year 1 Machinery	40 000	12 000	28 000
Year 2 Machinery	40 000	20 400	19 600
Year 3 Machinery	40 000	26 280	13 720
Year 4 Machinery	40 000	30 396	9 604
Year 5 Machinery	40 000	33 277	6 723

Exercise 3 Joel

(a)

Machinery at Cost

2004		$	2004		$
Jan 1 Balance	b/d	18 000	May 7 Disposal of Machinery		6 000
Jun 3 Bank		7 000	Jun 3 Disposal of Machinery		12 000
Disposal of Machinery		3 000	Dec 31 Balance	c/d	10 000
		28 000			28 000
2005					
Jan 1 Balance	b/d	10 000			

(b)

Provision for Depreciation of Machinery

2004		$	2004		$
May 7 Disposal of Machinery		2 400	Jan 1 Balance b/d) (2400 + 7200		9 600
Jun 3 Disposal of Machinery		7 200	Dec 31 Profit and Loss		1 000
Dec 31 Balance c/d		1 000			
		10 600			10 600
			2005		$
			Jan 1 Balance b/d		1 000

(c)

Disposal of Machinery

2004		$	2004		$
May 7 Machinery at Cost		6 000	May 7 Provision for Depreciation of Machinery		2 400
			Bank		1 500
			Profit and Loss (loss)		2 100
		6 000			6 000
Jun 3 Machinery at Cost		12 000	Jun 3 Provision for Depreciation of Machinery		7 200
			Machinery at Cost		3 000
			Profit and Loss (loss)		1 800
		12 000			12 000

11.11 Multiple-choice questions

1 D **2** C **3** A **4** A

Chapter 12

Exercise 1 Saul

(a) 2000: $(4000 + 1150) = $5150
    2001: $(6400 + 1375) = $7775
    2002: $(7500 + 1125) = $8625
    2003: $(3000 + 1250) = $4250
    2004: $(8300 + 1420) = $9720

(b)

Provision for Doubtful Debts			
	$		$
31 Mar 2000 Balance c/d	5150	31 Mar 2000 Profit and Loss A/c	5150
31 Mar 2001 Balance c/d	7775	1 Apr 2000 Balance b/d	5150
		31 Mar 2001 Profit and Loss A/c	2625
	7775		7775
31 Mar 2002	8625	1 Apr 2001 Balance b/d	7775
		31 Mar 2002 Profit an Loss A/c	850
	8625		8625
31 Mar 2003 Profit and Loss A/c	4375	1 Apr 2001 Balance b/d	8625
Balance c/d	4250		
	8625		8625
31 Mar 2004 Balance c/d	9720	1 Apr 2003 Balance b/d	4250
		31 Mar 2004 Profit and Loss A/c	5470
	9720		9720
		1 Apr 2004 Balance b/d	9720

12.9 Multiple-choice questions

1 C   **2** B   **3** D   **4** B

Chapter 13

Exercise 1 $475 Cr

Exercise 2 $540 Dr (overdrawn)

Exercise 3 (a) Revised cash book balance: $80 – $210 = $130 overdrawn
(b) Bank reconciliation: Balance per bank statements $(650 + 220) Cr – $1000 = $130 overdrawn (per cash book).

Exercise 4

	$	$
Trade debtors (1055 – 420 + 323)	958	
Trade creditors (976 – 360)		616
Rent (800 + 200)	1000	
Bank (1245 – 360 + 420 – 200 – 323)	782	

13.5 Multiple-choice questions

1 C   **2** D   **3** B   **4** A   **5** B

Chapter 14

Exercise 1

Byit Ltd Purchase Ledger Control				
2004		$	2004	$
Mar 1	Balance b/d	16	Mar 1 Balance b/d	10 000
Mar 31	Purchases returns	824	Mar 31 Purchases journal	33 700
	Bank	27 500	Balance c/d	156
	Discounts received	1 300		
	Balance c/d	14 216		
		43 856		43 856
Apr 1	Balance b/d	156	Apr 1 Balance b/d	14 216

Exercise 2

Soldit Ltd
Sales Ledger Control

2004		$	2004		$
May 1	Balance b/d	27 640	May 1	Balance b/d	545
31	Sales journal	109 650	31	Sales returns	2 220
	Bad debt recovered	490		Bank	98 770
				Discounts allowed	3 150
	Balance c/d	800		Bank – bad debt recovered	490
				Purchases ledger contra	2 624
				Balance c/d	30 781
		138 580			138 580
Jun 1	Balance b/d	31 271	Jun 1	Balance b/d	800

Exercise 3

(a)

Rorre Ltd	**Purchases ledger balances**			**Sales ledger balances**		
		Debit	Credit		Debit	Credit
		$	$		$	$
Before amendment		64	7 217	Before amendment	23 425	390
Deduct invoice entered twice			(100)	Correction of invoice		
Debit balance incorrectly listed as credit balance		50	(50)	$326 entered as $362	(36)	—
				Corrected balances	23 389	390
Corrected balances		114	7 067			

(b)

Corrected Purchases Ledger Control

2003		$	2003		$
Dec 31	Cancellation of invoice	100	Dec 31	Balance b/d	7847
	Discounts Received	84		Balance c/d	114
	Sales Ledger contra – Trazom	710			
	Balance c/d	7067			
		7961			7961
2004			2004		
Jan 1	Balance b/d	114	Jan 1	Balance b/d	7067

Corrected Sales Ledger Control

2003		$	2003		$
Dec 31	Balance b/d	22 909	Dec 31	Purchases Ledger Contra – Trazom	710
	Sales journal	800		Balance c/d	23 389
	Balance c/d	390			
		24 099			24 099
2004			2004		
Jan 1	Balance b/d	23 389	Jan 1	Balance b/d	390

(c)

Amended net profit	$
Profit per draft Profit and Loss Account	31 000
Add reduction in purchases	100
discounts received omitted	84
increase in sales	800
Amended net profit	31 984

(d)

Balance Sheet extract at 31 December	$	$
Debtors		
Sales ledger	23 389	
Purchases ledger	114	23 503
Creditors		
Purchases ledger	7 067	
Sales ledger	390	7 457

14.10 Multiple-choice questions

1 B   **2** C   **3** C

Chapter 15

Exercise 1
(a)

Lee
Suspense account

	$		$
Sales	90	Difference on trial balance	58*
Doyle	18	Bad debt	50
	108		108

*Balancing figure

(b) Journal entries

	Debit	Credit
	$	$
Purchases*	150	
Bilder		150
Invoice from Bilder omitted from the books.		
*This should *not* be posted to Stock account.		
Machinery at Cost	400	
Machinery Repairs		400
Capital expenditure incorrectly posted to Machinery Repairs account.		
Profit and Loss Account	40	
Provision for depreciation of machinery		40
Additional depreciation on machinery.		

(c) Calculation of corrected net profit for the year ended 30 June 2004

	Decrease (Dr)	Increase (Cr)	
	$	$	$
Net profit per draft accounts			3775
(1) Increase in sales		90	
(2) Increase in purchases	150		
(4) Increase in bad debts	50		
(5) Decrease in machinery repairs		400	
(5) Increase in provision for depreciation of machinery	40	—	
	240	490	
		(240)	250
Corrected net profit			4025

Exercise 2
(a) Journal entries

		Jayesh	
		Dr	Cr
		$	$
1.	Suspense		2700
	Note. No debit entry is required.		
2.	*Note. The trial balance was not affected because the closing stock was not shown in it.*		
3.	Repairs to machinery	3500	
	Suspense	1800	
	Machinery at cost		5300
4.	Suspense	800	
	Sales		800
5.	Suspense	126	
	Note. No credit entry is required.		

(b)

Suspense account

	$		$
Machinery at cost	1800	Trial balance difference	26
Sales	800	Adjustment of opening	
Adjustment to creditors	126	stock	2700
	2726		2726

(c) Calculation of corrected net working capital at 31 December

	$
Net working capital per draft Balance Sheet	3200
Add Increase in closing stock	2000
Deduct: Credit balance $63 extracted as debit balance	(126)
Corrected net working capital at 31 December	5074

15.7 Multiple-choice questions

1 A		**2** B		**3** C		**4** B	
5 C		**6** C		**7** A			

Chapter 16

Exercise 1 Lian

Statements of affairs

	at 1 January	at 31 December
	$	$
Premises at cost	4 000	9 000
Motor van at cost	5 000	4 000
Motor car at cost	–	3 000
Plant and equipment	1 100	1 300
Stock of parts	400	200
Debtors for work done	700	800
Balance at bank	1 300	900
	12 500	19 200
Less		
Owing to suppliers	170	340
Capital	12 330	18 860
Less capital introduced: motor car		(3 000)*
		15 860
Add drawings ($120 × 52)		6 240
		22 100
Deduct capital at 1 January		12 330
Profit for the year ended 31 December		9 770

*The cost of the car is deducted because it was capital introduced during the year.

Exercise 2 Ammar

Trading Account for the year ended 30 June

	$	$
Sales (balancing figure)		35 000
Less		
Opening stock	4 000	
Purchases (balancing figure)	31 000	
(balancing figure)	35 000	
Closing stock	7 000	
Cost of sales		28 000
Gross profit (Margin 20%, so mark-up is 25%)		7 000

Exercise 3 Neha

Proforma Trading Account for the period 30 June 2003 to 5 November 2003

	$	$
Sales (122 000 – 16 000 + 37 000 + 17 000)		160 000
Less Cost of sales		
Stock at 30 June 2003	47 000	
Purchases (138 000 – 23 000 + 28 000)	143 000	
	190 000	
Less Stock at 5 November 2003 (balancing figure)	70 000	120 000
Gross profit (25% of 160 000)		40 000

Cost of stock lost in fire: $(70 000 – 12 000) = $58 000

16.7 Multiple-choice questions

1 B   **2** B   **3** C   **4** A   **5** C   **6** B

Chapter 17

Exercise 1
(a)

The Wellington Drama Club
Income and Expenditure Account for the
year ended 31 December 2004

	$	$
Subscriptions		2 400
Sales of tickets		20 000
Sales of programmes		3 000
Sales of refreshments	3 500	
Less Cost of refreshments	2 200	1 300
		26 700
Less		
Hire of costumes	4 700	
Hire of hall	2 600	
Copyright fees	1 400	
Printing	180	
Subscriptions for 2003 written off	80	8 960
Surplus of income over expenditure		17 740
Donation to Actors Benevolent Fund (50%)		8 870
Balance carried to Accumulated Fund		8 870

(b)

Balance Sheet extracts at 31 December 2003

Current asset	Subscriptions owing	$400
Current liability	Subscriptions in advance	$360

Exercise 2
(a)

The Hutt River Dining Club
Statement of Affairs at 1 January 2004

		$
Catering equipment		8 000
Stock of food		200
Stock of books		1 100
Subscriptions owing		180
Bank		1 520
		11 000
Less Creditors	40	
Subscriptions in advance	60	(100)
Accumulated fund at 1 January 2003		10 900

(b)

Receipts and Payments account for the
year ended 31 December 2004

2004		$	2004		$
Jan 1	Balance brought forward	1 520	Dec 31	Staff wages	39 000
Dec 31	Subscriptions	5 000		Purchase of food	24 980
	Restaurant takings	73 760		Purchase of books	4 840
	Sales of books	12 150		Catering equipment	3 750
				Heating and lighting	8 390
				Sundry expenses	2 270
				Balance carried forward	9 200
		92 430			92 430
2005					
Jan 1	Balance brought down	9 200			

(c)

Subscriptions

2004		$	2004		$
Jan 1	Balance b/f	180	Jan 1	Balance b/f	60
Dec 31	Income and Expenditure	4 780	Dec 31	Bank	5000
	Prepaid subscriptions c/d	140		Subscriptions owing c/d	40
		5100			5100
2005			2005		
Jan 1	Balance b/d	40	Jan 1	Balance b/d	140

(d)

Book Trading Account

		$	$
Sales			12 150
Less Cost of sales			
Stock at 1.1.04		1100	
Purchases		5040	
		6140	
Stock at 31.12.04		965	5 175
Transferred to Income and Expenditure Account			6 975

(e)

Restaurant account		
	$	$
Takings		73 760
Less Cost of food		
Stock at 1.1.04	200	
Purchases	25 300	
	25 500	
Stock at 31.12.04	270	25 230
Gross profit		48 530
Staff wages	39 000	
Depreciation of catering equipment	1 475	40 475
Transferred to Income and Expenditure Account		8 055

(f)

The Hutt River Dining Club Income and Expenditure Account for the year ended 31 December 2004		
	$	$
Subscriptions		4 780
Profit on sales of books		6 975
Profit on restaurant		8 055
		19 810
Heating and lighting	8 390	
Sundry expenses	2 270	10 660
Surplus of income over expenditure		9 150

(g)

Balance Sheet at 31 December 2004			
	$	$	$
Catering equipment	(8000 + 3750)	11 750	
Less Depreciation		1 475	10 275
Current assets			
Stocks: Books		965	
Food		270	
		1 235	
Subscriptions owing		40	
Bank		9 200	
		10 475	
Current liabilities			
Creditors: Food	360		
Books	200		
Subscriptions in advance	140	700	9 775
			20 050
Accumulated fund at 1 January 2004			10 900
Surplus of income over expenditure			9 150
			20 050

17.6 Multiple-choice questions

1 B   **2** B   **3** C   **4** B

Chapter 18

Exercise 1

Geeta
Trading and Profit and Loss Account for the year ended 31 March 2004

	Ladies' $	Ladies' $	Men's $	Men's $	Children's $	Children's $	Total $	Total $
Sales		100 000		120 000		80 000		300 000
Less Cost of sales								
Stock at 1.4.03	14 000		17 000		5 000		36 000	
Purchases	50 000		63 000		42 000		155 000	
	64 000		80 000		47 000		191 000	
Stock at 31.3.04	18 000	46 000	22 000	58 000	4 000	43 000	44 000	147 000
Gross profit		54 000		62 000		37 000		153 000
Wages	20 000		20 000		12 000		52 000	
Rent	11 200		11 200		5 600		28 000	
Heating & lighting	2 400		2 400		1 200		6 000	
Advertising	1 667		2 000		1 333		5 000	
Administration	12 000		9 000		6 000		27 000	
Depreciation	3 200	50 467	2 400	47 000	1 600	27 733	7 200	125 200
		3 533		15 000		9 267		27 800
Managers' commission		(168)		(714)		(441)		(1 323)
Net profit		3 365		14 286		8 826		26 477

18.5 Multiple-choice questions

1 A   **2** D   **3** C   **4** B

Chapter 19

Exercise 1

The Fabricating Company
Manufacturing, Trading and Profit and
Loss Account for the year ended 31 March 2004

	$000	$000
Raw materials: Stock at 1.4.03	10	
Purchases	130	
Carriage in	14	
	154	
Stock at 31.3.04	20	134
Direct labour		170
Direct expenses		16
Prime cost		320
Factory overheads	128	
Depreciation of machinery	12	140
		460
Work in progress: 1.4.03	12	
31.3 04	(22)	(10)
Factory cost of goods produced		450
Factory profit (20%)		90
Transferred to Trading Account		540
Sales		700
Less Cost of sales		
Stock of finished goods at 1.4.03	24	
Transferred from Manufacturing Account	540	
	564	
Stock of finished goods at 31.3.04	36	528
Gross profit		172
Office overheads	96	
Office depreciation	3	99
Net profit on trading		73
Factory profit	90	
Less Provision for unrealised profit $(36 - 24) \times \frac{20}{120}$	(2)	88
Net profit		161

Exercise 2

Glupersoo
Manufacturing, Trading and Profit and Loss Account
for the year ended 30 April 2004

	$	$
Direct materials: Stock at 1.5.03	11 250	
Purchases	132 000	
Carriage inwards	11 505	
	154 755	
Stock at 30.4.04	13 125	141 630
Direct labour		146 250
Prime cost		287 880
Indirect wages	19 500	
Rent $\frac{3}{4}$ (45 000 + 3750)	36 563	
Heating and lighting $\frac{2}{3}$ (42 300 + 2700)	30 000	
Insurance $\frac{9}{10}$ (3150 - 900)	2 025	
Motor vehicle expenses $(6000 \times \frac{1}{2})$	3 000	
Depreciation: Factory	3 000	
Machinery	10 000	
Motor vehicles $(8000 \times \frac{1}{2})$	4 000	108 088
		395 968
Work in progress: at 1.5.03	18 000	
30.4.04	15 750	2 250
Factory cost of goods produced		398 218
Factory profit (20%)		79 644
Transferred to Trading account		477 862
Sales		800 000
Less Cost of sales		
Stock of finished goods 1.5.03	27 000	
Transferred from Manufacturing account	477 862	
	504 862	
Less Stock of finished goods 30.4.04	24 000	480 862
Gross profit		319 138
Wages	51 450	
Rent $\frac{1}{4}$ (45 000 + 3750)	12 187	
Heating and lighting $\frac{1}{3}$ (42 300 + 2700)	15 000	
Insurance $\frac{1}{10}$ (3150 - 900)	225	
Carriage outwards	2 520	
Advertising (7000 - 3500)	3 500	
Motor vehicle expenses $(6000 \times \frac{1}{2})$	3 000	
Depreciation: Office machinery	4 000	
Motor vans $(8000 \times \frac{1}{2})$	4 000	8 000	95 882
Net profit on trading		223 256
Add Factory profit	79 644	
Reduction in Provision for Unrealised Profit		
$\frac{1}{6}$ (27 000 - 24 000) 500		80 144
Overall net profit		303 400

Chapter 20

Exercise 1 Fiford Ltd

Stock of fifolium at 31 October					
October	1	10	15	22	29
Price ($)	5.00	5.20	5.24	5.28	5.32
Quantity (kilos)	100	80	50	70	100
Sales					
3	(40)				
	60				
12	(60)	(15)			
	–	65			
14		(50)			
		15			
17		(15)	(30)		
		–	20		
30			(20)	(50)	——
31			–	20	100
Value				$105.60	$532.00
				Total	$637.60

Exercise 2 L.I. Fortune Ltd

Stock of lifoxium at 31 August					
August	1	12	18	25	30
Price ($)	1.50	1.75	1.90	2.00	2.15
Quantity (kg)	40	100	75	120	90
Sales					
5	(20)				
	20				
14		(60)			
		40			
19		(5)	(75)		
		35	–		
23		(25)			
		10			
27				(65)	
				55	
31					(60)
					30
Value ($)	30.00	17.50		110.00	64.50
				Total	$222.00

Exercise 3 A.V. Co. Ltd

Stock of digital hammers at 30 June					
Date		Quantity	Price per unit ($)	Average price $	Balance $
Jun 1	Balance b/f	200	5.00	5.000	1000
4	Purchased	100	5.20		520
	Balance	300		5.067	1520
10	Sold	(75)			(380)
	Balance	225			1140
13	Purchased	100	5.35		535
	Balance	325		5.154	1675
20	Sold	(150)			(773)
	Balance	175			902
26	Purchased	80	5.40		432
	Balance	255		5.231	1334
30	Sold	(90)			(471)
	Balance	165		5.230	863

Chapter 21

Exercise 1 (a)

Tee and Leef
Trading and Profit and Loss and Appropriation Account
for the year ended 31 March 2004

		$	$	$
Sales				215 000
Less Cost of sales:	Stock at 1.4.03		16 000	
	Purchases		84 000	
			100 000	
	Less Stock at 31.3.04		20 000	80 000
Gross profit				135 000
Selling expenses			24 000	
Administration expenses			46 000	
Depreciation: Fixtures and fittings		4 800		
Office equipment		5 400	10 200	
Interest on loan			600	80 800
Net profit				54 200
Share of profit	Tee ($\frac{1}{2}$)		27 100	
	Leef ($\frac{1}{2}$)		27 100	54 200

(b)

Partners' Current accounts

2004	Tee $	Leef $	2003	Tee $	Leef $
Mar 31 Drawings	29 000	31 000	Apr 1 Balances b/d	5 000	10 000
			2004		
Balances c/d	3 100	6 700	Mar 31 Interest on loan		600
			Share of profit	27 100	27 100
	32 100	37 700		32 100	37 700
			Apr 1 Balance b/d	3 100	6 700

(c)

Balance Sheet at 31 March 2004

	Cost $	Depn $	NBV $
Fixed assets			
Fixtures and fittings	48 000	12 800	35 200
Office equipment	27 000	10 400	16 600
	75 000	23 200	51 800
Current assets			
Stock		20 000	
Trade debtors		24 000	
Prepayment		6 000	
Bank		85 000	
		135 000	
Current liabilities			
Trade creditors	11 000		
Expense creditor	4 000	15 000	120 000
			171 800
Long-term liability: Loan – Leef			12 000
			159 800
Capital accounts: Tee	100 000		
Leef	50 000		150 000
Current accounts: Tee	3 100		
Leef	6 700		9 800
			159 800

Exercise 2 (a)

Tee and Leef
Trading and Profit and Loss and Appropriation Account
for the year ended 31 March 2004

	$	$	$
Sales			215 000
Less Cost of sales: Stock at 1.4.03		16 000	
Purchases		84 000	
		100 000	
Less Stock at 31.3.04		20 000	80 000
Gross profit			135 000
Selling expenses		24 000	
Administration expenses		46 000	
Depreciation: Fixtures and fittings	4 800		
Office equipment	5 400	10 200	
Interest on loan		1 200	81 400
Net profit			53 600
Interest on drawings: Tee	2 900		
Leef	3 100		6 000
			59 600
Interest on capitals: Tee	10 000		
Leef	5 000		
	15 000		
Salary Leef	4 000		19 000
			40 600
Share of profit Tee $\frac{3}{5}$	24 360		
Leef $\frac{2}{5}$	16 240		40 600

(b)

Partners' Current accounts

2004		Tee $	Leef $	2003		Tee $	Leef $
Mar 31	Drawings	29 000	31 000	Apr 1	Balances b/d	5 000	10 000
	Interest on			2004			
	drawings	2 900	3 100	Mar 31	Interest on capital	10 000	5 000
	Balances c/d	7 460	2 340		Interest on loan		1 200
					Salary		4 000
					Share of profit	24 360	16 240
		39 360	36 440			39 360	36 440
				Apr 1	Balances b/d	7 460	2 340

(c)

Balance Sheet at 31 March 2004

		Cost $	Depn $	NBV $
Fixed assets				
Fixtures and fittings		48 000	12 800	35 200
Office equipment		27 000	10 400	16 600
		75 000	23 200	51 800
Current assets				
Stock			20 000	
Trade debtors			24 000	
Prepayment			6 000	
Bank			85 000	
			135 000	
Current liabilities				
Trade creditors		11 000		
Expense creditor		4 000	15 000	120 000
				171 800
Long-term liability: Loan – Leef				12 000
				159 800
Capital accounts:	Tee	100 000		
	Leef	50 000	150 000	
Current accounts:	Tee	7 460		
	Leef	2 340	9 800	
				159 800

21.5 Multiple-choice questions

1 C   **2** D   **3** A

Chapter 22

Exercise 1 (a)

Journal entries

	Dr $	Cr $
Freehold premises	25 000	
Fixtures and fittings		3 000
Office equipment		2 000
Stock		3 000
Debtors Control		1 000
Revaluation account		16 000

Revaluation of assets at 1 September 2004 as agreed by partners.

Revaluation account	16 000	
Tee Capital account		8 000
Leef Capital account		8 000

Apportionment of profit on revaluation of assets to partners in profit-sharing ratios

(b)

Tom and Tilly
Balance Sheet as at 1 September 2004

	$	$	$
Fixed assets at net book values			
Freehold premises			65 000
Fixtures and fittings			15 000
Office equipment			5 000
			85 000
Current liabilities			
Stock		14 000	
Debtors		3 000	
Bank		6 000	
		23 000	
Current liabilities			
Creditors		3 000	20 000
			105 000
Capital accounts			
Tom			56 000
Tilly			49 000
			105 000

Exercise 2 Vera and Ken
(a) Value of net assets

	$
Premises	140 000
Fixtures and fittings	65 000
Motor vehicles	35 000
Office equipment	15 000
Stock	6 500
Debtors	11 800
Bank	3 620
	276 920
Less	
Creditors	5 830
Net asset value	271 090

Value of Goodwill: $(300 000 − 271 090) = $28 910

(b) Amounts to be credited to Capital accounts for Goodwill

Vera ($\frac{3}{5}$ of $28 910):	$17 346
Ken ($\frac{2}{5}$ of $28 910):	$11 564

Exercise 3 Punch and Judy
(a)

	Old profit-sharing ratios	New profit-sharing ratios	Capital accounts
	$	$	$
Punch	12 000	10 800	1200 credit
Judy	6 000	7 200	1200 debit
	18 000	18 000	

(b)

Capital accounts

2004		Punch $	Judy $	2004		Punch $	Judy $
Oct 1	Punch – Capital		1 200	Oct 1	Balance b/f	36 000	14 000
	Balance c/d	37 200	12 800		Judy – Capital	1 200	
		37 200	14 000			37 200	14 000
				Oct 1	Balance b/d	37 200	12 800

Exercise 4

Hook, Line and Sinker
Trading and Profit and Loss and Appropriation Accounts
for the year ended 31 December 2004

						$
Sales						129 500
Less Cost of sales						66 500
Gross profit carried down						63 000

	6 months to 30 June 2004		6 months to 31 December 2004		Year to 31 December 2004	
	$	$	$	$	$	$
Gross profit brought down		31 500		31 500		63 000
Wages	7 000		7 000		14 000	
General expenses	1 750		3 500		5 250	
Interest on loan	200		400		600	
Depreciation	875	9 825	875	11 775	1 750	21 600
Net profit		21 675		19 725		41 400
Salary – Hook			3 000	3 000		3 000
				16 725		38 400
Share of profit: Hook ($\frac{3}{6}$)	10 838		($\frac{1}{3}$) 5 575		16 413	
Line ($\frac{2}{3}$)	7 225		($\frac{1}{3}$) 5 575		12 800	
Sinker ($\frac{1}{6}$)	3 612	21 675	($\frac{1}{3}$) 5 575	16 725	9 187	38 400

Exercise 5

(a)

Bell, Booker and Candell
Trading, Profit and Loss and Appropriation Account
for the year ended 31 December 2004

	$
Turnover	600 000
Less Cost of sales	330 000
Gross profit carried down	270 000

	8 months to August 2004 $	8 months to August 2004 $	4 months to 31 December 2004 $	4 months to 31 December 2004 $	Year to 31 December 2004 $	Year to 31 December 2004 $
Gross profit brought down		180 000		90 000		270 000
Wages and salaries[1]	76 000		30 000		106 000	
Rent	28 000		14 000		42 000	
Heating and lighting	4 000		2 000		6 000	
Sundry expenses	8 000		4 000		12 000	
Interest on loan – Bell	–		800		800	
Depreciation						
Freehold premises	4 800		2 800		7 600	
Plant & machinery	12 000		1 800		13 800	
Motor cars	5 000		1 000[2]		6 000	
Office equipment	1 400	139 200	200	56 600	1 600	195 800
Net profit		40 800		33 400		74 200
Interest on capitals						
Bell	6 667		5 444		12 111	
Booker	4 000		3 322		7 322	
Candell	–		1 567		1 567	
	10 667		10 333		21 000	
Salary – Booker	10 000	20 667	6 000	16 333	16 000	37 000
		20 133		17 067		37 200
Profit: Bell ($\frac{2}{3}$)	13 422		($\frac{2}{5}$) 6 827		20 249	
Booker ($\frac{1}{3}$)	6 711		($\frac{2}{5}$) 6 827		13 538	
Candell	–	20 133	($\frac{1}{5}$) 3 413	17 067	3 413	37 200

1 Wages and salaries: Paid $106 000, less paid to Candell for 8 months $16 000 = $90 000

                 January to August ($\frac{2}{3} \times$ $90 000 + $16 000) = $76 000

                 September to December $30 000

2 Depreciation of motor cars September to December: $(3000 + 9000) \times 25\% \times \frac{3}{12}$ = $1000

(b)

Partners' Capital accounts

2004		Bell $	Booker $	2004		Bell $	Booker $
Aug 31	Balance c/d	187 333	103 667	Jan 1	Balance b/d	100 000	60 000
				Aug 31	Profit on revaluation[3]	47 333	23 667
					Goodwill	40 000	20 000
		187 333	103 667			187 333	103 667

3 Profit on revaluation: $(210 000 + 27 000 + 3000 + 6000) – $(135 000 + 30 000 + 34 000 + 7000)
 = $71 000

Partners' Capital accounts

2004		Bell $	Booker $	Candell $	2004		Bell $	Booker $	Candell $
Sep 1	Goodwill[4]		4 000	12 000	Sep 1	Balance b/d	187 333	103 667	–
	Loan a/c	20 000				Bank			50 000
Dec 31	Balance c/d	183 333	99 667	47 000		Motor cars			9 000
						Goodwill[4]	16 000		
		203 333	103 667	59 000			203 333	103 667	59 000
					2005				
					Jan 1	Balance b/d	183 333	99 667	47 000

4 Goodwill: Bell ($\frac{2}{5}$) $24 000 (reduction of $16 000); Booker ($\frac{2}{5}$) $24 000 (increase of $4 000); Candell entitled to ($\frac{1}{5}$) ($12 000).

Partners' Current accounts

2004		Bell $	Booker $	Candell $	2004		Bell $	Booker $	Candell $
Dec 31	Drawings	30 000	40 000	4 000	Jan 1	Balance b/d	16 000	12 000	
	Balance c/d	18 360	8 860	980	Dec 31	Int. on caps	12 111	7 322	1 567
						Salary		16 000	
						Profit	20 249	13 538	3 413
		48 360	48 860	4 980			48 360	48 860	4 980
					2005				
					Jan 1	Balance b/d	18 360	8 860	980

Exercise 6

(a)

Wilfrid, Hide and Wyte
Profit and Loss and Appropriation Account for the year ended
30 June 2004

		6 mos. ended 31.12.03		6 mos. ended 30.6.04	
		$	$	$	$
Gross profit			93 500		93 500
Wages		45 500		45 500	
Rent		6 000		6 000	
Electricity		4 200		4 200	
Interest on loan		–		3 750	
Sundry expenses		4 500	60 200	4 500	63 950
Net profit			33 300		29 550
Interest on capital: Wilfrid		4 000		–	
Hide		2 500		1 650†	
Wyte		1 500	8 000	325†	1 975
			25 300		27 575
Share of profit	Wilfrid $\frac{3}{6}$	12 650		–	
	Hide $\frac{2}{6}$	8 433		$\frac{1}{2}$ 13 788	
	Wyte $\frac{1}{6}$	4 217	25 300	$\frac{1}{2}$ 13 787	27 575

† Based on capitals of $33 000 and $6500 respectively.

(b)

Partners' Capital accounts

2004		Wilfrid $	Hide $	Wyte $	2003			Wilfrid $	Hide $	Wyte $
Dec 31	Goodwill		10 000	20 000	Jul 1	Balance b/d	80 000	50 000	30 000
	Revaluation				2004				
	of assets	10 500	7 000	3 500	Dec 31	Goodwill	30 000		
	Loan a/c	75 000				Current a/c	5 650		
	Bank	30 150							
Jun 30	Balance c/d	_____	33 000	6 500			_____	_____	_____
		115 650	50 000	30 000			115 650	50 000	30 000
					Jul 1	Balance b/d		33 000	6 500

Partners' Current accounts

		Wilfrid $	Hide $	Wyte $				Wilfrid $	Hide $	Wyte $
2004					2003					
Dec 31	Drawings	23 000			Jul 1	Balance b/d	12 000	3 000	4 000
	Capital a/c	5 650			Dec 31	Interest	4 000		
2004						Profit	12 650		
Jun 30	Drawings		28 000	18 000	2004				
	Balance c/d		1 371	5 829	Jun 30	Interest		4 150	1 825
						Profit	_____	22 221	18 004
		28 650	29 371	23 829			28 650	29 371	23 829
					Jul 1	Balance b/d		1 371	5 829

22.9 Multiple-choice questions

1 C   **2** C   **3** D   **4** B   **5** A

Chapter 23

Exercise 1 Seesaw Ltd
(a) Non-cumulative preference shares

Year	1998 $	1999 $	2000 $	2001 $	2002 $	2003 $
Profit	10 000	5 000	7 000	4 000	7 000	12 000
Preference dividend paid	6 000	5 000	6 000	4 000	6 000	6 000
Profit left for ordinary shareholders	4 000	nil	1 000	nil	1 000	6 000
Maximum ordinary dividend payable	4%	–	1%	–	1%	6%

(b) Cumulative preference shares

Year	1998 $	1999 $	2000 $	2001 $	2002 $	2003 $
Profit	10 000	5 000	7 000	4 000	7 000	12 000
Preference dividend for year	6 000	5 000	6 000	4 000	6 000	6 000
Arrears of dividend carried forward	–	–	1 000	–	1 000	1 000
Profit left for ordinary shareholders	4 000	nil	nil	nil	nil	5 000
Maximum ordinary dividend payable	4%	–	–	–	–	5%

Exercise 2 Premium Shares Ltd

Journal

	$	$
Bank	120 000	
10% Preference Share Capital		100 000
Share Premium account		20 000

The issue of 100 000 10% preference shares of $1 at $1.20 per share.

Exercise 3

Journal

	$	$
Freehold Premises at Cost	20 000	
Provision for Depreciation of Freehold Premises	18 000	
Freehold Premises Revaluation Reserve		38 000

Revaluation of freehold premises from net book value of $42 000 to $80 000.

Exercise 4 Gracenote Ltd

Total of ordinary share capital and reserves: $(200 000 + 50 000 + 100 000 − 40 000) = $310 000

Value of 100 ordinary shares $= \frac{\$310\,000}{200\,000} = \$155$

Exercise 5 (a)

Molly Coddle Ltd
Profit and Loss Account for the year ended 30 April 2004

		$	$
Turnover			300 000
Cost of sales:	Stock at 1 May 2003	20 000	
	Purchases	113 000	
		133 000	
	Stock at 30 June 2004	31 000	102 000
Gross profit			198 000
Selling and distribution			
Sales staff salaries		57 000	
Selling expenses		39 000	
Depreciation of warehouse machinery		8 000	104 000
Administration			
General office wages		32 000	
Other general expenses		35 000	
Depreciation of office machinery		10 000	77 000	181 000
Operating profit			17 000
Debenture interest			500
			16 500
Transfer to General Reserve		10 000	
Dividends: Preference		600	
Ordinary		3 750	14 350
Retained profit for the year			2 150

(b)

Balance Sheet as at 30 April 2004

	Cost $	Depreciation $	Net book value $
Tangible fixed assets			
Warehouse machinery	70 000	38 000	32 000
Office machinery	42 000	30 000	12 000
	112 000	68 000	44 000
Current assets			
Stock		31 000	
Trade debtors		38 000	
Bank		28 000	
		97 000	
Creditors: amounts falling due within one year			
Trade creditors	11 000		
Debenture interest	500		
Preference dividend	600		
Ordinary dividend	3 750	15 850	
Net current assets			
			81 150
Total assets less current liabilities			125 150
Creditors: amounts falling due after more than one year			
10% debentures 2006/2008			5 000
			120 150
Share capital and reserves			
50 000 Ordinary shares of $1			50 000
10 000 6% Preference shares of $1			10 000
Share premium			15 000
General reserve (25 000 + 10 000)			35 000
Retained profit (8000 + 2150)			10 150
			120 150

Exercise 6 (a)

Shillyshally Ltd
Profit and Loss Account for the year ended 30 June 2004

	$	$	$
Turnover			1 000 000
Less Cost of sales			
Stock at 1 July 2003		46 000	
Purchases		630 000	
		676 000	
Less Stock at 30 June 2004		38 000	638 000
Gross profit			362 000
Selling and distribution			
Sales staff salaries	79 000		
Delivery van expenses (38 000 + 2000)	40 000		
Advertising (34 000 – 6 000)	28 000		
Depreciation of delivery vehicles	13 000	160 000	
Administration			
Wages	36 000		
Office expenses (24 000 + 3000)	27 000		
Depreciation of office machinery	7 000	70 000	230 000
Operating profit			132 000
Less Debenture interest (6000 + 6000)			12 000
Profit before taxation			120 000
Taxation			16 000
Profit after taxation			104 000
Transferred to General Reserve		50 000	
Dividends paid and proposed:			
preference paid	4 000		
proposed	4 000		
ordinary paid	3 000		
proposed	24 000	35 000	85 000
Retained profit for the year			19 000

(b)

Balance Sheet at 30 June 2004

	Cost or revaluation	Depn	NBV
	$	$	$
Fixed tangible assets			
Freehold property	1 200 000	–	1 200 000
Delivery vehicles	80 000	41 000	39 000
Office machinery	70 000	28 000	42 000
	1 350 000	69 000	1 281 000
Current assets			
Stock		38 000	
Trade debtors		82 000	
Prepayment		6 000	
Bank		67 000	
		193 000	
Creditors: amounts falling due within one year			
Trade creditors	33 000		
Expense creditors (2000 + 3000)	5 000		
Debenture interest	6 000		
Taxation	16 000		
Dividends (4000 + 24 000)	28 000	88 000	
Net current assets			105 000
Total assets less current liabilities			1 386 000
Creditors: amounts falling due after more than one year			
12% debentures 2006/2008			100 000
			1 286 000
Capital and reserves			
800 000 ordinary shares of $1			800 000
100 000 8% preference share of $1			100 000
Capital Redemption Reserve			260 000
General reserve			100 000
Retained profit (7000 + 19 000)			26 000
			1 286 000

23.16 Multiple-choice questions

1 A 2 B 3 B 4 A 5 C 6 A 7 A
8 D 9 D 10 D

Chapter 24

Exercise 1

Contraflo Ltd
Reconciliation of operating profit to net cash flow from operating activities

	$000	$000
Operating profit		94
Add depreciation of fixed assets: (see working 1 below)		50
Profit less losses on sale of fixed assets (see working 1 below)		(10)
Decrease in stocks		15
Increase in trade debtors		(12)
Increase in trade creditors		8
Net cash inflow		145

Cash flow statement for the year ended 30 June 2004

	$000	$000
Net cash flow from operating activities		145
Servicing of finance		
Interest paid on debentures	(8)	
Preference share dividends paid (see working 2 below)	(6)	(14)
Taxation (see working 3 below)		(36)
Capital expenditure		
Payment to acquire fixed assets (see working 1 below)	(160)	
Proceeds for disposal of fixed assets $(50 + 1 + 4)K	55	(105)
		(10)
Equity dividends paid (see working 2 below)		(34)
		(44)
Financing		
Redemption of debentures	(30)	
Issue of 50 000 ordinary shares of $1	55	25
Decrease in cash		19

Reconciliation of net cash flow to movement in net funds

	$000	$000
Decrease in cash	19	
Debentures redeemed	(30)	(11)
Net debt at 1 July 2003 (55 – 100)		45
Net debt at 30 June 2004 (36 – 70)		34

Workings

1. Fixed assets

Freehold buildings at cost	$000	Freehold building disposal	$000	
At 31 December 2003	400	Cost	(36)	
Disposal	(36)	Proceeds	50	
At 31 December 2004	364	Profit on disposal	14	14

Plant and machinery at cost	$000	Plant and machinery depreciation	$000	Disposal	$000	
At 31 December 2003	80	At 31 December 2003	35	Cost	20	
Disposals	(20)	On disposals	(16)	Depreciation	(16)	
Additions (balancing figure)	90	Provided in year (balancing figure)	20	Proceeds	(1)	
At 31 December 2004	150	At December 2003	39	Loss on disposal	3	(3)

Motor vehicles at cost	$000	Motor vehicles depreciation	$000	Disposal	$000	
At 31 December 2003	120	At 31 December 2003	90	Cost	30	
Disposals	(30)	On disposals	(25)	Depreciation	(25)	
Additions (balancing figure)	70	Provided in year (balancing figure)	30	Proceeds	(4)	
At 31 December 2004	160	At 31 December 2004	95	Loss on disposal	1	(1)

Additions at cost $(90 + 70)K = $160 000   Net profit of disposals credited to Profit and Loss Account $10 000

Total depreciation provided in the year: $(20 + 30)K = $50 000

2.

Dividends	$000	
B/f at 1 January 2004	30	
Debited in P & L A/c	45	
C/f at 31 December 2004	(35)	
Paid in year	40	of which $6000 was preference dividend and $34 000 was ordinary dividend

3.

Taxation	$000
B/f at 1 January 2004	39
Debited in P & L A/c	40
C/f at 31 December 2004	(43)
Paid in year	36

Exercise 2

Horsa Ltd
Balance Sheet at 31 July 2004

Tangible fixed assets

	At cost	Depn	Net Book Value
	$000	$000	$000
Freehold premises	300	142	158
Plant and machinery	143	117	26
			184

Current assets

Stock	40	
Debtors	98	
Cash at bank	118	
	256	

Creditors: amounts due within one year

Trade creditors	(49)		
Dividends (ordinary)	(20)	69	187
			371

Creditors: amounts due after more than one year

10% debenture stock 2003/2006	(30)
	341

Share capital and reserves

Ordinary shares of $1	120
10% Preference shares of $1	50
Share premium	40
General Reserve	60
Profit and Loss Account	71
	341

Exercise 3

Cox Ltd
Balance Sheet as at 30 September 2003

	$000	$000	$000
	Cost	Depn	NBV
Fixed assets			
Intangible: Goodwill	180	–	180
Tangible: Freehold premises[1]	700	100	600
Plant and machinery[2]	622	557	65
Motor vehicles[3]	208	115	93
	1530	772	758
Total fixed assets			938

Current assets

Stock (154 + 71)	225	
Debtors (106 – 32)	74	
Bank (83 – 65)	18	
	317	

Creditors: amounts falling due within one year

Trade creditors (79 – 18)	61		
Preference dividend	4		
Ordinary dividend	35	100	217
			1155

Creditors: amounts falling due after more than one year

10% debentures 2002/5 (250 + 50)	300
	855

Share capital and reserves

Ordinary shares of $1 (600 – 100)	500
6% Preference shares of $1	80
Share Premium account (100 – 50)	50
(Revaluation reserve)	–
General reserve (240 – 40)	200
Retained profit (59 – 34)	25
	855

1 Freehold premises at cost (given) $700 000.

The Revaluation Reserve has been made up as follows:

Increase in freehold promises at cost $300 000

Depreciation at 31 May 2003 $100 000

2

Plant and machinery at cost	$000	Depreciation of P & M	$000	Disposal of P & M	$000		$000
At 30 September 2004	742	At 31 May 2004	526	Cost	180		
Less additions in 2004	(300)	Provided in 2004	(120)	Proceeds	(20)		
Add disposal in 2004	180	On disposals	151	Loss on disposal	(9)		
At 31 May 2003	622	At 31 May 2003	557	Depreciation to sale	151		

3

Motor vehicles at cost	$000	Depreciation of MVs	$000	Disposals of MVs	$000		$000
At May 2004	220	At May 2004	116	Cost	72		
Less additions in 2004	(84)	Provided in 2004	(70)	Proceeds	(11)		
Add disposal in 2004	72	On disposal	69	Profit on sale	8		
At 31 May 2003	208	At 31 May 2003	115	Depreciation to sale	69		

24.8 Multiple-choice questions

1 B   **2** C   **3** D   **4** A

Chapter 25

Exercise 1 Otago (Bonus Offers) Ltd

	$000
Fixed assets	1400
Net current assets	350
	1750
Ordinary shares of $1	1400
Share Premium	200
General Reserve	100
Retained profit	50
	1750

Note. The Share Premium account could have been used with $400 000 of the Revaluation Reserve, but the Share Premium account can be used for purposes not available to the Revaluation Reserve. (See chapter 23.)

Exercise 2 Bonarite Ltd

(a)

	$000
Net fixed and current assets	2000
Share capital and reserves	
Ordinary shares of $1	1800
General reserve	120
Retained profit	80
	2 000

(b)

	$000
Net fixed and current assets	2750
Share capital and reserves	
Ordinary shares of $1	2400
Share premium	150
General Reserve	120
Retained Profit	80
	2750

Exercise 3 Choppers Ltd
(a)

Balance Sheet	
	$000
Fixed assets	1300
Net current assets	550
	1850
Ordinary shares of $1	1150
Share premium	350
General reserve	200
Retained profit	150
	1850

(b)

Balance Sheet	
	$000
Fixed assets	1300
Net current assets	250
	1550
Ordinary shares of $1	1000
Share premium	200
Capital Redemption Reserve	300
Retained profit	50
	1550

(b)

Balance Sheet	
	$000
Fixed assets	2000
Net current assets[1]	720
	2720
Ordinary shares of $1[2]	2200
Share Premium account[3]	200
Capital Redemption Reserve[4]	50
Profit and Loss Account[5]	270
	2720

1 Net current assets have been increased by the amount received on the new issue ($220 000) but reduced by the cost of redeeming the preference shares ($300 000).

2 Ordinary share capital has been increased by the nominal value of the new ordinary shares.

3 The Share Premium account has been credited with $20 000 premium received on the new issue, and debited with $20 000 (the maximum amount permissible) of the premium paid on the redemption.

4 A Capital Redemption Reserve of $50 000 must be created to cover the difference between the nominal value of the redeemed shares and the nominal value of the new issue.

5 The Profit and Loss Account has been reduced by the transfer to Capital Redemption Reserve and the amount of the premium on redemption that was not covered by the premium on the new issue.

Exercise 4 Twist Ltd
(a)

Balance Sheet	
	$000
Fixed assets	2000
Net current assets (800 – 300)	500
	2500
Ordinary shares of $1	2000
Share Premium account	200
Capital Redemption Reserve	250
Profit and Loss Account[1]	50
	2500

1 The balance on the Profit and Loss Account has been reduced by the transfer of $250 000 to Capital Redemption Reserve and a debit of $50 000 for the premium paid on redemption.

(c)

Balance Sheet

	$000
Fixed assets	2000.0
Net current assets[1]	812.5
	2812.5
Ordinary shares of $1[2]	2250.0
Share Premium account[3]	212.5
Profit and Loss Account[4]	350.0
	2812.5

1 Net current assets have been increased by the proceeds of the new issue ($312 500) but have been reduced by the cost of redeeming the preference shares ($300 000).

2 Ordinary share capital has been increased by the nominal amount of the new issue.

3 The Share Premium account has been increased by the premium on the new shares ($62 500) and reduced by the premium on the redemption ($50 000), all of which is allowed because it is less than the premium on the new issue.

4 The cost of redeeming the preference shares has been completely covered by the proceeds of the new issue; it has not been necessary to create a Capital Redemption Reserve, or to charge any of the premium on redemption to the Profit and Loss Account.

Exercise 5

Downsize Ltd
Balance Sheet after capital reduction

	$000
Fixed assets	
Freehold property	340
Fixtures and fittings	80
Office furniture	70
	490
Net current assets	210
	700
1 000 000 ordinary shares of $0.70[1]	700

1 It is important to show the nominal value of the new shares.

25.12 Multiple choice questions

1 C   2 D   3 C   4 D   5 B

Chapter 26

Exercise 1 Hamil Ltd

(a)

Journal

	$	$
Goodwill	29 000	
Freehold property	70 000	
Plant and machinery	12 000	
Office furniture	4 000	
Stock	2 500	
Debtors	5 500	
Creditors		3 000
Cash		20 000
Ordinary share capital		80 000
Share Premium account		20 000
	123 000	123 000

Purchase of Abdul's business for $120 000 and settlement by $20 0000 in cash and 80 000 ordinary shares if $1 in Hamil Ltd at $1.25.

(b)

Hamil Ltd
Balance Sheet at 30 June 2004 immediately after the purchase of Abdul's business

	$	$
Intangible fixed asset: Goodwill		29 000
Tangible fixed assets		
Freehold property (100 000 + 70 000)		170 000
Plant and machinery (60 000 + 12 000)		72 000
Office equipment		14 000
Office furniture		4 000
		260 000
Total fixed assets		289 000
Current assets		
Stock (10 000 + 2500)	12 500	
Debtors (7000 + 5500)	12 500	
Bank (25 000 – 20 000)	5 000	
	30 000	
Current liabilities		
Creditors (6000 + 3000)	9 000	21 000
		310 000
Share capital and reserves		
Ordinary shares of $1 (150 000 + 80 000)		230 000
Share Premium account (20 000 + 20 000)		40 000
Retained profit		40 000
		310 000

Exercise 2 Carol

(a) $\$60\,000 \times \frac{5}{8} = \$37\,500$

(b) $\$60\,000 \times \frac{5}{4} = \$75\,000$

Exercise 3

Digger Ltd
Balance Sheet immediately after the acquisition of the partnership of Spaid and Shuvell

	$	$
Fixed assets		
Intangible: Goodwill		25 000
Tangible		
Land and buildings (90 000 + 60 000)		150 000
Fixtures and fittings (30 000 + 14 000)		44 000
Office machinery (15 000 + 10 000)		25 000
		219 000
Total fixed assets		244 000
Current assets		
Stock (20 000 + 15 000)	35 000	
Debtors (5000 + 6000)	11 000	
Bank (60 000 − 28 000)	32 000	
	78 000	
Current liabilities		
Creditors (16 000 + 12 000)	28 000	50 000
		294 000
Long-term liability		
8% debenture (12 000 × $\frac{10}{8}$)		15 000
		279 000
Share capital and reserves		
Ordinary shares of $1 (200 000 + 60 000[1])		260 000
Share Premium account		15 000
Retained profit		4 000
		279 000

1 Shares issued:	Purchase consideration		$118 000
	Less cash	$28 000	
	debenture	$15 000	$43 000
	Value of shares		$75 000
	No. of shares at $1.25 per share		60 000
	Share premium		$15 000

26.7 Multiple-choice questions

1 C   **2** D   **3** D

Chapter 27

27.20 Multiple-choice questions

1 B   **2** A   **3** A   **4** D   **5** D   **6** B

Chapter 28

Exercise 1 Najim

(a)

(i)	Gross profit percentage	2004	$\dfrac{\text{gross profit}}{\text{sales}} \times 100 = \dfrac{60\,308}{172\,308} \times 100$	$= 35\%$
		2005	$\dfrac{60\,000}{187\,500} \times 100$	$= 32\%$
(ii)	Net profit percentage	2004	$\dfrac{\text{net profit}}{\text{sales}} \times 100 = \dfrac{21\,539}{172\,308} \times 100$	$= 12.5\%$
		2005	$\dfrac{27\,322}{187\,500} \times 100$	$= 14.57\%$
(iii)	Fixed asset turnover	2004	$\dfrac{\text{sales}}{\text{fixed assets}} \quad \dfrac{172\,308}{78\,322}$	$= 2.2$ times
		2005	$\dfrac{187\,500}{93\,750}$	$= 2$ times
(iv)	Stockturn	2004	$\dfrac{\text{cost of sales}}{\text{average stock}} = \dfrac{112\,000}{(12\,000 + 16\,000) \div 2}$	$= 8$ times
		2005	$\dfrac{127\,500}{(16\,000 + 14\,000) \div 2}$	$= 8.5$ times
(v)	Debtors' days	2004	$\dfrac{\text{trade debtors}}{\text{credit sales}} \times 365 = \dfrac{9914}{60\% \text{ of } 172\,308} \times 365$	$= 35$ days
		2005	$\dfrac{12\,511}{60\% \text{ of } 187\,500} \times 365$	$= 40.59$ days or 41 days
(vi)	Creditors' days	2004	$\dfrac{\text{trade creditors}}{\text{credit purchases}} \times 365 = \dfrac{13\,984}{116\,000} \times 365$	$= 44$ days
		2005	$\dfrac{17\,192}{125\,500} \times 365$	$= 50$ days
(vii)	Current ratio	2004	current assets : current liabilities $= 30\,765 : 13\,984$	$= 2.2 : 1$
		2005	$33\,696 : 17\,192$	$= 1.96 : 1$
(viii)	Liquid ratio (acid test)	2004	current assets – stock: current liabilities $= 14\,765 : 13\,984$	$= 1.06 : 1$
		2005	$19\,696 : 17\,192$	$= 1.15 : 1$

(b)

(i) Sales have increased by over $15 000 or nearly 9% but gross profit percentage has decreased from 35% in 2004 to 32% in 2005, a reduction of 3%. This may be due to

- a reduction in selling prices to increase turnover
- an increase in the cost of sales not passed on to customers
- sales made at less than the normal mark-up (seasonal sales or disposal of old or damaged stock)
- some stock valued at less than cost because it is old or has deteriorated
- stock which has been stolen.

Whether or not the gross profit percentage is acceptable depends upon the normal margin expected on sales, but information about this is not given in the question.

(ii) Net profit percentage has improved from 12.5% in 2004 to 14.57% in 2005. This is in spite of a reduction of 3% in the gross profit margin. This has been achieved by tighter control on overhead expenditure, down from $38 769 in 2004 to $32 678 in 2005, a reduction of 15.7% although sales have increased by 8.8%.

(iii) Fixed asset turnover has remained almost steady (2.2 times in 2004; 2 times in 2005). Without further information about the nature of the business, it is not possible to comment on this ratio. There has been a considerable increase in the value of fixed assets employed in the business in 2005 and the additional assets would appear to have been brought into use early in the year for the full effect to have been felt.

(iv) Stockturn has increased slightly from 8 times in 2004 to 8.5 times in 2005. The average time that goods remain in stock is 6.5 weeks which may seem reasonable, but as nothing is known about the type of business, further comment is not possible.

(v) The period of credit taken by debtors has increased by 6 days, from 35 in 2004 to 41 in 2005. This deterioration may be due to one or more of the following factors:

- more lenient terms for debtors, to promote sales
- a deliberate policy to attract customers from competitors
- general economic conditions
- poor credit control.

A deterioration in the debtors' ratio incurs the risk of an increase in bad debts as old debts usually become bad. Najim should monitor the situation carefully.

(vi) The time taken to pay creditors has increased by 6 days, from 44 days in 2004 to 50 days in 2005. While this may help the cash flow at a time when debtors are taking 6 days longer to pay, care must be taken to retain the goodwill of suppliers, otherwise the suppliers may insist that future orders will only be accepted on a cash basis and this would greatly harm Najim's cash flow.

(vii) The current ratio has decreased slightly from 2.2 : 1 in 2004 to 1.96 : 1 in 2005. It remains satisfactory by normal standards.

(viii) The liquid ratio has remained almost steady at 1.06 : 1 in 2004 and 1.15 : 1 in 2005. As 60% of sales are on credit, the very low ratios on which businesses such as supermarkets work are not appropriate for Naji's business and his present ratios may be considered satisfactory.

General comments There are no indications that the business is not a going concern. Its cash position is positive and there are no bank loans or overdrafts that could cause embarrassment in the near future.

There is no sign of overtrading as stock and debtors are not excessive. Overtrading places businesses at great risk.

Note. Part (b) requires more than a simple repetition of the ratios already calculated in part (a) if marks are to be earned. It is necessary to *compare* the ratios and to recognise *trends* and their significance. Avoid irrelevant comments and repetition. Statements which cannot be supported by information given in the question should be avoided, but *possible* reasons for an improvement or deterioration in a trend may be *suggested*.

Exercise 2 Dunedin Ltd and Wellington Ltd

(a)

(i) Gearing

Dunedin Ltd $\frac{600 + 100}{400 + 600 + 100} \times 100 = 63.64\%$

Wellington Ltd $\frac{1000 + 750}{2050 + 1000 + 750} \times 100 = 46.05\%$

(ii) Interest cover

Dunedin Ltd $\frac{300}{60} = 5$ times

Wellington Ltd $\frac{420}{120} = 3.5$ times

(iii) Earnings per share

Dunedin Ltd $\frac{240 - 6}{200\,000} = 117$ cents

Wellington Ltd $\frac{300 - 60}{750} = 32$ cents

(iv) Dividend per share

Dunedin Ltd $\frac{90}{200} = \$0.45$ (45%)

Wellington Ltd $\frac{150}{750} = \$0.20$ (10%)

(v) Dividend cover

Dunedin Ltd $\frac{240 - 6}{90} = 2.7$ times

Wellington Ltd $\frac{300 - 60}{150} = 1.6$ times

(vi) Price earnings ratio

Dunedin Ltd $\frac{2.70}{1.17} = 2.31$ times

Wellington Ltd $\frac{3.60}{0.32} = 11.25$ times

(vii) Dividend yield

Dunedin Ltd $\frac{0.45}{2.70} \times 100 = 16.67\%$

Wellington Ltd $\frac{0.20}{3.60} \times 100 = 5.56\%$

(b)

(i) Gearing. Dunedin is highly geared (63.64%) and Wellington is low geared (46.05%). This makes Dunedin a little more risky from the point of view of shareholders and creditors, but neither company is far from neutral gearing (50%) and they are only separated by about $17\frac{1}{2}\%$.

(ii) Interest cover. Dunedin's interest is covered 5 times by the operating profit but Wellington's is only covered $3\frac{1}{2}$ times. Both ratios are satisfactory. Dunedin's ordinary shareholders are at less at risk of having their dividend curtailed if profits fall than Wellington's shareholders.

(iii) Earnings per share. Dunedin's EPS is much higher at 117 cents than Wellington's at 32 cents. This is mainly due to Wellington having issued more shares than Dunedin (3.75 times). This suggests that Dunedin is potentially the better company for dividend/capital growth.

(iv) Dividend per share. Dunedin is paying an ordinary dividend of $0.45 per $1 share, equal to 45% of the nominal value of the shares. Wellington is paying $0.20 per $2 share, equal to 10% of the nominal value of its shares. This makes Dunedin's shares seem the more attractive, but the yield on the amount invested is a better ratio.

(v) Dividend cover. Dunedin Ltd's dividend cover is 2.7 times, which is generally considered to be satisfactory. Wellington Ltd's dividend is covered 1.6 times and may be at risk if profits decline in the future.

(vi) Price earnings ratio. Dunedin Ltd's PER is 2.31 times and Wellington Ltd's PER is 11.25 times. This seems strange when the dividend covers of the two companies are compared. The share prices may be influenced by factors not mentioned in the question. Wellington Ltd's future trading prospects may be affected by various favourable factors not mentioned in the question.

(vii) Dividend yield. Dunedin's dividend yield based on the current market price is 16.67% compared with the yield of 5.56% on Wellington's shares. This makes Dunedin's shares more attractive from an income-earning viewpoint. However, it should be considered along with the potential for capital growth and, as has already been stated, Dunedin's earnings per share has permitted adequate profits to be retained for capital growth especially if a conservative dividend policy is continued in future.

Conclusion. Every ratio except gearing is favourable to Dunedin Ltd and even the gearing should not give rise to serious concern. Although Dunedin's dividend policy is more conservative than Wellington's, it still offers a better return on capital invested.

Exercise 3

(a)

Patience
Trading and Profit and Loss Account for the year ended 31 December 2004

			$	$
Step 6	Sales (495 000 × 100/65)			761 538
	Cost of sales			
Step 2	Stock at 1.1.04	(54 000 × 5/6)	45 000	
Step 5	Purchases	(balancing figure)	504 000	
Step 4		(balancing figure)	549 000	
Step 1	Stock at 31.12.04	(given)	54 000	
Step 3		(65% of sales)		495 000
Step 7	Gross profit	(35% of 761 538)		266 538
Step 9	Expenses	(balancing figure)		99 000
Step 8	Net profit	(22% of 761 538)		167 538

Balance Sheet at 31 December 2004

			$	$
Step 10	Fixed assets	(761 538 ÷ 4)		190 385
	Current assets			
Step 11	Stock		54 000	
Step 12	Trade debtors	(761 538 × 34/365)	70 938	
Step 16	Bank	(balancing figure)	20 050	
Step 15		(balancing figure)	144 988	
Step 13	Trade creditors	(504 000 × 42/365)	57 995	
Step 14				86 993
Step 17				277 378
Step 22	Capital at 1.1.04	(balancing figure)		249 840
Step 18	Net profit			167 538
Step 21		(balancing figure)		417 378
Step 19	Drawings	(given)		140 000
Step 20		(from step 17)		277 378

(b) Virtue and Patience

(i) Virtue's stockturn is 12 compared with 10 for Patience. Virtue earns his profit at a faster rate than Patience. His cash flow is improved by the higher stockturn.

(ii) Virtue's gross profit margin of 40% is more than Patience's 35% which indicates that he earns a higher margin on his sales. He may have cheaper sources of supply than Patience, or Patience's mark up may be lower than Virtue's. Without more information about their individual circumstances, further comment is not possible.

(iii) Virtue's net profit margin (20%) is 2% lower than Patience's (22%). This shows that Patience's overheads are comparatively lower than Virtue's. Not all overheads are easily controllable, and Virtue may have to pay higher rent, for example, because of the situation or size of his premises.

(iv) Virtue's turnover is 5 times his fixed assets but Patience's turnover is only 4 times. Virtue is using his fixed assets more efficiently and making them more profitable.

(v) Virtue's debtors' ratio is 31 days, which is 3 days less than that of Patience (34 days). This indicates that Virtue controls his debtors more efficiently and his cash flow is improved as a result.

(vi) Virtue pays his creditors 6 days earlier than Patience pays hers (36 days compared to 42 days). No information is provided regarding the credit terms each receives. If Virtue obtains his goods more cheaply than Patience, as suggested in (ii), the period of credit he is allowed may be less than Patience receives. On the other hand, if Virtue is not taking the full period of credit he is allowed, he is not managing his cash flow to the best advantage.

Conclusion. With the exception of the net profit margin and the possible exception of his payment of creditors, Virtue appears to be running his business more efficiently than Patience.

28.12 Multiple choice questions
1 D **2** B **3** C **4** D **5** C **6** D **7** B **8** A

Chapter 29

Exercise 1 See § 29.2.

Exercise 2 See § 29.3.

29.8 Multiple choice questions
1 C **2** B **3** C **4** C

Chapter 30

Exercise 1 Teepops Ltd
(a)

Expense	Basis	Total	Machining	Painting	Assembly	Packing
		$000	$000	$000	$000	$000
Indirect labour	actual	125	51	32	28	14
Factory: Rent	floor area	90	45	18	18	9
Heating & lighting	floor area	70	35	14	14	7
Maintenance	floor area	30	15	6	6	3
Insurance	floor area	20	10	4	4	2
Plant & machinery:						
Depreciation	cost	80	45	20	5	10
Repairs	cost	32	18	8	2	4
Insurance	cost	16	9	4	1	2
Total overhead		463	228	106	78	51

(b)

Expense	Basis	Total	Machining	Painting	Assembly	Packing
		$000	$000	$000	$000	$000
Direct materials	allocation	117	80	20	5	12
Direct labour	allocation	323	136	74	68	45
Overhead	apportioned	463	228	106	78	51
Total cost		903	444	200	151	108

Exercise 2 Luvlibix Foods

	Mixing	Bakery	Packaging	Stores	Canteen
	$000	$000	$000	$000	$000
Overheads	165.00	124.00	87.00	80.00	90.00
Re-apportion stores	54.55	14.54	3.64	(80.00)	7.27
Re-apportion canteen	32.42	43.23	21.62	-	(97.27)
	251.97	181.77	112.26	-	-

Exercise 3 Trimble Ltd

(a) No. of direct labour hours required:
Dimbles: $5000 \times 1.3 = 6500$
Gimbles: $7000 \times 0.7 = \underline{4900}$
$11\ 400$

$$\text{OAR} = \frac{\$129\ 276}{11\ 400} = \$11.34 \text{ per hour}$$

(i) OAR per unit: Dimble $\$11.34 \times 1.3 = \$14.742$
(ii) OAR per unit: Gimble $\$11.34 \times 0.7 = \$7.938$

(b) Overhead absorbed:

			$
Dimbles	$5000 \times \$14.742$ =		73 710
Gimbles	$7000 \times \$7.938$ =		55 566
Total overhead			129 276

Exercise 4 Makeit-by-Robot Ltd

(a) Total number of machine hours in a 13 week period
$$= 10 \times 7 \times 6 \times 13 = 5460$$
$$\text{Machine hour OAR} = \frac{\$141\,960}{5460} = \$26$$

(b) Each unit requires $\frac{5460}{1200}$ machine hours to make =
4.55 machine hours.
Therefore each unit absorbs 26×4.55, or $118.30
overhead.
(Proof: $118.30 \times 1200 = \$141\,960$)

Exercise 5 Egbert Ltd

(a) OARs

Moulding   Direct labour hourly rate $\frac{\$301\,857}{34\,500} = \$8.75$

Machining Machine hourly rate $\frac{\$115\,200}{18\,000} = \$6.40$

Painting   Direct labour hourly rate $\frac{\$47\,250}{9000} = \$5.25$

(b) Overhead absorbed per unit

	Sovrin		Ginny
	$		$
Moulding (4 × $8.75)	35.00	(3½ × $8.75)	30.625
Machining (2 × $6.40)	12.80	(2 × $6.40)	12.800
Painting (1 × $5.25)	5.25	(1 × $5.25)	5.250
	53.05		48.675

(c) Total overhead recovery

	Sovrin		Ginny		Total
	$		$		$
Moulding	(6000 × $35.00) 210 000	(3000 × $30.625)	91 875		301 875
Machining	(6000 × $12.80) 76 800	(3000 × $12.800)	38 400		115 200
Painting	(6000 × $5.25) 31 500	(3000 × $5.250)	15 750		47 250
	318 300		146 025		464 325

(d) Total cost per unit

	Sovrin	Ginny
	$	$
Direct material	102.00	85.000
Direct labour	190.00	151.000
Overhead	53.05	48.675
	345.05	284.675

Exercise 6 Upandown Ltd

	3 months to 31 March	3 months to 30 June	3 months to 30 September	3 months to 31 December
OAR	$124	$128	$130	$131
Overhead recovered	$111 600	$134 400	$143 000	$128 380
(Under-)/over-recovery	($16 400)	$9 400	$13 500	($4 420)

30.10 Multiple-choice questions
1 B   **2** D   **3** A

Chapter 31

Exercise 1 Luvlibrek

	$
Direct materials	398 000
Direct labour	996 000
Overheads	1 687 250
	3 081 250

Cost per unit of 1000 packets: $= \frac{\$3\,081\,250}{425} = \$7250$

Exercise 2 Geoffrey Pannell

	$
Labour: Geoffrey (200 × $100)	20 000
Susan (100 × $60)	6 000
Overhead recovery (300 × $40)	12 000
	38 000

Exercise 3 Wipup Ltd

No. of rolls = 6000
No. of labour hours = 10

(a)

	$
Raw materials (6000 × $0.08)	480
Labour (10 × $6)	60
Setting up machinery	30
Machine hour overhead recovery	93.50
Cost of batch of 1000 rolls	663.50

(b) Cost of one roll: 663.50/6000 = $0.1106

31.5 Multiple-choice questions
1 B   **2** A

Chapter 32

Exercise 1 The Sitrah Processing Company

Process I

	$000		$000
Direct material	10 000	Output transferred to process II	11 300
Direct labour	400		
Overhead	900		
	11 300		11 300

Process II

	$000		$000
Material transferred from process I	11 300	Output transferred to process III	16 514
Added material	4 000		
Direct labour	350		
Overhead	864		
	16 514		16 514

Process III

	$000		$000
Material transferred from process II	16 514	Output transferred to finished stock	24 212
Added material	7 000		
Direct labour	275		
Overhead	423		
	24 212		24 212

Exercise 2

Total processing costs to separation: $(21\,000 + 11\,000 + 23\,000) = \$55\,000$

(a) Joint cost of 3400 litres of Animo: $\$55\,000 \times \dfrac{3400}{8500} = \$22\,000$

Cost to completion of 1 litre of Animo: $\$ \dfrac{22\,000 + 4624}{3400} = \$7.831$

(b) Joint cost of 5100 litres of Lactino: $\$55\,000 \times \dfrac{5100}{8500} = \$33\,000$

Cost to completion of 1 litre of Lactino: $\$ \dfrac{33\,000 + 13\,362}{5100} = \$9.091$

Exercise 3 Okara Quality Carpets Ltd

Process 1 (2000 units)

	$		$
Material (2000 × 4 × $12)	96 000	Sale of by-product	1 630
Labour (2000 × 3 × $14)	84 000	Production transferred	
Overhead (6000 × $36)	216 000	to process 2	394 370
	396 000		396 000

Process 2 (1200 complete units; 800 incomplete units)

	$		$
Materials from process 1	394 370	Finished goods	474 372
Added materials			
(9750 + 4875)	14 625		
Labour (66 000 + 22 000)	88 000		
Overhead (162 000 + 54 000)	216 000	Work in progress c/d	238 623
	712 995		712 995

Note	Finished goods		Work in progress
	$		$
Material from process 1 ($394 370 × $\frac{1200}{2000}$)	236 622	($394 370 × $\frac{800}{2000}$)	157 748
Added material (1200 × 2.5 × $3.25)	9 750	(800 × 2.5 × 0.75 × $3.25)	4 875
Labour (1200 × 5 × $11)	66 000	(800 × 5 × 0.5 × $11)	22 000
Overhead (1200 × 5 × $27)	162 000	(800 × 5 × 0.5 × $27)	54 000
	474 372		238 623

32.7 Multiple-choice questions
1 B   **2** B

Chapter 33

Exercise 1

(i) Contribution from 1 unit = $146 250 ÷ 3000 = $48.75
Contribution from 3000 units = $(48.75 × 3000)
= $146 250
Profit from 3000 units = $(146 250 − 82 000)
= $64 250

(ii) Contribution from 4000 units = $(48.75 × 4000)
= $195 000
Profit from 4000 units = $(195 000 − 82 000)
= $113 000

(iii) Contribution from 1200 units = $(48.75 × 1200)
= $58 500
Loss from 1200 units = $(82 000 − 58 500) = $23 500

Exercise 2 Product Q

(a) (i) Contribution per unit = $(95 − 65) = $30
Break-even point = $\frac{\$75\,000}{\$30}$ = 2,500 units;

break-even revenue = $\frac{\$75\,000}{0.31579}$ = $237 500

(or 2500 × $95 = $237 500)

(ii) Margin of safety = $\frac{2500}{5000}$ × 100 = 50%

(b)

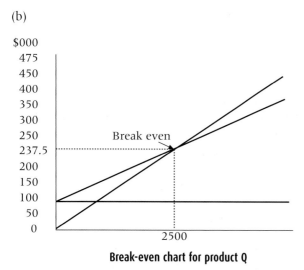

Break-even chart for product Q

Exercise 3 Veerich Ardson Ltd

No. of phones	(i) 10 000	(ii) 15 000	(iii) 20 000
	$	$	$
Contribution (50 – 41)	90 000	(48 – 41) 105 000	(42 – 41) 20 000
Fixed overheads	70 000	70 000	70 000
Profit/(loss)	20 000	35 000	(50 000)

Exercise 4 El Dugar Peach Ltd

Marginal cost per 1000 cans of fruit: $14 250
(i) Additional contribution from order for 5000 cans at $16 000 per 1000 cans:

$$5 \times \$(16\ 000 - 14\ 250) = \$8750 \text{ profit}$$

The order should be accepted.
(ii) Loss if order for 3000 cans at $14 100 is accepted:

$$3 \times \$(14\ 100 - 14\ 250) = \$450 \text{ loss}$$

The order should not be accepted unless it will prevent the company from having to lay off valuable skilled staff because of a temporary slump in trade.

Exercise 5 Canterbury Planes Ltd

Present position (tools produced by Canterbury Planes Ltd)	
	$
Price per tool	16.0
Direct costs: Material	3.0
Labour	2.5
Other expenses	1.0
Marginal cost of production	6.5
Variable selling expenses	2.0
Marginal cost of sales	8.5
Contribution	7.5

Contribution from sale of 15 000 tools = $112 500

Profit on sale of 15 000 tools = $(112 500 – 74 000) = $38 500

Break-even point: $\frac{\$74\ 000}{7.5}$ = 9867 tools

(a) (i) North Island Tool Co.
Cost per tool $6. This is $0.50 less than the present cost of production
Effect on profit: Increase by (15 000 × $0.5) $7 500 to $46 000

Effect on break-even point: $\frac{\$74\ 000}{\$8}$ = 9250 tools

(ii) South Island Tool Co.
Cost per tool $6.80 This is $0.30 more than the present cost of production
Effect on profit: Decrease by (15 000 × $0.3) $4 500 to $34 000

Effect on break-even point: $\frac{\$74\ 000}{\$7.2}$ = 10 278 tools

(b) Tools should be purchased from Northern Island Tool Co. because

- the cost will be $0.50 less than the cost of production
- profit will increase by $7500 to $46 000
- the break-even point will be reduced from 9867 tools to 9250 tools.

Tools should not be purchased from South Island Tool Co. because

- the cost will be $0.30 more than the cost of production
- profit will decrease by $4500 to $34 000
- the break-even point will increase from 9867 tools to 10 278.

Exercise 6 Castries Ltd

Revised production budget to maximise profit

	Gimie	Gros	Petit
Per unit	$	$	$
Selling price	14	25	20
Direct material	5	6.50	8
Direct labour	5	14.00	6
Marginal cost	10	20.50	14
Contribution	4	4.50	6
Contribution per litre of material	1.6	1.38	1.5
Ranking	1	3	2

Revised production budget:

	Units	Litres	Contribution
			$
Gimie	1000	2 500	4 000
Petit	800	3 200	4 800
Gros	1500	4 875	6 750
		10 575	15 550
Less fixed expenses			10 000
Profit			5 550

Exercise 7 Castries Ltd

Revised production budget to maximise profit

	Gimie	Gros	Petit
	$	$	$
Contribution	4	4.50	6
Contribution per direct labour hour	8	3.21	10
Ranking	2	3	1

Revised production budget

	Units	Labour hours	Contribution
			$
Petit	800	480	4 800.00
Gimie	1000	500	4 000.00
Gros	1725	2415	7 762.50
		3395	16 562.50
Less Fixed expenses			10 000.00
Profit			6 562.50

Exercise 8

((i) Fixed costs increase by $12 000 and profit is reduced to $23 000.

$$\text{Break-even} = \frac{\$92\,000}{\$5.75^*} = 16\,000 \text{ units;}$$

* contribution = $(8.75 − 3)

(ii) Variable costs increase by $9000 and profit is reduced to $26 000

$$\text{Break-even} = \frac{\$80\,000}{\$5.3^*} = 15\,095 \text{ units}$$

* contribution = $(8.75 − 3.45)

(iii) Costs and revenue increase by $21 000 and profit is maintained at $35 000.

$$\text{Break-even} = \frac{\$92\,000}{\$6.35^*} = 14\,489 \text{ units.}$$

* Costs have increased by $21 000; sales revenue becomes $196 000 ($9.80 per unit)
Unit marginal cost is $3.45; contribution = $(9.80 − 3.45) = $6.35

Exercise 9 Cohort Ltd

(a)

Products	Legion	Centurion	Praefect
Per unit	$	$	$
Material	20	40	50
Labour	36	60	72
Marginal cost	56	100	122
Selling price	80	130	150
Contribution	24	30	28
Budgeted contribution	24 000	60 000	112 000
	$		
Total contribution	196 000		
Less fixed expenses	115 000		
Profit	81 000		

(b) Revised production budget

Products ranked	Contribution per kg	Units produced	Materials required	Total contribution
	$		kg	$
1 Legion	12.0	1000	2 000	24 000
2 Centurion	7.5	2000	8 000	60 000
3 Praefect	5.6	3600	18 000	100 800
			28 000	184 800
		Less Fixed expenses		115 000
		Profit		69 800

(c) Reconciliation of profit per revised budget with profit in original budget

		$
Profit per original budget		81 000
Budgeted production of Praefect (units)	4000	
Revised budget for Praefect	3600	
Reduction in production	400	
Loss of contributions 400 × 28		11 200
Revised profit		69 800

Exercise 10 Cockpit Country Industrial Co. Ltd

(a)

(i)

15 000 units	
Per unit	$
Direct material (4 × $4.10)	16.4
Direct labour ($\frac{1}{3}$ × $12)	4.0
Variable overhead	1.8
Marginal cost	22.2
Selling price	25.0
Contribution	2.8

Profit: $(15 000 × 2.8) – $30 000* = $(42 000 – 30 000) = $12 000
(*$1.5 × 20 000 = $30 000)

(ii)

18 000 units	
Per unit	$
Material	16.4
Labour	4.0
Variable overhead	1.7889*
Marginal cost	22.1889
Selling price	25.0000
Contribution	2.8111

*(16 000 × $1.8 + 2000 × $1.7) ÷ 18 000

Profit = (18 000 × $2.8111) – $30 000 = $(50 6000 – 30 000) = $20 600.

(b) Break-even point

		$
Material per unit		16.4
Labour per unit		4.0
Variable overhead		
16 000 × $1.8	28 800	
4 000 × $1.7	6 800	
	35 600	
per unit		1.78
Marginal cost		22.18
Selling price		25.00
Contribution per unit		2.82

$$\text{Break-even point} = \frac{\$30\,000}{\$2.82} = 10\,639 \text{ units;}$$

(c)

20 000 units sold at $24 per unit		$	$
Sales revenue			480 000
Material (20 000 × 4 × $4.1)		328 000	
Labour (20 000 × $4)		80 000	
Variable overhead			
16 000 × $1.8	28 800		
4 000 × $1.7	6 800	35 600	443 600
			36 400
Less Fixed overheads			30 000
Profit			6 400

(d) A selling price may be lowered with advantage to:
- increase demand for the good
- undercut the prices of competitors
- maintain full production
- sell slow-moving stock
- introduce a new product.

Possible disadvantages are:
- the start of a price war with competitors
- fixed overheads may not be covered
- the product may be sold below the cost of production if the marginal cost is not known.

(e) The following assumptions are made when break-even charts are prepared.

- Fixed costs remain fixed at all levels of activity. *But* costs are only fixed within certain limits of activity and are more likely to be 'stepped' as activity increases.
- All costs may be classified as either fixed or variable. *But* many costs cannot easily be classed as fixed or variable.
- Variable costs vary directly with the output in units. *But* variable costs may decrease with the level of activity because quantity discounts are received on purchases of materials, or labour costs increase because overtime has to be paid to workers to achieve the level of activity.
- Sales revenue will increase proportionately to the volume of sales. *But* it may be necessary to discount prices to achieve the desired volume of sales.
- All the resources required for production will be available. *But* there may be limiting factors affecting materials, labour or demand for the product.

33.11 Multiple-choice questions
1 C   2 D   3 D   4 D

Chapter 34

Exercise 1 Flannel and Flounder Ltd

Sales budget for 6 months ending 30 June 2005

	January	February	March	April	May	June
Units sold	1000	1200	1300	1500	1700	1800
Price	$20	$20	$20	$22	$22	$22
Sales revenue	$20 000	$24 000	$26 000	$33 000	$37 400	$39 600

Exercise 2 Flannel and Flounder Ltd

Production budget for the 7 months from December 2004 to 30 June 2005

	2004	2005					
	December	January	February	March	April	May	June
Sales (following month in units)	1000	1200	1300	1500	1700	1800	2000
Add 10%	100	120	130	150	170	180	200
Monthly production	1100	1320	1430	1650	1870	1980	2200

Exercise 3 Flannel and Flounder Ltd

Purchases budget for the period November 2004 to May 2005

	2004		2005					
	November	December	January	February	March	April	May	June
Units of production	1100	1320	1430	1650	1870	1980	2000	2100
Material required (litres)	2750	3300	3575	4125	4675	4950	5000	5250
Price per litre	$4.10	$4.10	$4.10	$4.10	$4.25	$4.25	$4.25	$4.25
Purchases	$11 275	$13 530	$14 658	$16 913	$19 869	$21 038	$21 250	$22 313

Exercise 4 Flannel and Flounder Ltd

Expenditure budget for six months ending June 2005

	January $	February $	March $	April $	May $	June $
Purchases	13 530	14 658	16 913	19 869	21 038	21 250
Wages	4 000	4 000	4 000	4 000	4 000	4 000
Bonus	-	-	160	240	520	696
Electricity	-	2 400	-	-	1 800	-
Other expenses	6 000	6 000	6 000	6 600	6 600	6 600
Interest on loan	-	-	500	-	-	500
Dividend	-	-	-	4 000	-	-
Purchase of machine	-	-	-	-	15 000	-
	23 530	27 058	27 573	34 709	48 958	33 046

Exercise 5 Flannel and Flounder Ltd

(a)

Cash budget for the six months ending 30 June 2005

	January $	February $	March $	April $	May $	June $
Receipts						
Cash sales	10 000	12 000	13 000	16 500	18 700	19 800
Debtors – 1 month	6 864	7 800	9 360	10 140	12 870	14 586
Debtors – 2 months	1 800	1 760	2 000	2 400	2 600	3 300
Proceeds from sale of plant	-	12 000	-	-	-	-
	18 664	33 560	24 360	29 040	34 170	37 686
Expenditure						
Purchases	13 530	14 658	16 913	19 869	21 038	21 250
Wages	4 000	4 000	4 000	4 000	4 000	4 000
Bonus	-	-	160	240	520	696
Electricity	-	2 400	-	-	1 800	-
Other expenses	6 000	6 000	6 000	6 600	6 600	6 600
Interest on loan	-	-	500	-	-	500
Dividend	-	-	-	4 000	-	-
Purchase of machine	-	-	-	-	15 000	-
	23 530	27 058	27 573	34 709	48 958	33 046
Net receipts/(payments)	(4 866)	6 502	(3 213)	(5 669)	(14 788)	4 640
Brought forward	31 750	26 884	33 386	30 173	24 504	9 716
Carried forward	26 884	33 386	30 173	24 504	9 716	14 356

(b) Trade debtors: $(15 444 + 3740 + 3960) = $23 144
Trade creditors $22 313
Accrued commission on sales ($19 600 × 0.04) = $784

Exercise 6 Greenfields Ltd

(a)

Cash budget for the four months ending 30 April 2005				
	January	February	March	April
	$	$	$	$
Cash sales	25 000	28 000	30 000	33 000
Debtors	42 500	37 500	42 000	45 000
	67 500	65 500	72 000	78 000
Suppliers	22 500	25 000	20 000	30 000
Selling and distribution	6 250	7 000	7 500	8 250
Administration	20 000	20 000	20 000	20 000
Purchase of plant	–	–	60 000	–
Dividend	–	–	–	6 500
	48 750	52 000	107 500	64 750
Net receipts/(payments)	18 750	13 500	(35 500)	13 250
Balance b/fwd	20 750	39 500	53 000	17 500
Balance c/fwd	39 500	53 000	17 500	30 750

(b)

Greenfields Ltd **Budgeted Profit and Loss Account for the four months ending 30 April 2005**		
	$	$
Sales		290 000
Cost of sales		
Stock at 1.1.05	30 000	
Purchases	112 500	
	142 500	
Stock at 30.4.05	22 500	120 000
Gross profit		170 000
Selling and distribution expenses	32 500	
Administration expenses	83 500	116 000
Operating profit		54 000
Interest on debentures		1 000
		53 000
Ordinary dividend	6 500	
Transfer to General Reserve	25 000	31 500
Retained profit for the year		21 500

(c)

Greenfields Ltd **Budgeted Balance Sheet at 30 April 2005**			
Fixed assets	Cost	Depreciation	Net
	$	$	$
Freehold premises	50 000	10 500	39 500
Plant and machinery	97 500	29 000	68 500
	147 500	39 500	108 000
Current assets			
Stock		22 500	
Trade debtors		49 500	
Balance at bank		30 750	
		102 750	
Current liabilities			
Trade creditors	37 500		
Debenture interest accrued	1 000	38 500	64 250
			172 250
Long-term liability			
12% debentures 2009/10			25 000
			147 250
Share capital and reserves			
Ordinary shares of $1			65 000
General reserve			55 000
Retained profit			27 250
			147 250

34.11 Multiple-choice questions
1 C **2** B **3** D **4** A

Chapter 35

Exercise 1 Brekkifoods Ltd

Flexed Budget for the production of 110 000 packets of Barleynuts	
	$
Variable expenses	
Direct materials	22 000
Direct labour	16 500
Production expenses	6 600
	45 100
Fixed expenses	
Production expenses	13 000
Administration	29 000
	87 100

Exercise 2 Flexers Ltd

No. of locks	9000
	$
Direct materials	22 500
Direct labour	54 000
Production overhead	34 000
Selling and distribution	30 000
Administration	80 000
	220 500

Exercise 3 Enigma Ltd

(a)

	Flexed budget
No. of units	4250
	$
Direct materials	21 250
Direct labour	48 875
Variable overheads	10 625
Fixed overhead	50 000
Total cost	130 750

(b)

(i)	Total cost variance	$5 136 (A)
(ii)	Quantity variance	$4 750 (A)
(iii)	Direct material variance	$2 150 (A)
(iv)	Direct labour variance	$1 639 (F)
		$5 261 (A)

(c)

Variable overhead variance	$ 125 (F)
	$5 136 (A)

Exercise 4 Underpar Ltd

(a)

	Flexed budget
No. of units	6300
	$
Direct materials	21 420
Direct labour	42 525
Variable overheads	3 150
Fixed overhead	62 000
Total cost	129 095

(b)

Total cost variance	$6345 (F)
Quantity variance	$7455 (F)
Direct material variance	$ 530 (F)
Direct labour variance	$1540 (A)
	$6445 (F)

(c)

Variable overhead variance	$ 100 (A)
	$6345 (F)

Exercise 5 Dandelion Ltd

Standard total material cost of 12 000 packets of Pickup =
3 litres × $5 × 12 000 = $180 000
Actual material usage = 12 000 × 2.8 = 33 600 litres
Direct material usage variance =
(36 000 – 33 600) $5 = $12 000 (F)

Direct material price variance =
($5 – $4.80)33 600 = $6720 (F)
(Check: Actual cost was 2.8 litres × $4.8 litres × 12 000 =
$161 280; total material variance = $18 720 (F): $(12 000
+ 6720) (as above))

Exercise 6 Dandelion Ltd

The standard total direct labour cost for the production of 12 000 packets of Pickup = $10 × 12 000 = $120 000
Actual hours taken 12 000 × 1.25 = 15 000
The direct labour efficiency variance =
(12 000 – 15 000) $10 = $30 000 (A)
The direct labour rate variance = $(10 – 8.50)15 000 = $22 500 (F)
(Check: Actual labour cost of production of 12 000 packets of Pickup = 1.25 hours × $8.50 × 12 000 = $127 500; Total labour variance = $7500 (A) = $30 000 (A) – $22 500 (F) (as above))

Exercise 7 Larabee Ltd

(a) Workings:

Direct material: standard cost per kg $\frac{\$7200}{300 \times 4}$ = $6

standard usage for 400 units:
4 × 400 kg = 1600 kg

actual material per unit: $\frac{\$9000}{\$6.25 \times 400}$

= 3.6 kg
actual usage 400 × 3.6 kg = 1440 kg

Direct labour: standard hours per unit $\frac{\$6600}{\$11 \times 300}$

= 2 hours
standard hours for 400 units = 800
actual hours for 400 units:
400 × 2.25 = 900

actual cost per hour $\frac{\$10\,890}{400 \times 2.25}$

= $12.10

(i) Direct material usage variance: (1600 – 1440)$6
= $960 (F)
(ii) Direct material price variance: $(6.00 – 6.25)1440
= $360 (A)
(iii) Direct labour efficiency variance: (800 – 900)$11
= $1100 (A)
(iv) Direct labour rate variance: $(11.00 – 12.10)900
= $990 (A)

(b) The favourable material usage variance may be due to a better quality of material being used resulting in less wastage during production. This view may be supported by the adverse price variance which suggests that a better quality of material was more expensive than standard.

Both of the labour variances are adverse. The higher hourly rate of pay has not resulted in a favourable efficiency variance, even though the workers may have been working with a better quality of material. The adverse efficiency variance does not suggest that the higher rate of pay was due to the employment of a more skilled work force. It is possible that a pay increase given to the workers was below their expectation and they are poorly motivated as a result. The reason for the adverse variances can only be discovered by further investigation.

Exercise 8 Cantab Ltd

Calculation of actual profit made in a three month period

	$	$
Profit per master budget		98 970
Add favourable variances		
Sales volume		6 210
Materials price		9 635
abour efficiency		10 500
		125 315
Deduct adverse variances		
Quantity	17 009	
Sales price	3 730	
Materials usage	6 280	
Labour rate	7 840	
Overhead expenditure	5 760	40 619
Actual profit		84 696

35.13 Multiple-choice questions
1 A **2** B **3** A **4** C **5** C **6** C

Chapter 36

Exercise 1 Baseball Ltd
Ignore the machine that was acquired some years earlier as it is a sunk cost.
Average profit = $150 000 ÷ 6 = $25 000

Average investment = $ $\left(\frac{120\,000}{2} + 25\,000\right)$ = $85 000

ARR = $\frac{25\,000}{85\,000}$ × 100 = 29.4%

Exercise 2 Mapleduck Ltd
Calculation of payback periods

	Duckbill	Kwak
	$	$
Year 0	(90 000)	(90 000)
1	30 000	40 000
2	36 000	40 000
3	24 000	10 000
Payback	$2\frac{24}{40}$ years	$2\frac{10}{40}$ years
	2+ $\left(\frac{24}{40} \times 12\right)$ years	
	2 years 7.2 months	
	2 years 8 months	2 years 3 months

Kwak should be chosen because it has the shorter payback period and its pattern of cash flows will benefit the liquidity of Mapleduck Ltd.

Exercise 3 Nomen Ltd

Year	Discounting factor	Machine	A		B		C	
				NPV		NPV		NPV
	12%		$	$	$	$	$	$
0	1.000		(135 000)	(135 000)	(135 000)	(135 000)	(135 000)	(135 000)
1	0.893		50 000	44 650	38 000	33 934	26 000	23 218
2	0.797		50 000	39 850	38 000	30 286	26 000	20 722
3	0.712		38 000	27 056	38 000	27 056	38 000	27 056
4	0.636		26 000	16 536	38 000	24 168	50 000	31 800
5	0.567		26 000	14 742	38 000	21 546	50 000	28 350
	Net present values			7 834		1 990		(3 854)

Nomen Ltd should choose machine A as it has the highest NPV. Machine C should not be considered because it has a negative NPV.

Exercise 4 Nomen Ltd
Calculation of internal rate of return

Year	Discounting factor	Machine	A		B	
				NPV		NPV
	20%		$	$	$	$
0	1.000		(135 000)	(135 000)	(135 000)	(135 000)
1	0.833		50 000	41 650	38 000	31 654
2	0.694		50 000	34 700	38 000	26 372
3	0.579		38 000	22 002	38 000	22 002
4	0.482		26 000	12 532	38 000	18 316
5	0.402		26 000	10 452	38 000	15 276
	Net present values			(13 664)		(21 380)

IRR for machine A: $12\% + \left(8\% \times \dfrac{7834}{7834 + 13\,664}\right) = 14.9\%$

IRR for machine B: $12\% + \left(8\% \times \dfrac{1990}{1990 + 21\,380}\right) = 12.7\%$

Exercise 5 Baxter Ltd
Workings

	Big Gee	Maxi-Shadbolt
Annual depreciation	$\dfrac{\$140\,000 - \$20\,000}{5} = \$24\,000$	$\dfrac{\$180\,000 - \$30\,000}{5} = \$30\,000$

Cash outflows	Big Gee		Maxi-Shadbolt	
		$		$
Year 1	$(70 000 – 24 000)	46 000	$(84 000 – 30000)	54 000
2	$(84 000 – 24 000)	60 000	$(98 000 – 30 000)	68 000
3	$(91 000 – 24 000)	67 000	$(105 000 – 30 000)	75 000
4	$(98 000 – 24 000)	74 000	$(112 000 – 30 000)	82 000
5	$(95 000 – 24 000)	71 000	$(100 000 – 30 000)	70 000

Net receipts	Big Gee		Maxi-Shadbolt	
		$		$
Year 1	$(98 000 – 46 000)	52 000	(101 000 – 54 000)	47 000
2	$(112 000 – 60 000)	52 000	(118 000 – 68 000)	50 000
3	$(126 000 – 67 000)	59 000	(126 000 – 75 000)	51 000
4	$(126 000 – 74 000)	52 000	(140 000 – 82 000)	58 000
5	$(100 000 – 71 000)		(110 000 – 70 000)	
	plus $20 000	49 000	plus $30 000	70 000

Average profit	Big Gee		Maxi-Shadbolt	
		$		$
Year 1	$(98 000 – 70 000)	28 000	$(101 000 – 84 000)	17 000
2	$(112 000 – 84 000)	28 000	$(118 000 – 98 000)	20 000
3	$(126 000 – 91 000)	35 000	$(126 000 – 105 000)	21 000
4	$(126 000 – 98 000)	28 000	$(140 000 – 112 000)	28 000
5	$(100 000 – 95 000)	5 000	$(110 000 – 100 000)	10 000
		124 000		96 000
	÷ 5	$24 800	÷ 5	$19 200

(a)(i)

	Big Gee	Maxi-Shadbolt
ARR =	$\dfrac{24\,800}{70\,000} \times 100 = 35.4\%$	$\dfrac{19\,200}{90\,000} \times 100 = 21.3\%$

(ii) Payback period

Year	$		$
0	(140 000)		(180 000)
1	52 000		47 000
2	52 000		50 000
	36 000	Year 3	51 000
Year 3 $\frac{36\,000}{59\,000} \times 12 = 8$ months			32 000
		Year 4 $\frac{32\,000}{58\,000} \times 12 = 7$ months	
Payback = 2 years 8 months		3 years 7 months	

(iii) Net present values at 10%

Year	Factor	Big Gee Net (payment)/ receipt $	NPV $	Maxi-Shadbolt Net (payment)/ receipt $	NPV $
0	1.000	(140 000)	(140 000)	(180 000)	(180 000)
1	0.909	52 000	47 268	47 000	42 723
2	0.826	52 000	42 952	50 000	41 300
3	0.751	59 000	44 309	51 000	38 301
4	0.683	52 000	35 516	58 000	39 614
5	0.621	49 000	30 429	70 000	43 470
Net present values			60 474		25 408

(iv) IRR (40%)

Year	Factor	Big Gee Net (payment)/ receipt $	NPV $	Maxi-Shadbolt Net (payment)/ receipt $	NPV $
0	1.000	(140 000)	(140 000)	(180 000)	(180 000)
1	0.714	52 000	37 128	47 000	33 558
2	0.510	52 000	26 520	50 000	25 500
3	0.364	59 000	21 476	51 000	18 564
4	0.260	52 000	13 520	58 000	15 080
5	0.186	49 000	9 114	70 000	13 020
Net present values			(32 242)		(74 278)

IRR: Big Gee $10\% + \left(30\% \times \dfrac{60\,474}{60\,474 + 32\,242}\right) = 29.6\%$

Maxi-Shadbolt $10\% + \left(30\% \times \dfrac{25\,408}{25\,408 + 74\,278}\right)$
$= 17.6\%$

(b) Baxter Ltd should purchase Big Gee because

- it has a higher accounting rate of return: 35.4% (Maxi-Shadbolt: 21.3%)
- it has the shorter payback period: 2 years 8 months, lower risk (Maxi-Shadbolt: 3 years 7 months)
- it has higher net present value: $60 474 (Maxi-Shadbolt: $25 408)
- it has higher internal rate of return: 29.6% (Maxi-Shadbolt: $17.6%)

Exercise 6

Net present value: $150 000 − $(50 000 × 3.169) = $8 450
The net present value will become negative if:

1. the cost of the machine rises by $8450, i.e. an increase of 5.6%, or

2. the annual savings in operational costs fall below $47 333, i.e. they fall short by 5.3%

36.8 Multiple-choice questions
1 C **2** A **3** D **4** B

Index